Readings for History of the of the Military Art

Fourth Edition

Department of History
United States Military Academy
West Point, New York

Professor Steve R. Waddell
Editor

HI302

KENDALL/HUNT PUBLISHING COMPANY
4050 Westmark Drive   Dubuque, Iowa 52002

Published with the permission and cooperation of the United States Military Academy.

ISBN 0-7872-4703-0

Printed in the United States of America

10 9 8 7 6 5 4 3 2 1

Table of Contents

Preface

The essays and articles contained herein are selected readings designed to support the second half of the one year survey course, The History of the Military Art, taught at the United States Military Academy. This issue of readings is not intended to be a thematic collection. Its sole purpose is to fulfill specific course requirements and is intended for the exclusive use of the Department of History, United States Military Academy.

Steve R. Waddell
Professor and Course Director
Department of History

Reading 1

The British Tank Detachment at Cambrai

Lessons Learned and Lost Opportunities

by Major David P. Cavaleri

"And therefore I consider that we were not beaten by the genius of Marshal Foch, but by 'General Tank,' in other words, a new weapon of war . . ."

General der Infanterie A.D.H. von Zwehl, Die Schlachten im Sommer, 1918, am der Westfront.

On September 15, 1916, the British Expeditionary Force under the command of General Sir Douglas Haig employed tanks in support of infantry operations during the Battle of the Somme. In a previous article (*ARMOR*, November/December 1995), I discussed the decision-making process behind Haig's commitment of tanks at that time. This article analyzes the British development of mechanized doctrine leading up to the November 1917 Battle of Cambrai and the impact of the lessons learned from that operation. In the final analysis, the British selectively applied certain lessons to immediate tactical problems, but failed to grasp the implications of mechanized operations for the future.

At the end of September 1916, Lieutenant Colonel Hugh Elles took command of the British Tank Detachment. He was described by his primary staff officer, Major J.F.C. Fuller, as "boyish and

Reprinted from *Armor, The Journal of the U.S. Armor Association*, Vol. 90, No. 6 (November–December 1996), pp. 26–31.

reckless in danger; perhaps a better soldier than a strategist, yet one who could profit from the cooperation of his advisors, and one who was universally loved and trusted by his followers."[1] Historian Douglas Orgill looked beyond Elles' personality and wrote that Elles represented a "bridge between the new military knowledge and the old soldierly virtues."[2] Despite Elles' personal leadership qualities, however, Major Fuller was the one responsible for developing doctrine and training programs.

At their first meeting in late 1916, Elles stated that "this show [the Tank Detachment] badly wants pulling together; it is all so new that one hardly knows which way to turn."[3] Elles charged Fuller with creating a sense of discipline and *esprit de corps* in the detachment. Fuller regarded this mission as a three-part problem. First, he had to instill a sense of discipline, which he pursued via a series of lectures on the subject. Second, he had to instruct the officers in new doctrine. And third, he had to reorganize the detachment so as to maximize the use of its equipment.

Fuller was an infantry officer with a reputation for being a highly efficient staff officer. In February 1917, he published a training manual entitled "Training Note #16," designed to standardize all training practices in the detachment.[4] Fuller organized the manual in nine sections: detachment organization, operations, tactics, cooperation with other arms, preparations for offensives, supply, communication, reinforcements, and camouflaging. Calling the tank "a mobile fortress, which could escort the infantry into the enemy's defenses, and from behind which they could sally forth and clean up his trenches,"[5] he believed that tanks were capable of a more offense-oriented role than had been demonstrated during the Somme operation.

In June 1917, Fuller produced a document entitled "Projected Bases for the Tactical Employment of Tanks in 1918." In this study, he drew on the results of ineffective tank employment during the battles of the Somme (September 1916), Arras (April 1917), and Messines (June 1917). Fuller advanced three points based on his analysis. The first was that the tank's effectiveness was related directly to the terrain over which it operated. The second was that, if properly employed, tanks were capable of executing a penetration which could allow for a breakthrough by follow-on cavalry and infantry forces. The third principle was that the success of any tank penetration required a surprise artillery bombardment not to exceed forty-eight hours in duration.[6] Fuller expanded on Ernest D. Swinton's concepts in his belief that tanks were capable of more than strongpoint and wire obstacle reduction. "He soon became the leading advocate," wrote B.H. Liddell Hart, "of the tanks' wider potentialities—as a means to revive mobile warfare, instead of merely as a modernized 'battering ram' for breaking into entrenched defenses."[7]

Later in 1917, Fuller proposed an operation to British General Headquarters designed to test the validity of his ideas. Fuller's initial recommendation proposed a raid of no more than a few hours duration, designed to penetrate enemy defenses, capture prisoners, and shake up the defenders. In an August 1917 paper entitled "Tank Raids," he summarized the objectives of just such a limited raid as "Advance, hit, and retire; its objective being to destroy the enemy's personnel and guns, to demoralize and disorganize him, and not to capture ground or hold terrain."[8]

Unfortunately, such a plan had little to recommend it to GHQ; the limited tactical gains were outweighed by the potential loss of surprise and vehicles. However, the Third Army Commander, General Julius Byng, read the proposal and recognized its potential. He developed a plan which incorporated Fuller's basic concepts but which had much larger objectives, especially regarding the capture of territory.

Byng wanted the focus of the operation to be the communications center at Cambrai; once that town was captured he could then release his cavalry to the northwest to raid behind German lines. Byng's plan relied on the tanks to penetrate the defense and assumed that such a break-in would automatically result in a cavalry breakthrough. His plan meticulously prepared for the initial break-in, but discounted the fact that at that stage of the year, he lacked adequate reserves to follow through. Even if the operation was successful in effecting a break-in of the "outpost" and "battle" zones, he would not be able to penetrate into the "rearward" zone to launch his cavalry.[9]

Haig ultimately decided on an advance with limited objectives in the vicinity of Cambrai, but not necessarily focused on the town itself. He revised Byng's plan to concentrate on the Bourlon Ridge which, if captured, would provide British forces with excellent observation of the "battle" and "rearward" zones. Unwilling to discount completely the possibility of a breakthrough, Haig nevertheless retained the option to terminate the operation at the end of forty-eight hours unless clear progress was evident.[10] By October 1917, Fuller had revised his original "Tank Raids" proposal to incorporate Byng's and Haig's guidance. These new plans featured the tank in a spearhead-type role.

By mid-November 1917, the staff at GHQ had finalized the plans for the Cambrai attack. The sector was constricted by two canals, the Canal du Nord on the left and the Canal de l'Escaut on the right, six miles apart. The initial attack area included a number of small villages and two dominant ridgelines, the Flesquieres and Bourlon. The Hindenburg trench system in this sector was over five miles deep, complete with dugouts, machine gun posts, wire obstacles, antitank ditches in excess of twelve feet wide, and supporting artillery batteries.[11]

The Hindenburg Line proper ran in a northwesterly direction for almost six miles from the Scheidt Canal at Banteux to Havrincourt. The line then turned north for four miles to Mouvres. Roughly one mile behind this first line lay the Hindenburg Reserve Line, and an additional three and a half miles behind that lay the Beaurevoir, Masnieres, and Marquian Lines.[12]

The final plan called for the tanks to penetrate the Hindenburg Line between the two canals, pass the cavalry through the gap, then continue forward and assist the infantry in seizing Bourlon Wood and the town of Cambrai. The tanks and infantry would continue to expand the penetration while the cavalry raided support units in the "rearward" zone and beyond.[13] Fuller expressed concern over the suitability of the terrain beyond the "battle" zone and over the lack of reserves available to exploit any breakthrough, but the plan stood as written.[14] The Cambrai plan was a mixture of traditional operation and innovative thinking. The plan of attack dispensed with the traditional long duration artillery bombardment and instead, the 1,003 supporting artillery guns were to conduct a brief suppressive bombardment, concentrating on counter-battery and smokescreen fire. Once the assault began in earnest, the artillery would shift to the creeping barrage pattern similar to that designed by General Rawlinson for the 1916 Somme operation. The tanks were assigned the mission of breaching the trenches and wire obstacles and leading the attack, precluding the need for an intense preparatory bombardment.

Byng anticipated a breakthrough which would allow the cavalry to pass through to the "rearward" zone in order "to raid the enemy's communications, disorganize his system of command, damage his railways, and interfere as much as possible with the arrival of his reinforcements."[15] The final plan reflected the level of development which British mechanized doctrine had reached under Fuller; Haig was willing to commit the tanks to a crucial role and expected them to accomplish more than obstacle reduction. At the same time, the exploitation and disruption role stayed with the cavalry who remained vulnerable on a battlefield replete with machine guns and artillery.

Fuller divided the six-mile-wide offensive sector into a series of objectives, each of which was further subdivided, based on the number of strongpoints, into "tank section attack areas." He assigned a three-tank section, along with an infantry section, to each attack area. Each tank carried a bundle of wood three or four feet in diameter and weighing over one ton. These were affixed to the front of each vehicle with chains. The wood was carried to fill in antitank ditches, thereby allowing the tank-infantry teams to negotiate three ditches as they leapfrogged through the defenses.[16]

On November 20, 1917, at 0620 hours, British artillery commenced a suppressive barrage along the six-mile-wide front. Unlike previous preparatory barrages, this forty-five minute barrage was predominantly smoke and high explosive. The artillery concentrated on suppressing the defenders' artillery and masking the tanks' advance. After less than one hour, the artillery began the creeping barrage and the tanks moved forward. The absence of a traditional preparatory bombardment probably contributed to the defenders' surprise and to the tanks' success in breaching the first defensive lines.

GHQ allocated 476 tanks to Byng's Third Army for the Cambrai attack. Out of this total, 378 were fighting tanks; 44 were devoted to communications, command, and control; and the remaining 54 were assigned resupply duties. These last tanks each carried two tons of supplies and hauled an additional five tons on sledges over the breached obstacle networks. Fuller estimated that it would have required over 21,000 men to carry a similar resupply load, which represents a significant savings in fighting troops who were not diverted from actual combat duties.[17] The tanks were accompanied and followed by elements of six infantry divisions. Waiting behind the safety of the British trenches were the five divisions of cavalry which Byng hoped to launch forward.

The opening stages of the attack were successful. Masked by smoke and the creeping barrage, the tanks tore holes through the wire obstacles and filled in ditches with the wood. Less than two hours after the attack began, the British captured the Hindenburg Main Line over the six-mile front between the two woods. By 1130, the Hindenburg Support Line, with the exception of the ridge at

Flesquieres, was in British hands as well. By the end of the day, the BEF had penetrated to a depth of just over four miles, capturing over 5,000 prisoners, with a loss of just over 4,000.[18] The first day's operation demonstrated the effects of coordinated tank, infantry, and artillery tactics over suitable terrain within the parameters of a well thought-out tactical plan.

But the success of November 20 was mitigated by several failures. The British lost 179 tanks that day to a combination of enemy fire and mechanical breakdown. The tank/infantry teams penetrated to a depth of over four miles, but not deep enough to qualify as a breakthrough into the "rearward" zone. The cavalry divisions in most sectors never even made it into the battle, and the few cavalry units committed failed to accomplish anything significant in terms of rear area exploitation. In addition, the operation experienced several instances of degraded coordination between the tanks, infantry, and artillery. The 51st Infantry Division fell so far behind the assaulting tanks that, when the tanks reached the Flesquieres Ridge, the infantry could not detect the breaches in the wire.

A short while later, 16 tanks, without the protection of their own infantry teams, were destroyed by a battery of German field guns which were out of range of the tanks' weapons.[19] This incident illustrates clearly that Fuller's tactics needed refinement. While he had proven that tanks were capable of rapid penetration, they were by no means capable of independent operations.

Haig terminated the Cambrai attack on November 22, just as he had promised if the offensive failed to result in a breakthrough. He recognized that the BEF lacked the reserves needed to continue the attack because of the previous diversion of five divisions to the Italian Front at Caporetto.[20] One week after the attack began, he wrote, "I have not got the necessary number of troops to exploit our success. Two fresh divisions would make all the difference and would enable us to break out. . . ."[21] This lack of reserves, combined with the cavalry's inability to achieve a breakthrough on their own, convinced Haig to end the attack after only limited gains. It is clear that no one, with perhaps the exception of Fuller himself, anticipated the extent or rapidity of success. Swinton reacted to the initial reports on November 20 with this comment: "I'm pleased all right, but I'm wondering. I bet that GHQ are just as much surprised by our success as the Boche is, and are quite unready to exploit it."[22]

The lack of available reserves resulted in the loss of British momentum at Cambrai. The Germans were able to fall back, regroup, and on November 30 launch a counterattack to eliminate the new British salient. The Germans began their attack at 0700 with an intense one-hour-long artillery bombardment, similar to the one used by the BEF on November 20th. Using proven *sturmabteilung* tactics, they succeeded in reducing the salient on an eight-mile front in just over three hours. Several minor successes followed, but they were unable to execute a rapid or violent breakthrough due to inadequate reserves, British reinforcements, and general troop exhaustion. The counterattack forced the BEF to withdraw partially to stabilize the lines, resulting in practically no net gain based on the success of November 20th. By December 7, the lines had stabilized. The Germans had, between November 20 and December 7, lost 41,000 men and 138 guns. The British had lost 43,000 men, 158 guns, and 213 of their available tanks.[23]

In strategic terms, the BEF had gained nothing. But from a tactical and developmental viewpoint, the battle of Cambrai represents a transition in BEF operations. Because of the complete tactical surprise and significant gains made in less than 12 hours, several contemporaries mark November 20, 1917, as a landmark of sorts in the history of warfare. Lloyd George later said that the battle "will go down to history as one of the epoch-making events of the war, marking the beginning of a new era in mechanized warfare."[24] Haig credited the use of tanks at Cambrai with making it possible "to dispense with artillery preparation, and so to conceal our intentions from the enemy up to the actual moment of attack,"[25] and stated that the tanks' penetration of the Hindenburg Line had "a most inspiring moral effect on the Armies I command . . . the great value of the tanks in the offensive has been conclusively proved."[26] Swinton, not surprisingly, claimed some credit for the success of November 20th. "It has an added interest," he wrote, "in that it was upon the lines here laid down [reference made to his February 1916 'Notes on the Employment of Tanks.'] that the epoch-making Battle of Cambrai was fought. . . ."[27]

The combination of surprise, suitable terrain, adequate numbers of tanks, coordinated artillery bombardment, resourceful preparation and, most importantly, comprehensive planning, resulted in a major penetration of enemy lines. The lessons learned in the areas of economy in men per weapon, in men per yard of front, in casualties, artillery preparation, cavalry personnel, ammunition, and battlefield labor were important.[28] While there was no denying the significance of the event, the British failed to convert the early success of November 20th, and Fuller set out to determine exactly why. Fuller and the General Staff of the Third Army developed a list of lessons learned based on the Cambrai operation.[29] Six of the most significant lessons, several of which remain applicable to present-day combined arms operations as well, appear below:

1. "Tank units and infantry units must maintain close liaison during offensive operations." Haig used the incident at Flesquieres Ridge as an example of this lesson: "This incident shows the importance of infantry operating with tanks and at times acting as skirmishers to clear away hostile guns. . . ."
2. "Keep large reserves of tanks to replace unexpected losses in any sector."
3. "The present model tank is mechanically unable to deal with enemy parties in upper stories of houses."
4. "Tanks must not outdistance supporting infantry—this allows enemy to hide and reappear." This was a contributing factor in the cavalry's failure on November 20th.
5. "Infantry must not expect too much from tanks—they must assist the tanks with protection—this requires continuous combined arms training."
6. "Tanks used in small numbers are only 'frittered' away. If it is desired to continue the advance with tanks on the second day, a completely new formation of tanks should be earmarked."[30] Historian John Terraine alluded to this when he stated "the tanks [at Cambrai] had shown their effectiveness for breaking into even a very elaborate and strong trench position. Breaking through was another matter."[31]

In May 1918, Fuller published an important doctrine study entitled "The Tactics of the Attack as Affected by the Speed and Circuit of the Medium D Tank," more commonly referred to as simply "Plan 1919."[32] His analysis called for the initial penetration of the "outpost" and "battle" zones by tanks. Once into the "rearward" zone, the tanks would seek out the enemy's command and control systems and artillery support, thereby assuming the role of the cavalry.[33] This plan represented a further innovation on tactics beyond those employed in September 1916 and November 1917. Fuller advocated the destruction of systems, rather than the elimination of enemy troop concentrations, and believed the end result would be the same: the crippling of the enemy's will and capacity to fight. His futuristic concept was based on the speed, maneuverability, and firepower capabilities of the Medium D tank, and he assumed, mistakenly, that the military establishment would agree with him. In order to execute his plan, Fuller required a force of over 5,000 tanks, an increase in Tank Corps personnel from 17,000 to 37,000, and a willingness on the part of the military to replace the horse-mounted cavalry with tanks.[34]

Despite the success of November 20, 1917, Fuller's "Plan 1919" was too radical for the leadership to endorse, and it never progressed beyond the theoretical stage. What "Plan 1919" represents is the continuing development of mechanized doctrine. The limited success of November 20th demonstrated the capabilities of tanks; in July 1918 at the Battle of Hamel, and later, in August 1918, at the Battle of Amiens, the British Tank Corps had opportunities to demonstrate the potential for tank operational success on an increasingly greater offensive scale.

The Battle of Cambrai provides a picture of the tanks' development from infantry support weapons with limited offensive potential to weapons employed on the point of the offensive. They had proven capable of clearing a path for the infantry into the main defensive zone and demonstrated the potential to advance further. During the inter-war period, mechanized doctrine would vacillate between those who believed tanks should remain auxiliary to the infantry and those who were willing to take the doctrine to a higher level. Interestingly enough, it was the British who elected to revert back to the early philosophy, while the Germans, under General Heinz Guderian, explored the potential for expanded mechanized operations. In retrospect, the decision by both sides is logical. The British had won the war using traditional strategies augmented by innovative equipment and tactics, and therefore had little inclination to change. The Germans, on the other hand, had lost; their tactics had proven ineffective on the large scale of the Western Front, and they had everything to gain by adopting new equipment and strategies.

Notes

1. J.F.C. Fuller, *Memoirs of an Unconventional Soldier,* (London: I. Nicholson and Watson, 1936), p. 88.

2. Douglas Orgill, *The Tank: Studies in the Development and Use of a Weapon,* (London: Heinemann Publishing Co., 1970), p. 31.

3. Fuller, *Memoirs of an Unconventional Soldier,* p. 87.

4. *Ibid.,* p. 96ff.

5. *Ibid.,* p. 97.

6. *Ibid.,* pp. 129–130.

7. B.H. Liddell Hart, *The Memoirs of Captain Liddell Hart, Vol. 1,* (London: Cassell and Company, Ltd., 1965), p. 87.

8. *Fuller, Memoirs of an Unconventional Soldier,* pp. 172–175; see also Trevor Wilson, *The Myriad Faces of War,* (New York: B. Blackwell, 1986), p. 488.

9. Orgill, pp. 35–36; see also Wilson, p. 488.

10. Wilson, pp. 488–489; see also J.H. Boraston, *Sir Douglas Haig's Despatches, Dec 1915–April 1919,* (New York: Charles Scribner's Sons, 1927, pp. 152–153.

11. *Ibid.*

12. Boraston, pp. 153–154.

13. *Fuller, Memoirs of an Unconventional Soldier,* pp. 181–182.

14. *Ibid.*

15. Boraston, p. 153.

16. J.F.C. Fuller, *Tanks in the Great War,* (London: John Murray, 1920), pp. 136–153; see also Wilson, p. 489.

17. Fuller, *Memoirs of an Unconventional Soldier,* p. 198.

18. Boraston, p. 157; see also Wilson, p. 490.

19. Fuller, *Memoirs of an Unconventional Soldier,* p. 209.

20. Robert Blake (ed.), *The Private Papers of Douglas Haig, 1914–1919,* (London: Eyre and Spottiswoode, 1952), p. 265.

21. *Ibid.*

22. Ernest D. Swinton, *Eyewitness: being personal reminiscences of certain phases of the Great War, including the genesis of the tank,* (New York: Arno Press, 1972), p. 266.

23. Wilson, p. 492; see also David Eggenberger, *A Dictionary of Battles* (New York: Thomas Y. Crowell Company, 1967), p. 73.

24. David Lloyd George, *War Memoirs of David Lloyd George,* (Boston: Little, Brown and Company, 1933), p. 102.

25. Boraston, p. 157.

26. *Ibid.,* p. 173.

27. Swinton, pp. 171–172.

28. Arch Whitehouse, *Tank,* (New York: Doubleday and Company, Inc., 1960), p. 93.

29. Fuller, *Memoirs of an Unconventional Soldier,* pp. 218–219.

30. Blake, p. 269.

31. John Terraine, *White Heat: The New Warfare 1914–1918*, (London: Sidgewick and Jackson, 1982), p. 242.

32. Fuller, *Memoirs of an Unconventional Soldier*, pp. 332–335.

33. Robert H. Larson, *The British Army and the Theory of Armored Warfare, 1918–1940*, (New York: University of Delaware Press, 1984), p. 90; see also Orgill, p. 89; see also Fuller, *Memoirs of an Unconventional Soldier*, p. 321.

34. Orgill, p. 89; see also Fuller, *Memoirs of an Unconventional Soldier*, Appendix I, pp. 334–335.

Reading 2

Maneuver by Riflemen: The American Campaign

by Rod Paschall

German officers had criticized the lack of tactical proficiency among the American Marines' leadership at Belleau Wood, and a similar comment about U.S. Army leadership was made by British soldiers. The observation was made by the officers of the veteran British Fifteenth (Scottish) Division upon relieving the U.S. First Division a little to the north of the American Marines. The First Division had been in the thick of an eighteen-division counter-attack that caused Ludendorff to call off his final offensive in Flanders and resulted in a fighting German withdrawal from the Marne salient to a position not far from where their third drive had begun. The British noted the American dead lying in rows on the battlefield, indicating costly human-wave attacks. It appeared to be a terrible waste of good men.

In visiting American units, Haig had privately remarked that, although the young U.S. officers and their soldiers were "active and keen to learn," some of the senior American officers were "ignorant of their duties." The British were particularly astute observers of the U.S. Army. They conversed easily with the American rank and file, and they could reflect back to two years earlier when they had quickly raised their own "New Army." Haig muffled his criticism. More than all the others, he knew the real meaning of fresh Allied units on the Western Front. And despite its shortcomings, the U.S. Army had an unabashed enthusiasm

From *The Defeat of Imperial Germany, 1917–1918* by Rod Paschall, edited by John S. Eisenhower. Copyright © 1989. Reprinted by permission of Algonquin Books of Chapel Hill.

and drive that could be contagious. In the coming months, the Allies would need all the esprit, energy, and élan they could muster.

Now, pushed back deep in their own territory, the Allied leadership began to formulate an overall strategy. For the time being, the effort would clearly be to reduce the threatening salients that had been produced by Ludendorff's spring offensive. The midsummer of 1918 would therefore be spent in counterattacks aimed at regaining lost territory. There was little discussion or controversy about this immediate task. The enemy intrusions were vulnerable, inviting attack. The Germans must not be given the time to construct formidable defenses in their newly won positions. The Allied generals were as alert as ever to the possibilities of a negotiated end to the war. The less French and Belgian soil occupied by the Germans, the more favorable would be the Allied bargaining position. The summer would be devoted to recovering lost ground.

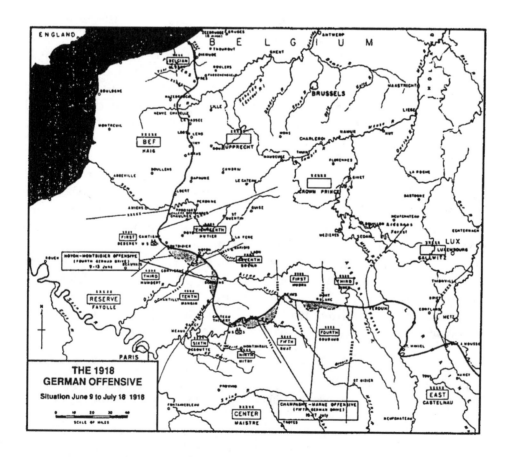

THE 1918 GERMAN OFFENSIVE

Situation June 9 to July 18 1918

The step beyond that, the Allied strategy for the fall, was now the special province of the senior Allied military authority, Foch. Several factors shaped his thinking. The foremost consideration centered on achieving the best political position for the Allied cause. That led the French general to insist on a continuous military offensive—all summer and through the fall. Once the Germans began to give up their gains, Foch believed, they must not be allowed to pause, to reorganize, to reconstitute and strengthen themselves.

The idea of a continuous offensive was, in 1918, somewhat novel. Military thinking was accustomed to planned battles that were limited by time and geography. Foch, however, became so wedded to the idea of a continuous offensive that he began to speculate that the war might be won in 1918. Coming from any other general, such a projection would be put down merely as an understandable but ill-founded encouragement to subordinates. Foch, however, was beginning to acquire a reputation for unfailing intuition.

A more objective analysis could not sustain such optimism. The Allies might have demonstrated an ability to slow and finally stop a German offensive, but there was little evidence to suggest that they could develop and maintain an offensive of their own. Even if the Germans were pushed back, it would be into the awesome defenses of the Hindenburg Line. Breaking that barrier would require the use of vast Allied resources. Then there were intelligence reports indicating that Ludendorff was bringing several more divisions from Russia to the Western Front, as well as all seven German divisions that had been employed heretofore in Italy. There was also a growing Allied industrial problem. Shortages of coal and iron had not only diminished the shipment of U.S. troops, but had placed the production rate of artillery ammunition behind the rate of spring and summer consumption. The Allies were becoming so desperate for iron that Foch had to advise the dismantling of British and American railroads; French industry could no longer supply the new rails needed for increasing lines of communication in France and Belgium. Finally, there was the ominous matter of manpower. The influenza epidemic had begun to wane, but the Allied counterattacks had been costly. American battle casualties per unit had been high in July, but Pershing still had few divisional-sized organizations in the fighting; the prime concern was over British and French casualties. The French were losing men at the rate of 112,000 per month, and the British loss rate was at about 70,000 per month. The British were now drafting men up to fifty years of age. Pessimists within Allied ranks had plenty of fuel for their arguments.

Foch, however, did not depend on mere hope and intuition. He countered the German Western Front reinforcement from Italy with the withdrawal of four of the six French divisions there and two of the five British divisions, adding to his force for the fall campaign. He even persuaded the reluctant Italians to send two of their own divisions. The sum of the Italian front redeployment had Foch one division up on Ludendorff.

He then attempted to check the flow of German troops westward from Russia. To pin down as many of his enemy's troops there as possible, he enthusiastically encouraged a doubting President Wilson to send American forces into the revolution-plagued land. His plea to the U.S. chief of state was wrapped in a piece of logic that he labeled "a decisive military argument." It worked. (The Russian scheme was destined to be of doubtful utility, an action that Americans prefer not to remember but one that Russians seldom forget.)

To cap it all off, Foch persuaded a willing Pershing to request a larger goal for the ultimate size of the American army in France, one hundred divisions in 1919 instead of the existing eighty-division plan. He then gathered the Allied leadership together on July 24 for a general planning session, a meeting that he used to imbue the French, British, and American senior commanders with a vision of final victory.

The enthusiastic French general began the conference with a relatively optimistic assessment. Foch claimed that they were now facing two armies, the well-trained but lightly equipped shock army that Ludendorff had prepared for his recently failed offensive, and another army, designed for defense. The leader of the Allied armies claimed that the shock army was spent, and the other force was being used up in the ongoing Allied counterattacks. Although not quite equal to their enemy in the number of divisions employed, the Allies were actually reaching a superiority in the numbers of combat battalions and reserve forces. The time was at hand, Foch declared, to consider an all-out offensive, one that would position the Allies for ultimate victory in 1919. They should help themselves in the severe iron and coal situation by aiming their offensive at German-occupied French and Belgian industrial districts, adding to Allied might while subtracting from the German industrial capacity. He concluded his appraisal with his firm belief that the reduction of the German salients must be extended to a campaign in which the enemy faced a succession of attacks that would prevent him from withdrawing barrier material, ammunition, and supplies.

The general's performance was wholly dedicated to inspiring a spirit of offense. It was vintage Foch. The supreme commander then asked the Allied leaders for a response. The reply was not encouraging. Haig, whose forces had been battling since late March, said his units were now disorganized. Pétain's appraisal was darker yet. The French leader described his army as "anemic," "worn out," and "bled white." The only glimmer of hope came from Pershing. The American claimed his elements were capable of fighting, although he warned that they were still in the process of being formed.

Despite the general air of caution, however, Haig, Pétain, and Pershing agreed with Foch that the only reasonable course of action was the continuation of the Allied counterattacks at the enemy salients and a transition into a general offensive. To lose the initiative once again to Ludendorff would have too many disadvantages. So, even though still without anything approaching superior numbers, with a critical industrial shortfall, and with no demonstrated ability to sustain an offensive, the Allied leaders set about mounting an attack.

Foch established the overall parameters for the offensive. The immediate actions were to be aimed at reducing the salients. Planning would be directed at final victory in 1919, when Allied numbers might weigh heavily. The fall 1918 offensive would feature a general advance in the center by Pétain's French forces, along with two aggressive and powerful thrusts, one in the north under Haig and another in the south by the Americans. A single bold thrust was never seriously considered, since that would be met by a similar concentration of Ludendorff's defense forces. The northern and southern arms of the offensive were to be aimed at securing industrial and transportation advantages. The British and American drives were therefore targeted on rail centers, coalfields, and iron deposits deep in the German rear. Although the outcome of the July 24 conference was perhaps predictable, there was at least one novel feature: there would be an American campaign.

Up to now, American troops had been fighting under British or French command, executing plans and using tactics that were compatible with those of the European units on the flanks. Pershing was in the process of creating the First Army headquarters, an organization designed to formulate and supervise American plans—plans intended to facilitate American doctrine, use American organizations, and take advantage of American training. Submitting to the coaching of French and British officers, Pershing's officers had patiently waited their turn. In private they had often criticized their European tutors, declaring that their allies were obsessed with the safety of trenches and cowed by enemy machine guns, and that they had become fatigued by Western Front conditions that produced an inordinate degree of reliance on artillery. The American style of moving would break the tactical deadlock and force the enemy out of the trenches and into open warfare; it would be a brand of combat that would see maneuver, rifle marksmanship, and rapid advance. To the Americans, it was going to be a different kind of war.

Some observers believed it already *was* a different war. Shortly after General Foch held his conference, a young British staff officer, Cyril Falls, a man destined to become one of the historians of the conflict, noted in his diary that if the Allies' forthcoming offensive failed after Ludendorff and his German infantrymen had shown how an attack was to be mounted, the British, French, and Americans might as well give up. For this young captain, the German spring offensive had clearly demonstrated a new and proven offensive method. Never before in this dreary, entrenched conflict had so much ground been covered so rapidly. In the end Ludendorff had been unable to sustain his drives, but the new German doctrine had pointed to methods that were worthy of emulation.

The Americans thought otherwise. American doctrine was based on the 1917 Field Service Regulations, which were hardly revised from the prewar 1911 version. The manual specified that the attack should be conducted under the conditions of fire superiority, with advance achieved by infantry rushes. Fire superiority was to be gained by accurate rifle fire. For the Americans, the bane of Western Front attackers—the machine gun—was viewed as a "weapon of emergency." Although the light machine gun had become the heart of German offensive doctrine, the American system gave it little notice. Machine guns were to be treated as obstacles, weapons to be destroyed by concentrated rifle fire. To be sure, artillery would assist the infantry, but the soul of an American assault was the rifleman.

The major readjustment that the U.S. Army had made in order to deal with the conditions of the Great War was in its huge divisional structure. Pershing had observed that European forces had often been forced to relieve their smaller divisions in the midst of an attack, thereby losing momentum and allowing the enemy to reinforce the threatened area. He insisted on a much bigger American organization, one that could sustain losses and press home an attack to reach open ground. Once there, Pershing believed the "independent character" of the American soldier would prevail over any adversary. To express the special American way of war, Pershing and his officers constantly used the catchphrase "open warfare." In sum, U.S. theory had three components: American independent character, superior riflemen, and a divisional organization especially created to absorb punishment in overcoming trench defense systems.

Not surprisingly, the American theory dominated the leadership of the newly created First American Army, despite an occasional flicker of doubt. One consistently raised concern was Pershing's dissatisfaction with the actual quality of the rifle marksmanship he found among his troops. This produced a flurry of messages back to the United States demanding better training. Unfortunately such messages were usually accompanied by others demanding accelerated troop deployment. Then, too, there was the matter of American performance in raids and patrols. General Robert Lee Bullard, commander of the most experienced U.S. unit, the First Division, had noted in the early spring of 1918 that although the U.S. "tradition of Indian and partisan warfare" should have made raiding and patrolling an "American speciality," actual practice indicated otherwise. Patrol and raid leaders had to be selected carefully, and their troops had to be rehearsed and practiced prior to engaging in these kinds of operations.

These two cautionary indicators—poor marksmanship and the need for careful selection and training of patrol and raiding parties—should have rung some alarm bells in an army that was basing its tactics on superior riflemen and "independence of character," but there was no indication of serious doubt at the higher levels of the U.S. command.

There was also the U.S. notion of "open warfare." One of the American combat leaders, General Hunter Liggett, observed in April 1918 that he could find no definitive U.S. instructions on open warfare. There was little doubt that all the U.S. officers talked about it, but when one attempted to find precise doctrine for its execution, the existing literature was a bit thin. Liggett made his concern known to Pershing's headquarters, and action was eventually taken. New doctrine was published—after the war was over.

In August the staff of the American First Army had little time to revise doctrine. Formally activated on the thirteenth of that month, the new headquarters supervised a massive consolidation of U.S. divisions on the right flank of the active portion of the Western Front, 120 miles east of Paris. The movement of the

Americans was a complex matter. During the German spring offensive, U.S. divisions had been plugged in where they were momentarily needed. As a result, fourteen of twenty-nine American divisions were in the French zone, five were in the British sector, and the remainder were in various stages of preparation. Nine of these American units had been involved in the fighting to reduce enemy penetrations, and had already sustained 50,000 casualties. Although Pershing would have preferred to consolidate all of his forces within the newly designated American sector, he yielded to Haig's argument that two U.S. divisions should stay in the north for the biggest of the planned Allied offensives. Two more joined the general reserve. The critical American shortage of transport greatly inhibited Pershing's planners.

The initial American-directed offensive was aimed at the surprise reduction of the St. Mihiel salient, a German-held protrusion that had existed since the early days of the war, and that interrupted direct French rail traffic from eastern industrial areas into Paris. It was in a quiet sector, usually defended by seven German divisions on line, with two additional divisions in reserve. The American staff calculated that the Germans could reinforce the salient with two more divisions in forty-eight hours and another two in seventy-two hours. Since the enemy held high ground overlooking the Meuse River valley on the northwestern face of the salient, the southern face became the selected area for the main American attack. The target date for the assault was September 10.

Pershing's First Army took over the St. Mihiel sector from the French on August 28, but the American commander still needed help from his allies. In addition to his own units, Pershing commanded four French divisions, a welcome role reversal for the Americans, many of whom had long been under French command. General Pétain also assisted Pershing by providing about half the tank crews for the 267 French light tanks, and 900 aircraft and pilots for the armada of approximately 1,500 airplanes scheduled to support the attack. The French also supplied a healthy percentage of the 3,000-piece artillery force that was being quietly assembled in the sector. All told, Pershing would have about 550,000 Americans and 110,000 Frenchmen involved in the operation. The great majority of the manpower was going to be American, but the material of war was almost wholly the product of the prodigious French armaments industry. There would be no U.S.-made aircraft, artillery pieces, or tanks on the battlefield.

The American design for the operation was simple and straightforward. While the French staged a holding action at the nose, the Americans would attack the two flanks of the salient. The assault on the northwestern shoulder of the enemy position would avoid the German-held high ground at the nose of the salient. This attack was the secondary effort under the American Fifth Corps, commanded by General George Cameron, who would have the U.S. Twenty-sixth and Fourth divisions as well as one French division. The main effort was to be on the southern flank of the salient, and would be conducted by two U.S. corps. The First Corps, under the command of General Liggett, had four U.S. divisions: the Eighty-second, Ninetieth, Fifth, and Second. On Liggett's left stood the U.S. Fourth Corps under General Joseph Dickman. This element had the First, Forty-second, and Eighty-ninth U.S. divisions. Additionally, there were six divisions in reserve.

Pershing's First Army staff, a large one of about 500 officers, had learned the vital nature of logistical preparation for a major offensive, and day planned well for the St. Mihiel operation. The attacking forces not only required support in their assembly and initial assault, but would need prepositioned resources to be used during the conduct of the offensive. This entailed 100,000 tons of crushed rock to lay or repair roadbeds, 295 miles of railroad line stock, the designation (and in some cases the construction) of facilities for 21,000 possible hospital patients, 40,000 tons of ammunition, and myriad other important considerations. Despite a host of complications, preparations appeared to be falling into place—until two major and disappointing events occurred.

The first setback had to do with resources; the second involved the entire strategic concept. Colonel George C. Marshall, an operations staff officer on whom Pershing increasingly relied, learned on August 24 that the British would not provide heavy tanks for the American assault. Only French light tanks would be available. The heavy tank was not only a powerful antidote for the machine gun, but a recognized device for coping with barbed-wire obstacles. The Americans would have to improvise.

The second blow came six days later and was directed at General Pershing himself. Arriving on August 30, Foch closeted himself with the American commander and began a carefully reasoned argument for a complete change in the American offensive. The concept involved a shift in the offensive from St. Mihiel to an area sixty road miles north and west, between the Meuse River and the Argonne Forest. The idea would require division of the American forces that were just now being brought together, and a diminished role for the new American command.

"Black Jack" Pershing listened as long as he could, then angrily replied to Foch. There would be no further division of U.S. forces. The United States recognized Foch as the senior Allied military authority, and would go to any area so ordered—but as a complete American force, commanded by an American officer, and to a U.S.-controlled sector. Foch pressed his case, saying, "I must insist." Pershing stood his ground, barking back, "You may insist all you please," but not yielding. Foch departed in a huff, leaving behind an unresolved, contentious issue and a steaming American general.

The essence of Foch's reasoning was that the American drive should start much farther to the north, closer to the vital parts of the German rear. Why not, for instance, let the Germans continue the defense of the St. Mihiel salient? It absorbed enemy troops, troops that could not be used to defend a more important sector. Besides, if the Americans started their drive well to the south, as presently contemplated, it would be some time before they could fight their way north. To the French general, all of this seemed reason enough to revise the plan.

Command and control issues aside, Pershing's reasoning conflicted sharply with that of Foch. It would take a considerable amount of time to pull units out of the gathering concentration at St. Mihiel. If Foch was concerned about continuous pressure on the Germans, he should consider lost time to be an intolerable enemy. However, that was not all. There was a sound operational factor to consider. The St. Mihiel salient lay on the right flank and rear of the proposed offensive in the Meuse-Argonne sector. What if the Germans allowed the new scheme to begin, and then used the St. Mihiel sector as a base to cut in behind the American offensive to the north? To the American commander, elimination of the St. Mihiel salient was an essential preliminary to the Meuse-Argonne operation.

The two generals did not allow the impasse to last. Both men gave ground. Although Pershing's plan for St. Mihiel was not allowed to stand unchanged, he did retain the authority for a consolidated U.S. command operating in a U.S. sector. But he would also have to conduct the Meuse-Argonne operation. The compromise involved limiting the time and depth of the St. Mihiel operation. The Americans were only to pinch off the salient, not continue the drive beyond it. After the reduction they would rapidly shift forces to the Meuse-Argonne and begin an attack there. All of this was to be done in the same month, September.

The immediate result was that Pershing's headquarters, still absorbed in the details of its first major operation, would have to begin concurrent planning for another large task. Because they used many of the same resources, the two undertakings had to be carefully coordinated. For any of the Allied armies the compromise solution would have involved a considerable military feat. For the Americans, with an inexperienced staff, it would be a tall order indeed.

Soon a third problem arose. An element of the planned French support, heavy artillery, could not be moved into place on schedule. For those American staff sections dealing with the new Meuse-Argonne plan, the delay seemed a disaster—there would be two days less to transfer units and supplies from St. Mihiel to the Meuse-Argonne. For those sections dealing only with St. Mihiel, however, it was a blessing, providing forty-eight more hours of planning time, much of which was devoted to the vexing problem of breaching enemy wire obstacles. Operating without the support of British heavy tanks, the Americans did not want to turn to the favored Allied alternative, a week-long "wire-cutting" artillery preparation. American tactical philosophy inclined to the sudden and violent surprise attack. George Marshall and his crew of young operations officers worked eighteen hours a day to find solutions.

Days before the massive September 12 American infantry assault, the scheme for the St. Mihiel operation began unfolding in accordance with a planned sequence of events. The first actions were centered on the French town of Belfort, one hundred miles to the southeast of the German-held salient, a city not far from the German border and the Black Forest. There an American officer took a hotel room in the town and set up a typewriter. Typing out two copies of a piece of correspondence suggesting a forthcoming American troop concentration near Belfort, the officer tucked away the completed letter in his tunic, deposited the carbon paper in the wastepaper basket, and went downstairs for a leisurely stroll. On his return to the room, he noted with satisfaction that the carbon paper had been removed from the basket.

Simultaneously, several U.S. radio detachments arrived near Belfort and began a series of coded messages back to the American headquarters. At the same time, a small element of American tank crews unloaded their light French tanks at a rail siding near the town and began driving the machines along the open edges of wooded areas, ensuring that the tracks would be clearly visible from the air. The bait was taken. Three German divisions began entraining for Mulhouse, twenty-five miles east of Belfort.

At 1:00 A.M. on September 12, 1918, the relative tranquility of the St. Mihiel salient, which had lasted for three years, was shattered by an enormous eruption of flames and shells. Three thousand artillery pieces began a four-hour pounding of German positions. At 5:00 A.M. thousands of American riflemen surged forward. Seventeen months after declaring war, the United States was at last launching its own offensive.

The enemy wire obstacles were overcome with bewildering speed. Each attacking unit seemed to have its own particular method to effect a breach, and every conceivable way was used to go through or over the wire. The novel techniques seemed to work—one and all. One method was not used: prolonged wire-cutting artillery fire. In some spots the bangalore torpedo, a long pipe filled with explosives, was rammed under a mass of wire, with the following explosion clearing a path. In other areas the American infantrymen carried folded mats of chicken wire to the obstacle, threw the mats on top of the German barbed wire, and simply walked across. There were even instances where the Americans physically tromped down the wire and passed beyond. Some units paused to use vintage wire cutters from the Spanish-American War. In other areas the attackers threaded their way through occasional gaps in the barriers. The lack of heavy tanks was soon forgotten.

Once past the wire, the U.S. infantrymen in the main (or southern) attack found the forward German positions lightly manned, or else discovered that the devastating artillery storm had done its grisly work. When the main defense works were reached, American casualties began to mount—but not for long. It was now daylight, and one amazed German soldier watching the U.S. attack described it as being conducted with "praiseworthy indifference" to danger. The Americans kept coming—and coming in astounding numbers.

In some areas of the main attack, the Americans had pounced on the defenders with such speed that they found their enemy still in bunkers, awaiting the final shells of the American and French artillery. That was the case with Sergeant Harry Adams of the Eighty-ninth Division. Spotting a German soldier darting into a bunker, the game Adams followed him, but the door slammed in his face. The eager American had almost exhausted all of his ammunition in the attack. He was down to his pistol—and had only two bullets left at that. Without hesitation (or perhaps forethought), Adams fired both rounds into the door. Essentially unarmed at this point, the determined sergeant shouted out an authoritative demand for surrender to his prey. The door cracked open. A timid German soldier appeared, hands held high. Adams waved his captive out of the doorway, the empty pistol thrust menacingly forward. Another German followed the first out of the bunker—then another, and yet still more. After Sergeant Adams had gathered his three hundred prisoners together under the rather impotent threat of his useless pistol, he became somewhat apprehensive about his own security. Nevertheless, without losing his stern and soldierly bearing, he herded his charges to the rear. At one point the horde of Germans with their obscure captor was mistaken for a massed German counterattack, but Adams and his small percentage of the kaiser's legions finally reached safety.

The main attack had gone well. The second day's objectives were almost all taken on the afternoon of the first day. To the north, however, the secondary attack had not matched the success of the main attack. The Germans fought harder there, since the attack was aimed nearer to the base of the salient and close to a vital supply corridor for the defenders. Only one unit of the U.S. Twenty-sixth Division gained its first day's objective by afternoon, and that only after the division's reserve was thrown into the fighting. The other elements of the secondary attack had ground to a halt far short of the planned advance. When Pershing learned that enemy troops were beginning to evacuate the salient, he quickly realized that a nighttime pause in the offensive might result in his enemy's escape. Grabbing the telephone, he ordered a night attack, with the goal of effecting a linkup with the main attack forces by dawn. The American commander was now demanding that the entire salient be pinched off in twenty-four hours.

The veteran Twenty-sixth Division sent its weary 102nd Infantry Regiment into the gathering darkness, on toward a front that had thus far successfully resisted the Allied assault. The hastily arranged plan was the soul of simplicity: an attack up a road in a narrow column. To the surprise of defender and attacker alike, the roadway was not blocked. The flanks of the road were defended but not the road itself. The American infantrymen marched forward, reaching the designated linkup point at a little past 2:00 A.M. on the morning of September 13. Along the way they captured an entire German ammunition train. A little before dawn, elements of the First Division arrived, closing off the route of escape for any enemy unit south of the juncture. Pershing's decisive intervention had paid off.

The American air arm had to contend with bad weather during the ground offensive, but its work was not wholly contingent on events below. The American race-car driver Eddie Rickenbacker had by now improved his ability to spot enemy aircraft. Flying a single-seater French fighter, the young captain was on patrol over the northeast part of the salient when he saw four German fighters closing in on a flight of American-piloted bombers returning from a raid over Metz. Climbing into the sun, Rickenbacker turned and dove his craft to the rear of the pursuing enemy, noting the well-known markings of Richtofen's old organization on the German planes. Catching the trailing fighter unaware, the American brought down the plane in a hail of machine-gun fire. Rickenbacker managed to elude the German pilot's three revenge-seeking comrades and save the bombers from probable destruction at the same time. It was his sixth "kill." There would be twenty others before the captain returned to the United States.

German observation balloons were a constant concern of the American attackers. The U.S. air service was hard pressed to destroy the balloons, since they were invariably well protected by antiaircraft defenses. If the balloons were allowed to float uncontested, enemy observers would have been amply warned about the forthcoming American attack. Moreover, elimination of the balloons was just as important after the attack, when the American and French troops established a defense. The better the German observation reports, the more casualties via German artillery. Fortunately, American, French, Italian, and Portuguese pilots in Colonel Billy Mitchell's air element for the St. Mihiel operation were becoming skilled in making rapid and deadly passes at the balloons. One of the best pilots at this dangerous game was Lieutenant Frank Luke. Luke got one balloon on the first day of the assault, two more on September 14, and another pair on the sixteenth. The lieutenant's big day was on September 18: two more balloons and three German fighters to boot. Luke would not return home.

On the ground the American offensive had ended less than forty hours after it had begun. The base of the salient had been reached, and that was the agreed-upon point at which the switch to the Meuse-Argonne deployment would begin. Some of the American officers believed the overall plan was flawed and that the original American concept should have been followed. With the Germans on the run, why not keep the momentum and continue the attack? One such officer, Douglas MacArthur, a brigade commander in the Forty-second Division, had slipped forward on the night of September 13 to a position well within what the Germans should have been defending. Seeing the fortress of Metz, MacArthur claimed his brigade could have pressed on for many miles.

On the surface, a continuation of the St. Mihiel operation appeared to be a sound idea, following the military dictum of reinforcing success. And there seemed to be a wealth of success to reinforce. The bag of prisoners was large. The short American attack had netted over 16,000 German and Austro-Hungarian captives. The haul of enemy weapons was also impressive: 443 artillery pieces and 752 machine guns. Two hundred square miles of French territory were liberated, and the rail line from Paris to northeastern France was no longer imperiled. The American doctrine seemed to be sound. The big divisions emerged from the fighting showing little need for relief. The American staff, no doubt with the British and French in mind, crowed that casualties had been light, only about 7,000 men. Congratulations poured in to the commander, Pershing.

On the evening of September 13, when he was certain all of the operational objectives had been achieved, Black Jack Pershing took a few moments to relax and enjoy the accolades. Reflecting on the success, he confided to his intelligence officer, Brigadier General Dennis Nolan, that the reason for the American triumph lay in the superior nature of the American character. Americans were the product, he said, of immigrants who had possessed the initiative and courage to leave the Old World. They were the descendents of those who had the drive, intellect, and daring to make a mighty nation out of a wilderness. Americans had the willpower and spirit that Europeans lacked. With military training equal to that given a European, the American soldier was superior to his Old World counterpart.

Even as the two American officers were speaking, however, evidence began to trickle in to headquarters that should have taken much of the euphoria out of Pershing's attitude—if the evidence were considered objectively. Through prisoner interrogations and captured documents, it was learned that the American attack had been staged against forces that were already in the process of withdrawal. The retreat had begun on September 10, big guns first, and the Germans had no heavy artillery within range of the attack. Although the defenders had forecast an offensive against the salient, their higher headquarters had not thought the area important enough to reinforce. Reserves had been positioned far to the rear, incapable of executing the standard German defense doctrine of immediate counterattack. Total withdrawal had been ordered as early as noon on the day of the attack. The barbed-wire obstacles had not been maintained for some time, a prime reason they were so easy to overcome. Some of the stakes held up little more than fragile belts of rust. Many of the prisoners taken came from the same unit, an Austro-Hungarian division that had little intention of carrying on the war. Numerous members of this unit simply slung their rifles over their shoulders and marched forward, looking for someone to accept their surrender.

An objective analysis would also have considered battle information derived from the Americans themselves. The American boast of light casualties was right—but only if the consideration was restricted to the amount of ground taken. Pershing's pronouncement of about 7,000 casualties did not take into account the French under his command, and was obviously meant to include only the two days of major offensive action. Even then, the casualty rate of 3,500 per day exceeded Haig's accurate prediction of his expected losses for a major offensive prior to the bloody Passchendaele push of 1917. In the next two days, during the consolidation phase, the Americans took over 3,000 more casualties.

An unbiased appraisal of losses would also have considered the intensity of the resistance. In the case of St. Mihiel, the enemy's retreat had as much to do with his desire to withdraw as it did with American pressure to do so. The optimistic conclusions drawn by the U.S. military leadership could be put down to inexperience—but there were Americans who had experience now. Some of the "old-timers" in the U.S. First Division did not regard the St. Mihiel affair as much of a battle. It was an American victory, but along with the elation it should have provoked concern.

Despite the pressing need to set the wheels in motion toward the Meuse-Argonne operation, First Army headquarters did conduct a brief, shallow analysis of the St. Mihiel operation. The results produced several important conclusions: first, there had been severe traffic congestion and confusion on the primitive road net supporting the offensive and second, there had been poor coordination between the American units. The traffic problem was a serious one. An inability to sort out the priorities between infantry reinforcement, ammunition supply, artillery displacement, and casualty evacuation could cripple future offensive actions. The liaison and coordination problem was just as serious. Combat efficiency depended on the ability of one unit either to support or else get out of the way of another unit. Pershing concluded that better training for the traffic control element was essential to rectify the first deficiency, and that more detailed instructions in operations orders were needed to enhance coordination between his forces. The basic American tactical doctrine, however, was not questioned.

Traveling at night in order to avoid enemy air reconnaissance, American units and logistical convoys made their way northward behind French lines to join in the Allies' great fall offensive. Pershing's army would be on the right flank of the French Fourth Army, and together their thirty-seven divisions would form the southern thrust that complemented Haig's massive assault in the north. The ultimate southern objective, the city of Mezieres, was located in the French-designated sector, about forty miles behind the thirty-six German divisions that were facing Pershing and his ally. Allied possession of this town would sever the vital German lateral rail line that serviced the great majority of Ludendorff's Western Front forces. Success in the southern advance would give the Allies important industrial facilities and deprive the Germans of a considerable amount of resources. There could be little doubt about the importance of the forthcoming offensive. It was not likely that the enemy would voluntarily withdraw this time, as they had from the St. Mihiel salient.

The Americans were taking over twenty-four miles of the front from the French, and the overall plan dictated an eventual U.S. occupation of about one-third of the entire Western Front, or about ninety-four miles. The idea was to feed in the incoming U.S. forces on the right of the French Fourth Army as they became available. Plans were already being drawn up to create another American army headquarters, the U.S. Second Army. Pershing would then become an army group commander and another officer would take over his duties with the First Army. The Meuse-Argonne offensive would therefore carve out the left flank of what was to be a large American sector in France.

The Meuse River formed the initial right extremity of the U.S. attack sector, and the Argonne Forest lay within the left extremity. The main American thrust would be made between the two, in the watershed of the Meuse and Aire rivers. The rolling terrain there was badly churned up and pockmarked from previous fighting around Verdun. During most of the action the Argonne Forest would overlook the main attack corridor, so that the eastern wood line would have to be occupied and dominated by U.S. units. The veteran Twenty-eighth Division was picked to handle this important task.

Possibly the most notable feature of the entire area was a missing element: adequate transportation arteries. There were only three roads in the region that ran parallel with the American direction of attack. Nine U.S. divisions would be using those roads—and that was counting only the front-line infantry formations that were to lead the assault.

Only four of the attacking divisions had any appreciable combat experience; the other five had not even completed their training. Three of these latter divisions had yet to receive their artillery units, and had to be provided with hastily arranged fire-support formations. Fifty percent of the untried Seventy-ninth Division was composed of enlisted men who had been in uniform for only four months. The Fourth, Twenty-eighth, and Seventy-seventh were veteran divisions, but the Seventy-seventh had to be fleshed out with infantry and was destined to receive four thousand riflemen who had been drafted in the United States in July. These new men would arrive only two days before the assault. Clearly Pershing was not putting his best foot forward for the grand offensive. How had it happened?

When Pershing was directed to plan for the Meuse-Argonne operation, he was already committed to St. Mihiel. There he had placed his experienced units in the lead, using his untried divisions for the reserve. Because the reserve force for St. Mihiel had not been used, it therefore remained untested. Three of those units could be shifted rapidly to the Meuse-Argonne sector, and they were. Several U.S. divisions were in the final stages of training during the St. Mihiel operation. Although they would not complete their training in time for the Meuse-Argonne operation, they were at least uncommitted, and therefore were used.

In essence, the First Army staff, having just received the order for the Meuse-Argonne operation on September 7, threw in what appeared to be the most available units. Since the attack was to be made on September 26, the staff had to work quickly. It was a matter of expediency.

The Meuse-Argonne operation was going to be bigger than the one at St. Mihiel, yet in some ways the support for the operation would be less than that used for the first U.S. effort. The perception of ally and enemy alike was that Blackjack Pershing was in command of a rapidly growing, strong army. In reality some facets of that force were showing increasing weakness with each passing day. In addition, there was less planning time than at St. Mihiel:

only nineteen days. At St. Mihiel there had been about 1,500 aircraft under Billy Mitchell's direction. For the new operation, only 820 aircraft, 600 of them flown by Americans, would participate on the Allied side. This time there would be only 189 tanks, 25 percent of them with French crews. There was more artillery—some 3,980 guns—but it could not all be brought to bear for the initial assault. More American troops were to be involved; about 600,000 would move into the sector. But these numbers were rapidly being eroded by the mystifying influenza. Beginning in early September, the epidemic returned with a vengeance. American hospital admissions climbed to almost 40,000 for that month. And this wave was deadly. About 2,500 of Pershing's soldiers died from the incurable malady in September. Both figures—hospital admissions and the death toll—far exceeded the wounded and killed for St. Mihiel.

The American intelligence estimate projected that five German line divisions were facing the nine U.S. assault divisions on the first day. Fixed defenses consisted of three well-maintained, well-constructed defense lines about one or two miles apart. Villages interspersed throughout the area had been heavily fortified. Carefully camouflaged machine-gun positions were often present in the basements of houses. While the number of German divisions on the line facing the Americans would be less than at St. Mihiel, the enemy reinforcement capability in the Meuse-Argonne was far greater. General Nolan's intelligence officers predicted the five enemy line divisions would be reinforced with four more in twenty-four hours, two more the second day, and there could well be a surge on the third day of nine additional divisions. If the intelligence estimate was correct, within ninety-six hours of the start of the offensive Pershing's men could be facing twenty German divisions.

To better the chances of success, Pershing and his First Army staff, now grown to 600 officers and 2,000 enlisted men, relied heavily on speed and stealth. The "Belfort ruse" had served well for St. Mihiel, but once fooled, Ludendorff might not be fooled a second time. The American general's intuition proved sound. The Germans actually expected to confront what Pershing *wanted* to do, not what he was *ordered* to do. The enemy staff was looking for the Americans to continue the St. Mihiel offensive. The night movement, front-line reconnaissance done in French uniforms, and other precautions designed to mask the replacement of 200,000 French troops with 600,000 Americans, largely worked, so that Ludendorff was not fully aware of what was about to take place in the Aire Valley. In order to beat those nine third-day German reinforcement divisions to the draw, Pershing directed his planners and commanders to gain about ten miles on the first day. That would put the lead divisions through the successive defense works and into the open ground. Once there, the American infantry was expected to be in its own element.

The First Army plan was once again a simple one. The artillery preparation, one hour shorter in duration than at St. Mihiel, was scheduled to begin at 2:30 A.M. on September 26. There would be less firepower—2,700 guns, used for less time—but the American strong card was thought to be its infantry, and less delay between the start of the artillery preparation and the beginning of the assault would enhance the chances of surprise and minimize the effect of early enemy reinforcement. In order to ensure that the Twenty-eighth Division would secure the wood line overlooking the valley to the east, Lieutenant Colonel George S. Patton's tank brigade was assigned to the First U.S. Corps, which had the attack corridor including both the Argonne Forest and the Aire River. The Seventy-seventh Division formed General Liggett's First Corps's left flank, joining the rightmost element of the French Fourth Army. Patton's 140 tanks would be advancing with the Twenty-eighth Division on one side of the Aire, as well as supporting the right flank element of the corps, the Thirty-fifth Division, on the other side of that river. General Bullard's Third U.S. Corps would form Pershing's right flank, attacking with three divisions. The rightmost division of this corps, and thus Pershing's easternmost unit, was the Thirty-third Division, which would be attacking up the west bank of the Meuse River. On the left of the Thirty-third Division was the Eightieth Division, and on its left was Bullard's last assault unit, the experienced Fourth Division.

General Cameron's Fifth U.S. Corps would make the main attack and was emplaced in the center, between Liggett's and Bullard's corps. The three divisions of the Fifth Corps, from left to right, were the Ninety-first, Thirty-seventh, and Seventy-ninth. Cameron had no rivers or major streams in his attack corridor or on its flanks, but there were a number of wooded areas, villages, and a few hills. The most prominent hill that the Fifth Corps had to contend with initially was a spot called Montfaucon (mount of the falcon), about five miles behind the German front line. Montfaucon was in the Seventy-ninth Division's sector, Cameron's right flank unit.

On September 26 at 2:30 A.M. the United States Army began its greatest battle to date. At 5:30 A.M. infantry and tanks moved forward in a dense mist made all the more murky by smoke and gas shells. In the main, surprise had been achieved and the forward German positions were lightly held. Through the first two or three hours there were few reports from the front. On the left, however, the Twenty-eighth Division was encountering great difficulty in the Argonne Forest. Trees had been knocked down by the artillery fire, forming obstacles for the attackers and welcome barriers for the defenders. Patton could hear the Twenty-eighth Division's fighting, and the sounds of his tanks with that unit on his left. Across the river, in the Thirty-fifth Division sector, he waited impatiently, but no reports from his tank crews came in. Gathering his party together, he picked up his long walking stick (a device used to gain the attention of his men inside their noisy machines) and marched forward toward the sound of battle. It was 6:30 A.M.

Soon the American tank brigade commander met a disorganized group of Thirty-fifth Division infantrymen walking to the rear. Stopping them, he learned that they had lost contact with their units in the mist and smoke. Adding them to his party, the determined lieutenant colonel continued his advance. Soon the mist began to lift and the group found themselves within range of a number of German machine guns. During the next three hours Patton would release a carrier pigeon with a report to his superior, organize digging parties to get tanks past ditches, direct his vehicles against enemy machine-gun positions, and lead a somewhat foolish two-man attack against one of these positions. While he was busily involved in the Thirty-fifth Division sector, his elements across the river with the Twenty-eighth Division were experiencing considerable problems in their first encounter with German pillboxes in the wood line. Patton was wounded in the leg and turned over his command to his most aggressive battalion commander, Major Brett. While being helped from the battlefield, he concluded that the Thirty-fifth Division was not doing well at all.

Although the left flank of the attack was falling far behind the scheduled advance, at least one unit with the right flank corps was pressing ahead. The Fourth Division had held together in the mist, and when the weather cleared it found itself about a mile and a half beyond, but to the east of, the key terrain feature, Montfaucon. The division's leadership could see that the prized position was still in German hands, but it was in the designated sector of the Seventy-ninth Division, and the detailed instructions cautioned them to stay in contact with flank units. So the Fourth Division settled in, awaiting the advance of the Seventy-ninth.

By late afternoon the offensive was far behind expectations on the left flank and about on schedule on the right. But what of the main attack and Cameron's Fifth Corps? The experienced U.S. units had a saying about the rolling barrage supporting an assault: "Keep your nose in it." In other words, follow it closely, so that you will be on the enemy machine guns before the German crews can react. The Seventy-ninth, an untried and partially untrained unit, had not learned that the prime support in the attack was not concentrated rifle fire but artillery. The new unit had lost the rolling barrage in its advance, and it paid the price. By 9:00 A.M. the lead regiments of the division were pinned down and without artillery support. A French tank unit was sent to assist the stalled division, but the renewed attack ground to a halt on the edge of Montfaucon at dusk. At the same time, Major Brett began counting his losses. Between enemy action and mechanical failure, he had lost 43 of his 140 tanks. With the darkness, the lead elements of the first German reinforcement division began arriving on the battle-field. Pershing's optimistic goal for the first day's gain faded with the sun.

The next day the offensive was resumed against a now fully alarmed and reinforced German defense. Luck was with the de-fenders; it began to rain. Brett threw in eleven tanks to assist the Twenty-eighth Division, but found that the enemy had begun a concentration of artillery batteries on the edge of the Argonne Forest, hitting the tanks and shelling the exposed American infan-try in the open area to the east. The Seventy-ninth Division man-aged to take Montfaucon at midday, but could not manage a further advance. By holding on to the high spot, Ludendorff's defenders had gained thirty hours. To compound Pershing's diffi-culties, the fragile routes of resupply and reinforcement began breaking down. Some of the light artillery got forward, but ammu-nition supply became a severe problem. One traffic jam was seven miles long. Not much was gained on September 27. Brett was now down to eighty-three operating tanks, and the Germans, having built their strength to ten divisions, began counterattacking.

By September 28 the defenders had massed thirteen batteries of artillery in the Argonne wood line. The Thirty-fifth Division, a prime target of the German gunners, began to give ground and to disintegrate as a cohesive fighting unit. The game Seventy-seventh and Twenty-eighth divisions kept hammering away in the forest, but they were not getting much help from the French Fourth Army in the open ground to their left. The rain continued; the roads became nearly impossible to traverse; enemy counterattacks increased; casualties mounted; Brett lost another thirty tanks. The American offensive was slowing to a halt.

It had gone wrong. Even in the best of conditions it was doubtful whether nine divisions could be supported over such a poor network of roads. The Americans were tied to a simple but inflexible plan that called for attacking on line, anchoring flanks with the advance of neighboring units, and keeping within the confines of divisional boundaries, a system that the Germans had learned to abandon long before. Montfaucon should have been taken on the first day, regardless of assigned boundaries. The weather precluded much support from the air, and the initial delay allowed the defenders to bring in reinforcements, six additional divisions by October 3. Most of all, the attack clearly demonstrated that a good percentage of Pershing's army, and particularly its leadership, was not yet ready for effective offensive combat.

The American commander acted. Ordering only local attacks, Pershing began a complex replacement operation over the tenuous lines of communication. The Eightieth Division was pulled out of the line. The inexperienced Seventy-ninth Division was pulled out of action, replaced by the veteran Third Division, the organization that had put up such a stout defense on the Marne River during the summer. The battle-wise ranks of the "Big Red One," the First Division, pulled into the line, replacing the badly mauled Thirty-fifth Division. The Thirty-seventh Division was relieved by the Thirty-second Division, a unit that had been fighting since late July.

Not satisfied with replacing units, Pershing also replaced leaders. The axe began to fall on generals. Several division commanders were replaced. Cameron, the Fifth Corps commander, would be reduced to division, not corps command. For the first time, the American command faced a problem their allies had long known: finding suitable officer replacements. Pershing had lost 521 of his officers, killed in battle during September.

There was little time to make adjustments. Full-scale resumption of the offensive was scheduled for October 4. Prior to the second effort, Pershing was beset with several problems. The fighting in the Argonne Forest was developing into a confused, knock-down-drag-out affair. One group of about 550 Americans from the Seventy-seventh Division had been cut off from American lines and was fighting a desperate battle for survival. The transportation problem had become so acute that the American commander ordered his line-of-communications trucks to the front to serve as troop and ammunition transports. And then there was an unwelcome visit in the form of a French general officer, carrying a proposal from Foch. The idea put forth was that the tactical situation in the Argonne Forest could be solved by moving in the French Second Army headquarters with some French troops and placing the American units fighting there under French command. Pershing dismissed the proposal and concentrated on the forthcoming battle.

It began at 5:00 A.M. on October 4. This time the order permitted division and corps commanders to act independently within their sectors, discarding the notion that each organization had to maintain alignment with its flanking units. Slow, grinding, and painful progress was made, especially by the veteran divisions, but the cost was high. One battalion of the First Division, the Third Battalion of the Sixteenth Infantry, lost 18 of its 20 officers and 560 of its 800 soldiers.

The enemy was not the only cause of losses. During the first week of October 16,000 new influenza cases were recorded. The medical crisis caused Pershing to cut into his requested troop deployments from the United States in order to transport 1,500 additional nurses to the crowded American hospitals in France. All of these losses, whether stemming from the endless heavy combat or a surging epidemic, were cutting into the American army's combat effectiveness.

The isolated unit in the Argonne was finally reached. There were only 195 unwounded survivors from the initial contingent of 550. There had now been 75,000 combat casualties since the offensive began on September 26, almost all in the infantry. Reluctantly, Pershing ordered two of his least-ready divisions to be dismantled, with their members to be used as replacements.

Along with the word of losses came reports of great bravery and skill. The most highly publicized report dealt with an acting corporal of the Eighty-second Division, Alvin York. Leading a seventeen-man element against several German machine-gun positions, York captured a German battalion commander and his party, only to come under attack by the enemy. After losing about half of his men, York set out by himself to reduce the odds. One by one, the skilled marksman dispatched 28 of his adversaries and returned to pick up his prize catch. Leading the defeated German officer around, York persuaded him with his pistol to encourage his men to surrender. In all, the corporal netted 132 prisoners. For those seeking good news from the American sector, it was a banner day.

October 8 also marked the day when the American sector started to expand. The Thirty-third Division secured a crossing over the Meuse River and American units began to form an entirely new attack corridor. By October 12 the American front stretched for ninety miles, and the Second U.S. Army was established. At last a trickle of American-made munitions started to arrive in France: 75-mm artillery shells. The United States was playing a much larger role in the war.

Losses continued to mount. The First Division had taken 9,000 casualties in the first eleven days of October. Such numbers could not be replaced with any sort of speed. Despite the rising number of wounded and killed, the American soldiers continued attacking in the Meuse-Argonne sector, in some cases with astounding results.

Less publicized than the York feat of arms was the case of a professional soldier, acting Captain Sam Woodfill. A veteran of the Philippine Insurrection and the 1916–17 adventure against Pancho Villa in Mexico, the former sergeant found himself on October 12 leading a company of Fifth Division riflemen against several German machine-gun positions near the right flank of the First Army offensive. Pinned down by fire in the middle of an open field, the captain took matters into his own hands. Moving forward, he jumped in a shell hole and determined that the most serious threat was an enemy automatic weapon in a church tower about 200 yards away. Raising up, he quickly fired five rounds from his rifle. The fire from the church tower ceased.

The next threat appeared to be coming from a stable. Locating the gun position, Woodfill repeated his technique—firing five quick rounds with great accuracy. Success once more. Next came the grazing machine-gun fire across the open field. The weapon was concealed in a bushy area, and Woodfill realized he could not use his previous procedure. The deadly machine gun was directly in front of him. He dashed to another shell hole and then began crawling toward a patch of woods on the flank of the enemy position, barely escaping death from artillery and small-arms fire. Reaching a ditch, he worked his way within ten yards of the German gun. Spotting the partially hidden gunner, Woodfill shot him. One soldier after another took the gunner's place, and the captain kept firing until four replacements had been killed. A fifth soldier showed himself and paid the price. Seeing one more, Woodfill brought him down with a pistol shot.

Moving farther into the woods, the veteran soldier bumped into a German officer, who made the fatal error of trying to grab the American's rifle and was shot then and there. Locating another machine gun and crew, the captain eliminated the crew with his now-proven method of picking off the gunner and his four replacements. Surprising two enemy soldiers, he sent them packing to the rear, hands up. Finding yet another machine-gun position, he repeated his technique—five more enemy soldiers died. Bringing his company forward, and still well in the lead, Woodfill was caught in a flurry of artillery shells. Diving into a nearby trench, he landed on top of two enemy soldiers. The ensuing tussle resulted in both Germans being killed—this time by their own pickax. With the enemy position now firmly held by his unit, the captain sent a messenger for reinforcements. His recommendation was disapproved. The company was "too far out front." So Woodfill withdrew from the hard-won ground and abandoned the penetration—the penetration of the Hindenburg Line.

Two days later the First American Army, under the command of General Liggett, began the next phase of the offensive. It was now facing thirteen enemy divisions in the Meuse-Argonne sector. The eight U.S. divisions were ordered to break the Hindenburg Line. Opposition stiffened even more. After forty-eight hours, on October 16, the Americans finally secured the objectives that Pershing had designated for the first day of the attack on September 26. Most of the original attacking divisions had been sent to the rear. The notion that the large U.S. unit could sustain its losses and continue an offensive had not proved out; in actual practice, the average length of stay at the front proved to be about two weeks. As both the Allies and the Germans had learned, divisions must be rotated out of the front in order to reconstitute, feed in replacements, and rest.

At this point, Pershing's problem was that there were not enough replacements to send to Bullard's Second and Liggett's First armies. Two steps were taken to provide an immediate solution. The American commander ordered a reorganization of the large American rifle company, reducing the authorized strength from 250 to 175 men. On the surface this appeared to be merely a paper solution, but in reality the order permitted units that had not been badly reduced by combat to transfer riflemen to divisions that were now seriously understrength at the company level. The reorganization also included measures to dismantle more divisions; the total number of divisions salvaged for replacements now stood at seven. Pershing also ordered an armywide crackdown on stragglers. There were thought to be about 100,000 men milling around the rear areas, either lost, confused, or shirking combat duty. Casualty replacement and filling in for the influenza victims became a major concern. By October 19 the Third, Fifth, and Eighty-second divisions were down to little more than 5,000 combat-effective infantrymen apiece.

The situation in the American sector did not escape the notice of the French political leader Clemenceau. The wily politician knew that Foch, in his position as the overall Allied military authority, had been in direct correspondence with President Wilson. Using his own political position, Clemenceau asked his countryman to take action seeking the replacement of General Pershing. The politician cited the heavy casualties being incurred by the Americans, and their lack of progress in comparison to the British attack in the north being commanded by Haig.

Clemenceau's motive may have been aimed more at diplomatic rather than military objectives. Serious negotiations were now under way with Berlin to end the war, and the basis for the exchange of notes revolved around President Wilson's earlier proposals for peace. Undercutting Pershing and his independent army on the Western Front would diminish the American influence at the bargaining table. Clemenceau had little trust in the American president, and believed that the terms of peace must, above all, suit the needs of France.

It was now October 21. Foch could not ignore Clemenceau's request. The French general had seen much of the American army and its leadership in the past eighteen months. Prior to 1917, American combat experience had largely been limited to minor, punitive campaigns—operations against Indians, Philippine insurrectionists, and various armed Mexican contingents. Some U.S. generals had exhibited an ability to learn their duties in the wholly different arena of Western Front combat, but others had not. None of them had ever commanded the vast number of soldiers they were now attempting to lead. Despite the fact that America had been in the war for a year and a half, their army had been raised quickly—and showed it.

To Foch and his fellow officers, the deployment of the U.S. Army to France had seemed slow indeed. It was clear that the United States had been unprepared to wage modern warfare. The most prominent indication was the lack of American matériel; almost everything had to be given to them—artillery, tanks, airplanes, and machine guns. Once these were in their hands, the Americans had to be taught how to use them. All of this had taken time.

Then there was the matter of American tactical doctrine. There was no question that the individual American soldier fought, and fought well. But the types of attacks they were conducting were extremely costly. Their leaders appeared to have no concern for losses. The American assault was little more than a human wave into the face of German machine guns, a weapon that the Americans treated with contempt. Their doctrine favored the rifle, yet except for a few highly skilled marksmen their use of that weapon appeared to be little different than that of their European counterparts. They insisted on huge divisions, perhaps because they knew they did not have the officers to direct a larger number of more reasonably sized units. However, they were now in the process of reducing the size of these organizations. Pershing was also eliminating some of his more inept generals. And, most important, they were attacking. Losses or not, the Americans kept coming on.

Foch knew the matter had to be handled carefully. The relief of General Pershing might cause a serious and unfavorable reaction in the United States, where the American general was regarded as a hero. The American attack might be slow, but the U.S. offensive was absorbing a growing number of German divisions and, while the American casualties were high, Ludendorff's losses could not be light either. Another 257,000 American troops had arrived in September, and 180,000 were due to reach France during October. No one could replace the casualties being sustained on the Western Front at this juncture—except the Americans.

Reading 3

Between the World Wars, 1919–39

by Larry Addington

I. The Failure of the Treaty Approach to Prevent Rearmament and War

The years between the wars saw the greatest effort to that time to control armaments and to discourage war through treaty. The approach varied in form all the way from the dictated armament clauses in the Treaty of Versailles with Germany to the voluntary renunciations of war as an instrument of national policy under the Paris Peace Pact of 1928. The greatest practical progress in limiting armaments during the interwar years was made through naval treaties, but ultimately all efforts through treaty failed of their purpose. The reason was not the approach or the terms of the treaties themselves, but the unwillingness of Nazi Germany, Fascist Italy, and Imperial Japan to abide by the status quo. Their revisionist policies in the 1930s finally resulted in a second global war worse than the first.

In June 1919, a German delegation was summoned to the Palace of Versailles outside Paris to sign, not to negotiate, a treaty of peace between Germany and her enemies of World War I. Though the Imperial German government which had waged the war had been replaced by the democratic Weimar republic, the peace terms were no less severe for that fact. They stripped Germany of its overseas empire and of a seventh of its territory in Europe. The loss of

From *The Patterns of War Since the Eighteenth Century* by Larry Addington, Copyright © 1986, Reprinted by permission of the publisher, Indiana University Press.

Alsace-Lorraine to France had been expected, and small territorial losses to Belgium and Denmark were tolerable, but the Germans deeply resented the large loss of territory to the new state of Poland. In addition, the Saarland was transferred to France for fifteen years (its return subject to local plebiscite), and Germany was saddled with a heavy reparations bill. The treaty made of the German Rhineland a demilitarized zone in which Germany was forbidden to station troops or to erect fortifications, but in which the Allies might station troops for up to fifteen years. Germany was also denied membership in the new League of Nations, founded at the Paris Peace Conference.

The Treaty of Versailles's limitations on the German armed forces are of special relevance to the study of the patterns of war. The postwar German army was reduced to the status of an *armée de métier* of one hundred thousand professional soldiers serving under long-term enlistments. All German military service had to be voluntary, and neither an army reserve nor paramilitary organizations were permitted. The army was denied tanks, poison gas, heavy artillery, and air forces, and technically it was not supposed to have any form of the traditional General Staff. The German navy was limited to fifteen thousand sailors, six old pre-dreadnought battleships, six light cruisers, twelve destroyers, and twelve torpedo-boats. The remainder of the High Seas Fleet, interned at Scapa Flow since the end of the war, was to be divided up among the Allies. (Much of it was scuttled by its crews when the terms of the peace treaty were learned.) The pre-dreadnought battleships could be replaced with ships displacing no more than ten thousand tons and carrying guns no larger than 11-inch. (The three built between the wars—the *Admiral Scheer*, the *Admiral Graf Spee*, and the *Deutschland*—were dubbed "pocket battleships" by the press.) An Inter-Allied Military Control Commission (IMCC) was to make periodic inspections in Germany, in order to insure German compliance with the armament provisions.

Ultimately, enforcement of the Treaty of Versailles depended upon cooperation among the United States, Britain, and France, but that cooperation proved lacking in the postwar period. The U.S. Senate rejected the treaty because it committed the United States to membership in the League. The state of war with Germany was ended by a joint resolution of both houses of Congress. In 1921, the American garrison in the Rhineland was withdrawn. Relations between Britain and France suffered after Germany defaulted on reparations payments in 1923 and French troops occupied the Ruhr in retaliation. By then Britain had come to realize that revitalized trade with Germany was worth more to her than reparations. The Ruhr Crisis ended in 1924, when American loans under the Dawes Plan allowed Germany to resume reparations payments to France. In 1925, the government of Gustav Stresemann in Germany signed the Locarno Pact, voluntarily recognizing Germany's new frontiers in the west and pledging not to change those in the east by force. The next year France sponsored Germany's entry to the League, and Britain withdrew her troops from the German Rhineland. The Young Plan in 1929 made it easier for Germany to pay reparations, and in 1930 the last French troops left the German Rhineland. That year too the IMCC made its final report on German armaments and was dissolved. The onset of the Great Depression caused Germany to default on reparations in 1932, and that summer a final settlement was made off the reparations issue. But in January 1933, Adolf Hitler and the Nazi Party came to power in Germany, and the era of the Third Reich began. In October 1933, Hitler took Germany out of both the World Disarmament Conference and the League, and it was widely suspected that Nazi Germany was covertly rearming.

In 1921–1922, representatives of many powers met at Washington, D.C., in order to seek a settlement in the Pacific and to head off the danger of a new naval race. From that conference emerged three treaties. The Nine-Power Treaty reaffirmed international support for the "Open Door" policy with China. The Four-Power Treaty obligated the United States, Britain, France, and Japan to respect each other's territory in the Pacific and the Far East, and limited fortification in the Pacific basin. Most important was the Five-Power or Washington Naval Treaty, which imposed limits on the world's leading navies.

The Washington Naval Treaty defined all warships larger than 10,000 tons displacement with larger than 8-inch guns as "capital ships." It decreed that, with specific exceptions, no capital ship could exceed 35,000 tons displacement or carry larger than 16-inch guns. A ceiling of 525,000 tons was placed on each of the capital fleets of the United States and Britain, and 310,000 tons on that of Japan (the so-called 5/5/3 ratio). In addition, France and Italy were each restricted to 178,000 tons in capital ships. A "battleship-building holiday" was put into effect for ten years, though some capital ships under construction could be completed. Except for specific exceptions, no aircraft carrier was to exceed 27,000 tons displacement, and the United States and Britain were allowed 135,000 tons in aircraft carriers, Japan was allowed 80,000 tons, and France and Italy were each allowed 60,000 tons. Although no agreement was reached on ratios for cruisers, it was agreed that "heavy" cruisers would carry 8-inch guns and "light" cruisers 6-inch guns. No agreement was reached on submarines, save that they would not be employed as weapons of *guerre de course* (France abstained from this pledge). Among the vessels exempted from the limits imposed by the treaty were the British battle cruiser *Hood*, which displaced over 40,000 tons and was the largest warship in the world for much of the interwar period; the American aircraft carriers *Lexington* and *Saratoga* (built on the hulls of ships originally intended to be finished as battle cruisers) which displaced 33,000 tons apiece when completed in 1927; and the Japanese carriers *Kaga* and *Akagi*, also converted ships, which, when completed, displaced 30,000 tons apiece.

At the London Naval Conference of 1930, the United States, Britain, and Japan agreed to a 10/10/7 ratio in cruisers, placed a limit of 57,200 tons on their respective submarine fleets, and extended the "battleship-building holiday" for another ten years. But Japanese militarists increasingly controlled Japan's policies after 1930, launching the invasion of Chinese Manchuria in 1931 and turning it into the puppet state of Manchukuo. When the League found Japan guilty of aggression, Japan left the League. In December 1934, Japan served the required two-year notice of withdrawal from the limitations of the Washington and London naval treaties. Formally, all multilateral treaty limitations expired on December 31, 1936. Meanwhile, the Italian invasion of Ethiopia in 1935 had led to League condemnation and then to Benito Mussolini's withdrawal of Italy from the League. In March 1935, Hitler disavowed the armament limitations of the Treaty of Versailles, and Britain resigned herself to German rearmament. However, Britain believed that she had headed off another Anglo-German naval race when, in June 1935, Hitler signed an Anglo-German Naval Treaty which limited the German surface navy to a ceiling equal to 35 percent of the British fleet and conferred parity in submarines. Actually, Hitler gave away nothing by the treaty, since it would be years before the expanding German navy would reach its limits. In the meantime, the treaty helped to convince British leaders that they could do business with Hitler. In March 1936, German troops entered the demilitarized zone of the German Rhineland in violation of the Treaty of Versailles, but Britain was unwilling to take action, and France was unwilling to act without British support. The Germans then began building the so-called West Wall—a line of fixed fortifications along Germany's western frontiers—the strongest segment of which was the Siegfried Line, opposite the

French frontier. Though the Siegfried Line was not completely finished even by September 1939, it served as a psychological, as well as a physical, barrier to French attack when Germany expanded to the east. Thus, one by one, all of the "bonds" of Versailles had been stripped away by 1937. Meanwhile, in 1936, Hitler and Mussolini had pledged, in the Axis Pact, that Nazi Germany and Fascist Italy would support each other's foreign policies.

In 1937, the Far East took the limelight when Japan launched an undeclared war on China, referred to as the "China Incident." Over the next three years, Japanese armies would occupy much of eastern China and imperil the interests of other powers in the Far East, in clear violations of the Nine-Power and Four-Power treaties made at Washington. In early 1938, Hitler's threats forced Austria—by then a landlocked country of only 6 million people—to accept union with Nazi Germany. Later in 1938, Hitler demanded cession of the Sudetenland, heavily peopled with Germans, from Czechoslovakia, and Prague called on its alliance with France. London and Paris were both appalled at the prospect of war over the Sudetenland issue and finally accepted proposals for a four-power meeting at Munich in September. The upshot of the Munich Conference was that Prime Minister Neville Chamberlain of Britain and French Premier Édouard Daladier of France agreed with Hitler and Mussolini that the Sudetenland would be transferred to Germany in return for Hitler's pledge that he would seek no more territorial changes in Europe. When Chamberlain returned to London, he thought he had brought with him "peace in our time." Actually, the Munich Pact only whetted Axis appetites and made Hitler and Mussolini contemptuous of Anglo-French leadership into the bargain.

Encouraged by the Anglo-French policy of appeasement, in March 1939, Hitler cast aside his pledge at Munich and ordered German troops to occupy the rest of Czechoslovakia and the port of Memel in Lithuania. In April, Mussolini seized the opportunity to invade Albania on the Adriatic Sea. The Anglo-French governments were so enraged at Axis perfidy that Britain adopted peacetime conscription for the first time in her history, and both governments pledged aid to Poland, Rumania, and Greece against future Axis aggression. But in May 1939, Hitler and Mussolini made the Pact of Steel—a full-fledged military alliance—and that summer Hitler began to make demands on Poland. Both Germany and the Anglo-French powers began to court Soviet Russia for a military alliance. On August 23, the Nazi-Soviet Pact was signed whereby, under its secret provisions, Hitler and Joseph Stalin agreed to attack and divide up Poland between them. Though Britain and France promptly made a military alliance with Poland in a last effort to deter Hitler, the peace of Europe was doomed. Treaties for peace had been replaced by pacts for aggression.

II. Armies

The principal topic of debate in the more advanced armies between 1919 and 1939 concerned the future of motorization and of armored warfare especially. Conservative soldiers held that the heavy tank was essentially an infantry-support weapon, while the light tank and armored car were properly assigned to cavalry for reconnaissance missions. Since conservatives held the upper hand in the British, French, and American armies after World War I, armor in each army was divided between the infantry and cavalry branches. But whereas the French army shared with other mass continental European armies the problem that resources were too scarce to dispense totally with horse-drawn vehicles for supply beyond the rail-heads, the smaller Anglo-American armies were able to motorize their logistics almost entirely over the course of two decades, substituting motor trucks for horse-drawn vehicles in their supply columns. Since completely motorized supply columns were denied to them, the French and other continental armies had only the choices of mixing what motorization they possessed with horse-drawn equipment and spreading it through the whole force, or, alternatively, of concentrating it in a completely motorized *corps d'élite* within a traditional mass army. Down to 1939, the French army chose to motorize completely only a very few light mobile divisions and to distribute the rest of its motorization among the infantry divisions and their supply trains as far as it would go.

All three of the French generals-in-chief between the world wars were cautious in their attitude toward the organization of armor and motorization, and in general favored a strategic defensive for France in the event of another war with Germany. Henri Pétain had made his reputation with his unconquerable defense of Verdun in World War I, and he continued to believe in the power of the defensive during the interwar years. Not only was he relatively indifferent to developments in motorization and armor, he may have played a decisive role in the French decision in 1930 to build a powerful line of fixed fortifications across the hundred-mile-wide Lorraine Gap, the traditional gateway from Germany into France. Though the Maginot Line was named for André Maginot, the French minister of war, when the credits were voted by the French parliament, it was really Pétain's monument.

General Maxime Weygand, Pétain's successor at the head of the French army, took relatively more interest in armor and motorization than Pétain, but under his administration French doctrine continued to stress that only traditional combinations of infantry and artillery could conquer and hold ground in a decisive fashion. Under Weygand, the French continued the practice of distributing heavy tank battalions piecemeal among the infantry divisions. Weygand did concentrate light tanks and armored cars in *Divisions Légère Méchanique* in anticipation that these divisions could carry out armed reconnaissance into Belgium in the event that France ever had to counter a second enactment of the German Schlieffen Plan, but once contact with the enemy was made and the battle developed, Weygand planned for the following French mass army to go on the defensive in the Belgian plains and to immolate German attacks on its firepower. General Maurice Gamelin, who succeeded Weygand as head of the French army, did not challenge the ideas of his predecessors down to 1939. The French war plan in 1939 called for the active army to serve as a *force de couverture* (covering force) for the mobilization of the reserve. Once mobilized, the mass army would remain on the defensive until its German opponent made some move, either through Belgium or against the defenses of the Maginot Line.

Among the critics of traditional thinking were the British general J. F. C. Fuller, Captain B. H. Liddell Hart, and Colonel Charles de Gaulle of the French army. Fuller, as chief-of-staff of the Royal Tank Corps in World War I, had extensive experience with armored operations, and he believed that a small, armored, and all-motorized army was preferable to maintaining the traditional branches. He visualized tanks of great speed and range penetrating the enemy's front and overrunning his centers of command, creating paralysis among his forces. Captain B. H. Liddell Hart visualized armored divisions composed of tanks and motorized infantry, which could make deep penetrations to sever communications and carry out strategic encirclements. De Gaulle, serving in a mass army, proposed the creation of armored divisions with as many as five hundred tanks apiece, manned by one hundred thousand long-service professional soldiers, which could not only act as weapons of offense, but could serve as a mobile reserve with which to counterattack enemy breakthroughs of the continuous front.

Soviet Russia was potentially a customer for the new ideas on armor and motorization after she survived a civil war and forced-draft industrialization under Joseph Stalin, Lenin's successor in power. Marshal Mikhail Tukhachevsky, the Red Army's commander-in-chief in the mid-1930s, carried out a number of experiments with armored motorized forces before his career, and innovation in the Red Army, was cut short by Stalin's great purges. The Russian generals who survived the purges became almost slavish adherents to Stalin's ideas on war, which relied on sheer quantities of armaments to offset their mediocre quality. Russian armored organization and tactics lagged well behind the German by 1939.

It seems ironical that Germany, denied armored fighting vehicles by the Treaty of Versailles and really without them until after 1933, should have developed the most advanced ideas on armored, motorized warfare of any army on the continent of Europe by 1939. Actually, the treaty stimulated Germany's interest in highly mobile forces by denying her fixed fortifications in the west and a traditional mass army. General Hans von Seeckt, Chief of the Army Command, encouraged experiments with trucked infantry and motor-towed artillery in the early 1920s. After his retirement in 1926, the Troop Office (the disguised Army General Staff of the period) set up a special section in 1928 to study the theoretical possibilities in armored warfare. Major Heinz Guderian, formerly an officer of light infantry, became familiar with the ideas of Fuller and Liddell Hart, both of whom had published books and articles in the 1920s, and in 1929 he hit upon his own conception of an armored or panzer division. Essentially, Guderian's panzer division was an armored-mechanized-motorized task force, one in which mobile infantry, artillery, engineers, and supply units were combined with a brigade of tanks in order to allow the tanks to fight with full effect. Guderian recognized that such armored-and-all-motorized divisions might serve to revive the tradition of the *Kesselschlacht*, or the battle of encirclement and annihilation, and thus lend decisiveness to ground warfare for the future. Guderian's ideas were supported by Oswald Lutz, later the first general-in-chief of German armored forces, though he retired before World War II. Lutz and Guderian took the first opportunity to impress Hitler with exercises of motorized troops, and in 1935 the Army High Command (OKH) agreed to set up three panzer divisions on an experimental basis. Despite the fact that these early formations were only equipped with the PzKw. I light tank, they looked so promising that by September 1939, the number had been increased to six panzer divisions and a panzer brigade. By then the principal tanks in use (about 300 to a division) were the PzKw. I and the slightly better PzKw. II, but the excellent PzKw. III and PzKw. IV would soon replace them as Germany's principal types. The best of the German tanks were good compromises of speed, range, protection, fire-power, and versatility, as suited their roles and missions. They stood in contrast to the overly specialized Anglo-French designs.

In addition to the panzer divisions, the German army had two other types of all-motorized divisions by 1939. The four so-called light divisions combined regiments of motorized infantry with a light tank battalion in each division, and represented a compromise between the panzer division and the French DLM. Six motorized infantry divisions completed the *corps d'élite* of a mass army of slightly more than a hundred divisions on the eve of World War II. The German infantry divisions, which made up the vast majority of the army in 1939, were not greatly different in their organization and capacities from those of 1918. Still, with the close air support of the *Luftwaffe*, this combination of new and old style forces constituted the essence of the *Blitzkreig* ("Lightning War") which Hitler unloosed on Europe in 1939 and which soon laid more of Europe at Hitler's feet than at any man's since Napoleon.

No similar blitzkrieg vision inspired the American army between the world wars. Part of the problem was that the army was starved for funds. In addition, few army leaders until the late 1930s foresaw another major American commitment to Europe. A war in the Pacific with Japan would require different kinds of ground forces than would a continental war. Still another hindrance was the National Defense Act of 1920, which arbitrarily defined tanks as infantry weapons and armored cars as cavalry weapons. An Experimental Mechanized Force (EMF) in 1928, modeled on a similar British experiment in 1927, never came to much, in part because it was forced to use World War I equipment. Though General Douglas MacArthur, while army chief-of-staff in 1934, set up a mechanized cavalry brigade by transferring tanks from the infantry (he called them "combat cars" to get around the 1920 Act), the result was more like the French DLM than the German panzer division. Actually, the American army did not hit upon the right organization until the German panzers rolled over France in 1940. Within a few weeks after the French defeat, the Americans had cobbled together the First Armored Division. Fortunately, it was not too late to change tank designs, and mass production began on the M-4 Sherman, like the best of the German tanks, a good compromise on speed, range, protection, firepower, and versatility.

Neither Japanese armor nor armored organization was outstanding when, in 1938–1939, they encountered the Red Army in Manchurian border clashes. But the demonstrated inferiority of Japanese machines and organization came too late to result in major policy changes before the outbreak of the war in the Pacific. In that contest, amphibious mechanization was more important than armor for continental warfare, and Japan could not in the long run compete in resources with the United States.

III. Navies

Because of the treaty limitations already discussed, by the time serious naval rearmament got underway in the 1930s, many of the world's battleships and battle cruisers were aging. In addition to sheer age, most had been designed and built when airpower was in its infancy, and it was not always practical to reconstruct them against the new threats of aerial bombs and torpedoes. Accordingly, the new battleships that appeared in the late 1930s and in the early 1940s were, in fact, a quantum leap in dreadnought design over the so-called treaty battleships. Such were the USS *North Carolina* class with a speed of thirty knots, nine 16-inch guns, horizontal sloped armor to deflect aerial bombs, and numerous dual-purpose 5-inch and other antiaircraft guns. The most impressive of the World War II dreadnoughts were the Japanese *Yamato* and *Musashi*, at 70,000 tons displacement the largest such ships ever built. Each had a main battery of nine 18-inch guns capable of hurling 3,200-pound shells up to twenty miles. Besides antiaircraft guns, each was protected by an 8-inch-thick steel deck impervious to bombs weighing less than a ton and dropped from below 10,000 feet. Armor protection at belt-line was 19 inches thick. While both ships were to be sunk by air power, it took veritable fleets of aircraft to do it.

When the Second World War broke out in September 1939, none of the new super-dreadnoughts was yet in service. The Germans possessed the *Scharnhorst* and the *Gneisenau*, displacing more than the three "pocket battleships" but armed with the same 11-inch guns. The five ships, taken together, were too few and too lightly armed to qualify as a battle line, and all of them were used in World War II as surface raiders. The *Bismarck*, a true dreadnought with 15-inch guns, was not launched until October 1939, and not ready for service until the spring of 1941, when she too was employed as a surface raider. Her sister ship the *Tirpitz*, Germany's only other true dreadnought battleship in World War II, had to be used in the same way. In 1939, France had seven battleships, but the *Dunkerque* and the *Strasbourg* carried 13-inch guns and had been designed to counter the *guerre de course* sorties of the German "pocket battleships." Italy had four battleships and two under construction. Japan had ten battleships and battle cruisers, but the most recent had joined the fleet in 1921 and the two super-battleships were still being built. Britain had fifteen battleships and battle cruisers, the most recent having joined the fleet in 1925. The United States had fifteen battleships, the newest—the *West Virginia*—having joined the fleet in 1923. As late as December 1941, the only new battleship in the American fleet was the *North Carolina*. All the battleships sunk or disabled at Pearl Harbor on December 7, 1941, were old.

Only France, among the European powers save Britain, launched an aircraft carrier between the world wars, the *Béarn* in 1927. The Germans laid down the carrier *Graf Zeppelin* in 1935, but after the *Luftwaffe* absorbed the German naval air arm the carrier was never finished. Five of Britain's six carriers in 1939 were modernized World War I vessels, but three new carriers were building. Part of the European indifference to aircraft carriers was based on the belief that carrier forces would be no match for land-based aircraft in Europe. Even Britain's carrier strength suffered from organizational and technical weaknesses. Until 1937, the Royal Navy owned the carriers and the Royal Air Force owned the planes and aircrews. By the time the Fleet Air Arm was wholly naval, it lagged behind the American and Japanese naval air services in both numbers of aircraft and in performance. Moreover, British carriers based only about half as many planes on the same tonnage as their American and Japanese counterparts. In December 1941, nine British carriers based 450 aircraft when seven American carriers based 500 planes and nine Japanese carriers based 700 aircraft.

Cruiser design also varied among the world's three leading navies. The American and Japanese navies preferred a lesser number of heavy cruisers armed with 8-inch guns to a greater number of light cruisers with 6-inch guns. The British view was just the opposite. The difference was caused by Britain's need to protect the largest merchant marine in all parts of the world, and this could best be done with a greater number of more lightly armed vessels. In September 1939, only fifteen of Britain's fifty-seven cruisers were heavy cruisers, and some of the others were classified as antiaircraft cruisers and armed with only 5-inch dual-purpose guns. Not even the British cruisers with 8-inch guns were a match for the five German ships armed with 11-inch guns in 1939, not to mention the battleships *Bismarck* and *Tirpitz* when they were ready for sea. The British had no choice after the outbreak of war but to escort all important convoys with battleships, battle cruisers, and aircraft carriers, as well as antisubmarine craft—a tremendous strain on British resources. Fortunately for the British, all of the large German ships were never available for commerce-raiding at one time. On the other hand, the German occupation of Norway and France in 1940 gave the Germans far better bases for a surface *guerre de course* than they enjoyed in World War I. In addition to hunting down the raiders which got to sea, Britain found the solution to this problem to be air attack on the raider bases, a kind of resurrection of the old close blockade.

Destroyers developed in diverse directions before 1939. Large destroyers, displacing up to 3,500 tons and carrying 5-inch guns, were launched for service with the battle fleets. Smaller destroyer escorts, corvettes, and frigates served to protect merchant ships from submarines. Antisubmarine warfare got a tremendous boost from the development of "sonar" ("asdic" in the British navy), sound navigation, and ranging. The device could detect and track underwater craft by bouncing sound waves off their hulls and measuring the "echoes." Combined with the traditional depth charge, sonar made the antisubmarine-craft a far greater threat to the submarine than even in World War I. On the other hand, the American and British navies, the first to possess sonar, became somewhat complacent that the device would largely negate the threat of submarine attack to merchant fleets. Actually, far more destroyer escorts and sonar sets were needed than were available at the outbreak of World War II. Also, new submarine tactics—such as the night surface attack—rendered sonar useless. Eventually, destroyerlike craft had to be equipped with both sonar and radar, and supplemented by land-based and sea-based aircraft, in order to deal adequately with the submarine.

Soviet Russia led the world in the number of submarines in service in September 1939—perhaps 150—but most of them were small craft intended for coast defense. Italy ranked second with 104 submarines, but its underwater forces were designed for operations in the Mediterranean Sea and lacked great range. With 100 submarines, the United States was third, but, in line with the traditional American opposition to submarine guerre *de course*, its underwater craft were intended for coast defense and operations with the battle fleet. However, the prospect of operations in the great distances of the Pacific led the United States to emphasize range in her submarines. France had 78 submarines, including the huge *Surcouf* (a 9,000-ton long-range submarine cruiser armed with two 8-inch guns and a catapult-launched seaplane), and Japan had 59 submarines (like the American, built for range but not *guerre de course*). Britain and Germany tied for sixth place with 57 submarines apiece in 1939, but only Germany's U-boat fleet had been designed with *guerre de course* in mind.

Between the world wars, German naval leaders had given much thought as to how to conduct a future *guerre de course*, even though after German rearmament commenced they hoped to create eventually a "balanced" fleet and one capable of commanding the sea. The relative paucity in submarines in September 1939, was due to both the lateness of German rearmament and to Hitler's earlier assurances to Admiral Erich Raeder, commander-in-chief of the navy from 1928 to 1943, that Germany would not be faced with war for many years. After 1933, Raeder had opted to give priority in shipbuilding to the larger vessels which took longer to complete, and when war came much sooner than expected Admiral Karl Dönitz's submarine fleet was excellent in many respects but small in numbers. Still, the U-boat command faced up to the task of waging *guerre de course*, even when Hitler was slow to place priority on building submarines. The German type of submarine called the IX-B sank more merchant tonnage than any other single type in the world. The IX-B displaced 1,200 tons submerged, had a surface speed of eighteen knots on diesel engines, and an underwater speed of seven knots on electric motors. It was armed with 21-inch torpedoes and a 4-inch deck gun, and later with an antiaircraft gun. But the problem of insufficient numbers was not overcome until 1942, by which time the Allied antisubmarine fleet was also swelling. A total of 1,178 submarines served Germany during World War II. Though they did tremendous damage to the Allied sea lanes, they finally failed of their purpose. On the other hand, some 300 American submarines, in a *guerre de course* strategy adopted after Pearl Harbor, finally decimated Japan's merchant marine. To be sure, the Japanese merchant fleet was far smaller than the Anglo-American counterpart which Germany's submarines attacked, and there were far fewer antisubmarine craft in the Japanese navy than in the Anglo-American.

Faced by the prospect of a war in the Pacific, both the United States and Japan took more interest in the problem of amphibious assault than did other countries. On the American side, the joint Army-Navy Board sanctioned the efforts of the U.S. Marine Corps to find a satisfactory doctrine beginning in 1927. In the early 1930s, the Marine Corps both issued the *Tentative Manual for Landing Operations*, which became the "bible" of American amphibious assault doctrine in World War II, and created the Fleet Marine Force (FMF) to operate as an integral part of the fleet for the purposes of capturing advanced bases. The Marine doctrine covered all aspects of amphibious assault, including command relationships between land forces and the supporting fleet, ship-to-shore movement and communications, air and gunfire support, and amphibious logistics. No other country in the world had such an advanced doctrine by 1939, except Japan, which came up with similar solutions. The U.S. Army, which had neglected the problem to the eve of the Pacific War, adapted the Marine doctrine to its own purposes in 1941. And thanks to sound doctrine, most of the prototype equipment necessary for amphibious assault had been developed by the United States before the war. Thus, there was no great delay in deciding on the mass production of such designs as the bow-ramped Landing Craft Infantry (LCI), the Landing Ship Tank (LST), and the amphibious tank and personnel carrier. Though the U.S. Marine Corps numbered only 18,000 troops in September 1939, and no more than 50,000 by December 7, 1941, the Corps was prepared to serve as the cornerstone of the greatest amphibious assault force of the Pacific War. By 1945, at its peak strength, the Marine Corps numbered 485,000 men, six amphibious-assault divisions, and as many supporting air wings.

IV. Air Forces

Land-based air power was the focus of heated debate between the world wars. Air-power enthusiasts, such as General Giulio Douhet of Italy and General William ("Billy") Mitchell of the United States, believed that not only would air forces dominate future land and sea operations but that strategic air power might strike the vital centers of the enemy homeland and bring about the rapid collapse of the opposing society. More conservative military thinkers believed that air power would certainly be important in future wars, but that it would be exercised in the forms familiar from World War I.

In 1922, just after Benito Mussolini became Fascist dictator of Italy, Douhet became Italian minister for air. His book *Command of the Air* (1921) had brought him to the attention of a government interested in overhauling Italian military power. Douhet was instrumental in organizing a separate Italian air force—the *Regio Aeronautica*—but his plans for making it an offensive striking force at the expense of the army and navy aroused so much opposition from the traditional services that he finally resigned his post and returned to writing on air power. In the aftermath, the *Regio Aeronautica* developed into a mediocre air service of about fifteen hundred airplanes by 1939, equipped to support the other two services and to carry out high-level pattern bombing to close the central Mediterranean. It never met Douhet's requirement for an air force capable of long-range air strikes against the urban centers of other European countries.

Mitchell served as assistant chief of the Army Air Service for operations in France during World War I, where he came into contact with Hugh Trenchar and witnessed with approval the creation of the Royal Air Force in 1918. After the war, Mitchell returned to the United States convinced that his own country should have a separate air force as well. In 1921, he rigged the "battleship bombing tests" of that year in such a way that they were more useful for propaganda for air power than as tests to show how well dreadnoughts would stand up to aerial bombing under combat conditions. Still, the sinking of the old German battleship *Ostfriesland* greatly impressed the American public. Mitchell's intemperate criticisms of American military and naval leadership in 1925 led to his court-martial. Sentenced to five years' suspension from the service, he preferred to resign his commission altogether and to spend his final years until his death in 1936 writing and speaking on air-power issues as he understood them.

Under less abrasive leaders than Mitchell, the Army Air Service made slow but steady progress during the interwar years. It was retitled the Army Air Corps in 1926, a step toward autonomy, and in 1933 its mission was expanded to include coast defense. Its combat components were placed under a single headquarters for the first time in 1935, and in the same year the new four-engine B-17 Flying Fortress was test-flown. Originally developed as a weapon of long-range coast defense, the B-17 was easily adapted to the role of strategic bomber. The B-17, and the later B-24 Liberator, were equipped with the Norden bomb sight, the best high-level optical aiming device to appear in World War II. Still, the AAC remained relatively small down to even the fall of France in June 1940. Then Congress untied the nation's purse strings, and Army air planners made preparations for an Air Corps of 400,000 men and 7,800 planes by June 1942. Meanwhile, in June 1941, the Army Air Corps was transformed into the Army Air Forces (AAF). General Henry H. Arnold served as both head of the AAF and as assistant chief-of-staff for air. By December 7, 1941, the AAF had a strength of 354,000 men and 2,864 aircraft. In the less than four years after Pearl Harbor, it had reached a strength of 2,400,000 men and 41,163 aircraft (13,930 of them four-engine, long-range bombers). In 1945, the AAF was the mightiest air force in the world.

Until 1933, Germany got around prohibitions in the Treaty of Versailles on air forces to a degree by exchanging technical knowledge on aircraft with the Russians in return for the use of an airfield near Lipetsk, where 180 German pilots had graduated by 1933. In some cases, German officers took up sport plane and glider flying. German aircraft companies inevitably learned much of military importance while building civilian aircraft of all kinds. Still, down to Hitler's accession to power, no real plans existed for a German air force in the future. Hitler gave responsibility for building the *Luftwaffe* to Hermann Göring, a pursuit pilot in World War I, and second only to Hitler in the Nazi Party by 1933.

Göring created the upper echelons of the *Luftwaffe* by transferring officers from the army and navy, and by commissioning civilian aviators. The *Luftwaffe* officially came into being in March 1935, at which time Göring, until then minister for aviation, took on the added title of commander-in-chief of the air force. Göring himself was an empire-builder rather than an idea man, but General Walther Wever, the first chief of the *Luftwaffe* general staff, wanted an air force capable of launching independent air operations as well as serving to support the other two branches of the armed forces (naval aviation was subsumed under the *Luftwaffe* after 1935). He started work on a four-engine, long-range bomber similar to the B-17, but Wever's death in an aerial accident in 1936 removed his influence from the *Luftwaffe's* higher circles. His successors as chief of the general staff were more interested in Ernst Udet's proposals for dive bombers for support of the army. Head of the *Luftwaffe's* technical office, Udet was a former pursuit pilot and postwar stunt flyer. Work on the four-engine bomber was cancelled, and from the new interest evolved the famous Junkers 87 Stuka, the gull-wing, fixed-gear plane that almost symbolized the blitzkrieg for a generation. The excellent Messerschmidt Bf 109 fighter held the world's speed record before the war, but it had a combat radius of only 125 miles. The Dornier 17 and the Heinkel 111 were twin-engine bombers which, like the Ju-87 dive bomber, had a combat radius of about 500 miles. None of the German bombers were heavily armed or armored, but *Luftwaffe* doctrine emphasized surprise air attacks to destroy the enemy air force on the ground at the start of hostilities. Germany had about 3,000 combat aircraft in September 1939, but was weak in reserves of pilots and aircraft.

The *Luftwaffe* was far superior in performance and capability to any other air force in Europe in 1939 except, perhaps, the British. The French *Armée de l'Air* had received its independence in 1933, but remained very much tied to the army's thinking and was less than half as numerous as the *Luftwaffe* by the showdown in 1940. Most of its aircraft did not compare with their German counterparts. The Soviet air force, organically part of the Red Army, was a great collection—ten thousand aircraft—of obsolescent machines. Newer planes were beginning to come off the production lines when the Germans attacked in June 1941. The other air forces, save the British, hardly counted.

As early as 1936, the British Air Staff had selected four-engine bomber designs that later evolved into the Stirling, Halifax, and Lancaster bombers. These bombers could carry from six to nine tons of bombs as far as a thousand miles and return to base in England. Not many of the new bombers had been produced by the outbreak of the war or, indeed, until about 1941. In the meantime, the British relied on two-engine bombers of mediocre qualities. But fear of *Luftwaffe* attacks on the British Isles resulted, before the war, in priority being placed on the development of formidable fighter-interceptors such as the Hurricane and the Spitfire. Britain also made more progress than any other country in the world in the 1930s in developing an early warning system based on radio-detection-and-ranging or "radar." Twenty radar stations monitored the European approaches to England by September 1939, and more were under construction. By the summer of 1940, British radar could detect and track aircraft as far away as seventy-five miles from the set, and Fighter Control using voice radio could vector the aircraft of Air Marshal Hugh Dowding's Fighter Command to intercept enemy planes short of their targets. In September 1939, Britain had 2,000 combat aircraft, of which 750 were fighters.

Save for a few special naval air squadrons, Japan's land-based aviation was organically part of the army. As such, it developed only short-ranged aircraft and no strategic bombers. The Japanese Zero fighter was superior to the American P-40 Tomahawk in 1941, and Japanese twin-engine bombers were about as good as their American counterparts, the B-25 and the B-26, but Japan could never compete with the United States in either aircraft or pilot production in a long war. Moreover, whereas the United States introduced a variety of new aircraft after December 7, 1941, Japan was hard pressed to mass produce even existing types. Accordingly, performance fell off as the war went on. In 1939, Japan had about two thousand combat, land-based aircraft.

Experiments with airborne landings began soon after World War I in Italy, when General Allesandro Guidoni took a special interest in landing soldiers by parachute. By 1927, nine-man squads were jumping from Italian transports, but the program went into temporary eclipse in 1928 when Guidoni was killed in a parachute accident. In 1938, Air Marshal Italo Balbo founded a parachute-training school in the colony of Libya, but Italy carried out no significant airborne operations in World War II. The Soviet Union founded a parachute-training school in 1930, and in army maneuvers in 1935 a total of 1,500 troops were put into action from the air. In 1936, the number rose to 5,200 soldiers. In 1939, the Red Army claimed to have five airborne brigades and 50,000 trained parachute-soldiers.

German military observers at Russian maneuvers were the first to press on their army and the *Luftwaffe* arguments for airborne forces. In January 1936, Göring ordered the formation of a *Luftwaffe* parachute battalion, and about the same time the German army created its own airborne unit. A struggle ensued as to whether airborne forces should be organically part of the army or the air force, one won by Göring in July 1938, when all German parachute and glider troops were concentrated in the *Luftwaffe's* Seventh Air Division under the command of General Kurt Student. The *Luftwaffe* also created the Twenty-Second Air-Landing Division, actually a force to be ferried to its objective and then landed in the aircraft. By September 1939, Germany claimed twelve thousand troops trained for airborne assaults by parachute or glider.

Neither the U.S. Army nor the British army took much interest in airborne forces between world wars. The first simulated American airborne assault took place on maneuvers in 1932 and consisted of a single infantry company landed behind "enemy" lines. Little more was done with the idea down to the war. The British gave parachute training to a few soldiers before 1939, but nothing resembling airborne forces existed prior to the summer of 1940. Then, in the wake of the successful German airborne landings in Norway and the Low Countries, both the United States and Britain took an intense interest in airborne operations. Before the end of the war, Anglo-American airborne divisions—three American and three British—were serving in Europe, and composed an airborne army under the command of General Lewis Brereton. As many as three divisions were actually used at one time. The largest German airborne operation of the war—that against Crete in May 1941—involved one division delivered by parachute and glider, and another division landed in airplane transports. The Russians never carried out an airborne operation with more than one division at a time, and the Japanese never employed more than one brigade delivered by parachute at a time.

The performance of air forces, of course, depended on the technical means at hand. By 1939, the airplane had come a long way from the primitive machine of World War I. The latest aircraft had fuselages of sheet metal, cantilever wings (struts and support-ing wires located internally), enclosed cockpits with more sophis-ticated instruments and oxygen masks for high attitude flying, retractable landing gear, and voice radio. Pursuit planes could fly in level flight at speeds up to about three hundred fifty mph, and bombers were fifty to a hundred mph slower. Two-engine air transports, such as the American C-47, could haul about three tons of supplies or thirty troops up to five hundred miles. The German DFS-320 glider carried up to fifteen soldiers. Navigation was by dead reckoning, corrected by ground observation and sometimes radio and celestial "fixes." Ground-attack aircraft were often pro-vided with armor protection for the pilot and vital parts, as well as with self-sealing fuel tanks. By the outbreak of World War II, the last of the bi-planes were fast disappearing from the skies, and the monoplane ruled the air in the second great conflict.

V. Electronic Warfare

Electronic warfare played a major role in World War II and in a variety of forms. Radar, originally used for early warning and fighter-control, could also direct the fire of ships at sea in darkness and in all kinds of weather. Airborne radar eventually aided the bombardier toward the end of the war. Another radar application was in the proximity or variable time (V-T) fuse. By constantly measuring the distance between the shell and the aircraft being fired at, the fuse determined the optimum moment for the shell's detonation. Since most shells brought down or damaged aircraft not by direct hits but from shell fragments, the V-T proved greatly superior to either chemical or mechanical fuses for antiaircraft artillery shells. In fact, the lethality of an antiaircraft gun was multiplied five times by using the proximity fuse. The V-T fuse was given much of the credit for the high percentage of German V-1 "buzz bombs" (pilotless cruise missiles) downed when Hitler's new weapons were launched against England in 1944. The V-T fuse played an equally important role in helping American ships in the Pacific to fend off Japanese *kamikaze* or suicide-plane attacks in 1944–1945. Anglo-American fears that Germany and Japan might learn the secrets of the V-T fuse from a dud caused a prohibition on V-T fused shells for surface-to-surface artillery until late in the war. Then V-T shells played a significant role in helping to repel the German Ardennes offensive in 1944, and in defeating Japanese forces on Luzon and Okinawa, where aerial bursts were especially effective.

An enormous increase in the use of the military radio took place between world wars. No other signal means had the radio's range, flexibility, and speed. But messages cast into the ether were easily intercepted by enemy radio monitoring and therefore depended upon encoding for their security. The most sophisticated encoding device between world wars was the German Enigma machine, a kind of complex electric typewriter which substituted other letters for the originals but never the same letter twice. Yet when an encoded message was received, it could be swiftly deciphered by typing it back into another machine with its rotors set in a prearranged fashion. German confidence in Enigma was such that all high commands used variations of the Enigma well before the war, and Japan even acquired still other variations for both its armed forces and its diplomatic service.

Polish intelligence made the first progress in breaking Enigma's secrets even before 1939, but not enough to save Poland from defeat. With the aid of the Poles who escaped to France and England with Enigma counterpart *Wicher* machines, still more penetration was made before the fall of France in 1940. Still, it was not until the summer of 1940 that the British Operation Ultra finally penetrated the secrets of the *Luftwaffe* Enigma. By 1944, the British could read messages from the Enigmas of any of the German armed forces and Hitler's headquarters. The American counterpart to Ultra was Magic, which concentrated on Japanese traffic. By December 1941, the Japanese diplomatic code known as Purple had been penetrated by the Army Signal Intelligence Service, though nothing in the final messages between Tokyo and its embassy in Washington, D.C., indicated where the first blow would be struck in the Pacific. The Office of Naval Intelligence broke a Japanese naval code sufficiently in April 1942, to allow U.S. commanders in the Pacific to anticipate correctly the Japanese drives into the Coral Sea and against Midway, and to a degree those American victories resulted from intelligence coups.

But radio intelligence successes were not always on the Allied side, and sometimes radio intelligence was ignored. A major German success was penetration of the American Black Code even before the United States formally entered the war but after American aid began to flow to Britain. Messages to Washington from the American military attaché in Cairo often contained information of value to the Germans about British forces in the Western Desert. Then, after the British deciphered the complete most-secret order from Hitler to his armed forces for the invasion of Russia in 1941, Stalin ignored their offering because he thought it was some kind of British trick to foment war between the Soviet Union and Nazi Germany. British agents captured in the Netherlands were used by the Germans to radio false and misleading information back to Britain. The list, of course, goes on and on. It suffices to say that the battle for information was continuous, sometimes favoring one side and sometimes the other, and only toward the end of the war clearly favoring the Allied powers. Still, Ultra and Magic, taken together, were perhaps the most important intelligence operations of the war, and highly influential to its outcome.

VI. The Wars between the World Wars

None of the wars between 1919 and 1939 gave much indication of the direction that World War II would take. They were either civil wars, in which the forces involved were not well equipped, or they were wars between states so unequal that no firm conclusions could be drawn. Certainly, none of them provided a thorough test of the new German conception of mass and mobility for decisive battle in the Napoleonic tradition, and none of them settled the debates over the proper role of air power and motorized-armored forces.

The Russian Civil War, which broke out just a few months after Russia left World War I, ended up involving foreign governments. It began in the summer of 1918 with rebellions against Lenin's government, led by former tsarist generals and admirals, and concentrated in the Baltic territories, in southern Russia, and in Siberia. Britain and France openly assisted the so-called White forces. The United States landed troops at Murmansk to keep supplies out of the hands of the Bolsheviks, and at Vladivostok in order to check the Japanese there. To combat the danger, Lenin's government founded the Red Army and appointed Leon Trotsky as commissar for war and as effective commander-in-chief of the forces in the field. Sometimes called the "Red Carnot," Trotsky put his considerable organizing talents into building an army of workers and peasants by propaganda and compulsion. He used former tsarist officers for technical positions when he found no better-qualified people at hand, and insured the army's political loyalty as a whole through a political commissar system similar to that of the deputies-on-mission of the French Revolution. Trotsky also founded schools for junior officers, which, by the end of 1919, had insured that four-fifths of all the Red Army's officers came from worker and peasant backgrounds. At its peak strength in the Civil War, the Red Army had a half million men.

The crest of the fortunes of the White forces was reached in 1919 and thereafter began to subside, but in 1920 Poland attacked Russia from the west and, aided by Ukranian nationalists, seized Russian territory as far east as Kiev. When a powerful Red Army counteroffensive drove the Poles back almost to the gates of Warsaw, French supplies and French general Maxime Weygand's advice made it possible for the Poles to counterattack and drive back the Red Army. Finally, in October 1920, an armistice was reached, which, when confirmed by the Peace of Riga in March 1921, left Poland with a large strip of territory which Soviet Russia still considered to be properly its own. By the end of the Russo-Polish war, the last of the White armies in the Crimea had been defeated and the Soviet regime was secure. Though some 9 million of the Tsar's subjects had been killed, wounded, or made ill in World War I, possibly more Russians, Poles, Balts, and Ukranians were victims of the Civil War. In any case, the Red Army emerged from the Civil War with a tradition of endurance in the face of adversity.

When the Chinese monarchy collapsed in 1911, an era of prolonged strife began in China that was to last nearly forty years. In 1921, Sun Yatsen founded the Kuomintang (National Democratic) Party and a shaky central government, but much of China was really ruled by generals or "war lords." The Nationalist government established ties with the Soviet Russian government in order to get foreign aid, and Soviet military advisers helped to establish Whampoa military academy in 1924. Upon Sun's death in 1925, General Chiang Kai-shek, superintendent of Whampoa and a close associate of Sun, took up leadership of the Nationalist government. Under Chiang, the Nationalist government made a sharp turn to the right in its ideology and ruthlessly purged leftist elements in the party. A Marxist faction under Mao Tse-tung and

Chu Teh retired to the hill country between Hankow and Ganton, where they organized a peasant guerrilla war against Chiang's regime. In 1927 Chiang's armies defeated the independent war lords of the Yangtze valley, and in 1928 they seized Peking, the traditional Chinese capital. In the early 1930s they so heavily defeated Mao's forces in southern China that they were forced to make the "Long March" northward in 1935 to find security at Yenan in Shensi province.

Chiang's efforts to unite China under his leadership was complicated by Japanese intervention, first by the invasion of Manchuria in 1931, and then by an undeclared war on China in 1937. Chiang's armies were no match for the Japanese, which captured Peking, Shanghai, and much of the populated region of southern China. In December 1937, the Japanese captured the Nationalist capital at Nanking, and in 1938 Chiang moved his capital to Chungking, the principal city in the remote Province of Szechuan province bordering Tibet. The Japanese empire in China was populated by 170 million, or more than twice as many people as lived in Japan's home islands. Japan claimed that by 1940 its forces had suffered only fifty thousand casualties, while inflicting eight hundred thousand on the Chinese armies. Still, Japan had not terminated the "China Incident," and Chiang's government received material aid from Britain, the United States, and the Soviet Union. In northern China, Mao's Communist armies also continued to resist the Japanese. Complicating matters for the Japanese, in 1938 and 1939 there were serious border clashes with the Russians in Manchuria. The largest, at Khalkhin-Gol in the summer of 1939, ranged a Japanese army of 75,000 troops, 180 tanks, 500 guns and 450 aircraft against a Russian army, under General Georgi Zhukov, with 100,000 troops, 498 tanks, 750 guns and 580 aircraft. After that battle, in which the Japanese got the worst of it, Japan's militarists showed no interest in expanding Japanese territory at Russian expense.

The Italian invasion of Ethiopia in 1935 at first miscarried, but in March 1936, a new Italian offensive with tanks, poison gas, and planes routed the primitive army of Haile Selassie, and the capital of Addis Ababa was occupied in May. But by far the most serious war involving European powers in the 1930s was the civil war in Spain. In July 1936, elements of the Spanish regular army rose, under the leadership of General Francisco Franco and other Spanish generals, against the left-leaning Spanish republic founded in 1931. Franco's forces, who called themselves the Nationalists, quickly seized the most important provinces in northern Spain save Catalonia, but they failed to carry either the capital at Madrid or most of the provinces in the south. The Loyalist supporters of the Spanish government included a minority of the regular forces and the militia. When both sides discovered that they lacked the means to win the war without foreign aid, the Nationalists appealed to Fascist Italy and Nazi Germany, while the Loyalists appealed to Britain, France, the United States, and the Soviet Union.

The three major democracies ended up taking official positions of neutrality and nonintervention in the Spanish Civil War, though thousands of Communists, socialists, and liberals in those countries volunteered for service in "international brigades" on the side of the Loyalists. Soviet Russia sent minor contingents of armor and aircraft, as well as Soviet military advisers, to the Loyalist side, but not on a scale to compare with the aid rendered the Nationalists by Fascist Italy and Nazi Germany. Mussolini's government was the most responsive to Franco's plea, finally sending 50,000 troops, 750 warplanes, and many tanks and other war material. Hitler dispatched 16,000 troops and military technicians, a Condor Legion of 200 aircraft, and a few battalions of tanks. While the Germans got some practical experience of war in Spain and tested out some of their weapons there, the conditions were not conducive to any real test of the blitzkrieg doctrine.

Even with foreign aid to both sides, the Spanish Civil War became a long, drawn-out struggle of attrition. The mountainous nature of much of the country favored defense, and, despite repeated Nationalist attacks, Madrid did not fall until March 28, 1939. Among the more modern aspects of the war were the Condor Legion's indiscriminate bombing of the Basque town of Guernica on April 26, 1937, an attack that may have killed 5,000 people, and the airplane-tank spearheads in the Nationalist drive down the Ebro valley in 1938. At peak strength, the Nationalist army may have numbered 700,000 men, the Loyalist army about 600,000. The Loyalists were increasingly short on arms and equipment toward the end of the war, while the Nationalists steadily improved in this regard. By the end of the war in the spring of 1939, perhaps 600,000 people had died from its effects, half of them on the battlefield and at least 100,000 as victims of atrocities. The balance perished from famine and disease.

Reading 4

Breakthrough on the Meuse

by B. H. Liddell Hart

On the 10th May, 1940, Hitler launched his long-expected invasion of the West.[1] It achieved a lightning victory that changed the course of history, with far-reaching effects on the future of all peoples.

The decisive act in this world-shaking drama began on the 13th—when the Meuse was crossed by Guderian's panzer corps near Sedan and by Rommel's panzer division near Dinant. The narrow breaches were soon expanded into a vast gap. The German tanks, pouring through it, reached the Channel coast within a week, thus cutting off the Allied armies in Belgium. That disaster led on to the fall of France and the isolation of Britain. Although Britain managed to hold out behind her sea-ditch, rescue came only after a prolonged war had become a world-wide war. The price of that mid-May breakdown in 1940 has been tremendous, and remains immeasurable.

After the catastrophe, the breakdown was commonly viewed as inevitable, and Hitler's attack as irresistible. But appearances were very different from reality—as has become clear from post-war revelations.

Instead of having an overwhelming superiority in numbers, as was imagined, the German armies were not able to muster as many as their opponents did. The offensive was launched with 136 divisions, and was faced by the equivalent of 156—French, British,

Belgian, and Dutch. It was only in aircraft that the Germans had a big superiority, in numbers and quality. Their tanks were fewer than those on the other side—barely 2,800 against more than 4,000. They were also, on the average, inferior in armour and armament, although slightly superior in speed. The Germans' main advantage, besides that in airpower, lay in the speed with which their tanks were handled and the superior technique they had developed. Their panzer leaders had adopted, and put into practice with decisive effect, the new theories that had been conceived in Britain but not comprehended by the heads of the British and French armies.

Of the 136 German divisions, only 10 were armoured—but that small fraction, used as spearheads, virtually decided the issue of the campaign before the mass of the German Army came into action.

The brilliant result of these panzer thrusts obscured their small scale, and also the narrowness of the margin by which they succeeded. That success could easily have been prevented but for the paralysis, and all too frequent moral collapse, of the opposing commanders and troops in face of a tempo and technique of attack for which their training had not prepared them. Even as it was, the success of the invasion turned on a series of long-odds chances—and on the readiness of dynamic leaders like Guderian and Rommel to make the most of such chances.

The original plan for the offensive in the West had been on the lines of the pre-1914 Schlieffen plan, with the main weight on the right wing, where Bock's Army Group "B" was to advance through the plain of Belgium. But early in 1940 the plan was changed—following the proposal of Manstein for a more daring, and thus more unexpected, thrust through the hilly and wooded Ardennes country of Belgian Luxembourg. The centre of gravity was now shifted to Rundstedt's Army Group "A," which faced that sector. It was given seven of the ten German panzer divisions and the largest part of the infantry divisions.

The main drive for the Meuse was led by Kleist's Panzer Group, which was in the van of List's 12th Army. It had two spearheads, the stronger one being formed by Guderian's corps (of three panzer divisions), which made the decisive thrust near Sedan, while Reinhardt's corps (of two panzer divisions) on its right aimed for the crossing at Monthermé. Farther to the right, operating under Kluge's Fourth Army, Hoth's panzer corps drove through the northern Ardennes as cover for Kleist's flank and with the aim of getting across the Meuse between Givet and Namur. This secon-

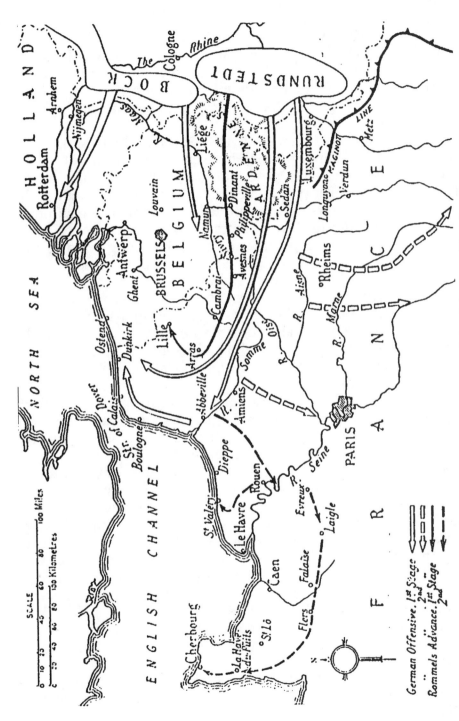

Map 1. The Advance from the Rhine to Cherbourg

dary thrust had two spearheads of smaller scale, formed respectively by the 5th and 7th Panzer Divisions.

The 7th was commanded by Rommel. This was one of the four "light" divisions that had been converted into panzer divisions during the winter. It had only one tank regiment instead of the normal two, although this regiment was given three battalions instead of two—making a total of 218 tanks. More than half of these were Czech-built.[2]

The conversion had been made in the light of the lessons of the Polish campaign. There Rommel, himself an ardent infantryman, had come to recognise the potentialities of the tank arm. It was only on the 15th February that he had taken over command of the 7th at Godesberg, on the Rhine, but he learned the new technique, and adapted himself to it, with extraordinary quickness. He had always been a thruster in the infantry field, handling infantry as if they were mobile troops, and he revelled in the much greater scope for mobility offered by his new command.

On the opening day of the offensive, little resistance was met. The mass of the Belgian Army was concentrated to defend the plain of Belgium, where the chief cities lie, and the defence of the hilly and wooded region of Belgian Luxembourg, beyond the Meuse, was left to the special *Chasseurs Ardennais*, whose role was simply to impose as much delay as possible until the French came up to cover this wide flank approach to their own frontier. Such was the calculation on which the Belgian plan was based.

The French plan, however, was based on a more offensive concept. The First and Seventh Armies, which comprised the bulk of the French mechanised divisions, drove far forward into the plain of Belgium, together with the British Expeditionary Force. Meanwhile, the Ninth Army, forming the hinge of this manoeuvre, made a shorter wheeling advance over the Belgian frontier to align itself along the Meuse from Meziéres to Namur. It consisted of seven infantry divisions (only one of which was motorised) and two cavalry divisions—these last being horse-mounted troops with mechanised elements. The cavalry were sent forward across the Meuse on the night of the 10th May, and next day pushed deep into the Ardennes, where they met the rapidly advancing panzer divisions, which had already overcome most of the Belgian defences there.

On the eve of the attack, during the last tense hours of preparation, Rommel wrote this brief letter to his wife, and then takes up the narrative:

9 May 1940

Dearest Lu,

We're packing up at last. Let's hope not in vain. You'll get all the news for the next few days from the papers. Don't worry yourself. Everything will go all right.

In the sector assigned to my division the enemy had been preparing obstructions of every kind for months past. All roads and forest tracks had been permanently barricaded and deep craters blown in the main roads. But most of the road blocks were undefended by the Belgians, and it was thus in only a few places that my division was held up for any length of time. Many of the blocks could be by-passed by moving across country or over side roads. Elsewhere, all troops quickly set to work to deal with the obstructions and soon had the road clear.

At our first clash with French mechanised forces, prompt opening fire on our part led to a hasty French retreat. I have found again and again that in encounter actions, the day goes to the side that is the first to plaster its opponent with fire. The man who lies low and awaits developments usually comes off second best. Motorcyclists at the head of the column must keep their machine guns at the ready and open fire the instant an enemy shot is heard. This applies even when the exact position of the enemy is unknown, in which case the fire must simply be sprayed over enemy-held territory. Observation of this rule, in my experience, substantially reduces one's own casualties. It is fundamentally wrong simply to halt and look for cover without opening fire, or to wait for more forces to come up and take part in the action.

Experience in this early fighting showed that in tank attacks especially, the action of opening fire immediately into the area which the enemy is believed to be holding, instead of waiting until several of one's own tanks have been hit, usually decides the issue. Even indiscriminate machine-gun fire and 20mm. anti-tank fire into a wood in which enemy anti-tank guns have installed themselves is so effective that in most cases the enemy is completely unable to get into action or else gives up his position. In engagements against enemy tanks also—which more often than not have been more heavily armoured than ours—opening fire early has proved to be the right action and very effective.

11 May 1940

Dearest Lu,

I've come up for breath for the first time to-day and have a moment to write. Everything wonderful so far. Am way ahead of my neighbours. I'm completely hoarse from orders and shouting. Had a bare three hours' sleep and an occasional meal. Otherwise I'm absolutely fine. Make do with this, please, I'm too tired for more.

Following up the retreat of the French 1st and 4th Cavalry Divisions, Rommel's advanced troops reached the Meuse in the afternoon of the 12th May. It was his aim to rush a crossing if possible on the heels of the French, and gain a bridgehead on the west bank. But the bridges at Dinant and Houx were blown up by the French—just as the leading tanks began to cross—and Rommel was thus compelled to mount a river-crossing assault with troops ferried over in rubber boats. This assault was launched early next morning, and suffered heavy casualties before it succeeded. Rommel writes:

On the 13th May, I drove off to Dinant at about 04.00 hours with Captain Schraepler. The whole of the divisional artillery was already in positions ordered, with its forward observers stationed at the crossing points. In Dinant I found only a few men of the 7th Rifle Regiment. Shells were dropping in the town from French artillery west of the Meuse, and there were a number of knocked-out tanks in the streets leading down to the river. The noise of battle could be heard from the Meuse valley.

There was no hope of getting my command and signals vehicle down the steep slope to the Meuse unobserved, so Schraepler and I clambered down on foot through the wood to the valley bottom. The 6th Rifle Regiment was about to cross to the other bank in rubber boats, but was being badly held up by heavy artillery fire and by the extremely troublesome small arms fire of French troops installed among the rocks on the west bank.

The situation when I arrived was none too pleasant. Our boats were being destroyed one after the other by the French flanking fire, and the crossing eventually came to a standstill. The enemy infantry were so well concealed that they were impossible to locate even after a long search through glasses. Again and again they directed their fire into the area in which I and my companions—the commanders of the Rifle Brigade and the Engineer Battalion—were lying. A smoke screen in the Meuse valley would have

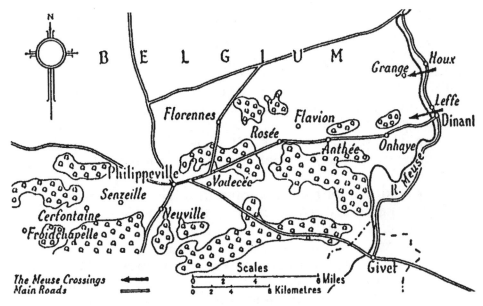

Map 2. The Breakthrough on the Meuse

prevented these infantry doing much harm. But we had no smoke unit. So I now gave orders for a number of houses in the valley to be set alight in order to supply the smoke we lacked.

Minute by minute the enemy fire grew more unpleasant. From up river a damaged rubber boat came drifting down to us with a badly wounded man clinging to it, shouting and screaming for help—the poor fellow was near to drowning. But there was no help for him here, the enemy fire was too heavy.

Meanwhile the village of Grange [*1-1/4 miles west of Houx (and the Meuse), and 3 miles north-west of Dinant*] on the west bank had been taken by the 7th Motor-cycle Battalion, but they had not cleaned up the river bank as thoroughly as they should have done. I therefore gave orders for the rocks on the west bank to be cleared of the enemy.

With Captain Schraepler, I now drove south down the Meuse valley road in a Panzer IV to see how things were going with the 7th Rifle Regiment. On the way we came under fire several times from the western bank and Schraepler was wounded in the arm from a number of shell splinters. Single French infantrymen surrendered as we approached.

By the time we arrived the 7th Rifle Regiment had already succeeded in getting a company across to the west bank, but the enemy fire had then become so heavy that their crossing equipment had been shot to pieces and the crossing had had to be halted. Large numbers of wounded were receiving treatment in a house close beside the demolished bridge. As at the northern crossing point, there was nothing to be seen of the enemy who were preventing the crossing. As there was clearly no hope of getting any more men across at this point without powerful artillery and tank support to deal with the enemy nests, I drove back to Division Headquarters, where I met the Army commander, Colonel-General von Kluge and the Corps commander, General Hoth.

After talking over the situation with Major Heidkaemper and making the necessary arrangements, I drove back along the Meuse to Leffé [*a village on the outskirts of Dinant*] to get the crossing moving there. I had already given orders for several Panzer IIIs and IVs and a troop of artillery to be at my disposal at the crossing point. We left the signals vehicle for the time being at a point some 500 yards east of the river and went forward on foot through deserted farms towards the Meuse. In Leffé we found a number of rubber boats, all more or less badly damaged by enemy fire, lying in the street where our men had left them. Eventually, after being bombed on the way by our own aircraft, we arrived at the river.

At Leffé weir we took a quick look at the footbridge, which had been barred by the enemy with a spiked steel plate. The firing in the Meuse valley had ceased for the moment and we moved off to the right through some houses to the crossing point proper. The crossing had now come to a complete standstill, with the officers badly shaken by the casualties which their men had suffered. On the opposite bank we could see several men of the company which was already across, among them many wounded. Numerous damaged boats and rubber dinghies lay on the opposite bank. The officers reported that nobody dared show himself outside cover, as the enemy opened fire immediately on anyone they spotted.

Several of our tanks and heavy weapons were in position on the embankment east of the houses, but had seemingly already fired off almost all their ammunition. However, the tanks I had ordered to the crossing point soon arrived, to be followed shortly afterwards by two field howitzers from the Battalion Grasemann.[3]

All points on the western bank likely to hold enemy riflemen were now brought under fire, and soon the aimed fire of all weapons was pouring into rocks and buildings. Lieutenant Hanke[4] knocked out a pill-box on the bridge ramp with several rounds. The tanks, with turrets traversed left, drove slowly north at 50 yards' spacing along the Meuse valley, closely watching the opposite slopes.

Under cover of this fire the crossing slowly got going again, and a cable ferry using several large pontoons was started. Rubber boats paddled backwards and forwards and brought back the wounded from the west bank. One man who fell out of his boat on the way grabbed hold of the ferry rope and was dragged underwater through the Meuse. He was rescued by Private Heidenreich, who dived in and brought him to the bank.

I now took over personal command of the 2nd Battalion of 7th Rifle Regiment and for some time directed operations myself.

With Lieutenant Most I crossed the Meuse in one of the first boats and at once joined the company which had been across since early morning. From the company command post we could see Companies Enkefort and Lichter were making rapid progress.

I then moved up north along a deep gully to the Company Enkefort. As we arrived an alarm came in: "Enemy tanks in front." The company had no anti-tank weapons, and I therefore gave orders for small arms fire to be opened on the tanks as quickly as possible, whereupon we saw them pull back into a hollow about a thousand yards north-west of Leffé. Large numbers of French stragglers came through the bushes and slowly laid down their arms.

Other accounts show that Rommel's intervention was even more crucial, and decisive, than he conveys. The German troops were badly shaken by the intensity of the defenders' fire when he arrived on the scene and organised the fresh effort, in which he himself took the lead. Fortunately for his chances, the French 18th Infantry Division, which was charged with the defence of the Dinant sector, was only in process of taking over the position after a lengthy march on foot, and was short of anti-tank guns, while the 1st Cavalry Division had not recovered from the tank-mauling it had received in the Ardennes. Thus the boldly led attackers were able to prise open the defence once they had gained sufficient space on the west bank to develop a manoeuvreing leverage.

I now went down with Most to the Meuse again and had myself taken back to the other bank, where I drove north with a tank and a signals vehicle to the 6th Rifle Regiment's crossing point. Here the crossing had meanwhile been resumed in rubber boats and was in full swing. I was told by Colonel Mickl, the commander of the anti-tank battalion, that he already had twenty anti-tank guns on the western bank. A company of the engineer battalion was busily engaged in building 8-ton pontoons, but I stopped them and told them to build the 16-ton type. I aimed to get part of the Panzer Regiment across as quickly as possible. As soon as the first pontoon was ready I took my 8-wheeled signals vehicle across. Meanwhile, the enemy had launched a heavy attack, and the fire of their tanks could be heard approaching the ridge of the Meuse bank. Heavy enemy shells were dropping all round the crossing point.

On arrival at Brigade Headquarters on the west bank I found the situation looking decidedly unhealthy. The commander of the 7th Motor-cycle Battalion had been wounded, his adjutant killed, and a powerful French counter-attack had severely mauled our men in Grange. There was a danger that enemy tanks might penetrate into the Meuse valley itself.

Leaving my signals lorry on the west bank, I crossed the river again and gave orders for first the Panzer Company, and then the Panzer Regiment to be ferried across during the night. However, ferrying tanks across the 120-yards-wide river by night was a slow job, and by morning there were still only 15 tanks on the west bank, an alarmingly small number.

At daybreak [*14th May*] we heard that Colonel von Bismarck had pressed through his attack to close on Onhaye [3 *miles west of Dinant*], where he was now engaged with a powerful enemy. Shortly afterwards a wireless message came in saying that his regiment was encircled, and I therefore decided to go to his assistance immediately with every available tank.

At about 09.00 hours the 25th Panzer Regiment, under the command of Colonel Rothenburg, moved off along the Meuse valley with the 30 tanks which had so far arrived on the west bank, and penetrated as far as a hollow 500 yards north-east of Onhaye without meeting any resistance. It transpired that von Bismarck had actually radioed "arrived" instead of "encircled"[5] and that he was now on the point of sending an assault company round the northern side of Onhaye to secure its western assault company round the northern side of Onhaye to secure its western exit. This move, as had been shown by an exercise we had carried out earlier in Godesberg, was of the greatest importance for the next stages of the operation. Accordingly, five tanks were placed under von Bismarck's command for this purpose—not to make a tank attack in the usual sense, but to provide mobile covering fire for the infantry attack on the defile west of Onhaye. It was my intention to place the Panzer Regiment itself in a wood 1,000 yards north of Onhaye and then to bring all other units up to that point, from where they could be employed to the north, north-west or west, according to how the situation developed.

I gave orders to Rothenburg to move round both sides of the wood into this assembly area, and placed myself in a Panzer III which was to follow close behind him.

Rothenburg now drove off through a hollow to the left with the five tanks which were to accompany the infantry, thus giving these tanks a lead of 100 to 150 yards. There was no sound of enemy fire. Some 20 to 30 tanks followed up behind. When the commander of the five tanks reached the rifle company on the southern edge of Onhaye wood, Colonel Rothenburg moved off with his leading tanks along the edge of the wood going west. We had just reached the south-west corner of the wood and were about to cross a low plantation, from which we could see the five tanks escorting the infantry below us to our left front, when suddenly we came under heavy artillery and anti-tank gunfire from the west. Shells landed all round us and my tank received two hits one after the other, the first on the upper edge of the turret and the second in the periscope.

The driver promptly opened the throttle wide and drove straight into the nearest bushes. He had only gone a few yards, however, when the tank slid down a steep slope on the western edge of the wood and finally stopped, canted over on its side, in such a position that the enemy, whose guns were in position about 500 yards away on the edge of the next wood, could not fail to see it. I had been wounded in the right cheek by a small splinter from the shell which had landed in the periscope. It was not serious though it bled a great deal.

I tried to swing the turret round so as to bring our 37 mm. gun to bear on the enemy in the opposite wood, but with the heavy slant of the tank it was immoveable.

The French battery now opened rapid fire on our wood and at any moment we could expect their fire to be aimed at our tank, which was in full view. I therefore decided to abandon it as fast as I could, taking the crew with me. At that moment the subaltern in command of the tanks escorting the infantry reported himself seriously wounded, with the words: "Herr General, my left arm has been shot off." We clambered up through the sandy pit, shells crashing and splintering all round. Close in front of us trundled Rothenburg's tank with flames pouring out of the rear. The adjutant of the Panzer Regiment had also left his tank. I thought at first that the command tank had been set alight by a hit in the petrol tank and was extremely worried for Colonel Rothenburg's safety.

However, it turned out to be only the smoke candles that had caught light, the smoke from which now served us very well. In the meantime Lieutenant Most had driven my armoured signals vehicle into the wood, where it had been hit in the engine and now stood immobilised. The crew was unhurt.

I now gave orders for the tanks to drive through the wood in a general easterly direction, a move which the armoured cars, which stood at my disposal, were of course unable to follow. Slowly Rothenburg's command tank forced its way through the trees, many of them tall and well grown. It was only the involuntary smoke-screen laid by this tank that prevented the enemy from shooting up any more of our vehicles. If only the tanks had sprayed the wood which the enemy was believed to be holding, with machine-gun and 37mm. gunfire during their advance, the French would probably have immediately abandoned their guns, which were standing in exposed positions at the edge of the wood, and our losses would almost certainly have been smaller. An attack launched in the evening by the 25th Panzer Regiment was successful, and we were able to occupy our assembly area.

A tight combat control west of the Meuse, and flexibility to meet the changing situation, were only made possible by the fact that the divisional commander with his signals troop kept on the move and was able to give his orders direct to the regiment commanders in the forward line. Wireless alone—due to the necessity for encoding—would have taken far too long, first to get the situation reports back to Division and then for Division to issue its orders. Continuous wireless contact was maintained with the division's operations staff, which remained in the rear, and a detailed exchange of views took place early each morning and each afternoon between the divisional commander and his Ia.[6] This method of command proved extremely effective.

By his advance that day Rommel had created a breach which had momentous consequences, particularly by its effect on the mind of General Corap, the commander of the French Ninth Army.

Three crossings of the Meuse had been achieved on the 13th, Rommel's being the first. In the afternoon, the leading troops of Reinhardt's panzer corps had got across at Monthermé, and Guderian's at Sedan. But Reinhardt's gained only a narrow foothold, and had a desperate fight to maintain it. Not until early on the 15th were they able to build a bridge over which his tanks could cross, and the exit from Monthermé ran through a precipitous defile that was easy to block. Guderian's troops were more successful, but only one of his three divisions gained an adequate foothold, and at daybreak on the 14th only one bridge had been completed. The bridge was lucky to escape destruction, as it was repeatedly attacked by the Allied air forces. Guderian's troops had little support from the Luftwaffe on this second crucial day, but his anti-aircraft gunners put up such a deadly canopy of fire that they brought down an estimated 150 French and British aircraft, and effectively upset the bomb-aiming. By the afternoon, all three of Guderian's panzer divisions were over the river. Holding off heavy counter-attacks from the south he wheeled west towards the joint between the French Second and Ninth Armies, which began to give way under his fierce and skilfully manoeuvred pressure.

That night the commander of the French Ninth Army made a fatal decision, under the double impact of Guderian's expanding threat to his right flank and Rommel's penetration in the centre of his front—wild reports conveyed that thousands of tanks were pouring through the breach there. Orders were issued for the abandonment of the Meuse, and a general withdrawal of the Ninth Army to a more westerly line.

On Rommel's front this intended stop-line ran along the railway east of Philippeville, and 15 miles behind the Meuse. It was penetrated by Rommel next morning, the 15th, before it could be occupied, and under his deep-thrusting threat the confusion of the withdrawal quickly developed into a spreading collapse. His renewed thrust also forestalled an intended counter-attack towards Dinant by the French 1st Armoured Division and 4th North African Division, which were just arriving on the scene. The former appeared on Rommel's right flank but ran out of fuel at this crucial moment, and only a small fraction of its tanks went into action. Rommel's advance swept past its front while it was at a standstill, and many of its tanks were subsequently captured before they could get away. Meantime, the North African Division was bowled over by the onrush of the panzers and the stream of fugitives.

Worse still, Corap's general withdrawal order had uncorked the bottleneck at Monthermé, where the right wing of the Ninth Army had hitherto blocked Reinhardt's panzer corps. Once a withdrawal began here, it quickly became a hopelessly confused retreat, and Reinhardt's leading troops were able to slip round the right flank of the Ninth Army—behind the back of the forces opposing Guderian—and then drove on westward many miles along an open path. By that evening, also, Guderian had overcome the last line of resistance that faced him, and broke through into open country. The breach in the French front was now 60 miles wide.

The significance of Rommel's story of the 15th May becomes all the clearer when set against the wider background of that decisive day.

My intention for the 15th May was to thrust straight through in one stride to our objective, with the 25th Panzer Regiment in the lead and with artillery and, if possible, dive-bomber support. The infantry was to follow up the tank attack, partly on foot and partly lorry-borne. The essential thing, to my mind, was that the artillery should curtain off both flanks of the attack, as our neighbouring divisions were still some way behind us. The 25th panzer Regiment's route, which was marked out on the map, led round the outskirts of Philippeville [*18 miles west of Dinant*], avoiding all villages, and on to our objective, the district round Cerfontaine [*8 miles west of Philippeville*]. It was my intention to ride with 25th Panzer Regiment so that I could direct the attack from up forward and bring in the artillery and dive-bombers at the decisive moment. To simplify wireless traffic—over which highly important messages often arrived late, due to the necessity for encoding—I agreed a "line of thrust" with the Ia and artillery commander. Starting point for this line was taken as Rosée church and finishing point Froidchapelle church. All officers marked the line on their maps. If I now wanted artillery fire on, for instance, Philippeville, I simply radioed: "Heavy artillery fire immediate round eleven." The artillery commander was delighted with the new system.

At about 09.00 hours I met a Luftwaffe major who informed me that dive-bombers could be made available for my division that day. As the tanks were already starting to move I called for them immediately, to go into action in front of the attack. I then moved over to Rothenburg's tank and instructed my *Gefechtsstaffel*[7] to follow up the tank attack from cover to cover with their armoured car and signals vehicle.

After a brief engagement with enemy tanks near Flavion, the Panzer Regiment advanced in column through the woods to Philippeville, passing on the way numerous guns and vehicles belonging to a French unit, whose men had tumbled headlong into the woods at the approach of our tanks, having probably already suffered heavily under our dive-bombers. Enormous craters compelled us to make several détours through the woods. About 3 miles north-west of Philippeville there was a brief exchange of fire with French troops occupying the hills and woods south of Philippeville. Our tanks fought the action on the move, with turrets traversed left, and the enemy was soon silenced. From time to time enemy anti-tank guns, tanks, and armoured cars were shot up. Fire was also scattered into the woods on our flanks as we drove past. Staff and artillery was kept closely informed of the progress of the attack by brief radio messages sent in clear, with the result that the artillery curtain functioned perfectly. The day's objective was soon reached.

With one of Rothenburg's panzer companies placed under my command, I then drove back over the tracks of the advance to establish contact with the infantry in the rear. On the high ground 1,000 yards west of Philippeville we found two of our tanks which had fallen out with mechanical trouble. Their crews were in process of collecting prisoners, and a few who had already come in were standing around. Now hundreds of French motor-cyclists came out of the bushes and, together with their officers, slowly laid down their arms. Others tried to make a quick getaway down the road to the south.

I now occupied myself for a short time with the prisoners. Among them were several officers, from whom I received a number of requests, including among other things, permission to keep their batmen and to have their kit picked up from Philippeville, where it had been left. It was greatly to my interest that the Philippeville garrison should surrender quickly and without fighting, so I granted the requests.

My escorting panzer company now drove for Neuville [*2 miles south of Philippeville*], with the object of cutting off the French retreat from Philippeville to the south. On arriving at the company with Most, I found it involved in fighting near Neuville, with the action moving south and threatening to turn into a pursuit. I had no intention of pushing any farther south, and so gave orders for the battle to be broken off and for the company to continue eastward from Neuville. About 500 yards south of Vocedée we ran into part of Panzer Company Hüttemann, which joined up with us. On the southern edge of Vocedée we had a brief engagement with a considerable force of French tanks, which was soon decided in our favour. The French ceased fire and were fetched out of their tanks one by one by our men. Some fifteen French tanks fell into our hands, some of them damaged, others completely intact. It being impossible to leave a guard, we took the undamaged tanks along with us in our column, still with their French drivers. About a quarter of an hour later we reached the main Dinant-Philippeville road, where I met the leading troops of the Rifle Brigade, with 8th M. B. Battalion under command, who were following up the tank attack. I took several officers into my armoured car and with the whole column behind me, drove at high speed along the dusty road through the northern outskirts of Philippeville. [*Rommel had turned about, and was heading westward again.*]

En route I described the situation to the commanding officers and instructed them in their new tasks. At the rate we were driving (average about 40 m.p.h.) the dust-cloud behind us was enormous. Near Senzeille [*4 miles west of Philippeville*], we met a body of fully armed French motorcyclists coming in the opposite direction, and picked them up as they passed. Most of them were so shaken at suddenly finding themselves in a German column that they drove their machines into the ditch and were in no position to put up a fight. Without delaying, we drove on at high speed to the hills west of Cerfontaine, where Rothenburg was standing with the leading units of Panzer Regiment. On its arrival, the column was deployed as quickly as possible and without halting into the surrounding district. Looking back east from the summit of the hill, as night fell, endless pillars of dust could be seen rising as far as the eye could reach—comforting signs that the 7th Panzer Division's move into the conquered territory had begun.

The fact that the enemy had been able to infiltrate between the Panzer Regiment and the Rifle Brigade during the afternoon had been solely due to the latter's delay in getting moving. The officers of a panzer division must learn to think and act independently within the framework of the general plan and not wait until they receive orders. All units had known the start time of the attack, and they should have formed up at that time.

Next day, the 16th May 1940, I received orders from Corps to stay at Divisional H.Q. The reason was unknown to me. It was about 09.30 hours before I at last received Corps' permission to move forward to the new H.Q. Shortly after my arrival the division received orders to thrust via Sivry through the Maginot Line and on that night to the hills around Avesnes.

This was not the Maginot Line proper, which ended near Longuyon, but its later westward extension—where the type of fortification was much less strong. But German accounts often draw no distinction between the original line and its extension.

Guderian's and Reinhardt's corps had encountered, and broken through, the Maginot Line extension shortly after crossing the Meuse, and were now racing westward behind it. But Hoth's corps, having crossed the Meuse farther north, in Belgian territory, had still to penetrate it in their south-westerly drive. Sivry is 12 miles west of Cerfontaine, and Avesnes 12 miles west of Sivry.

I had just discussed the plan for our attack on the Maginot Line with my Ia, when the Army Commander, Colonel-General von

Kluge, walked in. He was surprised that the division had not already moved off. I described to him our plan. The intention was first to gain frontier near Sivry, while, at the same time the Reconnaissance Battalion reconnoitred the Maginot Line over a wide front and the mass of the artillery moved into position round Sivry. Then the Panzer Regiment, under powerful artillery cover, was to move in extended order up to the French line of fortifications. Finally, the Rifle Brigade, covered by the tanks, was to take the French fortifications and remove barricades. Not until all this was accomplished was the breakthrough to Avesnes to be made, with the armour in the lead and the mass of the division following closely behind. General von Kluge gave complete approval to our plan.

Soon the leading battalion was moving rapidly forward towards Sivry, which was reached without fighting. Artillery and anti-aircraft went into position and received instructions to open fire immediately into certain areas on the other side of the frontier to see whether the enemy would reply. Meanwhile, the 25th Panzer Regiment arrived at Sivry and received orders to cross the frontier and take Clairfayts [3 *miles beyond*].No enemy battery had replied to our artillery fire on their fortified zone.

I rode, as on the previous day, in the regimental commander's command tank. Soon we were across the French frontier and then the tanks rolled slowly on in column towards Clairfayts, which was now only a mile or so away. When a report came in from a reconnaissance troop that the road through Clairfayts had been mined, we bore off to the south and moved in open order across fields and hedges in a semi-circle round the village. There was not a sound from the enemy, although our artillery was dropping shells at intervals deep into their territory. Soon we found ourselves among orchards and tall hedges, which slowed up the advance. Rothenburg's tank was among the leading vehicles, with Hanke, my aide-de-camp, following behind in a Panzer IV. His orders were to open fire quickly on a sign from me and thus act as a lead-gun for the rest. It had been very evident in the previous days' fighting that frequently far too much time elapsed before the tank crews opened fire on fleeting targets.

Suddenly we saw the angular outlines of a French fortification about 100 yards ahead. Close beside it were a number of fully-armed French troops, who, at the first sight of the tanks, at once made as if to surrender. We were just beginning to think we would be able to take it without fighting, when one of our tanks opened fire on the enemy elsewhere, with the result that the enemy garrison promptly vanished into their concrete pill-box. In a few moments the leading tanks came under heavy anti-tank gunfire from the left and French machine-gun fire opened over the whole area. We had some casualties and two of our tanks were knocked out. When the enemy fire had quieted down again, reconnaissance established the existence of a very deep anti-tank ditch close beside the enemy fortification, which had not so far opened fire. There were more defence works in the enemy rear and the road from Clairfayts towards Avesnes was blocked by high steel hedgehogs (anti-tank obstacles).

Meanwhile, elements of 25th Panzer Regiment had joined battle with the enemy west and 2,000 yards south of Clairfayts; the artillery had also opened a heavy fire at my orders and was laying smoke over various sections of the Maginot Line. French artillery now began to bombard Clairfayts and Sivry. Soon the motor-cyclists arrived with the engineer platoon of the 37th Armoured Reconnaissance Battalion. Under covering fire from tanks and artillery, infantry and engineers pushed forward into the fortified zone. The engineer platoon began to prepare the demolition of the steel hedgehog blocking the road to our advance.

Meanwhile, an assault troop of the Panzer Engineer Company overcame the concrete pill-box. The men crawled up to the embrasure and threw a 6-pound demolition charge in through the firing slit. When, after repeated summonses to surrender, the strong enemy garrison still did not emerge, a further charge was thrown in. One officer and 35 men were then taken prisoner, although they shortly afterwards overcame the weak assault troop and escaped, after French machine-guns had opened fire from another pill-box.

Slowly the sky darkened and it became night. Farms were burning at several points in Clairfayts and farther west. I now gave orders for an immediate penetration into the fortified zone, and a thrust as far as possible towards Avesnes. Staff and artillery were quickly informed by wireless, and then it was time for us to climb into the command tank and get under way. Taking our place immediately behind the leading panzer company, we were soon rolling across the demolished road block towards the enemy.

During the time that the sappers of the 37th Reconnaissance Battalion had been demolishing the steel hedgehogs, more violent fighting had broken out against anti-tank guns and a few field guns located near a cluster of houses 1,00 yards west of Clairfayts. Round after round had been fired over open sights at our tanks and infantry standing near Clairfayts. Finally, the enemy guns had been silenced by a few rounds from a Panzer IV.

The way to the west was now open. The moon was up and for the time being we could expect no real darkness. I had already given orders, in the plan for the breakthrough, for the leading tanks to scatter the road and verges with the machine and anti-tank gunfire at intervals during the drive to Avesnes, which I hoped would prevent the enemy from laying mines. The rest of the Panzer Regiment was to follow close behind the leading tanks and be ready at any time to fire salvoes to either flank. The mass of the division had instructions to follow up the Panzer Regiment lorry-borne.

The tanks now rolled in a long column through the line of fortifications and on towards the first houses, which had been set alight by our fire. In the moonlight we could see the men of 7th Motor-cycle Battalion moving forward on foot beside us. Occasionally an enemy machine-gun or anti-tank gun fired, but none of their shots came anywhere near us. Out artillery was dropping heavy harassing fire on villages and the road far ahead of the regiment. Gradually the speed increased. Before long we were 500—1,000—2,000—3,000 yards into the fortified zone. Engines roared, tank tracks clanked and clattered. Whether or not the enemy was firing was impossible to tell in the ear-splitting noise. We crossed the railway line a mile or so south-west of Solre le Château, and then swung north to the main road which was soon reached. Then off along the road and past the first houses.

The people in the houses were rudely awoken by the din of our tanks, the clatter and roar of tracks and engines. Troops lay bivouacked beside the road, military vehicles stood parked in farmyards and in some places on the road itself. Civilians and French troops, their faces distorted with terror, lay huddled in the ditches, alongside hedges and in every hollow beside the road. We passed refugee columns, the carts abandoned by their owners, who had fled in panic into the fields. On we went, at a steady speed, towards our objective. Every so often a quick glance at the map by a shaded light and a short wireless message to Divisional H.Q. to report the position and thus the success of 25th Panzer Regiment. Every so often a look out of the hatch to assure myself that there was still no resistance and that contact was being maintained to the rear. The flat countryside lay spread out around us under the cold light of the moon. We were through the Maginot Line! It was hardly conceivable. Twenty-two years before we had stood for four and a half long years before this self-same enemy and had won victory after victory and yet finally lost the war. And now we had broken through the renowned Maginot Line and were driving deep into enemy territory. It was not just a beautiful dream. It was reality.

Suddenly there was a flash from a mound about 300 yards away to the right of the road. There could be no doubt what it was, an enemy gun well concealed in a concrete pill-box, firing on 25th Panzer Regiment from the flank. More flashes came from other points. Shell bursts could not be seen. Quickly informing Rothenburg of the danger—he was standing close beside me—I gave orders through him for the regiment to increase speed and burst through this second fortified line with broadsides to right and left.

Fire was opened quickly, the tank crews having been instructed in the method of fire before the attack. Much of our ammunition was tracer and the regiment drove on through the new defence line spraying an immense rain of fire far into the country on either side. Soon we were through the danger area, without serious casualties. But it was not now easy to get the fire stopped and we drove through the villages of Sars Poteries and Beugnies with guns blazing. Enemy confusion was complete. Military vehicles, tanks, artillery, and refugee carts packed high with belongings blocked part of the road and had to be pushed unceremoniously to the side. All around were French troops lying flat on the ground, and farms everywhere were jammed tight with guns, tanks, and other military vehicles. Progress towards Avesnes now became slow. At last we succeeded in getting the firing stopped. We drove through Semousies. Always the same picture, troops and civilians in wild flight down both sides of the road. Soon the road forked, one going right to Maubeuge, which was now only about 10 miles away, and the other left down into the valley towards Avesnes. The road was now thick with carts and people, who moved off to the side of the tanks or had to be directed into the side by us. The nearer we came to Avesnes the greater was the crush of vehicles through which we had to fight our way. In Avesnes itself, which had been shelled by our artillery shortly before, the whole population was on the move, jammed between vehicles and guns on both sides of the road in front of our moving tank column. It was obvious that there were strong French forces in the town.

I did not have the column halted, but drove on with the leading battalion of tanks to the high ground west of Avesnes, where I intended to stop and collect up prisoners and captured equipment. On the way a scouting party of two tanks was detached in the southern outskirts of Avesnes and dispatched down the main road to the south. Some 500 yards outside the town on the road to Landrecies, we made a halt, marshalled our units and rounded up the French troops in the immediate neighbourhood. Here, too, farmyards and orchards beside the road were jammed full of troops and refugee carts. All traffic down the road from the west was halted and picked up. Soon a prisoner-of-war cage had to be constructed in the field.

Meanwhile, firing had started behind us in Avesnes—tank guns by the sound of it—and soon we saw flames rising, probably from burning tanks or lorries. We had lost contact with the tank battalion behind us and with the 7th Motor-cycle Battalion.

This did not yet cause me any concern, as, in the confusion of ownerless refugee carts, it was only too easy for a traffic jam to pile up. We had reached our objective and that was the main thing. However, the enemy in Avesnes—there must have been at least a battalion of tanks—made good use of the gap in the Panzer Regiment, and French heavy tanks soon closed the road through the town. The 2nd Battalion of the 25th Panzer Regiment at once tried to overcome the enemy blocking the road, but their attempt failed with the loss of several tanks. The fighting in Avesnes grew steadily heavier. Intermittent wireless contact was established between the 2nd Battalion and ourselves. The battle in Avesnes lasted until about 04.00 hours [*17th May*]. Finally, Hanke, who, on my orders, advanced from the west against the powerful enemy tanks with a Panzer IV, succeeded in disposing of the French tanks. Dawn was slowly breaking when the battle ended and contact was reestablished with the 2nd Battalion.

Meanwhile, I had sent repeated signals to Corps through the divisional staff asking whether, in view of the success of our breakthrough of the Maginot Line, we should not now continue our advance over the Sambre. Receiving no reply—wireless contact had not been established—I decided to continue the attack at dawn with the object of seizing the Sambre crossing at Landrecies and holding it open. I issued orders by wireless to all other units to follow up the Panzer Regiment's advance to Landrecies [*11 miles west of Avesnes*].

At about 04.00 hours I moved off towards Landrecies with the leading battalion of Rothenburg's Panzer Regiment. The 7th Motor-cycle Battalion, which had now closed up, followed behind, and I was firmly convinced that behind them again the remaining units of the division would take part in the attack. The failure of the wireless had simply transmitted all orders into the blue.

As no supplies had come up during the night, we now had to be sparing with ammunition and drove westwards through the brightening day with guns silent. Soon we began to meet refugee columns and detachments of French troops preparing for the march. A chaos of guns, tanks, and military vehicles of all kinds, inextricably entangled with horse-drawn refugee carts, covered the road and verges. By keeping our guns silent and occasionally driving our cross-country vehicles alongside the road, we managed to get past the column without great difficulty. The French troops were completely overcome by surprise at our sudden appearance, laid down their arms and marched off to the east beside our column. Nowhere was any resistance attempted. Any enemy tanks we met on the road were put out of action as we drove past. The advance went on without a halt to the west. Hundreds upon hundreds of French troops, with their officers, surrendered at our arrival. At some points they had to be fetched out of vehicles driving along beside us.

Particularly irate over this sudden disturbance was a French lieutenant-colonel whom we overtook with his car jammed in the press of vehicles. I asked him for his rank and appointment. His eyes glowed hate and impotent fury and he gave the impression of being a thoroughly fanatical type. There being every likelihood, with so much traffic on the road, that our column would get split from time to time, I decided on second thought to take him along with us. He was already fifty yards away to the east when he was fetched back to Colonel Rothenburg, who signed to him to get in his tank. But he curtly refused to come with us, so after summoning him three times to get in, there was nothing for it but to shoot him.

We drove through Maroilles [*8-1/2 miles west of Avesnes*], where the street was so crowded that it was not easy for the people to obey our shouts of "A droit!" On we went, with the sun on our backs through the thin morning mist to the west. The road was now just as full of troops and refugees outside the villages. Our shouts of "A droit!" had little effect and progress became very slow, with the tanks driving through the fields alongside the road. At length we arrived at Landrecies, the town on the Sambre, where there was again a vast crush of vehicles and French troops in every lane and alley, but no resistance. We rolled across the Sambre bridge, on the other side of which we found a French barracks full of troops. As the tank column clattered past, Hanke drove into the courtyard and instructed the French officers to have their troops paraded and marched off to the east.

Still in the belief that the whole division was rapidly approaching Landrecies behind us, I continued the attack towards Le Câteau [*8 miles west of Landrecies*]. We drove through a long wood, which the enemy was using as an ammunition dump. Against the

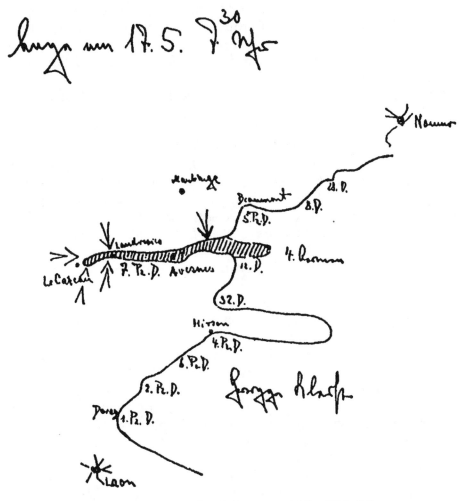

Map 3. Rommel's Advance, 16th–17th May

Map drawn by Rommel showing his advance in the 24 hours to 7.30 a.m. 17th May—in relation to those of the neighbouring divisions and of von Kleist's Panzer Group. This map brings out the extraordinary depth, narrowness, and audacity of his thrust—from Cerfontaine to Le Câteau.

rising sun, the sentries were unable to identify us until we were on top of them. Then they surrendered. In Pommereuille, too, the French troops stationed in the village laid down their arms. I kept the advance going until the hill just east of Le Câteau, where we finally halted. It was 6.15 a.m. My first task was to assure myself that contact with the rear still existed, after which I intended to make another attempt to get in touch with Division Headquarters.

Rommel's division had advanced nearly 50 miles since the previous morning. Then way he had driven on with his tanks during the night was a daring act. Then, and later, most commanders considered that, even in exploiting a victory, the continuation of a tank advance in the dark was too great a hazard.

On Rommel's left, the leading troops of Reinhardt's and Guderian's Panzer Corps were racing level with him. Early that day Guderian's left wing division reached the Oise at Ribemont, 20 miles south of Le Câteau. That was the breadth of the swathe that had been cut by the tank torrents that were sweeping west towards the sea, across the rear of the Allied armies in Belgium. All attempts to block them proved too late, for each time that the French Command chose a new stop-line it was overrun by the German tanks before the slower-moving French reserves arrived, or before they settled into position.

It was now high time that the country we had overrun was secured by the division, and the enormous number of prisoners—approximately two mechanised divisions—was collected. I had kept the division staff constantly informed of our progress, but all messages had been transmitted blind from the Panzer Regiment's command tank and there was no way of telling whether they had been received. Even so, I was not very pleased when I heard shortly afterwards that only a small part of the Panzer Regiment and part of the Motor-cycle Battalion had come through as far as the hill east of le Câteau. An officer was sent off to the rear immediately. Then I tried myself to drive back to establish contact, but soon came under anti-tank gun fire from Le Câteau and had to return. Meanwhile, Rothenburg with part of Panzer Battalion Sickenius had been in action with French tanks and anti-tank guns on the hill east of le Câteau, but had soon disposed of them. I returned to the Panzer Battalion, which had meanwhile formed a hedgehog, and waited there until the arrival of part of the Motor-cycle Battalion which was placed under his command. I then started back in my signals vehicle, with a Panzer III as escort, to bring up and deploy the rest of the division. On the way we came across several stranded vehicles belonging to the Motor-cycle Battalion and Panzer Regiment, whose crews told us that it was wise to go carefully in Landrecies as a number of our vehicles had been fired on there by enemy tanks. I then drove on [*eastward*] at high speed to Landrecies, where the Panzer III, which was in the lead, lost its way in the town. When at last we reached the road to Avesnes, we saw a German vehicle standing in the road a hundred yards ahead, where it had been shot up by enemy guns. There must have been a French tank or anti-tank gun somewhere around, but we had no time for a long palaver and so—through! As we drove past, wounded motor-cyclists shouted frantically to us to take them along. I could not help them, unfortunately—there was too much at stake. Both vehicles crossed the danger zone at top speed and won through to the Maroilles road. Then the escorting Panzer III dropped out with mechanical trouble.

Vehicles now stood everywhere, all over and across the road. Alongside the road there were French officers and men bivouacked close beside their weapons. But they had apparently not yet recovered from the fright which the German tanks had spread and so we put them on the march so far as we could by shouts and signs from the moving vehicles. There were no German troops to be seen. On we went, at top speed, through Maroilles. East of the village we suddenly discovered a Panzer IV, which had been stranded by mechanical trouble and had its 75 mm. gun in working order. We sighed with relief. A Panzer IV was a strong protection at such a moment.

There were now French troops everywhere, on both sides of the road, most of them bivouacked beside their vehicles. There was no chance, unfortunately, of getting them on the march as prisoners as we had no men to form an escort. Where we did manage to get them moving, they marched only so long as our armoured car was with them, and then vanished into the bushes the moment we drove on ahead.

I gave the Panzer IV orders to hold the hill east of Maroilles and to send any prisoners who came from the west on to the east. Then we drove on, but had only gone a few hundred yards when the driver reported that he had to stop for petrol. Fortunately, he still had several full cans aboard. Meanwhile, I was informed by Hanke that he had heard from the crew Panzer IV that the village beyond had been reoccupied by the enemy. There could be no question of tackling French tanks and anti-tank guns with my lightly armoured vehicle, so I drove back Panzer IV with the idea of making wireless contact from there with all parts of the division and organising a quick move into the territory we had overrun. Fortunately, there was no sound of fighting anywhere in the vicinity.

I had barely arrived back at the Panzer IV when a motor rifle company appeared on the horizon, travelling fast down the road from Marbaix [*5 miles west of Landrecies*]. There now being a hope that further detachments would be following in the wake of this company, I drove off again in the direction of Avesnes, but found nothing.

A short distance east of Marbaix a French car came out of a side-turning from the left and crossed the road close in front of my armoured car. At our shouts it halted and a French officer got out and surrendered. Behind the car there was a whole convoy of lorries approaching in a great cloud of dust. Acting quickly, I had the convoy turned off towards Avesnes. Hanke swung himself up on the first lorry while I stayed on the cross-road for a while, shouting and signalling to the French troops that they should lay down their arms—the war was over for them. Several of the lorries had machine-guns mounted and manned against air attack. It was impossible to see through the dust how long the convoy was, and so after 10 or 15 vehicles had passed, I put myself at the head of the column and drove on to Avesnes. Shortly before the town we had to make a detour across country where the road was closed by burning vehicles.

At length we arrived at the south-west entrance to Avesnes, where we found part of the Battalion Paris [*the commander's name*] installed near the cemetery. Without halting, Hanke led the lorry convoy on to a parking place and there disarmed the enemy troops. We now found that we had had no less than 40 lorries, many of them carrying troops, behind us.

Staff H.Q. of the division arrived in Avesnes at about 16.00 hours, and now unit after unit began to move into the territory we had overrun during the night and early morning. In the course of this move, the 2nd Battalion of the Artillery Regiment successfully prevented 48 French tanks from going into action just north of Avesnes. The tanks stood formed up alongside the road, some of them with engines running. Several drivers were taken prisoner still in their tanks. This action saved the 25th Panzer Regiment an attack in their rear by these tanks.

The 7th Panzer Division's losses during the breakthrough of the Maginot Line extension (on the 16th/17th May) are given in the division's official history as 35 killed and 59 wounded. In the division's sector the prisoners taken were approximately 10,000 men, together with 100 tanks, 30 armoured cars, and 27 guns.

The account concludes, "The division had no time to collect large numbers of prisoners and equipment."

After settling the layout of the division between Le Câteau and the French frontier west of Sivry, I took an hour and a half's rest. Shortly after midnight orders came in for the attack to be continued next day, the 18th May, towards Cambrai. At about 07.00 hours next morning the adjutant of the 25th Panzer Regiment arrived at headquarters and reported that a powerful enemy force had established itself in Pommereuille Wood [*midway between Landrecies and Le Câteau*]. He had managed to break through from west to east in an armoured car under cover of night. The 25th Panzer Regiment, which was still holding its position east of Le Câteau, urgently needed petrol and ammunition and the commander had instructed him to get them brought up as quickly as possible.

At about 08.00 hours I put the remaining panzer battalion on the march for Landrecies and Le Câteau with orders to push through to the regiment and get the ammunition and petrol up to it. The 37th Armoured Reconnaissance Battalion was to follow up behind. With Most and Hanke, I later caught up with the Panzer Battalion in the woods half a mile east of Pommereuille, and found them in action against French tanks which were barring the road. Violent fighting developed on the road and there was no chance of outflanking the enemy position on either side. Our guns seemed to be completely ineffective against the heavy armour of the French tanks.

The French tanks had from 40 mm. to 60 mm. of armour whereas even the German medium tanks had only 30 mm., and the light tanks had even less protection.

We stood for some time watching the battle from close range, until I finally decided to take the battalion south through the woods via Ors [*4 miles south-west of Landrecies*]. We again came up against the French in the northern outskirts of Ors and progress became slow while we fought our way forward. For some unknown reason the Panzer Regiment's ammunition and petrol column did not follow up behind the battalion. It was midday before we finally reached Rothenburg's position. He reported that his force had held the position against heavy enemy tank attacks, but that he was now incapable of further movement and in urgent need of petrol and ammunition. Unfortunately, I was not at that moment in a position to help him.

The necessary forces were now dispatched to Pommereuille to open the shortest road to Landrecies. Meanwhile, French heavy artillery had begun to lay down a heavy barrage on our hedgehog position. Their fire was accurate and part of the position had to be vacated. Confident that the fighting at Pommereuille would soon be decided in our favour, I now gave orders for the Panzer Regiment to form up for their attack on Cambrai. By 15.00 hours the situation had cleared up sufficiently for the attack to open.

The passages that follow in Rommel's narrative have more detail than significance, and may therefore be summarised. The ammunition and petrol column which had been left south-east of Pommereuille Wood did not reach 25th Panzer Regiment's two battalions located near Le Cateau until some hours later. By the time these tanks had filled up with ammunition and petrol, the one Panzer Battalion which Rommel had brought up was already far ahead on the road to Cambrai.

I now gave orders to the reinforced Battalion Paris to secure the roads leading from Cambrai to the north-east and north as quickly as possible. Led by its few tanks and two troops of self-propelled A.A. guns, the battalion advanced over a broad front and in great depth straight across the fields to the north-west, throwing up a great cloud of dust as they went. Tanks and A.A. guns scattered fire at intervals into the northern outskirts of Cambrai. The enemy in Cambrai, unable in the dust to see that most of our vehicles were soft-skinned, apparently thought that a large-scale tank attack was approaching the north of the town and offered no resistance.

Nothing could have been more futile than the way that the French Command used its armoured forces. It had 53 tank battalions compared with the Germans' 36. But all the German battalions were formed into divisions (of which they had ten) while nearly half the French were infantry-support units. Moreover, even their seven divisions of armoured type were used piecemeal.

Before the war the only French armoured formations had been the so-called "light mechanised division" (200 tanks), of converted cavalry. The French had three of these, which were employed for the advance into Belgium. There were also four "armoured" divisions (of 150 tanks only) which had been formed during the winter. These four were thrown separately and successively against the seven German armoured divisions (averaging 260 tanks apiece) that drove across the Meuse like a vast phalanx. The 1st French Armoured Division was directed towards Dinant, but ran out of fuel and was overrun—as already related. The 3rd was directed against Sedan, but distributed to support the infantry there; the fragments were swamped by Guderian's three divisions. The 4th (under de Gaulle), recently formed and still incomplete, went into action against Guderian's flank as he swept on towards the Oise, but was brushed aside. The 2nd was spread along a 25-mile stretch of the Oise, and Guderian's two leading divisions quickly burst through this thin string of static packets.

The three French mechanised divisions from Belgium were assembling just north of Cambrai, and although two of them had been mauled in their fight with Hoeppner's Panzer Corps in the Belgian plain they were still a powerful force. They were ordered to strike south towards Cambrai and St. Quentin on the 19th, but the order was not executed—as a considerable proportion of the tanks had been detached to aid the infantry at various places.

As for the British, they had only ten tank units in France, and these were all split up among the infantry divisions. The first armoured division was not embarked for France until after the German offensive had started.

Notes

1. This introductory note is supplied by the Editor, Captain B. H. Liddell Hart. Elsewhere all his editorial comments apart from footnotes are set in italics.

2. The 7th Panzer Division comprised:

   Armour

   > 25th Panzer Regiment (of 3 tank battalions)

   > 37th Panzer Reconnaissance Battalion

   Motorised Infantry

   > 6th Rifle Regiment

   > 7th Rifle Regiment

   > 7th Motor-cycle Battalion

   Engineers

   > 58th Pioneer Battalion

   Artillery

   > 78th Field Artillery Regiment (of 3 battalions, each of 3 four-gun batteries)

   > 42nd Anti-Tank Artillery Battalion

3. In the Germany Army, units and formations were often called by the name of their commanders.

4. *Note by Manfred Rommel.* Hanke was a prominent member of the Nazi party and an official of Goebbels's Propaganda Ministry. He appears to have been very unpopular with the other officers on account of his high-handed behaviour, and Rommel finally removed him from the Staff after an incident in the Mess when he suggested that he had the power to have Rommel himself removed from his command. Rommel made a long report later to Hitler's Adjutant.

Later in the war, Hanke became Gauleiter of Silesia and achieved noto-
riety for his defence of Breslau to the last stick and stone. However, when
the devastated city finally capitulated, Hanke did not stay to meet the
invading Red Army, but escaped in an aeroplane, leaving the population
to the tender mercies of the Russian troops. He has never been heard of
since.

5. Translator's note: *eingetroffen* instead of *eingeschlossen*.

6. "Ia" is the operations side of the staff, and is also used for the officer in
    charge of it.

7. The *Gefechtsstaffel*, to which Rommel refers through his campaigns, was a
    small headquarters group consisting of signals troops and a small combat
    team, together with the appropriate vehicles (including a wireless lorry),
    which always accompanied him in action.

Reading 5

Destroying the Wehrmacht: January 1944–May 1945

by Ronald J. Wright

The Red Army conducted a series of major offensive operations along the entire strategic front in 1944–45, inflicting mortal blows upon the *Wehrmacht*. Firmly in control of the strategic initiative, the Soviets chose the time and place for a major strike and massed superior forces at the point of decision. In three major campaigns— the winter campaign of 1944 (January–April), the summer–fall campaign of 1944 (June–November), and the winter campaign of 1945 (January–May)—the Soviet armed forces broke the back of the German Army, swept the invaders from Soviet soil, and secured hegemony over Eastern Europe.

To better understand the success of Soviet mobile forces in the last year and a half of the war, it is necessary to place them within the context of the strategic situation in 1944. As the year began German armies still occupied the Baltic states, Belorussia, portions of Western Ukraine, and the Crimea but had insufficient forces to hold a front 2,000 kilometers in length. The Soviets outnumbered the Germans in manpower and weaponry, and the difference in strength levels increased month by month. Germany's allies were weak and faltering, while the Soviet Union's allies, especially the United States, applied increasing pressure on the German War Machine and nourished the Red Army with war materiel. The

From *Historical Analysis of the Use of Mobile Forces by Russia and the USSR*. Occasional Paper Number 10. The Center for Strategic Technology, The Texas Engineering Experiment Station, The Texas A & M University, 1985.

Soviets were fully in control of the strategic initiative, and their skill in conducting operations was, at the least, equal to the Germans. The Germans probably retained the tactical edge on the Eastern Front, but the advantage was less pronounced than it had been earlier in the war.

The Red Army possessed a substantial advantage in men and materiel over the *Wehrmacht* in January 1944. In the field armies the Soviets counted 5,568,000 troops. They fielded 480 rifle divisions (each averaging a strength of 6,000–7,000 men), thirty-five tank (mechanized) corps, forty-six independent tank brigades, eighty artillery and mortar divisions, over 5,600 tanks, and close to 9,000 combat aircraft. These forces were organized into sixty combined-arms armies, five shock armies, six tank armies, or were in *STAVKA* Reserve. German forces on the Eastern Front numbered 4,906,000 men (including 706,000 allies, mostly Rumanians, Hungarians, and Finns), 5,400 tanks and self-propelled guns, and 3,000 planes. German ground forces were formed into 236 divisions, including twenty-five panzer and eighteen motorized divisions.—By 1945 the Soviets had twice as many troops, three times the tanks and self-propelled guns, four times as many guns and mortars, and eight times the planes possessed by the Germans. The growing disparity between the forces wielded by the Soviets and the Germans meant that the Red Army enjoyed a favorable, sometimes overwhelming, correlation of forces in every major operation in the third period of the war.

Although most of Germany's manpower and economic resources went to the Russian Front in 1944–45, fighting a two-front war seriously hindered German efforts to stave off defeat in the east. In early 1944, the Eastern Intelligence Branch of the German Army High Command concluded that at least thirty percent of Germany's military resources went to defend Western Europe, while the Soviet Union diverted only seven percent of its strength to the passive Far Eastern theater. Increasing numbers of men and weapons were employed in defending the Reich against Allied air raids. German and German-allied divisions in Western Europe and the Balkans totalled 102 in January 1944. This number would grow, to the detriment of German armies in the east, as the Western Allies landed additional troops in Europe, especially after June 1944.

Both the Germans and the Soviets had suffered grievous losses in two-and-a-half years of war, but the Soviets could more easily replace their losses because of their larger manpower reserves. Also, success in battle engendered replacement, for the Red Army drafted males in the territories it captured. Throughout 1944, the Red Army added thousands of Poles, Rumanians, Czechoslovakians, and Bulgarians to its ranks. By 1945, their number totaled 320,000 men. The Soviets outproduced the Germans in important categories of war materiel, as well. Nearly 107,000 tanks and self-propelled guns rolled out of Soviet factories during the war, while the Germans managed to produce but 76,000.

By the beginning of 1944, the Soviets benefited substantially from Lend-Lease, although post-war Soviet writings generally dismiss the importance of Lend-Lease to their war effort. Zhukov writes, "I do not wish completely to deny its value though as in some degree it did help the Soviet Army and our war industry. However, it did not amount to much and hence cannot be considered of much significance." Throughout the war the Soviet Union produced most of its own tanks, self-propelled guns, artillery, and aircraft. Soviet production in 1943 totaled 24,100 tanks and self-propelled guns, 130,300 artillery pieces, and 29,900 aircraft. However, a significant number of the trucks, railroad cars, telephones, boots, and canned food needed to enhance the transport, mobility, and communications of the Red Army were obtained from the West. According to a list published by the Commissariat of Foreign Trade in Moscow, the United States, Great Britain, and Canada shipped to the USSR the following items from June 1941 through April 1944: 220,817 trucks and armored personnel carriers; 1,154 railroad cars; 245,000 telephones; and 5,500,000 pairs of army boots. Especially important for the Red Army's tactical, operational, and logistical mobility were the trucks received from Lend-Lease. One Western historian calculated that by the end of the war fifty percent of all vehicles in service in the Soviet armed forces were made in the United States. However, there never were enough trucks. The Soviets stripped the civilian sector, but even at the end of the war elite Soviet tank armies remained ten to twenty-five percent short of their authorized complement of trucks.

With large numbers of tanks, self-propelled guns, and other weapons coming off assembly lines, the Soviets reorganized their armored forces once again at the end of 1943. Tank and mechanized corps were reinforced with a new medium tank model, the T-34/85. This was an upgraded version of the T-34 with an 85mm gun. When practicable, the corps were equipped with tanks of the same type, mainly medium T-34s. The tank and mechanized corps retained their basic structure and mission but had more tanks, more artillery, and a larger complement of support personnel. A

1944 tank corps contained: 12,010 men, 207 medium tanks, 63 self-propelled guns, 36 artillery pieces, 94 mortars, and 8 truck-mounted multiple-rocket launchers, the famous *Katyushas*. A tank corps was authorized 1,456 trucks, tractors, and armored personnel carriers. A 1944 mechanized corps had: 16,422 personnel, 183 medium tanks, sixty-three self-propelled guns, eighty artillery pieces, 154 mortars, and eight *Katyushas*. A mechanized corps had at its disposal 1,849 trucks, tractors, and armored personnel carriers. For a representative example of a late 1944–early 1945 guards tank corps, see Table 1.

Table 1: Table of Organization of 4th Guards Tank Corps (1945)

12th, 13th, and 14th Guard Tank Brigades

29th Guards Heavy Tank Regiment

3d Guards Motorized Rifle Brigade

293d Guards Self-Propelled Artillery Regiment

298th Guards Self-Propelled Artillery Regiment

1660th Antitank Artillery Regiment

264th Mortar Regiment

120th Guards Antiaircraft Artillery Regiment

240th Guards Mortar Battalion

76th Motorcycle Battalion

106th Engineer Battalion

413th Communication Battalion

3d Aviation Element

165th Medical Battalion

226th Chemical Defense Company

85th Mobile Tank Repair Base

92d Mobile Automotive Repair Base

17th Motor Transport Company

24th Field Bakery

2135th Gosbank Field Disbursement Unit

Tank brigades, the building blocks of the tank and mechanized corps were also reorganized late in 1943. The brigades were strengthened by the addition of an additional tank battalion. Gradually, light tanks were removed and each of the three tank battalions in a brigade were equipped with medium tanks. PA full strength a 1944–45 tank brigade numbered: 1,354 troops, sixty-five T-34 or T-34/85 tanks, 121 trucks, and a small number of support vehicles and weapons.

Technological developments improved the battle performance of Soviet mobile ground forces in 1944–45. Not only were more armored vehicles available, the new models of tank and self-propelled guns had greater firepower, armor protection, and mobility. Killing power was increased by mounting larger guns, and armor protection was improved by the addition of high quality steel plate. An increase in speed and range gave tanks and self-propelled guns more mobility and maneuverability. The increased depth of offensive operations in the third period of the war coincided with the extended range of new Soviet tank models, which had a radius of action twenty to fifty percent greater than earlier types.

Soviet tank and self-propelled guns produced in 1944–45 were designed to counter newer models of more powerful German tanks, as well as overcome stronger and deeper enemy defenses. In October 1943, the Soviets terminated light tank production. A few months later they began the mass production of medium T-34/85 tanks, Joseph Stalin heavy tanks, and the SU-122 and SU-152 assault guns. The latter two vehicles were allocated primarily for use in the tank and mechanized corps. They followed in the wake of an attack, providing support fire for infantry and tank units within the enemy's defense system.

Armored formations were the heart of Soviet mobile forces. Units built around the tank, self-propelled gun, and truck continued to grow, and their impact on the battlefield increased. By the end of the war the Red Army fielded six tank armies (each of two to three tank or mechanized corps), twenty-three independent tank (mechanized) corps, fifty-nine independent tank brigades, fifty-three independent tank regiments, and 128 self-propelled artillery regiments; a force of approximately 14,500 tank; and 7,000 self-propelled guns. The number of tanks and self-propelled guns employed in Soviet offensive operations rose dramatically during the war. At Moscow in December 1941, the Soviets deployed only 774 tanks; at Stalingrad in November 1942, they assembled 1,463 tanks and self-propelled guns; during the Belorussian offensive in June 1944, the Soviets massed over 5,200 tanks and self-propelled guns.

The Soviet Union expended a great deal of labor and resources to build up their tank forces. At the end of 1943, 17.8 percent of the USSR's annual steel production went to the manufacture of tanks.

Soviet general and historian, I. Krupchenko, observed, "The experience of World War II demonstrated that a high rate of advance, mobility of combat actions and scale of operations, all other conditions being equal, were directly dependent on the number of tanks involved." Soviet armored formations were intentionally designed to be tank-heavy throughout the war, in part to offset heavy losses on the battlefield.

The construction of great numbers of tanks, while certainly justified from the Soviet point of view, affected the production of armored personnel carriers, a vehicle the Soviet Union never produced in substantial numbers during the war. The absence of such vehicles in mobile units to protect troops from small arms and artillery fire not only hindered tactical maneuverability, but also led to high losses among supporting infantry, who often rode unshielded on tanks. Immediately after the war the Soviets made a major effort to design and mass produce effective armored personnel carriers.

In 1944–45, the Soviets consistently implemented pre-war theories of the offensive-battle in depth. Successful offensive operations consisted of a series of battles in which Soviet forces encircled and eliminated large enemy formations or fragmented the enemy line into isolated segments which were destroyed in detail. The Red Army carried out mobile operations on a broad front, in great depth, and within short periods of time. For example, the Belorussian Offensive (23 June–29 August 1944) was conducted along a front one thousand kilometers wide and reached a depth of six hundred kilometers, with most of the distance attained within the first month of the attack. During the Vistula-Oder operation (12 January–3 February 1945) Soviet forces advanced along a front five hundred kilometers wide and achieved a penetration of five hundred kilometers in three weeks. During successful offensive operations of the third period of the war, armored forces advanced fifty to sixty kilometers per day, while infantry units managed twenty to thirty kilometers per day.

These successes were attained by implementing pre-war theories of deep operations, augmented by the battlefield experiences of 1941–1943. Mass and maneuver remained the guiding principles employed to achieve tactical and operational success. Combined arms "shock groups," consisting of infantry, tank, artillery, and engineer units, and supported by combat aircraft, massed on narrow frontages to penetrate the enemy's tactical defenses with battering rams of men and machines. Mobile groups, made up of tank, mechanized, and cavalry formations, exploited the shock group's breakthrough, pursuing the retreating enemy, encircling his units, engaging his reserves, and disrupting his command and supply networks.

Soviet offensives in the third period of the war repeatedly shattered German defenses and hurled the enemy line back on a wide front and in great depth. However, operations on a particular sector of the front eventually stalled and a pause ensued, as the Germans regrouped, counterattacked with reserves, and established a new front line. Soviet forces, weakened by losses, exhausted from a lengthy advance, and ill-nourished from a long and tenuous supply line, halted to reorganize, receive replacements, repair transportation lines, and plan fresh assaults.

Transformation of operational success into strategic victory required a succession of in-depth offensives. When *STAVKA* launched one or more major offensives, they planned future attacks, timed to commence upon the conclusion of the earlier drives. For example, as the Belorussian Operation lost momentum at the end of July 1944, the Soviets initiated a preplanned assault far to the south in Rumania in mid-August.

The Soviet front line advanced westwards in a series of staggered leaps, the Red Army assailing different sectors of the front in consecutive blows to keep the Germans off balance. Through attrition and maneuver, the Soviets bled the Germans and captured territory, until Hitler no longer had the manpower, resources, nor space to carry on the war. The Soviets never seriously overreached themselves strategically in 1944–45. From the experience of earlier offensive operations which ended in disaster, both their own and the enemy's, the Soviets had learned well the folly of going too far, too fast, with too little.

A major offensive operation in the third period of the war generally involved several Fronts. For example, four Fronts conducted the Belorussian Operation in June–August 1944, two Fronts launched the Jassy-Kishinev Offensive in August 1944, and three Fronts carried out the Vistula-Oder Offensive in January–February 1945. The forces assembled for the largest offensives numbered from 163 to 193 divisions, 3,000 to 6,000 tanks and self-propelled guns, 28,000 to 42,000 guns and mortars, and 3,000 to 7,000 aircraft. *STAVKA* planned the timing and objectives of an offensive, while a representative, or representatives, of the High Command coordinated the actions of a "group of Fronts." Soviet offensive operations in 1944–45 often followed this pattern: Two or more Fronts, echeloning their armies and corps into breakthrough forces, exploitation forces, and reserves, initiated powerful assaults at sev-

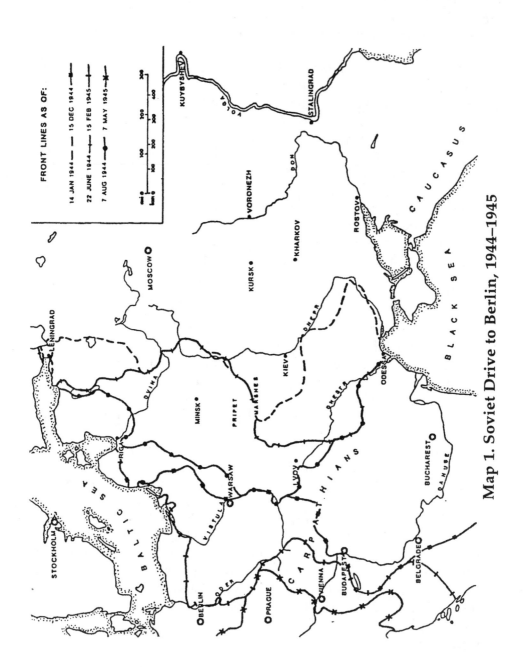

Map 1. Soviet Drive to Berlin, 1944–1945

eral points. Breaching the enemy's tactical defenses and developing the attack in depth, Soviet forces encircled large enemy formations, split them into several parts, and destroyed them in detail.

Certain aspects of the pre-war theories of a battle in depth were not successfully implemented during the third period of the war. There were no major airborne operations in 1944–45. Airpower, assigned the function of sealing off the enemy's rear during offensive operations, was inconsistently employed in deep interdiction missions. Generally, air operations were designed to win air superiority over the battlefield and to provide close air support for ground forces. Only five percent of Soviet air resources were used for attacks on the enemy's strategic transportation system and reserves.

The Soviets considered encirclement operations to be the most effective way of smashing large formations. Soviet general and historian, S. Shtrik, writes, "Encirclement and subsequent destruction of large enemy groupings was frequently the main task of all offensive operations and such operations were considered the most effective method of defeating the enemy." During the war the Soviets conducted ten large-scale encirclements in which they eliminated, according to their calculations, approximately 200 divisions. Most of the large encirclement operations occurred in the third period of the war. In the Korsun-Shevchenkovsky, Belorussia, Jassy-Kishinev, Budapest, East Prussia, Berlin, and Prague operations, all conducted by two or more Fronts, Soviet forces destroyed from ten to thirty enemy divisions in each offensive.

John Sloan has written of Soviet encirclement operations in World War II:

> From the German successes and failures at encirclement warfare the Soviets learned the necessity of combining the high speed and mobility of the forces that strike deep to develop an encirclement with the ability to occupy the ground with sufficient density of forces that must fill out the arms of the encirclement.

In order to concentrate the strength necessary for a large-scale double envelopment, the Soviets generally employed the forces of at least two Fronts. Of thirty encirclement battles, twenty-two were carried out by groups of Fronts. In such operations each Front organized its forces into "assault groups" of combined-arms and mobile formations which broke through the enemy's defenses and formed all or part of the force encircling a number of his divisions.

The Red Army executed a successful encirclement operation in phases: penetration of the tactical defense zone; exploitation of the breakthrough; link-up and encirclement of an enemy grouping; formation of inner and outer rings of encirclement. While Soviet aviation and air defense forces blockaded the surrounded units from supply by enemy aircraft, forces on the inner ring eliminated the pocket by splitting it into segments which were destroyed piecemeal. The exterior perimeter repelled counterattacks or developed the offensive deeper into the enemy's territory. In most encirclement operations during the war half or more of the attacking forces went to the interior ring. However, in the third period the Soviets increasingly allocated a greater proportion of men and materiel to the exterior front.

In encirclement operations in which Soviet and German forces were roughly equal in strength (as at Stalingrad in November 1942), or when the Germans had strong reserves beyond the exterior front (as at Korsun-Shevchenkovsky in February 1944), Soviet units on the exterior ring assumed a defensive stance. The distance between the interior and exterior fronts in such cases was generally seventy to eighty kilometers. If, on the other hand, the enemy did not have substantial forces in the immediate vicinity of the encirclement, Soviet forces pressed the attack, moving the exterior front 100–150 kilometers from the interior front. Such tactics created greater maneuver room for Soviet units and frustrated German attempts to relieve their forces trapped in the pocket.

In 1944–45, the Soviets not only conducted encirclement operations with increasing frequency, they expended less time in eliminating surrounded enemy forces. It took the Red Army over two months to annihilate the encircled 6th Army at Stalingrad in 1942–43, while only eight days were used to destroy German-Rumanian formations in the Jassy-Kishinev Operation in 1944, and only nine days to vanquish the encircled forces in Berlin in 1945. Swifter reduction of pocketed enemy forces resulted from the overwhelming strength the Soviets brought to bear in battle in the latter stages of the war and from their attempts to fuse the phases of an encirclement operation into a single process of "encircle, divide, and annihilate." During the last year of the war the Red Army frequently shattered the enemy defense line with powerful frontal assaults, exploited the breakthrough in depth, and surrounded enemy units without establishing a stable exterior front of encirclement. Surrounded and isolated German formations, labelled "wanderers," were subsequently destroyed by Soviet second echelon forces.

A basic principle of warfare, the concentration of maximum force at the point of decision, was a key element of the Red Army's offensive success in the third period of the war. "Regrouping of forces" was the method by which the Soviets realized the principle of mass. From the strategic down to the tactical level, Soviet commanders regrouped forces to shift operations from one axis to another, alter the composition of formations, reinforce offensive success, or overcome failure.

Prior to offensive operations, Front commanders reshuffled their forces, thinning-out secondary sections of the line and reinforcing the sector, or sectors, of the main drive. Major regroupings within the Fronts in 1944–45 were accomplished in six to fourteen days over distances of one hundred to four hundred kilometers, involving forces in excess of 500,000 men, 9,000 guns, and 1,000 tanks.

STAVKA shifted units from one Front to another or allocated forces from the strategic reserve to Armies and Fronts. These reserves became the primary means by which the Soviets insured numerical superiority over the enemy in major operations. Primary units of *STAVKA* Reserve included tank armies, tank and mechanized corps, independent tank brigades and regiments, infantry divisions, air corps and divisions, artillery corps and divisions, and Katyusha rocket brigades. The large number of these units retained in strategic reserve enabled the Soviets to form powerful shock and exploitation forces before initiating an offensive. In the third period of the war the Soviets steadily increased the proportional amount of strategic reserve forces used to create assault groups in the Fronts. In January 1945, fifty-seven percent of the infantry and sixty percent of the tanks in the 1st Belorussian Front during the Vistula-Oder operation came from the strategic reserve.

In combat, mass is more effective when combined with surprise; thus, a primary consideration was given to deceiving the enemy when the Soviets regrouped men and materiel. Usually, large bodies of troops moved near the front only at night. The Soviets employed elaborate deception and camouflage schemes in regrouping operations. When artillery was brought up by rail during the preparations for the assault on Berlin, for example, over 1,200 guns and mortars and 4,000 vehicles were disguised as hay and building materials loaded upon flatcars.

Strategic movements of troops and equipment were generally conducted by rail. Operational regroupings, those within Fronts and between Fronts advancing along the same axis, were most often accomplished by the "combined method"—some personnel marched, others traveled in vehicles, and the railroads moved heavy equipment. The Soviets favored the combined method because movement by rail, in comparison to motor transport, had both advantages and limitations. Railroads could carry more men and material, were capable of traveling longer distances per day, and were relatively independent of inclement weather. However, rail lines were vulnerable to air attack and to destruction by enemy sappers as the Germans retreated. Destruction of great lengths of track hindered regrouping operations, for the rate of advance of Soviet troops during offensives often exceeded the rate of repair of damaged rail lines, which in the third period averaged ten to twelve kilometers per day.

Men and equipment were also ferried by air. During the offensive in Belorussia in 1944, military and civilian aircraft airlifted 54,000 men to the front. Aviation offered a rapid and mobile means to regroup substantial forces rapidly, but the Soviets used airplanes for such a purpose only rarely.

Regrouping operations grew in scope in 1944–45, as STAVKA shuffled entire Armies and Fronts. For example, the 2nd Belorussian Front moved over three hundred kilometers from the East Pomeranian to the Berlin sector in fifteen days during April 1945. Included in the regrouping operation were five combined-arms armies, one air army, one tank army, a cavalry corps, and a large number of guns. Trains and motor transport, numbering 1,200 vehicles, moved the troops and equipment by the combined method. The combined-arms armies completed the transfer in five to eight days, averaging forty to sixty kilometers per day.

A major reason for regrouping forces was to mass sufficient strength so that the enemy's tactical defenses could be breached. Breaks in the line enabled mobile forces to surge through the gaps and wreak havoc in the enemy's rear areas. To accomplish this aim, Soviet Fronts and Armies in the third period attacked with greater depth and power. Soviet commanders divided their forces between one or more echelons and massed units on narrow breakthrough sectors.

In 1941–1943, the trend in the Red Army had been to form single echelons within Fronts and Armies. During the third period of the war, single echelons were still employed in offensive operations if conditions were appropriate, such as assaults against shallow, unprepared defenses. However, Fronts and Armies generally formed up into two echelons for sustained operations against prepared positions. On the strategic defensive after the summer of

1943, the Germans constructed stronger tactical defense positions which were organized in depth. The Soviets, possessing a mightier army than in 1941–43, echeloned their forces in depth to overcome the deeper German defenses.

A Front commander, echeloning his forces to a distance of seventy to one hundred kilometers, usually allocated from seventy to eighty percent of his men and equipment to the combined-arms armies of the first echelon. The mission of the first echelon was to penetrate the enemy's tactical defense zone as quickly as practicable. Second echelon forces generally consisted of one or two combined-arms armies in reserve and mobile groups of one or two tank armies and one or more tank, mechanized, or cavalry corps. These formations completed the breakthrough of the tactical defenses, maintained the momentum of the attack, and exploited success in depth.

The Soviets increased the density, as well as the depth, of assault forces in 1944–45. Continuing the trend established in the second period, they massed their men and equipment on even narrower breakthrough sectors. Front commanders concentrated from forty to seventy-five percent of their infantry, up to seventy percent of their artillery, and sixty to ninety percent of their armor and aircraft on breakthrough sectors representing but seven to sixteen percent of the width of the Front's lateral boundaries. Breakthrough sectors of a Front were thirty to sixty kilometers wide while those of an Army averaged ten to fifteen kilometers. This was a decrease in breadth of two to three times compared to the first period of the war.

Tactical density increased substantially. In major offensives in 1944 the Soviets massed 1–1.5 rifle divisions, from 180 to 310 guns and mortars, and up to forty-five tanks and self-propelled guns per kilometer of front selected for a breakthrough. The number of tanks and self-propelled guns rose to 95–104 per kilometer by 1945. Comparing the density of forces concentrated on breakthrough areas in 1944–45 with those of the first period of the war, the quantity of guns increased three to ten times, while the number of tanks rose five to ten times.

Combat experience in the first two periods of the war confirmed the tenet stated by Major General A. Ryayansky, "Modern battle is a combined-arms battle and is waged by the combined efforts of all combat arms." When adequate numbers of men and equipment were available and leadership was sound, infantry-sapper-tank assault teams, supported by intensive artillery bombardments and extensive air strikes, spearheaded Soviet assaults in 1944–45.

Armor carried the burden as the "main striking force" in attacks. With stronger, deeper German defenses to overcome in the third period, the role of infantry-support tanks and self-propelled guns was even greater than before. By 1944, independent tank brigades (regiments) and self-propelled gun regiments, held in *STAVKA* Reserve and parcelled out for specific operations, contained forty percent of the tanks and self-propelled guns in the Red Army. Front and Army commanders employed much of their available armor for direct infantry support during assaults. For example, forty-four percent of the armor strength of the four Fronts engaged in the Belorussian offensive in June 1944 was allocated to the first echelon for infantry support. The use of greater numbers of armored vehicles, when adequately supported by air, artillery, and engineer assets in breaching the enemy's tactical defenses, was a primary reason why both the depth of penetration and the rate of advance by Soviet forces increased in 1944–45.

The Red Army Air Force dominated the skies over the battlefield after mid-1943. In all major offensives Soviet aircraft enjoyed a highly favorable margin of strength over the enemy, as during the Belorussian Operation where the ratio of Soviet to German planes was 4.1:1. The Soviets used their greater air resources much more effectively than they had in 1941–42. During the first year and a half of the war they dispersed aircraft across a wide area and launched weak, periodic sorties over the battlefield. In 1944–45 they concentrated their air strength and sent up large formations in support of ground forces during the breakthrough and exploitation phases of an offensive.

The Soviets massed planes as well as troops in preparation for offensive operations. At the strategic level *STAVKA* maneuvered air units in support of a Front, or Fronts, initiating a major drive. With many more planes of higher quality available in 1944–45, the Soviets were better able to maintain the principle of mass. Whereas in the first and second periods of the war a Front conducting an offensive had only 300–400 or 650–1,000 aircraft, respectively; Fronts in the third period commanded up to 3,000 planes and sometimes more.

Air armies were the largest operational units of the Red Army Air Force, and they controlled the air operations for a Front. An air army in the third period averaged 1,400 planes, 41,000 men and 3,500 to 4,000 trucks. The latter vehicles enabled the air army commander to shift personnel and equipment rapidly to new airfields. In preparation for offensive operations an air army, often reinforced with additional aircraft from the strategic reserve, concentrated its forces near the sector (or sectors) of the enemy front targeted for a breakthrough. In the L'vov-Sandomierz operation during the summer of 1944, for example, the 2nd Air Army assigned eighty-eight percent of its strength in support of the two assault groups of the 1st Ukranian Front. The Soviets used air armies primarily as an adjunct to ground operations. The vast majority of Soviet aircraft flew air superiority or close support missions during the war—thirty-five percent in the battle to win control of the air and 46.5 percent in direct support, i.e., bombing and strafing targets for the troops on the battlefield.

In the third period, Soviet assault forces generally penetrated the main positions of the enemy's tactical defense zone within the first day of an offensive. Sometimes, rifle divisions of the first echelon, supported by tanks, self-propelled guns, artillery and aircraft, were able to break completely through the tactical zone (usually eight to twelve kilometers but extending to fifteen to twenty kilometers in some cases) on the first day, quickly opening the way for second echelon units and mobile groups to drive through the gap into the enemy's rear areas.

A number of factors explain the success of Soviet assaults in 1944–45. The Soviets regrouped their forces to concentrate strength at the point of decision, massed units to create high tactical densities, and echeloned their forces to insure depth. They attained numerical superiority in attacks throughout the period, consistently achieving favorable ratios over the enemy of three or five to one in troops, five or six to one in tanks, and five or seven to one in artillery. Beyond gaining the advantage of numbers on the battlefield, the Soviets credit much of their offensive success to their ability to achieve strategic and tactical surprise over the enemy. Undertaking elaborate deception and camouflage schemes, coupled with repaid regrouping of forces, they often deceived the Germans as to the time of an assault, the direction of the main blow, and the size of the attacking forces. A study by the Soviet General Staff entitled *The Ten Crushing Blows of 1944* stated, "The success of our offensive operations was achieved in significant degree by their surprise." Trading off problems in command control for the benefits of surprise, the Soviets launched forty percent of their attacks at night, a higher percentage than in 1941–43.

Soviet success paralleled German decline. Prowess in the tactics of "defense in depth" depended upon the troops' skill in separating enemy armor from supporting infantry and thus defeating each force separately. With a decline in strength and training, however, German tactical ability degenerated perceptively in 1944–45. Meanwhile, the Red Army improved the coordination between units, as its forces attacked in tailored assault groups employing combined-arms tactics. Strategically, the Germans played into Soviet hands, defending long stretches of territory with inadequate force. They compounded this problem by placing much of their tactical and operational strength near the front line within range of massive artillery barrages and air strikes.

When combined-arms assault forces penetrated the enemy's front, the decisive moment in offensive operations came with the commitment of Front and Army mobile groups to exploit the breach. Successful engagement of mobile ground formations drove the attack's momentum deep into the enemy's rear areas. The offensive entered a phase in which the mobility and maneuverability of units often meant the difference between victory and defeat.

Front-level mobile groups in the third period of the war were generally composed of one or two tank armies, one or two tank (mechanized) corps, and, where conditions were appropriate, one or two "cavalry-mechanized groups." These latter *ad hoc* formations consisted of a cavalry corps mated with a tank or mechanized corps and placed under a common headquarters. They combined the firepower and staying power of tanks and motorized infantry with the off-road capability of horses. One or two tank (mechanized) corps often made up the mobile group force of an Army. These tank, mechanized, and cavalry formations were the High Command's strategic mobile units and were held in *STAVKA* Reserve until released to Front or Army commanders for use in offensive operations. As an offensive wound down towards the inevitable strategic pause, mobile group forces were regrouped, reconstituted, and sometimes shuffled off to another sector of the front for a new drive on a different strategic axis.

Large armored units were the key to successful deep operations in 1944–45. Tank (mechanized) corps and tank armies combined firepower, shock, and maneuverability in independent formations able to operate at a swift pace apart from the slower-moving combined-arms armies. These mobile units had already proven their value in the second period of the war—the independent tank (mechanized) corps in the Stalingrad campaign and subsequent operations, and the tank armies in the Kursk engagement and the battle for the Dnieper River. The Soviets employed their six tank armies with even greater success in the third period. In offensive operations averaging fifteen days, tank armies advanced 150–750 kilometers along a zone thirty to thirty-five kilometers wide and sometimes advanced up to seventy-five kilometers in one day. General Pavel Kurochkin wrote of the importance of tank armies:

> World War II experience has shown that tank armies, correctly used as echelons in the composition of the front for the exploitation of success, were one of the most important means of successfully solving the problem of carrying out offensive operations at high speeds in comparatively short periods.

The composition and size of tank armies in 1994–45 remained similar to the organizational scheme of January 1943. At full strength a tank army had approximately 600–700 tanks and self-propelled guns, 500–600 field pieces and mortars, and 30,000–35,000 men in its two or more tank (mechanized) corps. However, the Soviets followed a flexible approach in the organization of the armies during the third period, altering the composition of a particular tank army to meet specific combat needs and conditions and in response to the availability of forces. For example, the make-up of the 5th Guards Tank Army varied noticeably from one operation to the next:

> Bolgorod-Kharkov (August 1943)—18th and 29th Tank Corps, 5th Guards Mechanized Corps

> Korsun-Shevchenkovsky (January–February 1944)—18th, 20th, and 29th Tank Corps

> Uman-Botsani (March–April 1944)—18th, 20th, and 29th Tank Corps

> Belorussia (June–August 1944)—3rd Guards and 29th Tank Corps

> East Prussia (January–February 1944)—10th Guards and 29th Tank Corps

The composition of the other five tank armies varied as much, with the most common combination being one or two tank corps and one mechanized corps. During the last months of the war, the Soviets sometimes joined one tank corps to two mechanized corps, in transition to the "mechanized armies" of the immediate post-war period.

Armored formations were the primary exploitation forces of the Red Army in the third period, but the Soviets sometimes employed cavalry units where conditions were appropriate. Cavalry divisions and corps were used as mobile groups in areas where terrain features or weather precluded the use of large mechanized forces. Cavalry units were capable of independent operations in marshlands, in areas covered with deep snow, or in regions with a poorly developed road net. A cavalry corps was made up of three cavalry divisions (each of 4,645 troops by 1945) supported by limited numbers of artillery pieces and tanks (two to four tank regiments of forty-one tanks each).

The primary function of Army and Front mobile groups was to exploit the breach made in the enemy's line by the rifle divisions of the combined-arms armies. Mobile groups were also used to complete the penetration of the tactical defense zone, if necessary, being committed on the first or second day of offensive operations. Typically, Army commanders first fed in independent tank (mechanized) corps. If that did not break the line, Front commanders threw in their armored assets, including tank armies. In effect, the Soviets traded off losses in the mobile groups for a more rapid penetration of the enemy's tactical defenses.

Penetration of the tactical defense zone by combined-arms armies depended directly upon the number of infantry support tanks in the first echelon. Generally, the density of close support vehicles in the second and third period of the war did not exceed twenty to twenty-five tanks per kilometer on breakthrough sectors. Against a defender echeloned in depth and supplied with sufficient numbers of anti-tank guns, at least forty to forty-five tanks per kilometer were needed to pierce the tactical defense zone before the enemy moved up reserves to counter the breakthrough attempt. Thus, in order to achieve penetration in less time, tank units from the mobile groups were called to perform close support work for the infantry. Increased availability of tanks and self-propelled guns in the latter stages of the third period alleviated, but did not completely resolve, this problem.

Tank and mechanized corps sometimes led the assault on the enemy's line. On a few occasions in 1944–45, notably at Korsun-Shevchenkovsky, Debrecen and Budapest, the Soviets positioned entire tank armies in the first echelon of a Front. Use of tank armies in this manner insured a powerful initial attack and offered the possibility of rapidly overwhelming the enemy's tactical defenses.

The Soviets preferred to employ tank armies in the first echelon only where defenses were shallow and weak in anti-tank artillery. The use of tank armies as spearheads in offensives had its consequences. The higher losses suffered in penetrating the entire depth of the tactical defense zone meant less momentum during the exploitation phase, in comparison with tank armies used as mobile groups.

The exploitation phase of an offensive began with the penetration of the enemy's tactical defense zone. Army and Front commanders moved mobile groups through the gaps, hoping to reap strategic benefits from tactical success. Army mobile groups maneuvered within fifty kilometers of the front to encircle and destroy enemy formations in cooperation with combined-arms army units. Front mobile groups, spearheading wedges into the enemy's operational defenses, attempted to unhinge an entire defense system in a wide area. Mobile groups had many missions to perform: smash tactical and operational reserves; disrupt communication and supply networks; seize important terrain objectives, such as crossroads and river crossings; overcome positions in the operational defense zone; seize and hold bridgeheads; cut enemy retreat routes and threaten encirclement; pursue retreating forces. In simple terms, Soviet mobile groups were to go deep, disrupt, and destroy.

Exploitation by mobile forces offered opportunities; it also presented problems. Besides enemy resistance, a number of factors could hinder a rapid advance. Success depended upon mobile forces' ability to overcome rear area defense lines and water barriers quickly. Fortunately for the Soviets, German operational defenses were generally hurriedly organized and inadequately manned. Rivers were a constant and serious impediment to mobile operations. Soviet tank and mechanized units crossed at least one river up to one hundred meters wide every forty to sixty kilometers. Rivers reaching two hundred meters in width were encountered each 100–150 kilometers, and a river up to three hundred meters in width occurred every 250–300 kilometers. If mobile groups entered into battle for large population centers, the daily rate of advance fell off precipitately, perhaps upsetting the entire timetable of an offensive.

Front commanders often reinforced successful mobile group breakouts by committing second echelon reserves to the battle. The missions of these forces included: covering the flanks of mobile groups, overcoming enemy positions in the operational defense zone, and securing the areas captured by mobile units. But the fact that the Red Army remained semi-motorized throughout the war meant that the bulk of a Front's forces often could not keep pace with mobile groups. A tank army, for example, might be separated from the main forces of the Front by forty to fifty kilometers on the fifth or sixth day of an offensive. At the end of the operation the distance could be as great as seventy to one hundred kilometers. A situation such as this created a whole array of difficulties for mobile forces. A mobile group advancing too far faced the possibility of being overwhelmed by superior enemy forces. The separation of mobile and nonmobile elements also fostered problems with command and control, logistics, and artillery support.

Front commanders experienced difficulties in maintaining contact with mobile groups when they pulled away from the main forces of the Front. Direct control was especially onerous when a Front included more than one tank army and several independent tank, mechanized, or cavalry corps. At great distances radio contact was lost and communications had to be continued through physical means, such as liaison aircraft. Advanced command posts were also set up to relay messages between a mobile group and the Front commander.

Supplying mobile groups during the exploitation phase was especially troublesome. Rail repair efforts generally could not keep up with a rapid advance and transport aircraft were relatively few in number. The Soviets had to rely primarily upon trucks to haul supplies forward to mobile units. Over 270 trucks were needed to meet the daily requirements of fuel and ammunition for a medium-sized tank army operating at distances of two hundred to three hundred kilometers from the original front line. The momentum of Soviet offensives slowed appreciably when mobile spearheads failed to receive needed supplies.

Technical support for tank and mechanized corps was also significantly affected during mobile operations. Because of breakdowns these formations sometimes lost up to fifty percent of their tanks in the first three days of battle. Tank and mechanized corps had organic repair units, but their effectiveness depended upon, in part, adequate supplies of spare parts, which were often not forthcoming when rapid advances extended supply lines. Mechanics resorted to cannibilizing parts from vehicles needing major repairs in order to get ones with minor maintenance problems back on the road. Tank and mechanized corps operating a great distance from Front or Army support units obtained forty to fifty percent of tank parts for repairs in this manner. It is instructive to note that the possession of the strategic initiative to the Soviets in 1944–45 gave them a tremendous advantage over the Germans in relation to the recovery of damaged or broken-down vehicles. Retaining possession of the battlefield after offensive operations, the Soviets recovered their disabled tanks, repaired them, and sent them once again into action. A tank lost by the Germans remained lost.

Artillery support for mobile groups fell off rapidly during the exploitation phase of an offensive. Most Soviet guns were towed and could not keep pace with mobile units. Even the self-propelled guns organic to tank armies and independent tank (mechanized) corps as well as those in special mobile artillery units from *STAVKA* Reserve could not attain the speeds reached by tanks during a rapid advance.

Aircraft sorties were the primary means of supporting mobile groups deep within the enemy's operational defenses. Adequate air cover was such a key element for success that when mobile formations were deprived of air support the rate of advance dropped sharply. Air missions in support of mobile groups included: preventing air strikes on ground units; destroying anti-tank strongpoints; securing the flanks of a mobile formation from enemy counterattacks. In turn, mobile groups captured airfields from which Soviet planes could support ground operations from bases closer to the front.

When a Front commander committed a tank army to action, he generally supported it with the aircraft of an air army. At times, units of an air army—usually a ground support corps and a fighter corps—were placed directly under the command of a tank army. To better coordinate operations, air division commanders from the air corps located their headquarters at the command posts of tank and mechanized corps.

Almost inevitably, the commitment of Soviet mobile groups to battle brought on confrontations with German armored forces in "meeting engagements" or "encounter battles." Such an action is defined by the Soviets as "a clash between opposing sides when they are simultaneously striving to fulfill assigned missions by means of offensive actions." During Soviet offensive operations, meeting engagements commonly occurred under the following conditions: in the breakthrough phase when the Germans threw in tactical and/or operational reserves to prevent penetration of the tactical defense zone; in the exploitation phase when enemy operational reserves counterattacked to defeat Soviet mobile formations and stem the momentum of the drive; during the concluding phase of an offensive when German operational and/or strategic reserves attacked depleted Soviet mobile units holding onto captured territory, such as bridgeheads. In defensive operations, meeting engagements ensued when Soviet mobile units counter-attacked enemy armored forces, attempting to thwart their advance.

Maneuver was a crucial element in meeting engagements and demanded a good measure of tactical skill on the part of commanders. The tactical prowess of the Germans gave them the edge in such battles in 1941–43. The Soviets were often able to tip the scales in their favor during 1944–45 due to the decline in German training, improved Soviet battle performance gained from the hard school of experience, and improved close air support by Soviet air forces.

Failure of German tactical or operational reserves to seal a major breach of the front line often meant that German units had to pull back or face encirclement by Soviet mobile forces. Pursuit of the retreating enemy was a critically important phase in Soviet offensive operations, for success or failure might mean the difference between a crushing defeat of substantial numbers of German troops or simply pushing the front line back a few kilometers.

Maneuverability and mobility were crucial elements in pursuit operations. The Soviets generally conducted a pursuit on as broad a front as possible, enabling mobile units to maneuver and strike retreating columns at their weakest points. "Since the enemy was often running for his very life, a rapid advance by pursuing forces was of the essence. Ideally, relentless pressure was put on the enemy day and night. The main forces of combined-arms armies and mobile groups pursued the enemy during daylight hours, and forward detachments continued the chase at night. Infantry units averaged rates of twenty to thirty kilometers per day in pursuit operations during the third period of the war, while tank and mechanized formations managed twice that rate and more. Soviet pursuit operations succeeded consistently in the concluding stages of the war because mobile forces were able to out pace and cut off slower-moving enemy infantry units.

Whenever possible, Soviet mobile groups advanced along routes parallel to the retreating enemy. While combined-arms army formations tangled with the enemy from the front and slowed his withdrawal, tank or mechanized units struck enemy columns in the flank and rear, or cut off their retreat entirely. Even when deep within the enemy's operational defenses and separated from the support of combined-arms army units, mobile group commanders preferred to employ this "combined method" of frontal and parallel pursuit. Small forces applied pressure from the front and at the same time the main forces of the group overtook the enemy using roads parallel to his withdrawal.

Forward detachments played a decisive role in Soviet offensive operations. These task forces, combining mobility and maneuver with firepower, spearheaded the exploitation of a breakthrough of the enemy's front. Detached from formations ranging in size from regiments to armies, forward detachments performed both tactical and operational missions. Advancing well ahead of their parent units, forward detachments captured important objectives and disrupted the enemy's attempts to organize a stable defense.

After the Soviets went over to continuous offensive operations in the latter half of 1943, forward detachments, steadily increasing in size, were used more extensively than they had been earlier in the war. By 1944, the forward detachments leading the drives of mobile groups were bigger and operated at greater distances from the main forces of the group. Through mid-1943, for example, the forward detachment of a tank corps generally consisted of a company or battalion-sized unit, while during the last two years of the war the forward detachment of a tank corps was primarily a tank (mechanized) brigade reinforced with a regiment of self-propelled guns, a battalion of *Katyushas*, a battalion of combat engineers, and anti-tank and anti-artillery units. During pursuit operations in 1942–43, the forward detachment of a tank (mechanized) corps advanced at a rate of twenty-five to thirty kilometers per day, and the distance between it and the main body of the corps might be fifteen to twenty-five kilometers. In the third period, the average rate of a forward detachment of an armored corps increased to forty to fifty kilometers per day. The distance between it and the main forces was forty kilometers and more, sometimes as high as one hundred kilometers.

Forward detachments detailed from mobile groups performed a number of operationally significant missions during offensive operations. They strove to keep the enemy off balance, disrupting his efforts to counter Soviet mobile thrusts. During a pursuit, forward detachments formed the leading edge of the mobile group, advancing parallel to the retreating enemy. Important objectives of forward detachments in such a situation were: striking enemy columns in the flank and rear; seizing river crossings; preventing the enemy from entering prepared positions; and cutting off retreat routes. Ranging well ahead of friendly forces, forward detachments were sometimes assigned raiding missions. They attacked command posts, overran airfields, and captured supply dumps, spreading confusion and destruction in the enemy's rear areas. One Soviet source notes, however, that raiding operations by forward detachments were the exception rather than the rule during the war.

Forward detachments maintained a rapid rate of advance because they normally avoided prolonged combat with superior enemy forces or strong points. Their mission was to push deeper into the enemy's operational defenses, although forward detachments sometimes deliberately engaged enemy forces, especially if the latter were small and could be overrun. Because successful tactical maneuver by forward detachments might preclude extensive and time consuming operational maneuvers by the main forces of a mobile group, forward detachments often served as the cutting edge in meeting engagements. In these actions the forward detachment attempted to forestall the enemy by the seizure of important tactical positions, hindering the enemy's deployment and ability to maneuver until the main Soviet forces came up to decide the issue. Before the main body of the mobile group arrived, the most important and sometimes the only support for the forward detachment came from Soviet air units.

One of the most important missions for forward detachments was the rapid forcing of rivers. At crossings where bridges were not intact, engineers moved up bridging equipment or constructed bridges from locally-procured materials. Aviation played a decisive role during the forced crossing of rivers by forward detachments. Soviet aircraft attempted to win air superiority, performed reconnaissance, and delivered strikes to isolate the area from enemy reserves. Successful negotiation of water barriers by forward detachments meant that when the main body came up a crossing could be made "on the run," maintaining the pace of the advance and outflanking enemy river defense lines. At the close of offensive operations, or in the face of determined resistance, forward detachments had the mission of holding onto bridgeheads in enemy territory until the main forces arrived to secure the position. Such bridgeheads served as valuable jumping-off points for subsequent offensive operations.

Although the Soviets retained the strategic initiative throughout 1944–45, the Red Army periodically had to go over to the defensive on some sectors of the front. Armies and Fronts assumed a defensive stance when preparing an attack, holding the exterior front of an encircled enemy force, repelling a major enemy thrust, or when consolidating gains at the end of an offensive. Whatever the reason for going over to the defense, it was considered to be only temporary; the goal of defensive operations was to create the conditions for subsequent offensive operations.

Defensive principles remained those refined by the Soviets at Kursk, although they never conducted a defensive battle with such elaborate preparations in 1944–45. Ideally, a Front or Army defense was one which was deeply echeloned, well supported by artillery, anti-tank, anti-aircraft, and aviation forces, and backed by powerful mobile reserves. The purpose of such a system was to retard the enemy's advance, inflict heavy losses upon him, and mount counterattacks leading to a counteroffensive which would complete the enemy's defeat.

Mobile formations played a key role in the defense. In most circumstances tank armies and independent tank (mechanized) corps deployed in support echelons, as part of Front or Army reserves, to launch counterattacks. Sometimes, as during the concluding stage of an offensive drive, tank armies and independent tank (mechanized) corps were assigned separate defensive zones on the front line. Defensive actions by mobile groups during offensive operations were often undertaken under unfavorable conditions. Mobile groups were forced onto the defensive when they failed to defeat enemy reserves in meeting engagements or at the conclusion of an offensive when they were on extended supply lines and had suffered substantial losses. In such cases, mobile groups were often separated from the support of Army or Front forces, and had to defend ground unprepared by engineers.

Attention will now be given to the employment of Soviet mobile forces in the Belorussian Offensive Operation (June–August 1944).

The Belorussian Offensive: 22 June–29 August 1944

The third period of the war opened with a series of major Soviet offensives along the entire strategic front from Leningrad to the Black Sea. During the winter campaign of 1944 most of the Red Army's striking power went to the outer flanks, in operations intended to relieve the German choke hold on Leningrad, throw the enemy out of the Crimea, and liberate the Ukraine. A secondary drive was conducted to destroy Army Group Center in the Vitebsk area.

The Ukrainian drive by four Fronts was the most important. In four months there were ten operations by Fronts or groups of Fronts. Both sides committed the cream of their forces in the

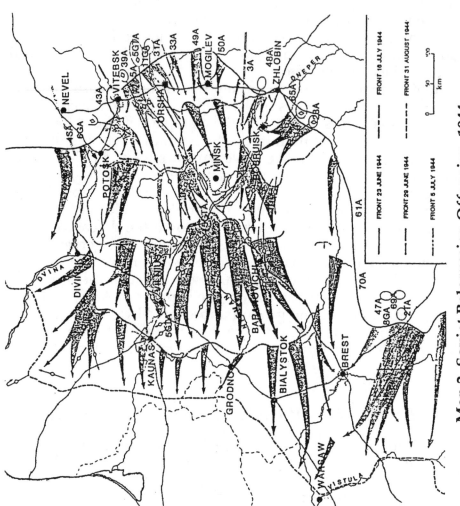

Map 2. Soviet Belorussian Offensive, 1944

decisive struggle for the western Ukraine. By the close of the winter campaign in April, the Red Army had forty percent of its infantry and eighty percent of its tanks in the southern sector. All six tank armies were south of the Pripet River. Only one-third of Soviet combat forces were on the central sector north of the river. By mid-April almost half of the German strength in the east, including seventy-five percent of the armored forces, was committed to the defense of the southern part of the front.

The Soviets achieved significant results from the winter campaign. They recaptured the Crimea and hurled the enemy back from the gates of Leningrad to the eastern borders of Estonia and Latvia. The Ukraine was retaken and the German southern wing split in two on either side of the Carpathian Mountains. The Red Army pushed one segment (Army Group North Ukraine) into southeastern Poland and the other part (Army Group South Ukraine) into Rumania. The Germans had suffered grave losses in men and materiel. Five armies—two in the north, two in the Ukraine, and one in the Crimea—had been smashed. On the southern sector alone, the Soviets estimated German casualties at close to a million.

Only on the central sector of the strategic front were the results disappointing. At great loss, Soviet armies had been unable to destroy Army Group Center nor advance any significant distance. The General Staff felt that the main cause for failure north of the Pripet Marshes was due not so much to the inherent strength of the enemy position but to mistakes in organization, supply, and operations by Soviet forces.

In April 1944 the front line, excluding the Russo-Finnish border, wound its serpentine way over 2,000 kilometers from the Baltic to the Black Seas. Two huge salients dominated the line. South of the Pripet River, Soviet Armies were in southeastern Poland, threatening to advance through L'vov and to capture the rich resource prize of Silesia. A drive north from here to the Baltic offered the prospect of a strategic envelopment of two German Army groups. North of the Pripet Marshes, Army Group Center occupied the "Belorussian Balcony." This position hung over the Soviet's southern strategic flank and threatened an envelopment of any Soviet thrust into Poland or Hungary. German forces in the salient also guarded the age-old Moscow-Minsk-Warsaw approach to the German border and protected Army Group North's southern flank.

In April a lull settled over the entire strategic front, due to the mud of spring thaws and the need of the Soviet Fronts south of the

Pripet to regroup and reinforce their forces before offensive operations could resume. In undisputed control of the initiative, the Soviets were free to chose the time and place for the next series of blows. The only question was, where would the Red Army strike next. In mid-April, after conducting a survey of every sector of the front, the General Staff drew up an outline plan for the 1944 summer-fall campaign. It envisioned a series of successive operations. In early June, two Fronts would attack to knock Finland out of the war, quickly followed by the main blow of the campaign—an offensive against Army Group Center in Belorussia. Success would undoubtedly pull German forces from south of the Pripet, in which case Soviet armies could renew the drive into Poland from the L'vov axis and the thrust into Rumania from the Jassy-Kishinev axis. Timing the offensive to commence in June was deliberate. It coincided with the planned Allied landings in France, which would catch the German High Command between two fires.

The Soviets had solid reasons for making Army Group Center the primary target of the summer offensive. The huge "Belorussian Balcony" offered a tempting opportunity to envelop the position, especially as the Red Army now possessed the strength to mass overwhelming forces for major attacks. Throwing the enemy out of the tangled forests and marshes of Belorussia would open a path to Germany along the plains of Poland. Lastly, and of critical importance, a major drive into Belorussia might catch the Germans off guard. Most of Germany's armored forces guarded the Pripet-Carpathian gap into Poland and the Carpathian-Black Sea gap into the Balkans. Army Group Center was firmly entrenched but had few operational mobile reserves to counter a Soviet breakthrough and exploitation.

The element of surprise played an important part in Soviet calculations. STAVKA ordered two Fronts, one north of Belorussia and the other south of the region, to feint preparations for an attack in June. Such a move, it was hoped, would draw German attention away from the center and pin down the enemy's armored forces. Further masking their plans, the Soviets retained their six tank armies in the Ukraine. Only one, the 5th Guards Tank Army, was to take part in the first phase of the Belorussia operation, and it did not begin to move north until late May.

The General Staff began operational planning for the Belorussian offensive in April, consulting with the Front commanders and their staffs who would direct the attack. Along a front nearly 1,000 kilometers in length, four Fronts would simultaneously assault on six sectors, breaking the enemy army group into segments which could be encircled and destroyed separately. Particular attention was given to the attacks against the fortified cities of Vitebsk and Bobruisk, the corners of the German bulge. The roads in the vicinity of these cities converged at Minsk, the major city in Belorussia and its capital. Tactical encirclements at Vitebsk and Bobruisk offered the promise of an operational envelopment of Army Group Center. With a breakthrough at the corners, Soviet mobile forces would drive from the northeast and southeast to join at Minsk, trapping the bulk of the German army group's forces east of the city.

STAVKA sent the final directive for the Belorussian Operation to the Front commanders on May 31. The missive specified the lines of advance, the objectives, and the forces to be employed in the offensive. The northernmost Front, the 1st Baltic under General Ivan Bagramyan, had two primary missions. It was to advance westward with three combined-arms armies guarding the northern flank of the drive, while also enveloping Vitebsk from the north. The Front had one tank corps to operate as a mobile group. General Polkovnik Chernyakovsky commanded the 3rd Belorussian Front with four combined-arms armies in position west of Vitebsk and Orsha. His forces were to envelop Vitebsk from the south in cooperation with 1st Baltic Front and penetrate the enemy's front between Vitebsk and Orsha. Mobile units would then push through the gap, envelop Orsha and advance across the Beresina River to Minsk. Three mobile formations were in position behind the infantry armies as mobile groups—a tank corps, the "Oslikovsky" Cavalry-Mechanized Group (one mechanized and one cavalry corps) and the 5th Guards Tank Army (two tank corps). The tank army was in the Front's second echelon and was to be committed after the enemy's tactical defense zone had been completely broken through. General Matvei Zakharov's 2nd Belorussian Front had a more modest, although important mission. Its three combined-arms armies, located east of the Dnieper, were to capture Mogilev and fix the German forces to their front, setting them up for the kill east of Minsk. With no significant exploitation role to perform, the Front had no armored or cavalry corps attached to it. However, a mobile group was formed by combining an infantry division, two tank brigades, and one anti-tank brigade. Its mission was to cut the Mogilev-Minsk road. The largest Front, General Konstantin Rokossovsky's 1st Belorussian, was to launch an enveloping attack on both sides of the Beresina against Bobruisk with its right-wing forces of four combined arms armies. Mobile forces consisted of two tank corps and the "Pliyev" Cavalry-

Mechanized Group composed of one mechanized corps and one cavalry corps. These forces were to assist in the encirclement of German forces in the Bobruisk area while also pushing on to Minsk from the south. The left wing of 1st Belorussian Front was to remain inactive until Soviet forces advanced westward past Minsk. Then the left wing was to launch an attack towards Brest. *STAVKA* appointed two representatives to oversee the drives of the four Fronts. Marshal Vasilevsky coordinated the actions of the 1st Baltic and 3rd Belorussian Fronts in the north, while Marshal Zhukov controlled the 2nd and 1st Belorussian Fronts to the south.

Three days before the assault was to commence, over 350,000 partisans were to carry out large-scale interdiction operations behind enemy lines. Thousands of demolition raids would demolish rail lines, bridges, and other key transportation links, paralyzing the enemy's rear areas in the crucial opening stages of the battle.

The terrain in the region presented difficult conditions for an attack, especially in Rokossovsky's zone where extensive woody, boggy areas would have to be negotiated. Belorussia seemed most inappropriate for the employment of large armored forces because mobility and maneuver was restricted by deep forests, marshes, and the lack of good roads. The terrain also offered advantages for the Soviets, however. The region was well known to them; Zhukov for example, remembered having hunted ducks in the marshes south of Bobruisk before the war. The paucity of roads would hinder the Germans in bringing up reinforcements and in retreat. Soviet planning placed great emphasis upon seizing the roads behind the German front. With road junctions and river crossings in Soviet hands, the Germans would flounder in the woods and marshes. Terrain conditions were not overly conducive to their employment, but mobile forces would play a crucial role in the operation. They had the mission of driving through the gaps created in the enemy's front by the combined-arms armies and controlling the road network behind enemy lines.

Some problems were mitigated by the types of forces the Soviets used in the operations. The number of tank corps was relatively small for the huge scale of the offensive. This was compensated for by the use of two cavalry-mechanized groups, whose horse units could better move through marshes and woods. In planning the attack, the General Staff placed a heavy reliance upon Soviet aviation. Because of the lack of roads, the Soviets knew that artillery units would lag behind as soon as pursuit operations commenced. The steady weakening of fire support as the offensive advanced was to be compensated for in part by the use of extensive numbers of ground-support aircraft on the major axes of advance.

The concentration of troops and equipment for the assault on Army Group Center began in late April. The buildup was accomplished less by moving whole armies into the zone of attack than by reinforcing those already there. Units drawn from other sectors of the front and from *STAVKA's* reserves reinforced the four Fronts in Belorussia. Within two months their manpower strength rose sixty percent, the number of tank and self-propelled guns three hundred percent, guns and mortars eighty-five percent, and air strength sixty-two percent. Draftees totalling 210,000 men moved up to the front to fill out the gaps in the ranks of veteran units. *STAVKA*-controlled air units began moving up to bases close to the front ten to twenty-five days prior to the attack. Thousands of train loads of troops and supplies rolled up to the front, but the Soviet rail system was so overtaxed that the original start date of the offensive, 19 June, had to be postponed to 22 June.

The Soviets implemented their usual artful camouflage and concealment measures to mask the buildup. They were successful. Up to the day of the attack, for example, German intelligence had not identified three new armies, including a tank army, which had moved into the Belorussian sector.

The Red Army massed overwhelming amounts of men and material for the offensive. On the eve of the attack the four Fronts had over a million and a half men, over 4,000 tanks and self-propelled guns, 24,000 artillery pieces and mobile heavy mortars, 2,300 *Katyusha* rocket-launchers, and nearly 9,500 aircraft. Making the initial assault would be 166 rifle divisions, eight tank or mechanized corps, and two cavalry corps. Army Group Center controlled forty infantry divisions, one *panzer* division and two *panzer* grenadier divisions, with forces totalling 700,000 troops supported by 775 planes. The Germans had approximately 900 tanks and self-propelled guns and 9,500 pieces of artillery. Soviet superiority in armor, artillery, and airpower at the major assault points reached ratios of ten to one over the enemy.

The Front assault groups, given the mission of breaking through the enemy's tactical defense zone and exploiting success, contained up to seventy percent of the total number of rifle divisions, nearly eighty percent of the guns, and virtually all of the tanks and aircraft allocated for the attack. On each Front, break through sectors comprised only about fifteen percent of the lateral zone of advance. On these sectors the Soviets massed one rifle division, 180–310 guns and mortars, and forty-five tanks per kilometer of front. Nearly half of the tanks in the assault groups were assigned to directly support infantry units in the initial attack. The Soviets were determined to break through the enemy's tactical defenses rapidly. Too often in the past, attacks against Army Group Center stalled along the last line of defense in the tactical defense zone.

The whole operation depended upon the violence and speed of the initial assault. German dispositions and Soviet superiority in forces promised success. Because the Germans massed so much of their strength in forward positions, an overwhelming Soviet assault could destroy much of the enemy's forces and hurl the remnants into the woods and marshes of Belorussia. With this achieved, Soviet forces would not have to engage in a lengthy destruction of a large, organized enemy grouping, as had occurred at Stalingrad. Also, with only a few enemy operational reserve units in front of them and broken enemy formations behind them, Soviet mobile forces would not have to form a stable outer front of encirclement but could push on into the operational depth of the German position.

The Red Army intended to blast the Germans out of their tactical defenses with a deluge of shells and bombs, combined with a well-rehearsed combined-arms assault. Soviet tank and infantry units trained rigorously. Each battalion in the front-line divisions of the 2nd Belorussia Front, for example, practiced its assault missions at least ten times. General Sergei Shtemenko, an officer on the General Staff in 1944, maintains that the tremendous victory that ensued from the Belorussian Operation resulted from the intensive preparations made before a shot was fired.

Army Group Center was ill-prepared for the avalanche that was about to come crashing down upon it. Four armies held a line that stretched for eight hundred kilometers. Third *Panzer* Army guarded Vitebsk. To the south, 4th Army clung to a vulnerable salient east of the Dnieper. Ninth Army was in position east and south of Bobruisk. The 2nd Army occupied a long front in the marshes to the west of that city. Of the army group's total of forty-three infantry and armored divisions, only two infantry and three armored divisions were in operational reserve. Eight weak security divisions were engaged in antipartisan operations in the rear.

The German High Command expected the main blow of the Soviet summer offensive to fall on Army Group North Ukraine protecting the Lvov gap which led into southern Poland. The attack in Belorussia took the Germans completely by surprise. The disposition of German armored forces on the Eastern Front readily indicates this. The two army groups south of the Pripet river had eighteen panzer or *panzer* grenadier divisions between them. Army Group Center had but three.

Soviet partisans opened the battle for Belorussia on 19 June. Thousands of explosions tore up the German rail network west of Minsk, delaying the movement of enemy troops and supplies to the front. The main Soviet attack jumped off on 22 June, the third anniversary of the German invasion. Massive artillery bombardments and air strikes preceded the infantry-tank assault waves of 1st Baltic and 3rd Belorussian Fronts. The forces of 2nd Belorussian and 1st Belorussian Fronts moved into action over the next two days. Almost everywhere the offensive got off to a good start. Overwhelming forces, coupled with effective combined-arms assault techniques, enabled the Soviets to penetrate German tactical defenses on the first day in a number of sectors.

Mobile groups were generally committed to action according to plan. The "Oslikovsky" Cavalry-Mechanized Group and the 5th Guards Tank Army, under the control of the 3rd Belorussian Front, are cases in point. On the second day of the attack the cavalry-mechanized group was sent through a gap in the enemy's front between Vitebsk and Orsha after the 5th Army had broken through the tactical defense zone to a depth of fourteen to fifty kilometers. Supported by planes from the 1st Air Army, the 5th Guards Tank Army moved into action on the third day, following the route taken by the "Oslikovsky" group. The Soviets were flexible in committing their mobile groups to battle. For example, plans had called for the 5th Guards Tank Army to pass through the 11th Guards Army on the Orsha axis. However, when that Army stalled in front of the city, the Front commander rerouted the tanks to pass through a gap created by the 5th Army to the north.

The breakthrough of the enemy's defenses and exploitation in depth by tank, mechanized, and cavalry units led to a rapid encirclement of German forces in the Vitebsk and Bobruisk areas. Infantry pincers from 1st Baltic and 3rd Belorussian Fronts quickly closed around Vitebsk, trapping four divisions. The mobile forces of Chernyakovsky's 3rd Belorussian Front mobile forces did not establish a stable outer ring of encirclement but pushed on to exploit the success of the breakthrough between Vitebsk and Orsha. The 2nd Guards Tank Corps cut off Orsha from the west, while the 5th Guards Tank Army and the "Oslikovsky" Cavalry-Mechanized Group advanced southwestward to the Beresina River.

The offensive went as planned for the two southern Fronts as well. General Zakharov's forces engaged the German 4th Army and wrested control of Mogilev, although at high cost. The 1st Belorussian Front attacked on both sides of the Beresina. The 1st and 9th Tank Corps and the "Pliyev" Cavalry-Mechanized Group raced ahead of the infantry armies to cut off Bobruisk from the west and north. Tanks operating in marshy areas carried brush and logs, which were laid to form carpets on the soft ground. By 27 June the Front's forces had closed in on Bobruisk, trapping 70,000 Germans within and east of the city.

Soviet aviation performed important missions during the attack. Enjoying undisputed air superiority, Soviet aircraft covered the advance of ground mobile units and pounded German artillery positions. Aviation also played a major role in interdicting enemy columns and assisting in the destruction of encircled forces. One Soviet historian insists that "it was actually the decisive factor in eliminating the grouping surrounded in the Bobruisk region."

The fall of Bobruisk marked the completion of the first phase of the offensive. After nearly a week of combat, the Soviets had made deep penetrations all along the front. Vitebsk, Orsha, Mogilev, and Bobruisk, the linchpins of the German defense, were in Soviet hands. Army Group Center had committed all of its reserves without delaying the Red Army anywhere for very long. Three German armies had been ripped away from each other, and two of the armies, 3rd *Panzer* and 9th, were virtually wrecked. The Germans had lost close to 200,000 men killed and captured. Nearly 900 burning or broken down tanks and thousands of trucks lay scattered about the battlefield. The 100,000 troops of the German 4th Army which was still intact had retreated west across the Dnieper, but the army was in mortal danger. Lead units of the 1st Belorussian Front to the southeast and units of the 3rd Belorussian Front to the northeast were both within eighty kilometers of Minsk, while the 4th Army was 120 kilometers to the east of the city. Much of the 4th Army was on foot. The forward units of the Soviet Fronts were rapidly advancing by track, wheel, and hoof to seal the fate of the Germans.

On 28 June *STAVKA* issued revised orders to the four Front commanders. The plan envisaged inner and outer pincers closing in on Minsk from the north, south, and the east. An inner perimeter of combined-arms armies and mobile units was to box in the German 4th Army and capture Minsk. Mobile formations from the 1st and 3rd Belorussian Fronts, forming an outer perimeter, were to advance to positions on the major roads west of the Belorussian capital. Specifically, STAVKA ordered the 1st Baltic Front to push on to Polotsk and secure the northern flank. The 3rd Belorussian Front was to push mobile forces on to Minsk and along the roads northwest of the city. The 2nd Belorussian Front was to press hard on the German 4th Army, preventing it from breaking away and forcing it into the trap. The 1st Belorussian Front was to eliminate the Bobruisk pocket containing 40,000 Germans of the 9th Army with part of its forces. The Front's mobile groups and two infantry armies were to continue the drive to the west and northwest, cutting the roads to Minsk at Slutsk and Baranovichi and pushing on to the capital itself. Minsk was to fall no later than 8 July.

The city fell sooner than *STAVKA* expected. With virtually no enemy forces of any significance in their way, Soviet mobile units were able to race down the roads and cut off Minsk. By 3 July the city was in Soviet hands, sealing 4th Army's fate. The commander of Army Group Center had too few operational reserves to counter-attack and break the encirclement. Of over 100,000 men trapped east of Minsk, the Soviets killed 40,000 and forced the rest to surrender. The last pocket of resistance collapsed on 11 July.

With the capture of Minsk the Red Army won one of its greatest victories of the war. In only twelve days Army Group Center lost twenty-five divisions, nearly sixty percent of its strength. For the first time in the war, the Soviets conducted a parallel and frontal pursuit operation, resulting in the encirclement and rapid annihilation of a large enemy force at a distance of two hundred kilometers from the start line. The speed and force of the Soviet drive, combined with the rigidity of the German defense and the paucity of enemy mobile reserves led to the victory. Marshal Zhukov noted that German countermeasures compounded the seriousness of the Soviet breakthroughs at Vitebsk and Bobruisk. Instead of immediately withdrawing and covering their flanks, the Germans prolonged the battle east of the Beresina with inadequate forces. Rapid exploitation by Soviet mobile forces multiplied the effect of this error and brought ruin upon Army Group Center.

Soviet historians recognize the impact that German errors had on their defeat at Minsk. But errors have to be exploited to bring results. The Soviets emphasize that their army did not simply crush Army Group Center by weight of numbers; maneuver and mobility multiplied the importance of superior forces. Powerful assault groups, combining the firepower and mass of combined-arms armies with the maneuverability of mobile groups, enabled the Fronts to encircle, divide, and destroy the enemy's forces in a single, rapid process. The deep striking power of aviation added another critical factor to the equation. A year and a half before the Belorussian Operation, it had taken the Red Army nearly three months to destroy the encircled 6th Army at Stalingrad. In June 1944, after the flanks of Army Group Center had been penetrated at Vitebsk and Bobruisk, Soviet forces encircled and annihilated the 4th Army east of Minsk in just over a week. The situation was such that Soviet mobile forces did not form stable outer fronts of encirclement at Vitebsk, Bobruisk, and Minsk but pushed deeper into the enemy's position, leaving the destruction of pocketed forces to the combined-arms armies. These methods of exploiting a breakthrough became standard Soviet practice for the rest of the war. They worked; especially in situations where a German army or army group possessed few mobile reserves or were slow in reacting to a Soviet attack.

STAVKA issued new orders to the Front commanders on 4 July. The one Baltic and three Belorussian Fronts were to continue the westward advance on a wide front. Any enemy pockets left in the rear would be eliminated by second echelon forces. This decision took the Germans by surprise. In the past, Soviet armies had generally paused to regroup and haul up supplies after advancing two hundred kilometers.

The Soviets had ripped open a four hundred kilometer gap in the German Front. Army Group Center had but a handful of divisions to dam the flood of Soviet units. Against light opposition, the pursuit rolled on at a good clip, averaging fifteen to twenty-five kilometers a day. Mobile formations attained even higher rates. The 5th Guards Tank Army advanced up to fifty-five kilometers per day, separated by forty kilometers at times from the combined-arms armies of the 3rd Belorussian Front. By mid-July the line had moved so far to the west that Rokossovsky brought the ten armies, including a tank army, on his left flank into action. They had the mission of attacking towards Lublin and enveloping Brest from the south.

Waking up to a debacle of undreamed of proportions, the German High Command rushed reinforcements to plug the yawning hole in the front. Twenty-eight divisions were taken from Army Group North Ukraine and Army Group South Ukraine and moved north. According to General Shtemenko this German countermove was exactly what the General Staff anticipated, and desired. For by weakening their strategic flanks to restore their center, the Germans opened themselves up to new blows.

Like a boxer, the Red Army pounded the opponent with consecutive body blows, never going for the knock-out punch with a single swing, but steadily sapping the antagonist's strength. When the enemy moved his guard to protect one area, the Soviets struck another. In mid-July, the Soviets dealt blows above and below Belorussia with a vengeance. In the north, the 2nd and 3rd Baltic Fronts opened an attack on Army Group North. On 13 July, *STAVKA* smashed another powerful fist into the reeling body of the *Wehrmacht*. Marshal Koniev's 1st Ukrainian Front, the most powerful Front in the Red Army with seven combined-arms armies, three tank armies, and two cavalry-mechanized groups, attacked towards L'vov, intending to wreck Army Group North Ukraine and gain a bridgehead across the Vistula River.

In late July and early August the expanded offensive rolled onwards, seemingly unstoppable. Soviet units crossed major rivers, and important communications fell to them—Divinsk, Vilnius, Kaunas, Grodno, Bialystok, Brest, and L'vov. At the end of July, Soviet Armies reached the Vistula. In the following weeks, they established and held onto bridgeheads south of Warsaw and north of the city on the Narew. This marked the high-water mark of the offensive. German reinforcements and sharp counterattacks by armored divisions stemmed the Soviet drive and even threw it back in places. Soviet forces had suffered substantial losses and were starved for fuel and ammunition. Having advanced over five hundred kilometers without a pause, they were deep in former enemy territory with a damaged rail system and blow bridges behind them. The summer campaign was far from over, however. As the Fronts north of the Carpathians went over to the defensive, *STAVKA* commenced an attack by two Fronts in Rumania.

Reading 6

OVERLORD Versus the Mediterranean at the Cairo-Tehran Conferences

by Richard M. Leighton

The long debate between U.S. and British leaders over the strategy of the European war reached a climax and a turning point at the great mid-war conferences at Cairo and Tehran late in 1943. Since the decision to invade North Africa, a year and a half earlier, the debate had focused on the war in the Mediterranean, the British generally advocating a bold, opportunistic strategy, the Americans a more cautious one. On the surface, they had disagreed on specifics rather than fundamentals. Few on the American side advocated complete withdrawal from the Mediterranean, and U.S. leaders were as quick as the British to respond to the opportunity offered by the disintegration of Italian resistance in early summer of 1943. They opposed the British primarily on the choice of objectives, especially east of Italy. For their part, the British never questioned the principle that the main attack against Germany in the West, and the decisive one, must eventually be made from the northwest (OVERLORD) not the south. In the meantime, they argued, aggressive operations in the Mediterranean were not merely profitable but even essential in order to waste the enemy's strength and to contain and divert enemy forces that might other-

From *Command Decisions* by Richard Leighton, Center for Military History, 1960.

wise concentrate on other fronts. But the debate was embittered by American suspicions that the British intended somehow to sidetrack, weaken, or indefinitely postpone the invasion from the northwest, subordinating it to peripheral and indecisive ventures in the Mediterranean that would serve their own long-range political ends. Since the British consistently disclaimed such intentions, the issue of OVERLORD versus the Mediterranean could not be deflated as such—and, indeed, cannot now be proved even to have existed outside the minds of the Americans. For them, nevertheless, it was the real issue, and the question actually debated at Cairo and Tehran, whether OVER-LORD should be postponed a few weeks in order to permit certain small-scale operations in the eastern Mediterranean, was only the shadow. From the American point of view, the great achievement of the conferences was not the compromise reached on the latter question—essentially a technical matter, worked out on the staff level—but the decision of the Big Three—Roosevelt, Stalin, and Churchill—to make OVERLORD and its southern France complement, ANVIL, the supreme effort of the Western Allies against Germany in 1944. After Cairo-Tehran, Mediterranean strategy continued to be a source of friction, but American leaders seemed to consider the cross-Channel invasion as assured and the issue of OVERLORD versus the Mediterranean as closed.[1]

Tools of Amphibious War

In November 1943 Allied military fortunes were high. On the Eastern Front Soviet armies had crushed the Germans' summer offensive against Kursk before it had got well under way, and had launched a series of powerful counteroffensives which by late November had driven the enemy across the Dnieper, isolated the Crimea, and, farther north, pushed almost to the Polish border. British and Americans in the Mediterranean had swept through Sicily in July and August, forced the capitulation of Italy, and invaded the peninsula in September, bogging down finally in the mountains south of Rome. (See Map 1.) The strategic bombing offensive against the German homeland continued with mounting intensity, despite heavy losses, and in early autumn the hitherto lagging build-up of American invasion forces in the British Isles swelled to massive proportions. In the Pacific war, the New Crimea offensive had reached the Huon Peninsula with the capture

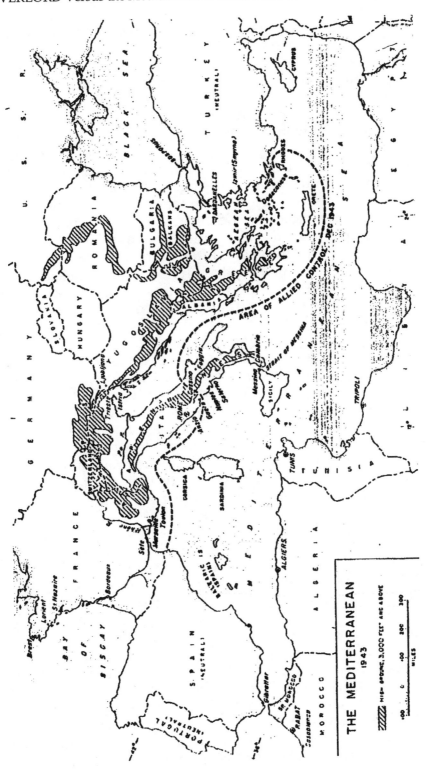

THE MEDITERRANEAN
1943

Map 1

of the important enemy base at Finschhafen, the South Pacific campaign had advanced to Bougainville in the northern Solomons, and the push across the central Pacific had begun with fiercely contested landings on Tarawa and Makin in the Gilberts. In the Atlantic, the U-boats had been decisively defeated, and shipping losses reduced to negligible proportions. On all fronts except Italy and Burma the Allies were advancing. Germany's defeat was now predicted for October 1944, and the American planning committees had been ordered to produce a scheme for ending the war against Japan within the year following. Optimism ran high.

Behind this optimism lay the realization that men and materials would be available on the scale needed to sustain and quicken the momentum already gained. The immense weight of Soviet manpower and industry, after more than two years of mobilization, was now making itself felt; Soviet armies, backed by masses of reserves and munitions, now had a capacity for sustained offensive warfare that the enemy no longer possessed. In the West, Britain's war effort had passed its peak, with armed forces fully deployed and manpower and industrial capacity fully engaged. American armed forces, on the other hand, though approaching the limits of their planned expansion, were still mostly uncommitted; the bulk of the U.S. Army was at home, waiting to be deployed overseas, and only a handful of divisions had actually seen action. American war industry by now had achieved a productivity that in many categories of munitions actually surpassed foreseeable needs. Military supply programs were already being cut back, and pressures were building up to expand production of civilian goods. The most spectacular achievement of American war production was in shipbuilding. American shipyards in this year poured out 19.2 million deadweight tons of merchant shipping, which was more than two and one-third times is much as had been built in 1942. Early in August, the Joint Chiefs of Staff informed the chairman of the War Production Board that they no longer expected merchant shipping to be the bottleneck of the overseas war effort.[2]

Only one category of supply—landing craft—threatened seriously to limit Allied strategy in 1944. At Cairo and Tehran, indeed, the apparent necessity of choosing between a postponement of OVERLORD and abandonment of planned or proposed amphibious operations elsewhere was dictated by the shortage of landing craft—more particularly, of one type of landing vessel, the Landing Ship, Tank (LST). Less than 300 LSTs were in existence in

November, almost all built in the United States. Of these, 139 were in the Mediterranean—67 of them allocated to the British under lend-lease—and except for a small contingent were all earmarked for transfer to the United Kingdom for OVERLORD as soon as the amphibious phases of the Italian campaign were completed. For OVERLORD, in addition, the United States had agreed the preceding spring to provide 62 more new LSTs during the coming winters. The remaining new production of LSTs was allocated to the war in the Pacific.[3]

Production of LSTs and other landing ships and craft in the United States had been late in going under way, reaching large volume only in the winter of 1942–43 and then rapidly falling off. This first wave of production, aimed originally at the now discarded plan for a cross-Channel invasion in spring of 1943 (ROUNDUP), had proved generally adequate, together with the smaller output of British factories and yards, to meet the rather modest needs of Allied amphibious operations before mid-1943.[4] Even the invasion of Sicily, in some respects the most massive amphibious operation of the entire war (eight divisions were landed simultaneously), was adequately mounted without drawing upon a substantial reserve of U.S. assault shipping in the Atlantic or interfering with planned deployments of craft to the Pacific.[5]

From the Navy's point of view the whole landing craft production program had been undertaken at the worst possible time—when the Navy was straining to rebuild sea power destroyed or immobilized at Pearl Harbor and in later engagements, in order to gain supremacy in the Pacific, while at the same time trying to break the stranglehold of enemy submarines upon the sea lanes in the Atlantic. The program competed with many other lines of war production for materials, above all for the steel, engines, and facilities needed to build other types of combatant vessels. A Navy official commented bitterly in April 1943 that the high rate of landing craft construction achieved late in 1942 had been obtained "only by cutting across every single combatant shipbuilding program and giving the amphibious program overriding priority in every navy yard and every major shipbuilding company. The derangement . . . will not be corrected for about six months."[6] As landing craft schedules were terminated or cut back that winter and spring, the Navy pushed the building of escort vessels to meet the revived menace of the German U-boats in the Atlantic, which in March reaped a harvest of more than a million deadweight tons of Allied shipping.[7] Navy officials candidly wanted no more emergency landing craft programs.

By August 1943, however, pressures were building up to increase the output of landing craft, at a time when, as a result of the abatement of the submarine menace, the Navy was cutting back its escort and antisubmarine vessel programs. While the landings on Sicily had been successful, with losses lower than anticipated, the greater part of the entire amphibious fleet in the Mediterranean was tied up for weeks after the initial landings moving supplies over the beaches and performing other administrative tasks. Other amphibious undertakings were in prospect in the Mediterranean, in southeast Asia, and on the two main avenues of advance toward Japan across the Pacific. The biggest prospective deficit of amphibious shipping, however, loomed in the planned cross-Channel assault, then scheduled, as a result of decisions at the Washington Conference of May 1943, for the spring of 1944. For this undertaking, against what was expected to be the most heavily defended coast line in the world, the assault as then tentatively planned was to be on a scale of only about three and a half divisions with two more afloat, a limit imposed arbitrarily by the predicted availability of assault shipping. At the Quebec Conference of August 1943 Prime Minister Churchill bluntly called for an immediate increase in American landing craft production, pledging at the same time a maximum effort in his own country, in order to strengthen the OVERLORD assault. The same demand was voiced on the American side in various quarters.

In September and again late in October, the Navy with JCS approval ordered large increases in landing craft production. Navy officials framed the new program, however, with an eye to the war in the Pacific, not the war in Europe. Large segments of the program were devoted to new types of vessels mainly adapted to warfare in the Pacific—notably armored amtracks (LVTs) and the new LCT(7), actually a small landing ship—inevitably at the expense of the older types desperately needed in Europe. Nor would the increases become effective in time to help OVERLORD if the operation were carried out early in May 1944. Allocations of new production to OVERLORD were limited to about three months' output, at current low rates, at the end of 1943. To this Admiral Ernest J. King, on 5 November, promised to add something less than a month's production of LSTs, LCI(L)s, and LCTS, and not all of these seemed likely to arrive in the United Kingdom in time to be used in the invasion.[8]

A month before the Allied leaders assembled at Cairo, U.S. representatives at a conference of foreign ministers in Moscow pointed to the new landing craft program as indisputable proof that the long-postponed second front would be opened the following spring. In Washington, by contrast, the British were being warned privately that no more new landing craft would be forthcoming for OVERLORD.[9] It was the latter assumption that shaped the options laid before the conferees at Cairo and Tehran.

Alarums and Excursions

American military leaders and their staffs, on the eve of the Cairo-Tehran Conferences, were in a mood to force a showdown on the strategy of the European war.[10] As they viewed it, Allied strategy since the decision to invade North Africa had been drifting steadily away from the northwestern Europe orientation, agreed on in April 1942, and into a peripheral line of action that could only end in stalemate. Preparations for a cross-Channel invasion in spring of 1943 had been suspended, the British Isles almost denuded of American troops, and American resources had been diverted into the development of a new line of communications and a new invasion base in North Africa. The decision at Casablanca in January 1943 to attack Sicily had ensured that the Mediterranean would continue to be the main theater in Europe during 1943 and that no cross-Channel invasion could be attempted until 1944 at the earliest. Since then British persuasion and the ineluctable logic of momentum had drawn the Allies deeper into the Mediterranean—into Tunisia, Sicily, Italy, Sardinia, Corsica—and a long, uphill struggle still loomed ahead in Italy. Most alarming to the Americans was the persistent effort of the British to broaden the Mediterranean front eastward—by pressure on Turkey to enter the war, by proposals to seize points on the Dalmatian coast and to step up aid to the Balkan guerrillas, and, most recently, by an ill-advised incursion into the Dodecanese Islands which had cost the British several thousand troops killed and captured and untold loss of prestige. Persistent dabbling by the British in this region raised, in American minds, the dread specter of military operations and political involvement in the Balkan peninsula, a land of inhospitable terrain, primitive communications, and turbulent peoples.

In the light of developments in the Mediterranean, American military leaders discounted the repeated pledges of loyalty by the British to the cross-Channel invasion strategy. They tended to gloss over or ignore the immense investment Britain already had in the cross-Channel operation, the heavy contributions of British shipping to the build-up of American invasion forces and material in the United Kingdom (almost half the entire tonnage used), and the persistent pleas of British leaders for a strengthening of the OVERLORD assault. It was widely believed in American official circles that British leaders feared to come to grips with the German Army on equal terms, that they were haunted, as Secretary of War Stimson put it, by the "shadows of Passchendaele and Dunkerque."[11] Army staff officers, wrestling with the paradox, could only conclude that the great Anglo-American invasion army amassing in the United Kingdom was intended by the British to be "a gigantic deception plan and an occupying force" after the expected German collapse.[12]

In recent weeks American suspicions of British intentions had quickened. At the Quebec Conference in August, the OVER-LORD plan prepared by the Anglo-American planning staff in London had been accepted by both sides with little discussion. But the British had rejected an American demand that OVER-LORD be given an "overriding" priority over operations in the Mediterranean. Prime Minister Churchill, then and subsequently, had stressed, to a degree that aroused American misgivings, the stipulations written into the OVERLORD plan to the effect that additional forces would be needed if German strength in France exceeded certain levels. As yet, the Americans had not made an issue of this point, since the JCS had approved the stipulations along with the plan. Then, late in October, a crisis had suddenly developed in Italy when it appeared that the Germans were winning the build-up race south of Rome and might soon be in a position to launch a crushing counterattack. Churchill and the British Chiefs had reacted with what the Americans considered unjustified alarm. The British had proposed the temporary retention in the Mediterranean of all assault shipping earmarked for OVERLORD, and, more disturbing, had intimated that if the situation in Italy continued to deteriorate it might be necessary to postpone OVERLORD beyond its present target date of 1 May 1944. After some discussion, it had been agreed that sixty-eight OVERLORD LSTs should remain in the Mediterranean until mid-December, as the theater commander, General Dwight D. Eisenhower, had requested, to help mount an amphibious turning movement around the enemy's right flank south to Rome. But the JCS and their staffs were still worried, as the time for the Cairo meetings approached, over the implied British threat to OVERLORD. For the British Chiefs had bluntly warned that they intended, at the forthcoming conference, to bring up for reconsideration "the whole position of the campaign in the Mediterranean and its relation to OVER-LORD."[13]

Finally, early in November, the Americans received a disturbing hint of the role the Soviet leaders might play at Tehran. At the foreign ministers' conference in Moscow late in October, Marshal Joseph V. Stalin had displayed a lively interest in the operations of his allies in the Mediterranean, and, to the astonishment of the Western representatives, had reacted with bland unconcern when British Foreign Secretary Anthony Eden had hinted that, owing to the worsening situation in Italy, it might be necessary to postpone OVERLORD. After the conference, Maj. Gen. John R. Deane, head of the U.S. military mission in Moscow, had been bombarded by complaints from the Soviet staff about Allied inaction in the Mediterranean. Deane had concluded from all this that the Soviets, as he informed Washington, "want to end the war quickly and feel they can do it," and therefore were less interested in OVERLORD, six months or more distant, than in immediate action to draw German strength from the Eastern Front. Deane warned his superiors to expect a Soviet demand at the forthcoming conference for a greater effort in the Mediterranean, including "some venture in the Balkans," even if that meant delaying OVERLORD.[14] Deane's warning caused a furor in Washington, where it was apparently taken at face value. Combined with the disturbing hints from London of an impending attack on OVERLORD, it conjured up nightmarish visions of a concerted Russo-British demand at Tehran for a major shift of effort to the Mediterranean—or worse, to the eastern Mediterranean—at the expense of OVERLORD.[15]

First Cairo: The Options

At Cairo, the Americans found that the British, too, were ready for a showdown. "It is certainly an odd way of helping the Russians," declared Churchill after a scathing review of recent setbacks in the Mediterranean, "to slow down the fight in the only theatre where anything can be done for some months."[16] The British Chiefs of Staff seized the initiative with a blunt criticism of American insistence on the "sanctity of OVERLORD."

> We must not . . . regard OVERLORD on a fixed date as the pivot of our whole strategy on which all else turns. In actual fact, the German strength in France next Spring may, at one end of the scale, be something which makes OVERLORD completely impossible and, at the other end, something which makes RANKIN not only practicable, but essential. . . . This policy, if literally will inevitably paralyze action in other theatres without any guarantee of action across the Channel . . . it is, of course, valuable to have a target date to which all may work, but we are firmly opposed to allowing this date to become our master. . . .

They were prepared, they asserted, to carry out the cross-Channel invasion "as soon as the German strength in France and the general war situation gives us a good prospect of success," but they insisted that unless the Allies pursued an aggressive course of action in the Mediterranean during the coming winter and spring, such conditions were unlikely to develop.[17]

The ominous implications of this manifesto were hardly borne out, however, by the British Chief's concrete program for the Mediterranean. They wanted to advance beyond Rome only as far as the Pisa-Rimini line (the same limit the JCS had in mind); to extend more aid to the Balkan partisan forces in the form of weapons, supplies, technical assistance, and commando raids; to try to bring Turkey into the war before the end of the year; and, with Turkish consent, to open the Dardanelles (shortest route to the USSR) to Allied shipping. The opening move, provided Turkey's support were assured, would be an attack about February 1944 on the largest of the Dodecanese Islands, Rhodes, which commanded the approaches to the Aegean and the Straits. Finally, control of the whole Mediterranean area would be unified under a British commander. (This last the Americans were already prepared to concede, in return for the appointment of a U.S. commander for OVERLORD.) In short, the British hoped by means of a major effort in Italy and what Ambassador Winant called "bush-league tactics" east of Italy to force the Germans back along the entire Mediterranean front. By the Prime Minister's reckoning, the eastern Mediterranean operations would involve not more than a tenth of the combined British and American resources in the whole theatre. But, while all the troops and other means needed were available in the area, the landing ships and craft were scheduled for early transfer to the United Kingdom. To retain them for the required time might mean postponing OVERLORD as much as six weeks or two months—that is, until about 1 July 1944.[18]

As far as Italy and the Balkans were concerned, the U.S. Chiefs had no quarrel with these proposals. They even saw certain advantages in gaining Turkey as an active ally, provided the price paid for intervention was strictly limited. But they doubted the ability of the Turks to hold their own if attacked by the Germans, and felt no enthusiasm for another try at Rhodes, so soon after the recent disaster. Moreover, the American staffs challenged the timetables and requirements of the British plan at many points. They doubted whether the Rhodes operation could be fitted into the LST movement schedules, even if OVERLORD were postponed to 1 July.[19]

The British, however, had an alternative proposal: the necessary assault shipping for the Rhodes operation might be taken from southeast Asia. In August a new Allied command had been set up in southeast Asia under Vice Adm. Lord Louis Mountbatten, embracing Burma, Ceylon, Siam, the Malay Peninsula, and Sumatra (but neither China nor India). Since then the basic divergence of British, American, and Chinese purposes in the area, not to mention the differences within each camp, had been sharpened. British aspirations looked primarily south and southeast, toward a restoration of Britain's prewar possessions and influence in Malaya and the East Indies. The Americans were more interested in increasing China's effectiveness as an ally and in gaining bases in China for bombing and, ultimately, invading Japan. For the British, therefore, Burma was a stage on the road to Singapore and beyond—one that might, perhaps, be bypassed—while for the Americans it lay on the route over the Himalayas into China. Although construction had begun early in 1943 on a road from Ledo, in India's Assam Province just over the Burmese border, to connect with the old Burma Road where it crossed into China, contact between China and her allies depended for the present on the airlift. Throughout 1943 supplies delivered over the Hump from India to China each month had not exceeded, on the average, what could be carried by a single medium-sized freighter. Competition for this trickle of cargo was fierce. Lt. Gen. Joseph W. Stilwell, Mountbatten's American deputy and Commander of the U.S. China-Burma-India theater (lying partly within Mountbatten's command), wanted to use the supplies mainly to equip Chinese forces in China in order to help in the reconquest of northern Burma, scheduled to begin early in 1944 before the onset of the spring monsoon. Maj. Gen. Claire L. Chennault, commanding the U.S. air forces in China, believed the airlift should be greatly expanded and devoted entirely to support of an air offensive against Japanese communications in China and with the home islands. Chennault's program, which promised quicker results at lower cost than Stilwell's long-range plan of regenerating Chinese armies and restoring land communications with China, appealed both to the President and to Chiang Kai-shek, though the latter naturally demanded an airlift large enough to support both programs. Since the preceding spring the bulk of supplies brought over the Hump had in fact gone to Chennault's air forces. However, Roosevelt's broader aims for China coincided with Stilwell's. His purpose in inviting Chiang to Cairo (over British objections) was, in part, to discuss further economic and military aid—which was imperative, Chiang said, if China were to continue fighting—and, in part, to enlist his co-operation in the forthcoming Burma offensive.

The general plan of this offensive was to launch converging drives into northern and central Burma—by British-Indian forces from the west, by Stilwell's American-trained Chinese from the northwest, and by Chiang's own armies from Southern China. Subsidiary features of the plan included a British naval demonstration in the Bay of Bengal by fleet units released from the Mediterranean after the Italian surrender, and an amphibious operation—although where this would be carried out was still somewhat uncertain. A year earlier Stilwell's plan for the reconquest of Burma had included a major amphibious attack on Rangoon; at the Washington Conference of May 1943 this had been scrapped, for lack of assault shipping, in favor of smaller landings near Akyab and on Ramree Island, along the Burma coast just below the Indian border. To mount these operations, a contingent of half a dozen attack transports, eighteen LSTs, and a number of smaller craft, had been sent to India, arriving there finally, after a protracted hold-over in the Mediterranean, early in the fall. Churchill, meanwhile, had come out strongly for an "Asiatic-style TORCH" in the form of a surprise descent on the northern tip of Sumatra (CULVERIN), which the Americans opposed as eccentric to the main effort and his own advisers thought would require more resources than were available. The theater commanders, finally, had proposed a more modest substitute in the form of landings on the Amdaman Islands, southwest of Rangoon, in March or April 1944. This operation (BUCCANEER) had been tentatively endorsed by both the British and the U.S. Chiefs of Staff, though it, along with the remainder, of the whole plan, still awaited formal approval. BUCCANEER was, then, the amphibious part of the general plan (CHAMPION) submitted to Chiang at Cairo.[20]

Immediately the plan ran into heavy weather. Hardly anyone, in fact, had much enthusiasm for BUCCANEER, except perhaps Chiang, who had not been informed of its objective, but who independently suggested the Andamans as a suitable objective. Its most serious defect was that it seemed to have little connection with the mainland operations it was intended to support, and hardly represented a threat serious enough to provoke a strong reaction. The U.S. Chiefs of Staff preferred it to CULVERIN, but were not committed to any particular operation; Admiral King himself favored a landing on the mainland near Moulmein with a view to cutting across the isthmus to Bangkok, but such an undertaking was not thought feasible with the assault shipping available. Evidently the most that could be said for BUCCANEER was that it would provide a base for future amphibious landings on the mainland and for bombing the new Bangkok-Moulmein railroad, which gave the Japanese in Burma direct overland connections with the Gulf of Thailand.[21] Churchill made no secret of his distaste for BUCCANEER and had earlier declared that if he could not have CULVERIN he would send the British assault shipping back to the Mediterranean. At Cairo he expanded on the idea: if the Americans would not accept CULVERIN, and if they refused to postpone OVERLORD the few weeks necessary to carry out the attack on Rhodes and move assault shipping back to the Mediterranean, then why not take the shipping needed for Rhodes from southeast Asia? BUCCANEER might be postponed rather than canceled. As Churchill remarked, "There really cannot be much hurry. The capture of the Andamans is a trivial prize compared with Rhodes, and also it can be undertaken at any time later in the year."[22]

That Churchill was willing to entertain the idea of doing BUCCANEER at all, despite his candidly expressed scorn for the operation, was the result of the position taken at Cairo by the Chinese Generalissimo. Chiang immediately branded the whole Burma plan (CHAMPION) as inadequate. As a price for his participation in a more ambitious one, moreover, he demanded an immediate increase in the airlift far beyond the capacity of available transport aircraft and explicit guarantees from the British that the land operations would be supported simultaneously by major coordinated naval and amphibious attacks. The unreasonableness of the airlift demand, and the arrogance shown by Chiang's subordinates in discussing it with the Western military leaders, caused the latter to close ranks, and drove even General Marshall to exasperation.[23] A moderate increase in the airlift was ordered, but the Chinese were told unequivocally that they must choose between an offensive in Burma and expanded ferry operations, since both competed for transport aircraft. As for BUCCANEER, the U.S. Chiefs of Staff did not at first take a strong stand, agreeing to postpone action pending decisions yet to be taken on the broader strategy of the war against Japan and the British role in it. In the CCS, therefore, Chiang's demand for an amphibious operation was carefully and noncommittally "noted," with a promise merely of future "consideration." Churchill, however, sharply challenged Chiang's view of the interdependence of the naval and amphibious phases of CHAMPION and the land operations. He pointed out that, in the absence of accessible bases and because of the time needed to refit and redeploy British naval forces from the Mediterranean, direct naval support could not be provided in the forthcoming spring campaign, even though he could promise that by March strong naval forces would be operating in the Bay of Bengal. Finally, he told Chiang emphatically that no definite undertaking to carry out an amphibious operation in conjunction with the land campaign could be given.[24]

Chiang thus faced defeat on all his demands. Early in the afternoon of the 25th he agreed to the CHAMPION plan as drawn, with the sole stipulations that the British should gain naval superiority in the Bay of Bengal—which Churchill had already promised—and that the plan should include an amphibious operation—to which Churchill was willing to agree if the Americans met his own conditions in the Mediterranean. At the same time, however,

Chiang was demanding that President Roosevelt give him something to show for having attended the conference.[25] The President obliged. On the same afternoon he told Stilwell and Marshall he had decided, as a further concession to Chiang, greatly to change the program of equipping Chinese divisions, and, some time on the same day, he seems to have given Chaing a pledge that BUCCANEER would be carried out on the scale and at the time planned.[26]

The President's pledge left his military chiefs very little room for maneuver. If the Soviet leaders at Tehran should insist, as the Joint Chiefs fully expected them to insist, on an immediate major effort by the Western allies in the Mediterranean, with or without OVERLORD, approval of the British program seemed assured. The assault shipping allotted for BUCCANEER, now sacrosanct, could not be made available for Rhodes. If OVERLORD shipping currently in the Mediterranean were used instead, how could it be replaced in time to meet the OVERLORD target date? New American production after January was allotted to the Pacific, and Admiral King bristled at the suggestion of further inroads on this source. The only remaining possibility seemed to be to postpone OVERLORD a few weeks as the British had proposed, thus giving more time to redeploy assault shipping and, incidentally, making available another one or two months' production of landing craft. As Admiral Leahy remarked, the problem was brutally simple: the JCS had to decide whether or not they could accept a delay in OVERLORD; if they could not, "the problem appeared insoluble."[27]

The President, at least, had been thinking of delay. Back in Washington Justice James F. Byrnes, Director of the Office of War Mobilization, had received on the 23d a "very urgent" message from him inquiring whether the output of landing craft could be increased, by means of an overriding priority, during the *first five months of 1944*—an inquiry that made sense only under the assumption that OVERLORD might be postponed beyond 1 May 1944. Byrnes' reply, dispatched on the 25th, indicated that substantial increases might be possible in April and later, but virtually none before then. Roosevelt probably knew, therefore, when he promised Chiang an amphibious operation, that if OVERLORD were postponed to July, it could be bolstered by the addition of some twenty-two new LSTs, not to mention ten more now allocated but unlikely to reach the United Kingdom in time for a May assault—and this without encroaching on existing Pacific allocations of February and later output.[28]

Final decision had to wait, then, until the Russians showed their hand. At the last Cairo meeting with the British (on the 26th) before going to Tehran, the U.S. Chiefs of Staff stressed the sanctity of BUCCANEER, but said little about OVERLORD or the Mediterranean. Sir Alan Brooke asked them whether they understood that "if the capture of Rhodes and Rome and Operation BUCCANEER were carried out, the date of OVERLORD must go back." Marshall assured him they did. Would it not be better, urged Brooke perplexedly, to postpone BUCCANEER rather than OVERLORD? What if the Russians should demand both a strong Mediterranean offensive and an early OVERLORD? The situation had become embarrassing. Finally, Admiral Leahy blurted out a broad hint: the U.S. Chiefs of Staff "were not in a position to agree to the abandonment of Operation BUCCANEER. This could only be decided by the President and the Prime Minister." There was little more to say. The Americans accepted the British program as a basis for discussion at Tehran, but on the contradictory assumption that it "would in no way interfere with the carrying-out of Operation BUCCANEER." The British left with the distinct impression, as Lt. Gen. Sir Hastings L. Ismay reported to the Prime Minister, that the Americans, now rigid against any tampering with BUCCANEER, contemplated a postponement of OVERLORD "with equanimity."[29]

Tehran: Enter ANVIL Compromise on OVERLORD

At the opening general meeting at Tehran, on 28 November, the three principals, at Stalin's brusque suggestion, promptly got down to business. Roosevelt noted in his opening remarks the possibility that OVERLORD might have to be postponed "for one month or two or three," and spoke of the various operations in the Mediterranean that were being considered to relieve enemy pressure on the Eastern Front—in the Aegean, at the head of the Adriatic, and in Italy. OVERLORD, he pointed out, would draw away more German divisions than any of these, and he urged that, if possible, it not be delayed "beyond May or June." Churchill presented the British case, elaborating on the promising opportunities that could be exploited in the eastern Mediterranean without detriment either to the campaign in Italy or to OVERLORD. How would the Soviet Union, he asked, regard this prospect "even if it meant as much as about two months' delay in OVERLORD?"[30]

Up to this point the atmosphere had been cordial. To the pleased surprise of the Westerners, Stalin opened his remarks with an almost casual promise that the Soviet Union would intervene in the war against Japan as soon as Germany was defeated. This confirmed and strengthened the more tentative offers the Soviet marshal had made on earlier occasions. But his next words brought the discussion abruptly to a tense climax. He declared bluntly that the whole Mediterranean program appeared to him to involve an excessive dispersion of forces. OVERLORD should be made the "basic" operation for 1944, and all other operations, however attractive, regarded as diversions. He saw only one useful possibility in the Mediterranean, an attack on southern France (which Churchill had mentioned in his opening remarks) followed by a drive northward toward an eventual junction with the main OVERLORD forces—the classic pincers formula, which the Russians had applied so often in their own theater. Why not, he suggested blandly, suspend the Italian campaign immediately in order to release forces for this operation, and then launch OVERLORD two or three months later?[31]

General Marshall must have been reflecting sardonically, while Stalin was dropping his bombshell, on an innocent remark he himself had made in a meeting of the Joint Chiefs that morning, to the effect that the Soviet demands, whatever they might be, "would probably simplify the problem."[32] Whatever the reasons for the sudden evaporation of Stalin's recently displayed interest in Mediterranean operations, and for his return to the old familiar insistence on a "second front"—perhaps because, with Soviet armies now at a standstill in the Ukraine, a grand convergence on southeastern Europe no longer promised quick victory—his proposals immeasurably complicated what had been an essentially simple, if baffling, dilemma. The Mediterranean was a "going" theater of war in which the Western allies had a heavy investment. To stop short on the present line in Italy would be almost as repugnant to the Americans as to the British, and Churchill promptly and emphatically asserted that from the British point of view the capture of Rome was both strategically and politically imperative. Stalin seemed, moreover, not to have grasped the limiting role of shipping and landing craft, or the central problem of timing and sequence that grew out of it. He had to be reminded that the troops in the Mediterranean, except for seven divisions already in transit to the United Kingdom, were irrevocably bound there for lack of shipping to deploy them elsewhere. He missed the point that the southern France operation and the landings in the Adriatic had been suggested as mutually exclusive alternatives and that the Rhodes operation was very modest in scope. When Churchill reminded him of this last fact, he conceded that on those terms the capture of Rhodes might be worthwhile. But if both the Rome and Rhodes operations were to be carried out, or even only the latter, how could a landing in southern France, two or three months before OVERLORD (for which Stalin had stipulated no date) be worked into the schedule—unless OVERLORD was postponed?[33]

At this juncture the President, who had been silent during the above exchange, suddenly interposed. Stalin's proposals, he said, had raised a serious problem of timing. A choice must be made: either undertake Churchill's Aegean operations, which would delay OVERLORD a month or two, or, as the Soviet premier had suggested, "attack [southern] France one or two months *before the first of May* and then conduct OVERLORD *on the original date.*" His own preference, Roosevelt added, was for the latter alternative.[34]

Churchill was caught off balance. Nothing in the President's earlier remarks had suggested any intention to insist on adherence to the 1 May target date for OVERLORD. He had, in fact, seemed to accept the idea of postponement, urging only that it be brief. His military advisers, by the end of the Cairo meetings, had seemed resigned to the inevitability of some delay. But by implying now that Stalin himself had demanded a 1 May date (which he had not, in fact, done), the President evidently hoped to enlist his support. If so, it was an adroit maneuver, for Stalin failed to challenge the President's implication. Its significance was not lost on Churchill, who immediately protested against the idea of condemning twenty or more divisions in the Mediterranean to inactivity "solely for the purpose of keeping the May date for OVERLORD," and chided the President for the "rigid timing" of the program he had proposed.[35]

The Russians had shown their hand. For the Americans the nightmare of an Anglo-Soviet demand for a shift to the Mediterranean had been dissipated in the comforting assurance that the Soviet leaders once more stood solidly for the primacy of OVERLORD and shared the American aversion for operations in the eastern Mediterranean. It quickly became clear, moreover, that the Russians also shared American suspicions as to

British motives, for in the course of the next day (the 29th) both Churchill and Brooke, under Soviet grilling, were repeatedly obliged to go through the ritual of affirming their loyalty to OVER-LORD.[36] At a meeting of the military representatives on this same day the Soviet leaders indicated no very specific notions as to what should be done in the Mediterranean or when. When Sir Alan Brooke pointed out the risk that a landing in southern France so long in advance of OVERLORD might be crushed before OVERLORD could get under way, the Soviet representative, Marshal Klementy Voroshiloff, merely reiterated rather woodenly his master's statement that the operation would be a valuable complement to OVERLORD. Anyway, he added, Stalin did not insist on a southern France operation. All other undertakings in the Mediterranean, "such as Rome, Rhodes, and what not," were diversions that, if carried out at all, should be "planned to assist OVERLORD and certainly not to hinder it." Evidently the Soviet leader intended to let his allies squabble unhindered over Mediterranean strategy. According to Voroshiloff, however, Stalin did insist on OVER-LORD—and "on the date already planned."[37]

Thus the issue was finally joined on the timing of OVERLORD. On this same 29 November Roosevelt, now committed to fight for a May OVERLORD and evidently confident that with Soviet support he could win, sent a message to Washington tardily instructing justice Byrnes to call off the proposed speed-up in landing craft production, since "the increase in critical types . . . does not become effective enough to justify change in present construction programs."[38] At the plenary meeting that afternoon, Stalin set forth his position in the language of an ultimatum. He also pressed for an early appointment of a commander for the operation. Soviet forces, he promised, would match the invasion from the west by a simultaneous offensive from the east.[39] Churchill held the floor for most of the session with a spirited defense of the British Mediterranean program. He vainly tried to draw out Stalin on his proposal for a southern France operation, for which, as he pointed out, no plan had yet been drafted, and he warned, as Brooke had already done, that if the attack were too weak or launched too early, it would invite disaster. If, on the other hand, a two-division amphibious lift could be left in the Mediterranean, bright possibilities opened up—turning movements along the Italian coasts, then a swift capture of Rhodes, and finally an invasion of southern France in conjunction with OVERLORD. This might mean setting back OVERLORD by six to eight weeks, or—and Churchill here introduced the alternative for the first time at Tehran—the needed assault shipping could be brought back from India. At all events, Churchill concluded, if the handful of vessels needed for Rhodes could not somehow be found, it was unreasonable to suppose that the larger number required for an invasion of southern France or any other diversionary operation in support of OVERLORD could be provided. He reminded the Soviet premier that OVERLORD could not be undertaken at all unless there was a reasonable expectation of success based on certain specified conditions of enemy strength. This brought from Stalin his celebrated query: Would OVERLORD be ruled out if there were thirteen instead of twelve mobile German divisions in France and the Low Countries on D Day? Churchill assured him it would not.[40]

Stalin made no effort to answer Churchill's arguments. He ignored the allusion to BUCCANEER, restated his demand for a May OVERLORD, and indicated his preference for a southern France invasion two or three months before OVERLORD; if this proved impossible, the operation might be launched simultaneously with OVERLORD or even a little later. All other operations in the Mediterranean he regarded as diversions. Roosevelt finally interposed to suggest a date for OVERLORD "certainly no later than 15 or 20 May, if possible." Stalin chimed agreement. Churchill promptly and emphatically dissented, and the atmosphere again became tense. Finally, the problem was referred to the military representatives to work out before the next afternoon, when final decisions would be reached.[41]

Despite the appearance of a deadlock, the germ of a compromise had already emerged. Both Stalin and Roosevelt had refrained from demanding a 1 May date. Before lunch the next day (30 November) Churchill decided to agree to a date sometime in May, and the British Chiefs of Staff came to the meeting with their American opposites that morning with specific proposals worked out on this basis.[42] General Eisenhower would be allowed to keep the sixty-eight OVERLORD LSTs in the Mediterranean until 15 January in order to ensure the early capture of Rome. This meant, by British calculations, that OVERLORD could not be earlier than June—but the British Chiefs were willing, in order to satisfy Stalin, to define this as "in May." They were also prepared to support an operation against southern France and, most important, to agree that no assault shipping earmarked for OVERLORD should be retained in the Mediterranean specifically for the Rhodes operation. The key to this last concession lay in their final proposition: as a result of Stalin's momentous pledge on the 28th to enter the war against Japan after Germany's defeat, they argued, the role of China in the coalition had been automatically reduced, and the whole case for an offensive in Burma in spring 1944, including BUCCANEER, had been weakened. The British now hoped, in short, to persuade the Americans to cancel BUCCANEER and send its assault shipping back to the Mediterranean, where it could be used to help mount the southern France operation—and, as a likely by-product, the attack on Rhodes as well. If the Americans refused to cancel BUCCANEER, the burden would be upon them to find the assault shipping for Southern France elsewhere, leaving the same probability that it could also be used for Rhodes.[43]

Meanwhile, the U.S. Chiefs of Staff, feeling confident in the assurance of Soviet support, had worked out their own position. The assault shipping already in the Mediterranean could be safely kept there until mid-January, as General Eisenhower had asked, to support the Italian campaign, without endangering an early May OVERLORD. With what remained after the withdrawals, the staff estimated, it would be possible to mount a two-division assault against southern France (now labeled ANVIL). This operation, for tactical and strategic reasons, should be launched no earlier than three or four weeks before OVERLORD rather than on the date suggested by Stalin. But the later date would not leave time, the Americans emphasized, to shift any of the landing craft over to the eastern Mediterranean for an attack on Rhodes and get them back to Corsica in time to refit for the ANVIL landings. *Ergo*—no Rhodes operation. The problem, as Admiral Leahy triumphantly summed up, "seemed to be a straightforward one of the date of OVERLORD."[44]

The argument that a southern France operation would be feasible but a Rhodes operation would not hinged on logistical calculations of an extremely speculative character. While these calculations, involving forward projections of landing craft availability, could not be positively disproved at the time—although the British challenged them at every point—the case for the ANVIL landings seemed particularly flimsy. Sir Alan Brooke could cite against it the verdict of General Eisenhower, a month earlier, that the assault shipping remaining in the Mediterranean would suffice for no more than a one-division lift, that the build-up following the assault would be very slow, and that no attack on such a scale would be likely to succeed.[45] The British did not believe the OVERLORD shipping could be moved back to the United Kingdom, after mid-January, in time for a May D Day, and they feared, incidentally, that the landing craft allotted for OVERLORD were inadequate.

Caught between contradictory logistical estimates, the discussion deadlocked. Nevertheless, the afternoon deadline was at hand, and the Russians had to be given an answer. The military leaders agreed, therefore (falling back on the subterfuge suggested by the British), that the Russians could be told "we will launch OVERLORD during May, in conjunction with a supporting operation against the south of France on the largest scale that is permitted by [available] landing craft," with a target date, for planning purposes, the same as that for OVERLORD. The advance in Italy would continue as far as the Pisa-Rimini line, and the sixty-eight LSTs requested by Eisenhower would be left in the Mediterranean until 15 January. The fate of BUCCANEER and the Aegean operations was reserved for discussion at Cairo.[46] Thus the difficult questions of timing and provision of means raised by Stalin's bombshell on the 28th were left unanswered, and no breath of discord ruffled the meeting of the principals on the afternoon of the 30th, when the military decisions were ratified. It was inconceivable, Churchill declared, "that the two nations, with their great volume of production, could not make the necessary landing craft available."[47]

Whatever else they did, the Tehran decisions did not spell defeat for the British program in the Mediterranean. The heart of that program—capture of Rome and advance to a defensible line beyond—now seemed assured, even though it had been the first target of Stalin's attack. The modest proposals for the Balkans had been accepted. American opposition had centered on the Aegean operations, for which Admiral King had warned he would not under any circumstances turn over American landing craft.[48] Nevertheless, the prospects of mounting the attack on Rhodes had been immeasurably improved by the introduction of an assault lift requirement for ANVIL, and Stalin had supported the British view, which was written into the formal conclusions of the Tehran Conference, that Turkey should, if possible, be brought into the war before the end of the year. The attitude of the Turks themselves, on which the whole enterprise would depend, was soon to be tested anew in negotiations at Cairo. At all events, the British left no doubt in American minds that they intended to press forward with their American plans, and that, in view of Stalin's firm pledge of participation in the war against Japan, they now regarded BUCCANEER as fair game.[49]

Second Cairo: Scratch BUCCANEER

Back at Cairo, the CCS faced the task of finding enough assault lift to carry out (1) a late May or early June OVERLORD, (2) a simultaneous southern France operation, (3) the British attack on Rhodes, as soon as possible following the impending landings South of Rome, and (4) BUCCANEER, still scheduled for March. The British promptly renewed their attack on BUC-CANEER. The operation was now even more vulnerable than before, since the receipt of Mountbatten's most recent plan which provided for a considerably stronger assault, with increased requirements for assault shipping and carrier-borne aviation. The ends in view seemed hardly commensurate with the cost, for more than 50,000 troops were to be concentrated against a garrison estimated at only about 5,000. The British insisted, moreover, on debating the larger issue of the whole campaign in Burma, which, in view of American plans for the Pacific and Stalin's firm promise to enter the lists against Japan, seemed to them to make little sense. The JCS were mainly worried lest, in the absence of an Allied offensive in Burma, the Japanese might seize the initiative and overwhelm the precariously defended American air bases in China. But they found it difficult to defend BUCCANEER on its merits. General Marshall candidly admitted that if the operation could be dropped without wrecking the mainland campaign, "he personally would not be seriously disturbed."[50]

Whatever the defects of BUCCANEER, the JCS were, of course, no more inclined than before to release its assault shipping if the craft were to be used to mount an attack on Rhodes. But the British adroitly shifted ground. They now soft-pedaled their Aegean plans (which depended mainly on the outcome of negotiations with the Turks, anyway), and concentrated on the problem of mounting an adequate attack against southern France, to which the Americans were firmly committed. ANVIL, they argued, must not be tailored to the leavings of other undertakings (as implied in the Tehran formula), but should be made strong enough to form a genuine complement to OVERLORD. This meant an assault by at least two divisions, perhaps three. But when the staffs checked their hasty Tehran estimates against the more ample data available at Cairo, they found that the residual assault lift in the Mediterranean, after OVERLORD withdrawals, would not exceed one and two-thirds divisions and might be even less. After a halfhearted attempt to hew to the Tehran line, the JCS conceded the need for at least a two-division assault, and on 4 December Admiral King, in a surprise move, offered to meet the ANVIL assault shipping deficit from new production previously allotted to the Pacific.[51]

King's offer opened no breach in the opposition of the JCS to the Rhodes operation, since, as he made clear, the new ships and craft could not reach the Mediterranean in time to be used for it. On the other hand, although they almost covered the calculated deficit against a two-division ANVIL assault, they did not guarantee this operation.[52] They left no margin for unforeseen contingencies, and many on the American as well as on the British side considered even a two-division assault too weak. There was, moreover, growing uneasiness over OVERLORD's own weakness, even after the allocations of 5 November. Time was growing short. OVERLORD and ANVIL were now designated the supreme operations for 1944; the responsible commanders were about to be named,[53] and few doubted that when they reviewed the existing plans they would demand a more ample provision of means. At the plenary meeting on 5 December Harry Hopkins elicited from the military leaders, after some sharp cross-questioning, the remarkable admission that although they had given the stamp of approval to a two-division ANVIL and a three and a half division OVERLORD, they believed nevertheless that both operations should be strengthened.[54]

After two days of discussion at Cairo, the problem had thus taken on new dimensions. It was no longer a question of mounting the ANVIL assault at a fixed scale. Now it seemed necessary to provide a pool of assault shipping large enough to mount both ANVIL and OVERLORD on a scale as yet undetermined but adequate to give each a reasonable margin of safety. Precisely how much shipping would be needed could not be known until the plans themselves were revised and developed in detail. The very uncertainty on this score lent force to the British argument that it would be folly to commit precious assault shipping irrevocably to a venture in southeast Asia that even the U.S. Chiefs of Staff conceded to be of secondary importance.

At the plenary meeting on the 5th, Churchill bluntly pointed out that only the President's unilateral pledge to Chiang stood in the way of agreement. He suggested that Chiang might be offered some lesser substitute for BUCCANEER, which itself would then be postponed until after the monsoon. The remainder of the campaign could be carried out as planned. Hopkins supported this idea. The President, obviously unhappy, finally agreed to the suggestion that Mountbatten's representatives, then in Cairo, and Mountbatten himself should be queried as to what small-scale amphibious operations might be undertaken if he had to give up the bulk of his assault lift. At the same time the CCS were ordered to reexamine forthwith the two main European operations "with a view to increasing the assaults in each case." Roosevelt's full capitulation swiftly followed. That same afternoon, after consulting with his advisers (only King, in the JCS, held out against postponing BUCCANEER), he sent Churchill a brief message: "BUCCANEER is off."[55]

The Joint Chiefs were not informed of the decision until the next day, but they must have realized, after their meeting with the President, that it could not long be delayed. What now had to be decided were the precise alternatives to be offered Chiang. On the night of the 5th the British and U.S. planners made a list of various amphibious operations that might be undertaken in Burma during the spring, assuming arbitrarily that the shipping to be withdrawn from the theater would comprise most of the LSTs, combat loaders, and small aircraft carriers. It was not an impressive list. The Joint Chiefs, studying it the following morning, were inclined to conclude that it might be better to give up serious amphibious ventures in the Southeast Asia Command altogether during this season, and transfer all the BUCCANEER assault shipping back to European waters. The British agreed. The CCS accordingly recommended that major amphibious operations in the Bay of Bengal be delayed until after the monsoon, and that Chiang Kai-shek be offered two alternatives: the mainland offensive as planned, with British naval control of the Bay of Bengal assured, but without BUCCANEER, for which would be substituted carrier strikes, commando raids, and bombardment of Bangkok and the railroad; or postponement of the mainland offensive, compensated for by increased airlift to China and more rapid development of the long-range bombardment program from bases in China. Later that day Mountbatten's reply came in, stating flatly that seaborne operations smaller than BUCCANEER would not be worth the effort. He proposed that, in anticipation of Chiang's probable reaction, only limited land operations in northern and central Burma and along the Arakan coast be undertaken, and that the aim of opening the land route to China during this season be abandoned.[56]

By evening of the 6th all knew that the President, without informing the JCS, had decided to abandon BUCCANEER and, moreover, had already cabled Chiang the bad news, presenting the same alternatives arrived at by the Chiefs of Staff that morning.[57] Ching's reply had not yet been received, but the President was due to leave Cairo the following morning and the conference decisions could not wait. Accordingly, the two alternatives presented to Chiang were both included in the final SEXTANT paper approved by the President and Prime Minister at the plenary meeting on the night of the 6th.

In the light of the Generalissimo's known attitude, there could be little doubt that he would reject the first; there was considerable doubt that he would accept even the second. Actually, by ruling out any worthwhile substitute for BUCCANEER, and so informing the Chinese leader forthwith, the President had thrown away an option that might have been acceptable to Chiang, inasmuch as the latter had never been told precisely what sort of operation was contemplated, but only that it would be a major one. At the time the conference decisions were approved, however, the leaders had Mountbatten's word for it that nothing less than BUCCANEER would serve. Later in the month Mountbatten changed his mind, but by then the President's message had left Chiang in no mood for compromise. In any case, Mountbatten's small residue of assault shipping was soon to be swallowed up in the maw of swelling European requirements. On 7 December the world-wide redeployment of assault shipping dictated by the SEXTANT decisions began as the CCS ordered Mountbatten to send fifteen LSTs and six assault transports—the bulk of his amphibious fleet—back to European waters.[58]

It has become almost a commonplace in American interpretations of World War II to say that at Tehran the British were forced to abandon their reservations concerning OVERLORD. Thus, it is asserted, the primacy of OVERLORD vis-à-vis the Mediterranean, and, indeed, its execution were finally assured.[59] Like the classic query, "When did you stop beating your wife?" this interpretation accepts as fact what is actually the nub of the issue, namely, the American allegation that the British, and Churchill in particular, had never intended to go through with OVERLORD and only resigned themselves to do so under Soviet pressure at Tehran. In reality, both Churchill and Brooke, forced repeatedly by the Russians to state their intentions concerning OVERLORD, held firmly to their position. At the end of the conference it was what it had been before: OVERLORD would be the main effort of the Western Allies in Europe, and, as far as the British were concerned, it would be carried out, as Churchill told Stalin on 30 November, "provided the enemy did not bring into France larger forces than the Americans and British could gather there."[60] In essence, this was the reservation already spelled out in the OVERLORD outline plan and accepted by the U.S. Chiefs of Staff themselves. Whether British leaders secretly harbored reservations of a more far-reaching nature is not known now (except by themselves) and probably will never be known. Certainly, the Americans had no basis at the time, other than hearsay, for suspecting that they did. The historian's position is likely to depend largely on where he decides to place the burden of proof—on the Americans to demonstrate that their suspicions were based on fact, or on the British to show that their professions were sincere.

As for Stalin's stand on OVERLORD, it was no more than a restatement of the familiar "second front" theme dinned into Western ears from the time of the German invasion of Russia down to the Moscow Conference of October 1943. It may be doubted whether Stalin was taken in by the transparently vague formula finally decided on to define the target date for the operation, but there is no indication that he attached any importance to it. His whole attitude at Tehran toward the timing of OVERLORD and supporting operations in the Mediterranean was one of lofty indifference. At all events, his pronouncements on OVERLORD added nothing to earlier Anglo-American agreements on the relation between the cross-Channel invasion and the Mediterranean. The most significant effect of Stalin's position was, not the essentially empty characterization of OVERLORD and ANVIL as "supreme" operation in 1944, but the CCS decision on 5 December to explore the possibility of strengthening the two assaults. This decision which virtually invited the responsible commanders to demand the means they considered necessary, formally recognized—what the JCS since spring of 1943 had refused to concede—that the limit placed on the size of the OVERLORD assault at the TRIDENT Conference was arbitrary and unrealistic. In principle, it represented a real vindication of the stubborn efforts by the British since early 1942 to obtain more American landing craft for OVERLORD.

How many would actually be forthcoming remained to be seen. For the present, over and above the allotments made at the TRIDENT and QUADRANT Conferences, the planners could count on the vessels released from southeast Asia, most of about two months of American production of LSTs, LCI(L)s, and LCTs, pledged by Admiral King on 5 November and 4 December, a handful of U.S. and British assault transports, and an indeterminate amount of new British LCTs. These additions, it was expected, "should provide a satisfactory lift both for OVERLORD and ANVIL." The expectation proved to be overoptimistic.[61]

With relation to the war in the Pacific, Stalin raised an issue that was welcome to the British and may have been embarrassing to the U.S. Chiefs of Staff. No debate on the question is recorded, but the CCS, in making OVERLORD and ANVIL the "supreme" operations for 1944, agreed that "nothing must be undertaken in any other part of the world" to jeopardize their success. Never before had the cross-Channel operation been underwritten in such sweeping terms; the statement wiped out provisos, insisted upon by the JCS at the TRIDENT Conference, that in the face of reverses in the Pacific the United States would be obliged to expand her operations there, even at the expense of the effort in Europe. In principle, at least, the war in the Pacific was now subordinate to the war in Europe.[62]

Coming at the time they did, the decisions at Cairo and Tehran relating to the war in Europe have inevitably taken on a retroactive luster from the dramatic events of the following summer—the invasion of Normandy and southern France, the advance up the Italian peninsula, the sweep across France to the Rhine. The decisions foreshadowed the events; it is less certain that they shaped them as well. To contemporaries, indeed, it seemed as though the whole conference program was going awry almost before the ink was dry. As the Cairo meetings ended, the outlook for the attack on Rhodes was good. The British could reasonably count on using for it the ex-BUCCANEER assault shipping now on its way back to the Mediterranean, since the conference agreements stipulated only that any operations undertaken in the Aegean must be "without detriment" to OVERLORD and ANVIL.[63] Negotiations with the Turks were going well. Less than a week later, the Turks suddenly raised the ante on military aid demanded as the price of intervention, and by the 25th Churchill had abandoned his Aegean plans. Similarly, by the middle of the month the planned landings south of Rome, taken almost for granted at

Cairo and Tehran, had been canceled owing to the failure of the American Fifth Army to reach positions within supporting distance of the target area. Later in the month, they were revived on a larger scale and, after a frantic search for the necessary assault lift, finally carried out late in January at Anzio. ANVIL, too, came under fire almost immediately, as the OVERLORD commanders laid claim to its allotted assault lift, and after protracted debate the plan was canceled. When the Allies finally invaded southern France in mid-August, the operation was no longer strategically related to OVERLORD and could not have been justified by the arguments used at Tehran.

As for OVERLORD itself, Stalin's unequivocal insistence upon the operation undoubtedly enhanced the likelihood that it would be carried out, even in the face of an unforeseen increase in German power. On the other hand, the massive preparations for the invasion had already generated a momentum difficult if not impossible to arrest. Any radical change of direction or of emphasis at this time—let alone later—would have caused an upheaval in plans and preparations more costly than many military defeats. As a practical matter, the war in Europe had progressed beyond the point of no return. Even the date was hardly any longer in the realm of strategic decision. After Tehran strategic planning was pointed toward a late May or early June OVERLORD (though the administrative staffs continued for some time to work toward an early May deadline), but in the end the actual date of the launching was shaped, as Churchill has remarked, mainly "by the moon and the weather."[64]

Notes

1. The present essay is condensed from several chapters of Richard M. Leighton and Robert W. Coakley, *Global Logistics and Strategy, 1943–1945*, a forthcoming volume in the series UNITED STATES ARMY IN WORLD WAR II, based on original research in the records of the Joint and Combined Chiefs of Staff, including the official minutes and papers of the Cairo-Tehran Conferences, and Army records in the custody of the Deputy Chief of Staff for Operations, G-3, filed in the Federal Records Center of the National Archives. A contrasting interpretation of the Cairo-Tehran Conferences will be found in another volume in this series, Maurice Matloff, *Strategic Planning for Coalition Warfare, 1943–1944* (Washington, 1959). The conferences are also described from various points of view in a number of other works in the series: Gordon A. Harrison, *Cross-Channel Attack* (Washington, 1951); Charles F. Romanus and Riley Sunderland, *Stilwell's Command Problems* (Washington, 1956); Forrest C. Pogue, *The Supreme Command* (Washington,

1954); and Louis Morton and Henry Morgan, The Pacific War: Strategy and Command, The Road to Victory (in preparation). Three other American studies deal with the Cairo-Tehran Conferences at some length: Herbert Feis, *Churchill, Roosevelt, and Stalin* (Princeton: Princeton University Press, 1957); William Hardy McNeill, *America, Britain, and Russia, Their Co-Operation and Conflict, 1941–1946* (London: Oxford University Press, 1953); and Robert Sherwood, *Roosevelt and Hopkins: An Intimate History* (New York: Harper & Brothers, 1948). The outstanding British interpretation is John Erhman, *Grand Strategy*, Vol. V, *August 1943–September 1944* (London: H.M. Stationery Office, 1956), in the official British *History of the Second World War*. (Permission to quote from this work has been received from the Controller of H.M. Stationery Office.) Of the large memoir literature, Winston S. Churchill's *Closing the Ring* (Boston: Houghton Mifflin Company, 1951) contains the most detailed and valuable account. The published memoirs of Admiral William D. Leahy, Admiral Ernest J. King, General Dwight D. Eisenhower, and Maj. Gen. John R. Deane are also useful, though sketchy on the conferences themselves. Arthur Bryant's two-volume biography of Lord Alanbrooke (General Sir Alan Brooke), *Turn of the Tide* and *Triumph in the West* (New York: Doubleday and Company, 1957, 1959), is also useful for the British position. Three American studies, recently published, contain brief, provocative analyses, from the American point of view, of the Anglo-American debate on European strategy in World War II: Kent Roberts Greenfield, *The Historian and the Army* (New Brunswick, N.J.: Rutgers University Press, 1954); Samuel Eliot Morison, *Strategy and Compromise* (Boston: Little, Brown and Company, 1958), and Trumbull Higgins, *Winston Churchill and the Second Front* (New York: Oxford University Press, 1957).

2. (1) Frederick C. Lane, *Ships for Victory: A History of Shipbuilding Under the U.S. Maritime Commission in World War II* (Baltimore, Md.: Johns Hopkins Press, 1951), pp. 601–05. (2) Gerald J. Fischer, *A Statistical Summary of Shipbuilding Under the U.S. Maritime Commission During World War II* (Washington, 1949), Table A-4. (3) Feighton and Coakley, Global Logistics and Strategy, 1943–1945, MS, Ch. X.

3. A few LSTs of special design were constructed in Britain early in the war. In origin, the LST was a British-designed vessel, like virtually all the landing ships and craft used in World War II. Under wartime agreements, the United States constructed most of the merchant and amphibious shipping used by both countries, thus enabling Britain, with limited building capacity, to concentrate on expanding its Navy.

    For figures on distribution of LSTs in November 1943 see CCS Memo for Info 175, 23 Nov 43, Landing Craft Reports, 1 Nov 43.

4. SLEDGEHAMMER, the tentatively planned emergency cross-Channel attack in fall of 1942, had been canceled, partly because of a shortage of assault lift, but for other reasons as well.

5. (1) Richard M. Leighton and Robert W. Coakley, *Global Logistics and Strategy, 1940–1943*, UNITED STATES IN WORLD WAR II (Washington, 1955), pp. 376–82, 602–03, 682–83. (2) George Mowry, *Landing Craft and the War Production Board* (WPB Study No. 11, July 1944), Ch. II. (3) Jeter A. Isley, and Philip A. Crowl, *The U.S. Marines and Amphibious War* (Princeton: Princeton

University Press, 1951), pp. 1–4, 47–48. (4) Harrison, *Cross-Channel Attack,* pp. 60–61. For a description of the various types of landing ships and craft, see *ONI 226, Allied Landing Craft and Ships* (Office, Chief of Naval Operations, April 1944).

6. JPS 152/1, 3 Apr 43, title: Production of Landing Craft.

7. Leighton and Coakley, Global Logistics and Strategy, 1943–1945, MS, Chs. I and III.

8. *Ibid.,* MS, Chs. X, XI.

9. *Ibid.*

10. This section is condensed from Leighton and Coakley, Global Logistics and Strategy, 1943–1945, MS, Chs. VI through X. For a good summary, see Harrison, *Cross-Channel Attack,* Ch. II.

11. (1) Henry L. Stimson and McGeorge Bundy, *On Active Service in Peace and War* (New York: Harper & Brothers, 1948), pp. 435–38. (2) Bryant, *Turn of the Tide,* pp. 573–76.

12. OPD paper [about 12 Nov 43], U.S. Courses of Action in Case Sextant Decisions Do Not Guarantee OVERLORD, Exec 5, Item 12a. See also various staff studies in ABC 381 Strategy Section Papers (7 January 1943), Numbers 131–95.

13. Memo, Representatives COS, in CCS 379, 26 Oct 43, Opns in Mediterranean.

14. (1) Msg 51, Deane to JCS, 9 Nov 43, with related papers in Exec 5, Item 15, Env. 3. (2) John R. Deane, *The Strange Alliance* (New York: The Viking Press, 1947), p. 35. (3) Churchill, *Closing the Ring,* pp. 286–89. (4) Cordell Hull, *Memoirs of Cordell Hull,* (New York: The Macmillan Company, 1948), Vol. II, p. 1301. (5) Ehrman, *Grand Strategy,* V, 100–101, 156–157.

15. Leighton and Coakley, Global Logistics and Strategy, 1943–1945, MS, Ch. XI.

16. Quoted in Churchill, *Closing the Ring,* pp. 332–33. The Cairo-Tehran meetings lasted from 22 November through 7 December 1943. At Cairo, Roosevelt, Churchill, and their military advisers met formally for the first time with Chiang Kai-shek. The Tehran meetings (28 November–1 December) brought the two Western leaders together with Premier Stalin for the first time. A second series of meetings, attended by British and Americans only, was held at Cairo on 2–7 December. See Matloff, *Strategic Planning for Coalition Warfare, 1943–1944,* Ch. XVI.

17. (1) CCS 409, Note by COS, 25 Nov 43, OVERLORD and the Mediterranean. (2) Ehrman, *Grand Strategy,* V, 109–12. RANKIN was one of several alternative plans for crossing the Channel in the event of a German collapse before the OVERLORD target date.

18. (1) CCS 409, cited n. 17(1). (2) Ehrman, *Grand Strategy,* V, 104–21, 165–67. (3) Min, 2d Plenary Mtg, SEXTANT, 24 Nov 43.

19. The discussion of these points is described in Leighton and Coakley, Global Logistics and Strategy, 1943–1945, MS, Ch. XI.

20. (1) Ehrman, *Grand Strategy,* V, 148–53. (2) Romanus and Sunderland, *Stilwell's Command Problems,* Ch. II. (3) [Mountbatten] *Report to CCS by Supreme Allied Commander, Southeast Asia, 1943–1945* (London: H.M. Stationery Office, 1951), p. 27. (4) Matloff, *Strategic Planning for Coalition Warfare, 1943–1944,* Ch. XVI, pp. 2–3.

21. (1) Mountbatten *Report,* p. 27. (2) Romanus and Sunderland, *Stilwell's Command Problems,* p. 51. (3) Ernest J. King and Walter Muir Whitehill, *Fleet Admiral King, A Naval Record* (New York: W.W. Norton & Company, Inc., 1952), pp. 509–10. (4) Ehrman, *Grand Strategy,* V, 162. (5) Min, CCS 129th Mtg, 24 Nov 43.

22. Msg, PM for CsofS Com, 21 Nov 43, quoted in Churchill, *Closing the Ring,* p. 686. (2) Ehrman, *Grand Strategy,* V, 114, 159. (3) Min, 2d Plenary Mtg, SEXTANT, 24 Nov 43. (4) Romanus and Sunderland, *Stilwell's Command Problems,* p. 66.

23. (1) See Marshall's outburst quoted in Joseph W. Stilwell, Theodore H. White, ed., *The Stilwell Papers* (New York: William Sloane Associates, Inc., 1948), p. 255. (2) Min, 129th Mtg CCS, 24 Nov 43. (3) Min, 130th Mtg JCS, 25 Nov 43.

24. (1) Churchill, *Closing the Ring,* p. 328. (2) Ehrman, *Grand Strategy,* V, 162, 164–65, 571. (3) Min, CCS 128th Mtg, 23 Nov 43. (4) Romanus and Sunderland, *Stilwell's Command Problems,* p. 65. (5) Min, 1st Plenary Mtg, SEXTANT, 23 Nov 43.

25. See Marshall's remark at the JCS meeting earlier in the day. Min, JCS 130th Mtg, 25 Nov 43.

26. The evidence on this last point is strong but not conclusive. Churchill (*Closing the Ring,* page 328) and Leathy (*I Was There,* page 201) both assert unequivocally that the pledge was given and Ehrman accepts this as fact (*Grand Strategy,* Volume V, page 165). Matloff (*Strategic Planning for Coalition Warfare, 1943–1944,* Chapter XVI) regards it as at least highly probable. Romanus and Sunderland, who give little attention to the amphibious phases of the war in Burma, do not mention the pledge, though they do mention the promise to equip more Chinese divisions. It may be significant that the President, in the interview with Stilwell and Marshall mentioned above, seemed from his remarks to have the Andamans operation on his mind. But the most convincing evidence is to be found, as shown below, in the abrupt change in the attitude and position of the JCS on the morning of 26 November.

27. Min, JCS 131st Mtg, 26 Nov 43.

28. (1) Msg, FDR to Byrnes, Dir OWM, 23 Nov 43, Exec 5, Item 14. (2) Msg, Byrnes to President, 25 Nov 43, in JCS Memo for Info 171, 27 Nov 43, ABC 561 (30 Aug 43). (3) Mowry, *Landing Craft and the WPB,* pp. 30–32.

29. (1) Min, CCS 131st Mtg, 26 Nov 43. (2) Ehrman, *Grand Strategy,* V, 166–67.

30. Min, 1st Plenary Mtg, EUREKA, 28 Nov 43.

31. (1) *Ibid.* (2) Ehrman, *Grand Strategy,* V, 174–76.

32. Min, 132d Mtg JCS, 28 Nov 43.

33. (1) Ehrman, *Grand Strategy,* V, 175. (2) Churchill, *Closing the Ring,* p. 355.

34. (1) Min, 1st Plenary Mtg, EUREKA, 28 Nov 43. (2) Ehrman, *Grand Strategy,* V, 176. [Italics supplied.]

35. (1) Min, 1st Plenary Mtg, EUREKA, 28 Nov 43. (2) Ehrman, *Grand Strategy,* V, 176.

36. (1) Min, Military Mtg, EUREKA, 29 Nov 43. (2) Min, 2d Plenary Mtg, EUREKA, 29 Nov 43. (3) See also Churchill's account of Stalin's attack on

General Brooke at the banquet on the evening of the 30th, *Closing the Ring*, pages 386–88.

37. Min, Military Mtg, EUREKA, 29 Nov 43.

38. (1) Quoted in Mowry, *Landing Craft and the WPB*, p. 31. See also pp. 32–33. Actually, the program had already been accelerated, in response to Roosevelt's message of the 23d, since certain measures had to be set in train immediately, without waiting for the President's order. (2) See Leighton and Coakley, Global Logistics and Strategy 1943–1945, MS, Ch. X.

39. Min, 2d Plenary Mtg, EUREKA, 29 Nov 43. This was hardly a compelling argument for a May OVERLORD since the Russians, as the British pointed out, had never launched a summer offensive in that month. According to Churchill, Stalin told him at lunch on the 30th that he wanted OVERLORD in May or in June in order for it to synchronize with the Soviet offensive. In the event, the latter jumped off on 23 June, two and a half weeks after OVERLORD. See Churchill, *Closing the Ring*, pp. 380, 383.

40. (1) Min, 2d Plenary Mtg, EUREKA, 29 Nov 43. (2) Churchill, *Closing the Ring*, p. 371. (3) Ehrman, *Grand Strategy*, V, 179.

41. (1) Min, 2d Plenary Mtg, EUREKA, 29 Nov 43. (2) Churchill, *Closing the Ring*, p. 370. (3) Ehrman, *Grand Strategy*, V, 180. (4) Sherwood, *Roosevelt and Hopkins*, p. 788. The British accounts indicate that both Roosevelt and Stalin gave the OVERLORD date as "in May," or words to that effect.

42. (1) Churchill, *Closing the Ring*, p. 376. (2) Ehrman, *Grand Strategy*, V, 181.

43. Ehrman, *Grand Strategy*, V, 181.

44. (1) Min, 132d Mtg CCS, 30 Nov 43. (2) Harrison, *Cross-Channel Attack*, p. 125. (3) James D. T. Hamilton, Threat to Southern France, in draft MS on the southern France operation, OCMH. The Americans had little reliable data on the southern France operation with them at Tehran. See Matloff, "The ANVIL Decision: Crossroads of Strategy," below.

45. (1) Min, 132d Mtg CCS, 30 Nov 43. (2) Msg NAF 492, Eisenhower to CCS, 29 Oct 43, quoted in Ehrman, Grand Strategy, V, MS, pp. 188–89.

46. (1) Min, 132d Mtg CCS, 30 Nov 43. (2) Ehrman, *Grand Strategy*, V, 182. (3) Msg FAN 281, CCS to Eisenhower, 1 Dec 43, Exec 3, Item 13.

47. Min, 3d Plenary Mtg EUREKA, 30 Nov 43.

48. (1) Min, JCS 131st Mts, 26 Nov 43. (2) See Hopkins' strong statement in Sherwood, *Roosevelt and Hopkins*, pages 793–96.

49. CCS Memo for Info 165, 2 Dec 43, Military Conclusions of the EUREKA Conference. It was also noted that Stalin had undertaken to attack Bulgaria if the latter attacked Turkey.

50. (1) Min, CCS 135th Mtg, 5 Dec 43. (2) Ehrman, *Grand Strategy*, V, 185–86. (3) Romanus and Sunderland, *Stilwell's Command Problems*, pp. 65–67. (4) Morton and Morgan, The Pacific War: Strategy and Command, The Road to Victory, MS, Ch. 1.

51. (1) Min, CCS 133d Mtg, 3 Dec 43. (2) Min, 3d Plenary Mtg, SEXTANT, 4 Dec 43. (3) CPS 131/1, 3 Dec 43, Amph Opns Against South of France. (4) Msg 10131, Adm Badger to VCNO, 5 Dec 43, Exec 5, Item 13. (5) CCS 424, Rpt by CPS and CAdC, 5 Dec 43, Amph Opns Against South of France. (3) Ehrman, *Grand Strategy*, V. 184, 187, 195.

King's offer was accompanied by a warning that it might result in setting back the operation against Truk, the main Japanese base in the Caroline Islands. He did not mention that the JCS had already decided, some three weeks earlier, to suspend the attack on Truk pending the results of carrier raids to test whether it might be feasible to bypass the fortress. See Min, JCS 123d Mtg, 15 Nov, and 124th Mtg, 17 Nov 43, and Robert Ross Smith, *The Approach to the Philippines,* UNITED STATES ARMY IN WORLD WAR II (Washington, 1953), p. 6.

52. The total extra lift required was figured at 3 XAPs (modified assault transports), 12 MT ships (freighters fitted for vehicle carriage), 26 LSTs, and 31 LCTs. King promised to provide the XAPs, the LSTs, and 26 of the LCTs. The MT ships were, or would be, available in the area; the five LCTs could be taken from craft earmarked for OVERLORD, to be replace by others in the contingent promised for OVERLORD on 5 November. See CCS 424, 5 Dec 43, cited. n. 51.

53. The President announced General Eisenhower's appointment as OVERLORD command on 6 December.

54. Min, 4th Plenary Mtg, SEXTANT, 5 Dec 43.

55. (1) Churchill, *Closing the Ring,* p. 411. (2) Min, 4th Plenary Mtg, SEXTANT, Dec 43. (3) Ehrman, *Grand Strategy,* V, 190–92. (4) King and Whitehill, *Fleet Admiral King,* p. 425. (5) William D. Leahy, *I Was There* (New York: Whittlesey House, 1950), p. 213. (6) Sherwood, *Roosevelt and Hopkins,* p. 801.

56. (1) Min, 136th Mtg JCS, 6 Dec 43. (2) Min, 136th Mtg CCS, 5 Dec 43. (3) Min, 137th Mtg CCS, 6 Dec 43. (4) CCS 427, Rpt by CPS, 5 Dec 43, title: Amph Opns in Southeast Asia Alternative to BUCCANEER. (5) Romanus and Sunderland, *Stilwell's Command Problems,* p. 70. (6) Ehrman, *Grand Strategy,* V, 192–93.

57. (1) Msg, President to Chiang, 5 Dec 43, Exec 10, Item 70. (2) Min, 5th Plenary Mtg, SEXTANT, 6 Dec 43. Since the CCS recommendations were those approved by the JCS and had been drafted by General Marshall, it is possible that Marshall had earlier shown this draft to the President and that the latter used it, but without informing Marshall. At all events it seems unlikely that the Chiefs of Staff could have known on the morning of the 6th that the President had already cabled Chiang, since they were discussing their own draft with a view to submitting it to the President. See Matloff, *Strategic Planning for Coalition Warfare, 1943–1944,* MS Ch. XVI, p. 60.

58. (1) Ehrman, *Grand Strategy,* V, 193, 211–12. (2) Mountbatten *Report,* p. 29. (3) Romanus and Sunderland. *Stilwell's Command Problems,* pp. 75ff.

59. For example, Sherwood (*Roosevelt and Hopkins,* page 788) states that Churchill at the plenary meeting on the 29th "bowed to the inevitable"— *i.e.,* accepted OVERLORD—by promising Stalin that "Britain would hurl every ounce of her strength across the Channel at the Germans." Admiral Leahy in his memoirs (*I Was There,* page 209) speaks of the decision on a May OVERLORD (which he represents as a capitulation by the British, not a compromise) in the same sense—*e.g.,* the British "fell into line." See also Harrison, *Cross-Channel Attack,* pp. 125–26; Cline, *Washington Command Post: The Operations Division,* UNITED STATES ARMY IN WORLD WAR II (Washington, 1951), p. 229; Matloff, *Strategic Planning for Coalition Warfare, 1943–1944,* Ch. XIII, pp. 71–72; "The Decision to Invade

SouthernFrance," MS, pp. 8–9; Greenfield, *The Historian and the Army*, p. 54; Higgins, *Winston Churchill and the Second Front*, pp. 212–13, 244.

60. Churchill, *Closing the Ring*, p. 380.
61. The additional lift was listed as follows:

	For OVERLORD	For ANVIL
LSTs	23 U.S. 3 British	36 U.S. 5 British
LCI(L)s	24 U.S.	
LCTs	19 U.S. 45 British	31 U.S.
Assault transports		3 U.S. 6 British

   See CCS 428 (Rev.), 15 Dec 43, Annex V.
62. CCS 426/1, 6 Dec 43, Annex V.
63. (1) CCS 428 (Rev.), 15 Dec 43, Annex V. (2) CCS 426/1, 6 Dec 43, Rpt to President and Prime Minister. (3) A summary of the Cairo-Tehran decisions prepared for the Army Service Forces on 15 December stated that Turkish intervention and surrender of Bulgaria were considered "probable," and that in this event it would be necessary "to mount such operations as may be practicable in the Eastern Mediterranean. . . ." See Memo, Gen Wood for various addressees, 15 Dec 43, sub: SEXTANT Decisions, ASF Planning Div Folder SEXTANT Decisions.
64. Churchill, *Closing the Ring*, p. 376.

Reading 7

Did Strategic Bombing Work?

by Williamson Murray

The most controversial aspect of the war that the United States and Great Britain waged against Nazi Germany was the Combined Bomber Offensive. The Harvard economist John Kenneth Galbraith, a member of the U.S. Strategic Bombing Survey, has articulated the arguments of those who dispute the contribution of strategic bombing to victory in the war. As he wrote in his memoirs:

> German war production had, indeed, expanded under the bombing. The greatly heralded efforts, those on the ball-bearing and aircraft plants for example, emerged as costly failures. Other operations, those against oil and the railroads, did have military effect. But strategic bombing had not won the war. At most, it had eased somewhat the task of the ground troops who did. The aircraft, manpower, and bombs used in the campaign had cost the American economy far more in output than they had cost Germany.

Galbraith's comment, that at most the Combined Bomber Offensive saved a few infantrymen's lives, suggests the pervasive view in much scholarly literature about World War II in Europe. That view contrasts the small savings with the wreckage of some of the world's most cultured and beautiful cities and the slaughter of innumerable civilians. Such criticisms reflect the fact that strategic bombing was not a pretty thing, and it laid waste to some of the great monuments of the Old World.

From *MHQ: The Quarterly Journal of Military History*, Vol. 8, No. 3 (Spring 1996).

But World War II was a matter of national survival, a war waged against a tyranny that represented a hideous moral and strategic danger. Consequently, any judgment on the Combined Bomber Offensive must rest on the grounds of expediency rather than on those of morality. As Clausewitz suggests, "It would be futile—even wrong—to try and shut one's eyes to what war really is from sheer distress at its brutality."

We need first to examine the conduct of the British and American campaigns from their intellectual and doctrinal origins to their actual implementation. The countries' theories of air power had much in common. Both held that aircraft represented the decisive weapon of the next war; that their only proper role was as strategic bombers that would directly attack an enemy nation's centers of population and industrial production; that strategic bombing would lead to quick victories and avoid the prolonged attrition that had characterized trench warfare; that cooperation with other services represented a mistaken diversion of air resources; that enemy fighters could not interfere in any significant manner with the conduct of a bombing offensive; and that the experience of previous war—in short, military history—had nothing to teach airmen.

Nevertheless, considerable differences developed between the British and American strategic-bombing doctrines that evolved during the period before the outbreak of World War II. The British emphasized attacks on enemy population centers, which they believed would destroy enemy morale. The Americans, however, favored a conception of strategic bombing that sought to destroy specific targets within the enemy's industrial system, leading to widespread economic dislocation and collapse.

War soon contradicted the assumptions with which airmen began the war. By the time the Royal Air Force initiated strategic bombing in May 1940, in response to the German attack on western Europe, the British already understood that their bombers could not survive in daylight against German fighters. Initially, they attacked specific industrial targets such as refineries or rubber plants at night, an approach more like the American one than their own interwar doctrine.

But in the summer of 1941, a detailed study of bombing raids brought depressing news to the RAF. Less than one-third of its bombers were dropping their loads within five miles of the specific industrial targets they were attacking. A target with a radius of five miles would contain over seventy-five square miles—yet two-thirds of the crews could not even come close to them. The obvious conclusion was that the only targets suitable for attack under nighttime conditions were German cities. Thus began Bomber Command's "area bombing" campaign, an effort that aimed to "dehouse" Germany's urban population and break the Nazi morale—which had been the original rationale of British strategic bombing. This effort represented the only possibility in 1941 of carrying the war to Germany. But in the face of defeats in North Africa and the Far East, it was more the strain on British morale than German that made some such campaign a political necessity.

The initial German response to the British night attacks was halfhearted. Some investment in a night-fighter force did occur, and the Germans did create an extensive radar and communication system. But two things prevented them from making major investments in air defense at this early date. First, their own offensive proclivities drove them to a strategy that aimed at paying the British back with attacks on British cities. The "Baby Blitz" of 1942 is a good example of an approach that in the long term was to have such a negative impact on German defenses. Second, given the difficulties the British were having in the early days of their attacks, the Germans for the most part failed to catch the significance of the long-term threat from the British bombing offensive. In early 1941 the British launched nighttime raids against Karlsruhe and Stuttgart; German radio reported British bombers over "Aachen, Eupen, Malmédy, Koblenz, Neuwied, Kreuznach, Frankfurt am Main, Wiesbaden, Limburg, Darmstadt, Mainz, Worms, Trier, Offenburg, Saarfels, Nuremberg, Erlangen, Bamberg, Bayreuth, Coburg, Pegnitz, Aschaffenburg, Schweinfurt, Würzburg, Regensburg, Weiden, and Chemnitz." It is not hard to see why some Germans might have underestimated the threat in 1941.

In February 1942, Arthur Harris was appointed head of Bomber Command. His name soon became synonymous with the conduct of the RAF's bombing campaign. At the beginning, substantial changes in the weaponry of the command aided Harris: coming into service were new four-engine bombers, the Sterling and the Halifax, and soon the first Lancasters, the best heavy bomber of the European war (with a bombload averaging over seven tons versus barely four for the B-17). As important was the fact that the RAF also acquired navigational aids and tactics that revolutionized the conduct of nighttime strategic bombing.

Bomber Command achieved a number of notable successes in 1942. Harris understood two crucial factors in that year: first, the technological limitations of his command were such that only area bombing offered potential that could be realized; second, he had to achieve significant successes immediately or the resources allocated to his command would shift elsewhere (such as to the Battle of the Atlantic). Consequently, Harris picked cities for their vulnerability rather than their economic or military significance. He first went after Rostock and Lübeck, which were easy to find because of their location on the Baltic. Then, in late May, Bomber Command put everything it had into the air, including the operational training squadrons. It launched 1,000 aircraft against Cologne and plastered that city's downtown area. Adolf Hitler himself recognized the significance of the raid. He remarked to his Luftwaffe aides that the British were opening up a second front in the West in support of the Soviets, who were struggling in the East.

Bomber Command's efforts over the rest of 1942 were less successful, which in the long term proved an unanticipated piece of luck. Because the air defense of Germany's cities never received Hitler's undivided attention, the Germans lost crucial time preparing for the coming storm. In January 1943, British and American air leaders agreed to wage a nonstop day-and-night offensive to break Nazi Germany, and by now the production to support it was beginning to flow from the factories of both nations.

In late winter and spring 1943, Bomber Command, largely reequipped with four-engine bombers, battered the population centers of the Ruhr, Germany's industrial heartland. Although its aircraft never reached hoped-for levels of destruction, they were now punishing the Germans severely. In late July, Bomber Command attacked the Baltic port of Hamburg with four major raids: it hit the jackpot. By using strips of aluminum, code-named Window, the British blinded the German night air defenses: radar stations, antiaircraft guns, and night fighters simply ceased to operate effectively. Conditions over Hamburg were ideal. Not only was visibility for marking the target nearly perfect, but the weather was dry and hot. The first markers went down on the great lumberyard into which Baltic timber arrived in Germany; within a relatively few moments, Hamburg's center was a raging inferno. Succeeding crews dropped their bomb and incendiary loads over the fire, spreading it. A tower of superheated air reached up to and over the bombers. The resulting vacuum sucked in masses of air from the surrounding countryside. Winds reached 300 miles per hour; temperatures, upwards of 1,000 degrees, in some cases incinerating those in shelters. Over 40,000 Germans died. The catastrophe came as a terrible shock to the German nation. The Nazi minister of armaments, Albert Speer, even warned Hitler that four or five more Hamburgs over the summer would lead to a general collapse of national morale.

But Bomber Command was not in a position to duplicate its success. In October it did create a second firestorm at Kassel, but a combination of bad weather and increasingly effective defenses, as the Luftwaffe countered the effects of Window, spelled increasing difficulty for the British.

As for the Americans, the first U.S. B-17s arrived in England in the summer of 1942 and immediately began attacking industrial targets in occupied France, such as the Renault factory outside Paris. Supported by British short-range fighters in their daylight raids, the American bombers suffered relatively low casualty rates. But the Americans never reached the level of 300 operational bombers that air leaders felt was necessary to strike beyond the range of fighter escorts. Moreover, the North African landings in November 1942 siphoned off U.S. bomber strength from England to the Mediterranean.

It was not until spring 1943 that Eighth Air Force in England reached sufficient strength to attempt deep penetration, daylight raids into German airspace beyond the range of Allied escort fighters. From the first, the Americans discovered that this was going to be a nasty business. The Germans had built their air defenses in depth. And the Luftwaffe began to bring significant numbers of its best fighter squadrons back to the homeland to defend the daytime skies over the Reich as the American effort expanded.

Throughout the summer and fall of 1943, a terrible attrition of Eighth Air Force aircrews took place, as its leaders struggled to prove that unescorted daylight missions against precision targets deep in the Reich could work. For the command, crew losses averaged over 30 percent per month over the summer and fall. Of thirty-five aircrews that arrived in England with the 100th Bomb Group at the end of May, only 14 percent of the crew members made it through the twenty-five missions required for rotation. The rest were dead, wounded, missing, psychological cases, or prisoners of war. Things were no better for the Luftwaffe. Although extravagant claims by Eighth Air Force gunners had little relationship to reality, Luftwaffe fighters suffered heavy losses throughout the period. To put it into perspective, a young American had a better chance of surviving the war by fighting with the Marines in the Pacific than flying in bombers over Germany in 1943; similarly, a young German had more chance of surviving the war by fighting in the Waffen SS than in a fighter in the skies over the Reich.

In August, Eighth Air Force launched its most ambitious deep-penetration mission thus far. Two separate formations, supposedly mutually supporting, attacked the ball-bearing factories at Schweinfurt and aircraft-production facilities at Regensburg in an effort to take out both those facilities with precision bombing. Unfortunately, because of fog over English air bases, the missions entered German territory at widely different times. After savaging the first formation, Luftwaffe fighters had time to land, rearm, and refuel. They shot down sixty bombers from both missions. But damage to Schweinfurt and Regensburg was considerable. That night, a major Bomber Command raid wrecked the research-and-development station at Peenemünde, where the V-1 cruise missile and the V-2 ballistic missile were under development. Underlining the strain that the German defenders were under, the Luftwaffe's chief of staff, General Hans Jeschonnek, committed suicide the next day.

After a slowdown in September to recover from heavy losses in midsummer, the Americans attacked in force in October. Again losses were high. On "Black Thursday," October 14, B-17s attempted to complete the destruction of the ball-bearing factories at Schweinfurt; again the attackers lost sixty aircraft. These air battles over targets deep in Germany represented a significant short-term victory for the Luftwaffe. The message was clear: bombers could not survive beyond the range of fighter escort. There was another problem. By the time the B-17s recovered enough from their losses in August to return to Schweinfurt in October, the Germans had already dispersed much of the production of ball bearings. And the losses that Eighth Air Force suffered in the second attack ensured that the B-17s would not be able to go back to Schweinfurt until February 1944.

As the fortunes of the American strategic bombing were skidding toward a low point, Harris launched Bomber Command in an all-out effort to destroy Berlin. From November 1943 through March 1944, his bombers hammered the German capital in hopes that they could break the morale of the government and the people. They broke neither, but their losses came close to wrecking the command. Though poorly supported by Hitler and Reichsmarschall Hermann Göring, the commander in chief of the Luftwaffe, German night defenses nevertheless rose to the occasion; British losses reached staggering proportions. In addition, on the night of March 30–31, 1944, Bomber Command lost 108 bombers in an attack against Nuremburg. Bomber Command had reached the same point that the Americans had reached in October 1943: bombers could not survive at an acceptable rate of attrition without protection from escort fighters.

By this point, however, Eighth Air Force was on the way to recovery. General Jimmy Doolittle replaced General Ira Eaker as its commander at the end of 1943, while a new fighter, the P-51 Mustang, which few in either the RAF or the U.S. Army Air Forces had believed could be built, provided the sought-for capability—long-range fighter escort. Eighth Air Force returned to attack the German aircraft industry in February 1944. The attacks had considerable impact on German aircraft production. Although German production of fighters rose significantly over the course of the year, the Germans achieved that only by stopping production of virtually all other aircraft types.

More significantly, Eighth Air Force's attacks forced the Luftwaffe to concentrate on defending its industrial base from American blows. For the four months between February and May 1944, a terrible battle of attrition occurred between the Americans and the Germans. Each month the former lost the equivalent of 25 percent of the bombers and approximately 30 percent of the crews with which they had begun the month. But such was American production strength that the number of operational bombers available in the squadrons actually climbed. On the other hand, the Luftwaffe was losing over 20 percent of its fighter pilots every month. The Allies could afford their aircraft and crew losses; the Germans could not. In May the German resistance collapsed. No longer was the Luftwaffe capable of defending even the Reich; on the frontiers of the Nazi empire, the Wehrmacht would now fight without any protection from the blows launched by Allied air forces.

In April, British and American strategic bombers came under the control of General Dwight Eisenhower, supreme Allied commander in Europe, and his chief deputy, the British airman Sir Arthur Tedder. They found themselves involved in a campaign to shut down the logistical support that the German army required to fight the coming battle in Normandy. Given the defeat in the Battle of Berlin, Bomber Command had no choice but to comply. The commanders of Eighth Air Force were less willing, but in the end they also played. Over the course of April, May, and early June, Allied air attacks smashed up the road and rail networks of northern France and Belgium. In early June, just before D-Day, a German logistical report admitted their effectiveness:

In Zone 1 [France and Belgium], the systematic destruction that
has been carried out since March of all important junctions of
the entire network—not only of the main rail lines—has most
seriously crippled the whole transport system (railway installations, including rolling stock). Similarly, Paris has been systematically cut off from long-distance traffic, and the most
important bridges over the lower Seine have been destroyed
one after another. As a result . . . it is only by exerting the
greatest efforts that purely military traffic and goods essential
to the war effort . . . can be kept moving. . . . The [enemy] aim
has so successfully been achieved—locally at any rate—that
the *Reichsbahn* [the German railroad] authorities are seriously
considering whether it is not useless to attempt further repair
work.

In the end, the campaign against the logistical network played
a crucial role in Allied victories in Normandy and eventually in
the reconquest of France and Belgium. Thanks to Allied air power,
the Germans had lost the battle that may have mattered most, the
battle of the buildup.

So overwhelming had Allied air resources become by spring
1944 that General Carl Spaatz, overall commander of the U.S.
strategic-bombing effort since the start of the year, persuaded
Eisenhower to allow his bombers to attack the German oil industry. Since Fifteenth Air Force in Italy was already bombing the
Romanian oil fields, it seemed likely that attacks on the German
synthetic-oil industry in the Reich would cripple Nazi fuel production. On May 12, 1944, some 935 B-17s and B-24s attacked synthetic-oil plants at Zwickau, Merseburg-Leuna, Brüx, Lützken-
dorf, Böhlen, Zeitz, and Chemnitz. Almost immediately, the
American air commanders received confirmation from Ultra de-
cryptions of the enemy's high-level ciphers that the Germans were
desperate about these attacks. From this point to the end of the
war, the Americans made the oil industry the focus of their air
campaign.

The collapse of the German position in the West in August and
the Allied advance to the German frontier wrecked the Luftwaffe's
early-warning network. Beginning in September, Bomber Command returned to its savaging of German cities. The emphasis of
American attacks remained on oil targets. But both bombing forces
cooperated in an additional effort to destroy Germany's transportation network. Tedder managed this campaign, as he had the one
in France. By February 1945 these attacks had finally broken Germany's ability to move and distribute its industrial and war pro-

duction; the inevitable result was the collapse in the West that began in March 1945.

Thus far, we have concentrated on the conduct of operations during the war. What impact did the extraordinary efforts of the British and American strategic-bombing offensive actually have on winning the war?

Regarding the British effort, it must first be noted that the bombing of Germany in the early war years was essential to bolstering British morale. With the string of German successes through 1942 in the land war, and the U-boat successes that threatened the very survival of Britain, the bombing of German cities was the only means of striking back at the enemy.

In a direct sense, the effectiveness of Bomber Command's offensive was more limited than that of the Americans. In its attacks on French transportation targets in spring 1944 the tactics, techniques, and technological capabilities developed in 1942 and 1943 allowed it to play the crucial role in breaking the Wehrmacht's transportation network in northern France. With effective navigational aids, British pathfinder bombers—the aircraft that dropped target markers to help following aircraft—were able to identify the transportation targets, and then, with each bomber dropping its load independently, the British were able to achieve more accurate patterns than their American counterparts. Ironically, Harris had made a thoroughly disingenuous effort to persuade Winston Churchill that Bomber Command could not strike precision targets in France—thereby reinforcing Churchill's fears that tens of thousands of French civilians might die in such raids, with serious political consequences for postwar Anglo-French relations. But a series of test raids had shown that Harris was wrong. Bomber Command followed with a series of devastating raids against the marshaling yards on which the French railroad system—and German logistics—depended.

Bomber Command's greatest contribution to the winning of the war came in an indirect fashion. By 1943, area bombing had caused a dramatic decline in the morale of the German populace. These ferocious attacks also caused considerable dislocations in Germany's economic performance. A German economy unburdened by such attacks and drawing on all of central and western Europe might have reached production totals close to those of the United States or the Soviet Union.

The impact on German morale seriously worried the Nazi leadership, particularly since that leadership blamed Germany's defeat in 1918 on the collapse of morale at home rather than on military defeat at the battlefront. Thus, the British assault on German morale led Hitler and Göring to base their decisions on political rather than military factors. As a result, they made two serious military mistakes.

Because Germany's population drew considerable psychological support from the comforting sound of antiaircraft artillery blasting at RAF bombers, Hitler and Göring emphasized that in their response to the bombing—even though the Luftwaffe knew as early as 1942 that these weapons were not cost-effective: antiaircraft guns expended more resources in shooting down a bomber than it took the British to build it.

By the summer of 1943, no less than eighty-nine flak batteries defended Berlin. From 791 batteries (88s, 105s, and 128s) defending the Reich in 1940, Germany's antiaircraft forces grew to 967 batteries in 1941, 1,148 in 1942, and 2,132 in 1943. All of these batteries used up ammunition in prodigious quantities and to little effect. For example, the 88mm flak 36 weapon required the expenditure of more than 16,000 shells to bring down a single aircraft, even when the enemy bombers attacked in a concentrated stream.

But intense pressure from Joseph Goebbels, the minister for propaganda, and the *Gauleiters*, Nazi Germany's political bosses, kept the emphasis on flak to meet the British bombing offensive. Obviously, the presence of somewhere around 10,000 antiaircraft guns, all of which were also highly capable as antitank weapons, and the half-million men to operate them would have had a significant impact on any of the battles in 1943 and 1944, whether one talks about Kursk, Salerno, or Normandy.

The second indirect impact of area bombing was in its influence on Nazi leaders who were making crucial choices about weapons production. To the end of the war, ironically, the Nazis remained firmly tied to the notion of air strategy that Giulio Douhet, the Italian air theorist, had articulated in the 1920s. As Douhet had argued, offense was the key, and except in the case of antiaircraft guns, the Nazis did not rely on defensive measures to try to ward off Allied air attacks.

Instead, the Nazis struck back with terror attacks of their own. Hitler set the tone. In the aftermath of Harris's 1,000-bomber raid on Cologne in May 1942, the führer warned that the only reply to such attacks was retaliation in kind. A year later, shortly after the Hamburg firestorm, he suggested that "terror can only be broken with terror. Attacks on German airfields made no impression on him [Hitler], but the smashing of the Reich's cities was another matter. It was the same with the enemy. . . . The German people demanded reprisals." In November 1943, believing that the V-1 and V-2 were close to operational use, Hitler proclaimed that "our hour of revenge is nigh! . . . Even if for the present we cannot reach America, thank God at least one country is close enough to tackle."

A number of senior Nazis, particularly Göring, echoed Hitler's comments. In October 1943, *Der Diche* ("the fat one," as most of the Luftwaffe's flying crews referred to their commander in chief, with less than admiration) announced that the German people did not care a whit whether the Luftwaffe attacked British airfields. "All they [the German people] wished to hear when a hospital or children's home in Germany is destroyed is that we have destroyed the same in England; then they [are] satisfied." One month later, during a conversation with Fritz Sauckel, slave-labor procurer for the Third Reich, Göring emphasized that the Luftwaffe needed bombers as well as fighters to meet the Allied air offensive. "I cannot remain on the defensive," he snorted; "we must also have an offensive [capability]. That is most decisive." Sauckel immediately agreed: "The only argument that makes an impression on a racial cousin [the British] is that of retaliation."

Such attitudes reinforced the emphasis on bomber and fighter-bomber production into the early months of 1944. Despite desperate warnings from senior Luftwaffe officers, Hitler and Göring refused to restructure the German aircraft industry in 1942 or 1943 to provide the level of fighter production necessary to meet the threat. Their decision rested on the belief that Germany had to reply to Allied strategic bombing in kind—with bombing attacks on British cities, attacks that continued sporadically from the "Baby Blitz" of 1942 into the winter of 1944. When the Luftwaffe's chief of production and logistics, Field Marshal Erhard Milch, urged Hitler in 1943 to accept a production program of 5,000 fighters per month for 1944, he received a contemptuous no for an answer.

Meanwhile, senior Nazi leaders pushed Germany's industry toward the development of rocket and jet technologies, almost exclusively for offensive purposes. In 1943 the Luftwaffe and the army rushed into production two separate weapons whose nomenclature—V stands for revenge weapon—underlines their purpose. A pulse jet engine powered the Luftwaffe's weapon, the V-1, while the army's answer, the V-2, was the world's first true ballistic missile. The latter weapon excited enormous interest on the part of the German leadership. Speer in particular waxed enthusiastic over the potential of the new weapon to strike at Britain. Having seen a test firing of the A-4 (the preproduction name for the V-2), he told a crowd of receptive Ruhr workers that "German mills of retribution may often seem to grind too slowly, but do grind very fine. . . ."

But the V-2, for all of its impressive technological accomplishments, represented a weapon that possessed little military capability. Like artillery shells (the army's artillery branch developed the V-2), it operated on the principle that what goes up must eventually come down. However, no one was sure where it would land. The circular area of probability seems to have been an area not much smaller than all of southern England.

The V-2 also represented a weapon that demanded considerable investments of time, scientific expertise, production resources, skilled labor, and scarce raw materials, all to produce a weapon that had a difficult time in hitting London with a conventional warhead. And unlike a bomber, which if it survived could bomb again, the V-2 flew on a one-way trip. Developmental demands for the V-2 soaked up much of the limited capacity that German industry possessed in the electronics and instrument spheres. By 1944, work on the V-2 was having a serious impact on research and development for Germany's radar programs and for production of the electronic components required by night fighters and ground-based radars.

As if this situation was not serious enough, the V-1 and V-2 programs seriously affected production levels of fighter aircraft. Yet it took only a film clip from a single V-2 test firing to persuade Hitler to approve plans to put the rocket into high-quantity production. On July 7, 1943, he decreed that V-2 production was to receive the highest priority of any weapons system. The U.S. Strategic Bombing Survey suggests that the industrial effort and resources expended on the V-2 were enough to have produced 24,000 fighters. A more recent study of the V-2 program has suggested that the Germans expended the equivalent in resources of one-third of what the Americans expended on the Manhattan Project. The payoff for the Germans was, however, minuscule in comparison to the atomic bomb. The V-2s achieved a paltry level of damage in strikes on London and Antwerp, and because it was impossible to defend against their descent, the British never bothered to divert military assets.

The impact of American precision bombing is easier to estimate. Since the Eighth and Fifteenth air forces were aiming at particular target sets—specific groups of targets that supported production in a single industry—it is possible to demonstrate their success or failure with some accuracy.

In 1943 the Americans targeted the German aircraft and ball-bearing industries. Given the resistance that the Luftwaffe mounted the former was an obvious choice. American planners also selected ball bearings because the industry possessed a limited number of production facilities concentrated in a few areas, and ball bearings were essential to the production of virtually every weapons system. In the first case, the Americans hoped to destroy the Luftwaffe's industrial structure. They were not fully successful, but they did substantially reduce production of new fighter aircraft. In July 1943, monthly German fighter production reached a high for the year, 1,263; thereafter, there was a steady decline that reflected the sustained pressure of U.S. bombing. By December, German production of new fighters was down to 687 for the month.

In the second case, however, the two great and costly raids on Schweinfurt, the center of the ball-bearing industry, had less impact. There were a number of reasons for this. First, the bombs the Americans used did less damage than planners had expected. Second, the Germans had higher inventories of ball bearings throughout their industrial structure than even they had calculated. In addition, they discovered that some factories could substitute roller bearings for many of the ball bearings used in weapons production. Finally, the neutral Swedes and Swiss were delighted to step in and sell large amounts of ball bearings to the Germans for hard cash.

In 1944 the Americans again selected several discrete target sets. This time, with better intelligence, luck, and greater resources, they achieved significant results. As suggested above, attacks on the aircraft industry did not prevent the Germans from increasing the numbers of fighters produced in 1944. But American bombing attacks placed considerable limitations on how much the Germans could increase fighter production and resulted in a considerable drop in the quality of that production. But the crucial contribution was that these attacks on the Luftwaffe's production facilities from February to May 1944 forced the Luftwaffe to come up to fight, and in the end the American escort fighters accompanying the bomber formations broke the German fighter force. By the end of May, the Luftwaffe had only a few extraordinarily skilled fighter pilots, while the great majority—well over 90 percent—could barely take off or land their aircraft. Whereas the Americans lost nearly a quarter of their bombers every month through May 1944, from that point on losses dropped significantly. Few of the 177,000 Allied troops who came ashore on June 6, 1944, would see a German aircraft. The situation would not change for the remainder of the Normandy campaign.

In May, Eighth Air Force began attacking Germany's synthetic-oil production centers. Along with the attacks that Fifteenth Air Force was making on the oil industry in Romania, the U.S. strategic bombing threatened the Wehrmacht's entire basis of mobile warfare. Immediately after the first American attacks on May 12, Speer cautioned Hitler that "the enemy has struck us at one of our weakest points. If they persist at it this time, we will soon no longer have any fuel production worth mentioning. Our one hope is that the other side has an air general staff as scatterbrained as ours!"

However, the American emphasis remained on oil, as Speer feared. That focus largely resulted from Ultra intelligence available to senior American commanders. On June 5, just hours before the D-Day landings, an Ultra message revealed the following:

> Following according to OKL [Oberkommando der Luftwaffe, the air force high command] on fifth [of June]. As a result of renewed interference with the production of aircraft fuel by Allied [bombing] action, most essential requirements for training and carrying out production plans can scarcely be covered by quantities of aircraft fuel available. [Normal] allocations only possible to officer for bombers, fighters, and ground attack. . . . No other quota holders can be considered in June. To assume defense of Reich and to prevent gradual collapse of readiness for German air force in the east, it has been necessary to break into OKW [Oberkommando der Wehrmacht, the German high command] reserves [of fuel].

By mid-June, systematic attacks were having a devastating impact: American raids had knocked out 90 percent of aviation-fuel production. By mid-July, desperate efforts by the Germans quadrupled that production, but to a rate that still was 50 percent under normal levels. And when Ultra alerted Eighth Air Force's commanders about German efforts to rebuild, a new series of raids lowered production back to 2 percent of normal aviation-fuel output.

For the Germans, the situation regarding other petroleum derivatives was not so desperate; nevertheless, it hardly allowed for optimism. By July, American attacks had reduced the synthetic-oil complex at Leuna to 70 percent of normal production, while other major facilities dropped to between 43 and 58 percent of normal production. By October the Germans not only had lost their access to Romanian oil, because the Soviets had captured the fields, but were producing only 43 percent of their normal total production of synthetic fuel.

Fuel shortages severely impeded the Luftwaffe's air operations and forced it to reduce the number of flying hours in training schools, thus making new pilots even less capable of defending themselves. The impact of such shortages on ground operations was also dramatic. The Battle of the Bulge saw Hitler launch his panzer forces into the Ardennes with only enough fuel to get halfway to their objectives, hardly an enviable logistical situation. Elsewhere, the impact of fuel shortages prevented the Germans from conducting a mobile defense. On the Eastern Front, the Germans possessed 1,800 tanks to defend Silesia in January 1945, but a lack of fuel virtually immobilized them. With the panzers incapable of movement, Soviet forces overran Silesia in less than a week.

But the greatest contribution of strategic bombing to the Allied war effort came in preventing a last battle on the ruins of Germany's cities. Whatever the impact of attacks on the Reich's petroleum industry, we must not believe that the oil campaign exercised the only impact on the last year of the war. With the exception of August 1944 on the Western Front and July–September on the Eastern Front, the Germans were able to wage a tenacious defense that held their opponents to relatively small gains and blocked any breakthroughs.

As the Western Front settled down to stalemate in late 1944, Allied air forces launched a massive aerial assault on the transportation network within Germany. Advocates of this transportation campaign were Eisenhower's chief deputy, Tedder, and his chief scientist, Solly Zuckerman. The two argued that a campaign against this network similar to that in Normandy would have more than just direct military consequences; it would result in the collapse of the German war economy.

However, control of the strategic bombers had returned from Eisenhower and Tedder to Eighth Air Force and Bomber Command in early September 1944. Spaatz and the American commanders now wanted to put their whole emphasis on Germany's faltering petroleum industry. Not surprisingly, Harris, with his devotion to attacking German morale, wanted to place his command's focus on attacking German cities.

In the end, Tedder, Spaatz, and Harris patched together a compromise. When the weather was not suitable for attacking petroleum facilities, Eighth Air Force would strike transportation targets. Similarly, Bomber Command would select as its aiming points such transportation targets as marshaling yards and the great railroad stations in the heart of major German cities. In addition, Tedder received support for the campaign from Allied tactical air forces, whose operating bases were now up on the German frontier.

Beginning in September, Allied air attacks fell with increasing severity on the structures of the German transportation network. Air planners divided the Reich into nine specific districts, five of which lay west of Kassel along the western frontier. The aim was to break the transportation system along these axes so that raw materials, finished goods, and parts could not move. The offensive hoped to block not only the Reichsbahn (the German railroad system) but also the canal and waterway systems.

The attacks had an immediate impact: loading of railroad cars in the Reich plummeted. For the week ending August 19, the Reichsbahn loaded and dispatched 899,091 carloads of material; by October 28 the figure for the preceding week had fallen to 703,580 cars; and by December 23 that number had fallen to 547,309, despite heavy demands from the Ardennes fighting. As early as October, Ultra indicated that "the Reich Minister for Equipment and War production reported that on account of the destruction of traffic installations and lack of power, from 30 to 50 percent of all works [factories] in west Germany were at a standstill." By December 1944 marshaling capacity in railyards had declined to 40 percent of normal; by February it had dropped to 20 percent. In effect, the U.S. Strategic Bombing Survey reported, the attacks on transportation "reduced the available capacity for economic traffic in Germany [to a level] which could not hope to sustain, over any period of time a high level of military production."

The breakdown of transportation meant that coal did not reach power stations, coke and iron-ore foundries, factories for tank turrets and engines, or plants for aircraft engines and aluminum subsections. Under such conditions, neither planning nor production could take place in an orderly fashion. The collapse of coal transportation suggests the extent of the damage. In January 1944, the Essen division of the Reichsbahn loaded an average of 21,400 cars daily. By September that average had dropped to 12,000, of which only about 3,000 were long-haul shipments. By February, Allied air attacks had cut the Ruhr off from the rest of Germany.

The Reichsbahn often had to confiscate what little coal was loaded and shipped just to keep its locomotives running.

Underlining the impact of transportation attacks was the state of coal production and stocks in the Ruhr between August 1944 and February 1945. Despite a dramatic decrease in coal production, stocks in the Ruhr collieries rose from 45,000 tons to 2,217,000 tons. Though the Ruhr was awash with its coal production, the transportation system could no longer move it to the industrial centers of the Reich.

The evidence thus points to a general destruction of the German war economy by midwinter 1945. Since the stoppage was not sudden and complete, it was difficult for even those conducting the bombing campaign to discern its full impact. In July and August 1944, German forces on both fronts had collapsed after suffering massive losses in equipment. Nevertheless, because armament production, outside of aircraft factories, remained largely untouched, the German army was able to reequip both surviving troops and new men (mostly boys) with excellent equipment. On the borders of the Reich, the Germans made a stand that brought the onrush of Allied forces to a halt and then even managed to launch an offensive into the Ardennes.

The resulting Battle of the Bulge, however, represented Germany's last shot. Beginning in the East in January 1945, followed within a month and a half in the West, the German armies gave way. Neither on the Rhine nor on the Oder were they able to pull themselves together for a last stand on the ruins of the Reich. There was no last-ditch *Götterdämmerung*. The cause of this collapse lay in the fact that the transportation campaign by Allied bombers had successfully shut down the German war economy; what little the economy produced could no longer move to the front. Without weapons and ammunition, even blind fanaticism could not maintain the struggle.

How, then, is one to judge the effectiveness of the Allied strategic-bombing campaign in achieving the defeat of Nazi Germany? It is impossible to separate the individual contributions of British and American bomber forces into distinct contributions. In the end, they achieved synergistic effects: the sum of their efforts was greater than the parts. Together, there is no doubt that strategic bombing played a crucial role in Nazi Germany's defeat. Victory over Germany was simply inconceivable without the Combined Bomber Offensive, just as it required the success of Allied navies in the Battle of the Atlantic, the Red Army on the Eastern Front, and the Allied ground forces in the Mediterranean theater and the great invasion of western Europe in spring 1944.

Much of the problem in evaluating the contribution of strategic bombing to Allied victory is that by claiming so much for air power before the war, and afterward as well, airmen created perceptions that historical evidence indicates are false. Perhaps the best way to address the question is to ask what alternatives existed for the Anglo-American powers. The answer is nothing. A greater emphasis on ground forces would not have made possible an earlier landing on the coast of France. And without total Allied superiority, which only the massive assault of the bombing offensive could give, such an invasion might have faced the same ignominious fate that the Dieppe landings suffered in August 1942.

Moreover, the capabilities developed by the earlier strategic bombing of Germany made possible the later transportation campaigns that in the first case wrecked the Wehrmacht's logistical support in France and in the second brought the German war economy to a grinding halt. One must also not forget that without strategic-bombing attacks in 1942 and 1943, the Germans would have had manpower and other resources available for use in North Africa and the Soviet Union that they instead devoted to the antiaircraft defenses of the Reich.

As for its impact on German war production, the evidence in the U.S. Strategic Bombing Survey suggests that it was considerable. What is hard to judge is how much better the Germans might have done with their war production had there been no bombing. It is well to remember that they could draw on the entire economy of continental Europe, with both its economic base and its industrial production. Certainly they could have rationalized production to a much greater degree than they did: instead of dispersing production, they could have concentrated it and used the same mass-production techniques that American industry was using to such effect.

The cost of the Combined Bombing Offensive was high indeed. In many ways the attrition that took place mirrored the terrible casualties of the Western Front in World War I. But now those charged with attacking Germany's population and economic structure measured progress by changes in the percentage of bombers lost per hundred sorties and in the number of tons of bombs dropped, rather than by the number of yards gained and artillery shells fired. The disastrous losses suffered by the two great raids in 1943 on the ball-bearing works in Schweinfurt and on Nuremburg in early 1944 have conditioned our historical memoirs. With hindsight, we can argue that airmen waged the Combined Bomber Offensive in an unimaginative fashion, that air forces often failed to adapt to changing tactical and technological conditions, and that the offensive often minimized rather than maximized the contributions that air power might have made. But could we not make these sorts of criticisms about military leadership in all wars?

What is certain is that strategic bombing was the only means with which the Western powers could strike at Germany in the dark early years of the war. And if such attacks did not achieve decisive results, the fact that they at least hit the Germans had a considerable impact on Allied morale. More important, the bombing offensive was crucial in military and operational terms in the winning of the war from 1943 on. An exact quantifiable measurement is impossible, but even the most cursory examination of the alternatives suggests the extent of the contribution.

Reading 8

The Logistical Bottleneck in Northwest Europe

by William Whipple

Introduction. Col. William Whipple, the chief logistical planner at SHAEF in World War II, provides an excellent overview of the planning and execution of logistical support for the Allied campaign in Northwest Europe after D-Day, with particular emphasis on the critical period from September through November 1944.

Much interest attaches to certain major decisions and conditions in Europe in the fall of 1944, particularly the lack of support for further operations of General Patton's victorious Third Army. There was considerable acrimonious debate at the time and argument still goes on.[1] The actual limiting conditions were of a somewhat technical nature and are still not generally understood.

The fact is that in September 1944 British 21st Army Group, U.S. Third Army, U.S. First Army, U.S. Seventh Army, and French First Army, too, all thought their operations were inadequately supported, particularly as regards supply. Both 21st Army Group and Third Army felt strongly that if they received full priority in use of available resources, they could end the war in a very short time.

At the time, and later on, the highly exasperating situation in which we could not continue our full pursuit of the shaken German Army has been variously blamed on Communications Zone, on

SHAEF, on "high level politics," on undue favoritism to the British, on the excessive strain on transport caused by Third Army's advanced position (a British view), on shortage of gasoline, on alleged preoccupation of service troops with black market activities and luxurious living, and still other more or less plausible causes. Certainly it was not to be expected that the reactions of victorious combat commanders, held up for lack of supplies, would be calm and objective. Indeed, apprehension of their healthy and uninhabited reactions was a strong incentive to responsible administrative staffs.

There were strong differences of opinion at the time among responsible staff officers regarding certain problems. There is plenty of ground for discussion as to how certain difficulties could have been avoided. It is true, however, that some of the later criticism has been based on ideas that were fully stated and fully considered by the proper staffs and then rejected, sometimes long in advance of the event. And not arbitrarily rejected, but simply through actual necessity proven by the basic arithmetic of logistics. The very serious operational consequences that these logistical difficulties brought about makes it important to understand just what the problem was and how it arose.

During the first three months after the Normandy landings extensive operations had been conducted without serious logistical troubles by virtue of effective and detailed advance planning over the preceding eighteen months. Again, after December 1944, all serious difficulties were overcome. But during the critical period of September–November 1944, all strategical or tactical decisions of importance were governed by the precarious situation of transport and supply. This article outlines some of the most awkward and inflexible of the difficulties and their effect upon the strategy of the campaign, as seen by the Allied Planning Staff.

Organization of the Allied Expeditionary Force

Both Allied and U.S. organization of the Allied Expeditionary Force was unorthodox during the initial phases, the OVERLORD period. The Ground, Air, and Naval Commanders in Chief had wide authority delegated to them. They functioned jointly and directly under the Supreme Commander, whose staff was not at the time operational, but was acting primarily in a planning capacity. The seizure of the lodgment area under the joint Commanders in Chief, which ended the OVERLORD period, was effected late in

August, and SHAEF then became operational. This new organizational stage was reached at a moment when the Allied forces were engaged in headlong pursuit.

After the formal inclusion of forces from the Mediterranean in mid-September, the whole force consisted of three U.S. armies and one French army, grouped under two U.S. army groups; one British and one Canadian army plus British line of communications troops, under a British army group; two U.S. communications zones; three tactical and two strategic air forces; and naval forces. The two U.S. communications zones, in accordance with orthodox U.S. doctrine, were responsible to the theater commander rather than to army group. This was necessary since the two communications zones were later to be combined.

As to major logistical questions, the U.S. elements of the SHAEF staff were responsible for theater-level coordination of communications zone operation and army group requirements. SHAEF also exercised a more general control on an Allied basis over British as well as U.S. forces.

Strategic Planning for Post-OVERLORD Operations

The SHAEF staff was not responsible for the original OVERLORD plans, except insofar as certain members of that staff had been members of earlier planning groups. Operations under these plans were mainly the responsibility of the three Commanders in Chief, acting jointly. The lodgment area, the objective of the OVERLORD operations, was considered achieved when our forces reached the line of the Seine River; and the SHAEF Planning Staff had devoted much thought before D-Day to operations after the OVERLORD phase for which SHAEF would be responsible.

The initiation and coordination of SHAEF strategical planning were effected through the Planning Staff. All Planning Staff papers and actions required anticipation by Operations, Air, Naval, and Logistical Head Planners, and usually Intelligence. Each Head Planner was responsible for straightening out and adjusting any conflicting national points of view, as well as for technically sound contributions to the plan, so that the finished paper could be cleared by higher staff officers and given final approval. If any one of the participants in a Planning Staff meeting objected to the action taken, he would present his objections through his own channels after the meeting and attempt to obtain his point at a higher level, but this, it should be recorded, was not often necessary. On the more complex problems, the Planning Staff always called for assistance of staff specialists. Initially, the Planning Staff handled mainly long-range planning rather than day-to-day matters, though later in the campaign it did consider many problems of immediate concern.

It was believed that the capture of either the Ruhr or Berlin would insure a German surrender, but that occupation of lesser objectives such as the Saar, or the cities of South Germany, would not necessarily do so. To reach the main objective, it was planned to move generally up the coast, which would have the further advantage of obtaining the great ports of the Low Countries as bases. In particular, the entire Ruhr lies within about 150 miles of the port of Antwerp, which has very extensive port facilities.

There were, of course, other considerations, including the desirability (not much talked about) of overrunning the V-weapon launching sites which had not yet been employed. It was evident also that there were unspoken political considerations on the part of the British planners, though the early liberation of the Low Countries was certainly not unwelcome to U.S. policy. Operations extending on both sides of the Ardennes were considered necessary in order to allow space for the large Allied forces to deploy and maneuver. After much study of operational, intelligence, and logistical aspects, the Planning Staff worked out approximate anticipated timing and approximate phase lines. These original basic plans, upon approval, formed the groundwork for all detail planning, including communications zone supply plans, for operations after the crossing of the Seine. They were eventually followed quite closely.

There were two major divergences from the progress anticipated. In August and early September the Allied Forces advanced much faster than had been expected. And German resistance in the final stages, after the capture of the Ruhr and Silesia, was more stubborn and prolonged than anyone had anticipated. Otherwise, the forecast of operations was generally accurate. There was one other significant divergence. Although ports were in general overrun earlier than anticipated, a number of the most important resisted capture for much longer than was expected.

Pre-D-Day Logistical Planning

The term Logistical Planning, as used in the ETO, covered mainly the broad aspects of supply and movement planning, and their coordination with tactical and strategical plans. The most urgent long-range objectives of such planning when initiated in SHAEF were three: (1) to determine the maximum number of divisions and supporting troops that could be moved to the Continent and maintained in combat; (2) to determine the tonnage of supplies required for their support; and (3) to verify that port and beach capacity would equal the tonnage of supplies to be landed. Obviously these results had to balance. The next problem was to determine how fast and far our forces could advance if, as actually happened, we made a break-through.

These logistical plans were made by an Allied staff, but were based on keeping U.S. and British lines of communication separate as far as practicable. Different factors were used for U.S. and British potentialities where experience so indicated this to be

Table 1: Planned Build-Up of U.S. Divisions

Date	Planned No. Divisions on Continent (excluding airborne)	Divisions Arriving Preceding Month	Routing of Divisions
1 Sep.	21	3	All staged in U.K.
1 Oct.	27	6	Two staged in U.K.
			Four direct from U.S. to Continent.
1 Nov.	34	7	One staged in U.K.
			Five direct from U.S. to Continent.
1 Dec	39	5	All direct from U.S.

1. This table refers to divisions to be brought in and supplied through Western French and Belgian ports only, and is exclusive of Sixth Army Group.

2. Divisions direct from U.S. in September–October were later scheduled for an increase, but this could not be effected.

3. Build-up shown in this table was a revision from the "OVERLORD" Plan which allowed for "two to four" divisions a month.

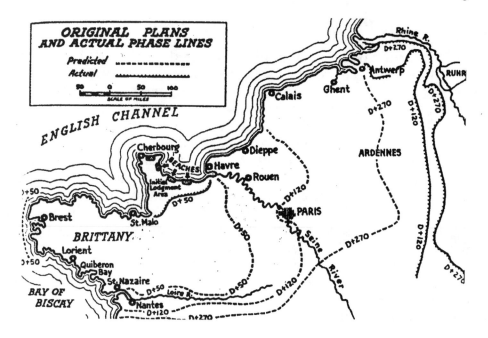

better. The plans considered only the landings in western France at this time, for the Anvil forces from the Mediterranean were to have entirely separate lines of communication, and stayed under the Mediterranean Theater until much later on.

Some results of this planning, as it concerned U.S. forces, are summarized in Table 1 which gives the planned U.S. build-up in divisions (each accompanied by 25,000 supporting and service troops), and Table 2, which shows the estimated U.S. tonnage requirements (exclusive of bulk p.o.l.) and the port capacity.

The estimated build-up and tonnage requirements proved quite accurate. With particular regard to build-up, an attempt was later made to speed up the planned arrivals of divisions from the U.S. in September and October. But the administrative difficulties proved so great that additional divisions had to be diverted, some to the Mediterranean and some, temporarily, to the United Kingdom. The result of this was that the effective build-up was practically as it had been originally planned. As regards tonnages the original planned figures in Table 2 still represent a fairly good statement of the actual requirements. It is true that the actual tonnages shipped from the U.S. and U.K. considerably exceeded these figures. But, as will be discussed in detail later, the tonnages landed at the ports during the critical months were much less.

The plan of port development outlined in Table 2 was the result of close figuring. Nominally, it indicated 5,000 tons of spare port

Table 2: Planned Tonnage Requirement and U.S. Port Capacity

Port	Capture Date		Est. Capacity at Aug. 6	Notes
	Estimated	*Actual*		
Beaches	D-Day	D	14,000	Good until end of September
Cherbourg	D plus 8	D plus 21	7,000	Reliable capacity to be increased to 10,000.
Minor Normandy Ports	D to D plus 17	D to D plus 57	4,400	Decreased at end of September.
St. Malo	D plus 25	D plus 73	2,500	
Brest	D plus 50	D plus 103	3,200	Potentially greater but inaccessible to rail.
Lorient	D plus 50	....	800	
Quiberon	D plus 40	....	4,000	New development. To be increased to 10,000.
Loire Ports			0	Latest intelligence indicated not worth developing.
Seine Ports	D plus 120	D plus 96	0	Anticipate capture about 1 October
Total estimated port capacity			6 Aug.	35,900
Estimated tonnage requirements:			6 Aug.	30,700
			1 Sept.	37,600
			1 Oct.	38,600
			1 Nov.	51,239

capacity at D plus 60, but this only if all ports were captured on schedule and were repaired on schedule. The estimate that an average of 14,000 tons a day could be put ashore on the bare flat beaches of Normandy, exposed to the Atlantic swell, was only a theoretical forecast, since no such large-scale operation of the kind had ever been conducted. Moreover, it was known definitely that open beach operation would have to cease entirely some time in October because of seasonal storms, although the artificial harbor could continue to function. This bad weather would also affect minor ports to a lesser degree. Cherbourg capacity, it was expected, would increase moderately; but it was not expected that the Seine ports would be captured in time to make up for the lost beach capacity, let alone to provide the 20,000-ton daily additional capacity needed by November 1.

To meet the indicated deficiency in the later months, use was planned of the only available expedients. Brest was a good port, but it was expected that it would have its rail communications broken by the demolition of the long rail viaduct at Morlaix, which would be impracticable to repair. Therefore, it could not be counted on as a supply port. However, it was safe to plan its use as a reception and staging area for troops arriving from the U.S. in September and later months. This appeared to be an ideal solution. The arrival each month of five divisions and other troops totaling 200,000 men, the unboxing and assembling of thousands of vehicles, the issuing of all equipment and supplies, and supply and administration while staging, would require a large area and several thousand tons a day of port capacity. The staged units, when ready, could move out on their own vehicles. The anticipated date of capture of Brest was late in July, which would allow time for necessary preparations.

Quiberon Bay was the other unorthodox potential development. This was a large natural harbor with good rail connections, but one not normally used as a port except by fishing vessels. Its development to handle up to 10,000 tons per day was planned by Communications Zone, approved by SHAEF and accepted by the U.S. War Department, and all necessary equipment was obtained. Piling and other heavy equipment was to be rafted around the Brittany Peninsula during the good summer weather, as soon as Brest and the German submarine base at Lorient were cleared. This plan would have been much simpler and easier to accomplish than the construction of the artificial harbors on the Normandy beaches and it would undoubtedly have been successful.

But the stubborn German defense of Brest and Lorient not only made it impossible to use Quiberon Bay; it denied us the port of Brest itself.

Thus, about the end of August, with our forces driving East across France at full speed, and the British about to start their rush to the North across the Seine, we were faced with the loss of these two projects—with the loss of about 14,000 tons per day of planned capacity needed to replace the supply movements across beaches, which would soon be stopped by the autumn storms. Moreover, the U.S. artificial harbor had been destroyed by a severe storm in June, which did not greatly affect us at the time but meant that its capacity could not be counted on for bad weather. The only re-

Table 3: U.S. Cargo Discharge in Ports of Western France (Daily average, long tons)

	Cherbourg	Normandy Minor Ports	Brittany	LeHavre	Rouen	Beaches	Total	Original SHAEF Est.	Approx. Deficit
July 1944	1,000	1,300				17,700	20,000		0
Aug. 1944	8,500	4,000	300			17,300	30,100	30,700	4,000
Sept. 1944	10,400	3,300	2,500			13,100	29,300	37,627	9,000
Oct. 1944	11,800	1,900	2,500	2,000	900	6,300	25,400	38,600	20,000
Nov. 1944	14,000	1,600	2,100	4,800	4,100	900	27,500	51,239	20,000

maining hope of avoiding administrative strangulation lay in the prompt opening of the Seine and Belgian ports.

Table 3 shows the actual cargo discharge through U.S. ports and beaches during the period before Antwerp opened, compared to the SHAEF estimates of requirements. The indicated deficiency in port capacity was 4,000 tons per day in August, rising to 20,000 tons a day in October and November. That this was a real deficiency and not a paper one was shown in two ways. The accumulation of shipping that awaited discharge in European waters rose to 150 ships on September 1 and 240 on October 20. And second, the Armies in September and October received only about two-thirds of the supplies tonnage they required for full-scale operations, even though not all the troops were at the front. It is true that most of the initial shortages were directly due to deficiencies in the inland transportation system. But the slow unloading of rolling stock, engineer supplies, and ordnance spare parts at the ports in turn slowed down the transportation system. Lack of port capacity was a bottleneck, in the truest sense of the word. The stubborn German defense of ports in Brittany, which prevented Brest and Quiberon Bay from being developed, cost U.S. forces each day up to 14,000 long tons of supplies, which accumulated offshore in ships that could not be unloaded. Finally the War Department was forced to cancel shipping.

From August onward the opening of Antwerp was plainly the one means of meeting an already serious situation, bound to become more acute as soon as the autumn storms shut down the beaches.

Development of Strategy

It was about this time [August 1944] or shortly before when the 12th Army Group plan for a quick drive by Third Army across the Rhine was advocated and carefully investigated. Logistical and movements studies in SHAEF before D-Day had shown that our advancing forces would probably be brought to a halt by lack of transportation not far from the line of the Seine, until rail transportation could be developed. This study had been the basis for a request to Communications Zone to increase the number of truck companies in the troop basis, which was done, as far as such companies were available. It was realized by the advocates of the Twelfth Army Group plan that, in view of the difficult existing situation as regards trucks, rail, and pipe lines, a further advance by Third Army to cross the Rhine and advance to the east of it could only be made by sacrificing the mobility of other forces. Truck columns and normal air transport were already strained, but much more could obviously be done for a limited force if four things were done:

1. If the other armies were held inactive near the ports or their divisions grounded;
2. If bombers and planes of airborne troops were used for air transport of supplies;
3. If Third Army were given priority on all available supplies;
4. If the British troops were held on the Seine or shortly beyond it.

Advocates of this plan maintained—and this was admitted in G-4 SHAEF—that by these emergency measures Third Army, with not more than ten or twelve divisions, could probably be supported in such an advance across the Rhine, possibly as far as Frankfurt. At the time there appeared to be no German forces that could prevent the advance.

It was further maintained by Twelfth Army Group planners, and this was the crux of the matter, that once the Third Army crossed the Rhine, the Germans would immediately surrender. In view of the ferocious last ditch defense the Germans made the following spring, it hardly seems probable that they would actually have surrendered, but it might possibly have happened. The attempt on Hitler's life had had very disturbing effects on the Reich government and on Hitler personally, and certain members of the German Army were involved. But early surrender did not appear at all probable at the time, and in any event there was no certainty as to what was going on in Germany.

There was nothing in such an advance across the Rhine to materially impair the strength of the Germans or force them to surrender. Frankfurt was the extreme limit of any advance logistically possible to a considerable body of troops, and Frankfurt is not even the principal city of southern Germany. The part of Germany the advance would occupy did not include much of either the governmental, military, or economic potential of Germany. Ten or twelve divisions seems a lot of troops in peacetime America. But they were only one of six Allied armies at the time and a very small force compared to the still existing German army. The advance would leave a northern flank 150 miles long through German territory, out of which German forces could move at any time to cut the Third Army's line of communications. The Allied Air Forces would have great difficulty in establishing adequate fighter cover so far forward, for time and supplies are needed to build up bases.

However, the most serious and certain consequence of undertaking such an operation, if the Germans did not surrender, would be the abandonment of operations to capture and open the port of Antwerp. Table 3 shows that without Antwerp U.S. forces would be short 20,000 tons a day of supplies, and this expected shortage was clearly evident in late August. The British had on their landing beach the Mulberry "B" artificial port, which together with Dieppe and some very minor ports might have been barely adequate for their winter needs. Without Antwerp, however, the U.S. forces could not receive, equip, and employ in operations the new divisions coming over every month. They would be forced by lack of supply to a static defense with reduced forces, and this on an extended front. There was no possibility whatever, in the minds of the staff, that Allied logistical resources, without Antwerp, could become sufficient to extend the proposed Third Army operations beyond Frankfurt to the Ruhr, or to Berlin, or even to Munich. The only chance of success lay in psychology. Such an advance might have frightened the Germans into surrendering at once. But if it did not work out that way, the operation would have brought the Allied forces to the brink of administrative disaster

The above is a summary of informal staff reaction at the time; the matter was never brought before the Planning Staff as such. General Eisenhower did not authorize the proposed Third Army drive farther to the east, but instead gave priority to 21st Army Group's two Armies and to First Army to continue their drive north, in order to clear the Channel ports and the V-weapon launching sites, and to open Antwerp. Third Army, deprived of supplies enough for an offensive, was held in place, while Sixth Army Group, with an independent line of supply, but equally low priority, came up on the flank.

Twelfth Army Group was not the only army group that believed Germany could be quickly defeated that fall. Field Marshal Montgomery, commanding 21st Army Group, has recorded that over the period August 23 to September 12, he discussed at length with General Eisenhower the plan of campaign, and attempted unsuccessfully to obtain approval of a plan to immediately concentrate all resources of U.S. and British alike for a single drive north of the Ruhr. This plan involved holding other portions of the line static and forcing a crossing of the Rhine before opening Antwerp. The 21st Army Group was allowed to stage a large airborne operation (Arnhem-Nijmegen), to attempt to seize a bridgehead across the Rhine before German resistance could form, but this was only a limited objective operation. The policy of opening Antwerp before attempting major operations east of the Rhine was maintained. Logistically, any other course seemed likely to gamble away our assurance of ultimate victory for a possible time advantage.

Logistical Stringency

The great drives of early September 1944, which furnished so many fine headlines, brought hectic days and sleepless nights to the Communications Zone staff, haunted by thought of the lengthening lines of communications and inadequate port capacity. On September 7, Third Army reached the Moselle in the Nancy-Metz area. On September 4, 21st Army Group, driving fast from the Seine, liberated the town of Antwerp; but the sea approaches up the Scheldt remained in German hands. British Second Army drove on to attempt their Rhine crossing at Nijmegen and Arnhem on September 17, with the aid of three airborne divisions. On September 13, First Army penetrated the famed Westwall in German territory. On September 11, Seventh Army, advancing up the Rhone Valley from Marseille, gained contact with Third Army and completed the Allied bunt. By October 1, lines of communication bringing supplies from Normandy and Marseille were 400 to 500 miles for U.S. front-line units and 350 to 400 for the British, as shown in Table 4. The basic loads of unit vehicles were largely

Table 4: Approximate Length of Lines of Communication October–December 1944

Army	From Normandy	From LeHavre	From Antwerp
First	500	350–400	125–150
Third	425	....	....
Ninth	500	350–400	125
Second British & First Canadian	350–400	Dieppe 200	125–150
Seventh Army & First French	450–500 miles from Marseilles		
	(Frankfurt 575 from Normandy)		

exhausted. Truck transport was stretched to the breaking point, and railroads, with bridges, yards, and shops all-too-well bombed by our air forces, were slow to repair. Stringencies in port unloading limited coal, rolling stock, and engineer supplies needed to extend rail communications, since immediate urgencies were reflected in priorities for food, ammunition, and p.o.l.

Favorable Circumstances

There was one major favorable circumstance, without which the situation would have been considerably worse. The great French coal fields of the Valenciennes area, largely demolished by the retreating Germans in World War I, were this time almost untouched. Coal still had to be imported from England but not so much as had been feared. It is not generally realized that the liberation of a great city as well as the operation of a railroad line requires coal. Paris, for example, without any space heating, requires some 7,000 tons of coal per day to keep the subway and necessary utilities going on a minimum scale. This coal had to be supplied or all sorts of consequences would have resulted inimical to our operations. If coal had not come from the Valenciennes fields, much more would have had to be imported, and other supplies would have had to be further cut down. It is not too much to say that the overrunning of the Valenciennes coal fields intact was by November equal to another major port, though there were few people who realized that fact.

Considering "might-have-beens," I often wondered at the time at the blindness of the Germans in wasting their V-weapons on London. London is so vast in extent, and the preparations for invasion were so decentralized, that no physical interruption of the invasion could result. Psychologically, also, it was a complete waste of effort. The British, about to realize their great hopes for an invasion of the Continent to make up for Dunquerque, were in no mood for defeatism. The cockney women reflected the national lack of excitement at Hitler's new mode of warfare by denying the new missiles a name—they were referred to, with stolid, contemptuous resentment, as "them."

The story might have been different if the V-weapons had been concentrated on the major English ports and staging areas where the enormously complicated business of mounting the greatest amphibious operation in history was in process. Movements specialists, considering this possibility before D-Day, could give no assurance that the operation would not be thrown out of balance and seriously hampered. The necessarily elaborate planning and the resulting rigidity in supply and shipping schedules, and the lack of administrative machinery at that time on the far shore, meant that it would have been very difficult to evaluate and replace any shortages resulting from bombing losses. Another serious possibility was that the V-weapons might be turned on the initial lodgment area, before the breakthrough, particularly on the beaches and dumps. Use of these new weapons against sensitive points in the logistical machinery might have been, militarily, much more effective than the blind and savage attacks on London, as it would have left our supply and transport system partially crippled and our build-up retarded.

The port of Le Havre proved to be badly damaged, even worse than had been expected after what was found at Cherbourg and elsewhere. The Germans, in general, devoted true Teutonic stubbornness and thoroughness to defense and demolition of ports, with far-reaching impact upon our operations. At this juncture, with rehabilitation of ports slow and difficult, the supply over beaches was maintained a few weeks longer than most of the experts had considered likely. However, early in October a heavy autumn storm interrupted operations, and by the end of the month beaches were virtually shut down, except the portion of the British beach behind the artificial harbor.

The Communications Zone staff, which could not meet the urgent supply requirements of First and Third Armies, and (later) Ninth Army, found itself in a difficult position. Everyone knew that the European Theater had been given consistently high War Department priorities as regards procurement and shipping, and the very real difficulties of Communications Zone in port and transport operations were not readily appreciated by field commanders and combat staffs. Third Army staff was particularly hard to reconcile, as it had been left with a low supply priority. General Patton's intolerance of administrative red tape or delays had given him, by sheer process of elimination, a supply staff that had usually managed to avoid curtailing his desired operations because of logistical limitations. No one was left in doubt at the time about his annoyance at being held up.

One further reason for Communications Zone's difficulties arose around the end of August when it had failed to protest against a plan to increase the planned flow of divisions from the U.S. Until September, all divisions and other troops had staged in the U.K., and, after a month or more of processing, come over to the Continent equipped and armed, with vehicles and basic loads, ready for immediate assignment The divisions direct from the U.S. were to begin to arrive in September, and owing to the failure to take Brest in time, they had to be crowded into the supply ports. It takes about a month to stage a division for combat after a trans-Atlantic crossing. As a result of the port congestion, some of the October arrivals had to be diverted to the U.K. for a later shipment to the Continent, and others were sent to Marseille.

In general, however, many of the supply difficulties blamed on Communications Zone at the time actually stemmed from German success in denying us the Brittany ports. Communications Zone was not responsible in any sense for the delay in reducing German resistance. The Corps assigned by Third Army to this task was all even the logistical planners felt could be spared to clear up German troops left in the Brittany Peninsula, in view of the wonderful opportunities at the time for enveloping and crushing the Germans to the east. Indeed, it was only as a result of strong pressure by the logistical planners that any troops were diverted for this purpose, but the one Corps was considered adequate. It was not known, of course, how strongly the ports would be held.

There is an element of poetic justice in the fact that Third Army, whose mission it was to clear the Brittany ports, later felt so stringently the lack of supply resulting partly from the failure to accomplish that mission. It would have been a rash man however, who would have suggested this thought to Third Army at the time.

The situation would have been much brighter if Antwerp could have been opened soon after its capture on September 4. Admittedly, both flanks of the Scheldt were strongly held and Walcheren Island on the north was accessible only by water. Also the Scheldt itself was so thickly sown with mines that seventeen days of concentrated effort were required to sweep it after the approaches fell, and Antwerp could not be reached by shipping until 26 November.

However, it is still difficult to understand why its reduction took so long. It certainly was recognized in SHAEF as a prime objective, for its use would reduce the average length of lines of communication for two U.S. Armies by about 300 miles and of the British and Canadian Armies by about 200 miles. It would increase port capacity at our disposal by twenty to 25,000 tons per day almost at once. Both British and U.S. officers agreed on the necessity of obtaining Antwerp without delay and it was listed as a prime objective in every SHAEF directive and planning staff paper for months.

The operation to reduce the approaches to Antwerp was complex. To clear the island of Walcheren ultimately required heavy bombing, a naval bombardment, landing craft, and commando elements, in addition to two divisions. Three divisions had previously reduced the resistance on the southern bank of the Scheldt in a relatively simple operation. Resistance on the Scheldt approaches would probably have been much less if they had been hit at once. Unquestionably, opening of Antwerp was delayed by 21st Army Group's preoccupation with the attempt to "bounce" across the Rhine for a quick bridgehead; but it seems that, even allowing for this operation, resources were available to allow simultaneous moves to open the Scheldt. If the Canadian Army had concentrated on this operation, reinforced by American troops if need be, this might have speeded up the use of Antwerp, perhaps by a month or more, and avoided some of the supply difficulties of the late autumn of 1944. However, it was noticeable that in all operations 21st Army Group assumed much of the detail planning and supervision of operations, down to include missions to be assigned individual divisions. It may be that they were unable to plan two such complex operations at once. In American practice much more responsibility for both planning and operations is delegated to Army Commanders.

It is appropriate to note that even taking the supply difficulties of this difficult period into account the U.S. Forces in Europe in 1944–45 were, on the balance, unquestionably by far the best supplied, equipped, and serviced major force which any country has ever maintained in any war. Even the forces of 21st Army Group were not so well provided for. British troops gladly ate American food but U.S. troops would only eat British rations with many complaints. Our artillery support was always greater than the enemy's, and our Engineer and Medical service were unquestionably outstanding by any standards. Twenty-first Army Group, for example, had to depend on U.S. Engineers for major bridges across the Rhine. There can be no question that our military vehicles were outstanding; particularly, the jeep and 2-1/2-ton truck. During the most stringent period, the U.S. truck companies with fifty-six 2-1/2-ton trucks actually outperformed in long hauls British truck companies with 120 3-ton trucks. This superiority was partly due, at least, to the vision of U.S. Transportation Corps in the theater, which had insisted on obtaining two drivers per truck. War is not an exact science; and the hardships of war are always very great and bear unequally on individuals, even under the most favorable conditions. However, in terms of other campaigns and standards of all countries our troops were on the whole well serviced.

Coalition Aspects

The four U.S. Armies, the British, Canadian and French Armies, the U.S. and British Air and Naval Forces, and the U.S. Communications Zone, which ultimately composed the Allied Expeditionary Force, constituted one of the largest and certainly the most complex and formidably equipped forces ever brought under a single commander. It ultimately included ninety divisions and 11,000 fighter and bomber planes. Of coalitions in general, Clausewitz said: "Generally the auxiliary force has its own commander who depends only on his own government, and to whom it prescribes an object such as best suits the shilly-shally measures it has in view." Clausewitz's bitter comment was fortunately not applicable to the Allied Expeditionary Force, but it is certainly true that all plans and decisions had to be obtained with more consideration and diplomacy than is necessary when only one nationality is involved. Many Americans, in fact almost all, complained at times that the high command was pro-British. It was curious, however, that no one ever mentioned the possibility that a British-led high command might have been designed or might have been more acceptable. It is no secret, in fact, that any such change would have caused widespread apprehension. The reaction to the later suggestion for a British ground force commander is ample evidence of that. History shows that any allied organization for a combined effort must of necessity be less efficient and less satisfactory than a single unified national force. And in Europe, the necessity for integrating ground force efforts with air operations and naval support added further complexity. The Allied coalition operations in 1917–18 certainly developed an abundance of organizational and administrative difficulties and conflicts of national interest. In perspective, the 1942–45 coalition will appear as a highly successful force, which without achieving anything approximating theoretical perfection, was still better managed on the whole than any comparable force of the past.

Notes

1. General Patton's *War As I Saw It* and Robert Allen's *Lucky Forward,* both published in 1947, have practically established as an American tradition that General Patton could have won the war in 1944 if his superiors hadn't held him back by refusing him enough supplies.

Reading 9

The Three Stages of the Protracted War

Excerpt from *On Protracted War* by Mao Tse-Tung

Since the Sino-Japanese war is a protracted one and final victory will belong to China, it can reasonably be assumed that this protracted war will pass through three stages. The first stage covers the period of the enemy's strategic offensive and our strategic defensive. The second stage will be the period of the enemy's strategic consolidation and our preparation for the counter-offensive. The third stage will be the period of our strategic counter-offensive and the enemy's strategic retreat. It is impossible to predict the concrete situation in the three stages, but certain main trends in the war may be pointed out in the light of present conditions. The objective course of events will be exceedingly rich and varied, with many twists and turns, and nobody can cast a horoscope for the Sino-Japanese war; nevertheless it is necessary for the strategic direction of the war to make a rough sketch of its trends. Although our sketch may not be in full accord with the subsequent facts and will be amended by them, it is still necessary to make it in order to give firm and purposeful strategic direction to the protracted war.

The first stage has not yet ended. The enemy's design is to occupy Canton, Wuhan and Lanchow and link up these three points. To accomplish this aim the enemy will have to use at least fifty divisions, or about one and a half million men, spend from one and a half to two years, and expend more than ten thousand million yen. In penetrating so deeply, he will encounter immense

From *On Protracted War* by Mao Tse-Tung, Foreign Languages Press, 1967.

difficulties, with consequences disastrous beyond imagination. As for attempting to occupy the entire length of the Canton-Hankow Railway and the Sian-Lanchow Highway, he will have to fight perilous battles and even so may not fully accomplish his design. But in drawing up our operational plan we should base ourselves on the assumption that the enemy may occupy the three points and even certain additional areas, as well as link them up, and we should make dispositions for a protracted war, so that even if he does so, we shall be able to cope with him. In this stage the form of fighting we should adopt is primarily mobile warfare, supplemented by guerrilla and positional warfare. Through the subjective errors of the Kuomintang military authorities, positional warfare was assigned the primary role in the first phase of this stage, but it is nevertheless supplementary from the point of view of the stage as a whole. In this stage, China has already built up a broad united front and achieved unprecedented unity. Although the enemy has used and will continue to use base and shameless means to induce China to capitulate in the attempt to realize his plan for a quick decision and to conquer the whole country without much effort, he has failed so far, nor is he likely to succeed in the future. In this stage, in spite of considerable losses, China will make considerable progress, which will become the main basis for her continued resistance in the second stage. In the present stage the Soviet Union has already given substantial aid to China. On the enemy side, there are already signs of flagging morale, and his army's momentum of attack is less in the middle phase of this stage than it was in the initial phase, and it will diminish still further in the concluding phase. Signs of exhaustion are beginning to appear in his finances and economy; war-weariness is beginning to set in among his people and troops; and within the clique at the helm of the war, "war frustrations" are beginning to manifest themselves and pessimism about the prospects of the war is growing.

The second stage may be termed one of strategic stalemate. At the tail end of the first stage, the enemy will be forced to fix certain terminal points to his strategic offensive owing to his shortage of troops and our firm resistance, and upon reaching them he will stop his strategic offensive and enter the stage of safeguarding his occupied areas. In the second stage, the enemy will attempt to safeguard the occupied areas and to make them his own by the fraudulent method of setting up puppet governments, while plundering the Chinese people to the limit; but again he will be confronted with stubborn guerrilla warfare. Taking advantage of the fact that the enemy's rear is unguarded, our guerrilla warfare will develop extensively in the first stage, and many base areas will be established, seriously threatening the enemy's consolidation of the occupied areas, and so in the second stage there will still be widespread fighting. In this stage, our form of fighting will be primarily guerrilla warfare, supplemented by mobile warfare. China will still retain a large regular army, but she will find it difficult to launch the strategic counter-offensive immediately because, on the one hand, the enemy will adopt a strategically defensive position in the big cities and along the main lines of communication under his occupation and, on the other hand, China will not yet be adequately equipped technically. Except for the troops engaged in frontal defence against the enemy, our forces will be switched in large numbers to the enemy's rear in comparatively dispersed dispositions, and, basing themselves on all the areas not actually occupied by the enemy and co-ordinating with the people's local armed forces, they will launch extensive, fierce guerrilla warfare against enemy-occupied areas, keeping the enemy on the move as far as possible in order to destroy him in mobile warfare, as is now being done in Shansi Province. The fighting in the second stage will be ruthless, and the country will suffer serious devastation. But the guerrilla warfare will be successful, and if it is well conducted the enemy may be able to retain only about one-third of his occupied territory, with the remaining two-thirds in our hands, and this will constitute a great defeat for the enemy and a great victory for China. By then the enemy-occupied territory as a whole will fall into three categories: first, the enemy base areas; second, our base areas for guerrilla warfare; and, third, the guerrilla areas contested by both sides. The duration of this stage will depend on the degree of change in the balance of forces between us and the enemy and on the changes in the international situation; generally speaking, we should be prepared to see this stage last a comparatively long time and to weather its hardships. It will be a very painful period for China; the two big problems will be economic difficulties and the disruptive activities of the traitors. The enemy will go all out to wreck China's united front, and the traitor organizations in all the occupied areas will merge into a so-called "unified government." Owing to the loss of big cities and the hardships of war, vacillating elements within our ranks will clamour for compromise, and pessimism will grow to a serious extent. Our tasks will then be to mobilize the whole people to unite as one man and carry on the war with unflinching perseverance, to broaden and consolidate the united front, sweep away all pessimism and ideas of compromise, promote the will to hard struggle and apply new wartime policies, and so to weather the hardships. In the second stage, we will have to call upon the whole country resolutely to maintain a united government, we will have to oppose splits and systematically improve fighting techniques, reform the armed forces, mobilize the entire people and prepare for the counter-offensive. The international situation will become still more unfavourable to Japan and the main international forces will incline towards giving more help to China, even though there may be talk of "realism" of the Chamberlain type which accommodates itself to *faits accomplis*. Japan's threat to Southeast Asia and Siberia will become greater, and there may even be another war. As regards Japan, scores of her divisions will be inextricably bogged down in China. Widespread guerrilla warfare and the people's anti-Japanese movement will wear down this big Japanese force, greatly reducing it and also disintegrating its morale by stimulating the growth of homesickness, war-weariness and even anti-war sentiment. Though it would be wrong to say that Japan will achieve no results at all in her plunder of China, yet, being short of capital and harassed by guerrilla warfare, she cannot possibly achieve rapid or substantial results. This second stage will be the transitional stage of the entire war; it will be the most trying period but also the pivotal one. Whether China becomes an independent country or is reduced to a colony will be determined not by the retention or loss of the big cities in the first stage but by the extent to which the whole nation exerts itself in the second. If we can persevere in the War of Resistance, in the united front and in the protracted war, China will in that stage gain the power to change from weakness to strength. It will be the second act in the three-act drama of China's War of Resistance. And through the efforts of the entire cast it will become possible to perform a most brilliant last act.

The third stage will be the stage of the counter-offensive to recover our lost territories. Their recovery will depend mainly upon the strength which China has built up in the preceding stage and which will continue to grow in the third stage. But China's strength alone will not be sufficient, and we shall also have to rely on the support of international forces and on the changes that will take place inside Japan, or otherwise we shall not be able to win; this adds to China's tasks in international propaganda and diplomacy. In the third stage, our war will no longer be one of strategic defensive, but will turn into a strategic counter-offensive manifesting itself in strategic offensives; and it will no longer be fought on strategically interior lines, but will shift gradually to strategically exterior lines. Not until we fight our way to the Yalu River can this war be considered over. The third stage will be the last in the protracted war, and when we talk of persevering in the war to the end, we mean going all the way through this stage. Our primary form of fighting will still be mobile warfare, but positional warfare will rise to importance. While positional defence cannot be regarded as important in the first stage because of the prevailing circumstances, positional attack will become quite important in the third stage because of the changed conditions and the requirements of the task. In the third stage guerrilla warfare will again provide strategic support by supplementing mobile and positional warfare, but it will not be the primary form as in the second stage.

It is thus obvious that the war is protracted and consequently ruthless in nature. The enemy will not be able to gobble up the whole of China but will be able to occupy many places for a considerable time. China will not be able to oust the Japanese quickly, but the greater part of her territory will remain in her hands. Ultimately the enemy will lose and we will win, but we shall have a hard stretch of road to travel.

The Chinese people will become tempered in the course of this long and ruthless war. The political parties taking part in the war will also be steeled and tested. The united front must be persevered in; only by persevering in the united front can we persevere in the war; and only by persevering in the united front and in the war can we win final victory. Only thus can all difficulties be overcome. After travelling the hard stretch of road we shall reach the highway to victory. This is the natural logic of the war.

In the three stages the changes in relative strength will proceed along the following lines. In the first stage, the enemy is superior and we are inferior in strength. With regard to our inferiority we must reckon on changes of two different kinds from the eve of the War of Resistance to the end of this stage. The first kind is a change for the worse. China's original inferiority will be aggravated by war losses, namely, decreases in territory, population, economic strength, military strength and cultural institutions. Towards the end of the first stage, the decrease will probably be considerable, especially on the economic side. This point will be exploited by some people as a basis for their theories of national subjugation and of compromise. But the second kind of change, the change for the better, must also be noted. It includes the experience gained in the war, the progress made by the armed forces, the political progress, the mobilization of the people, the development of culture in a new direction, the emergence of guerrilla warfare, the increase in international support, etc. What is on the downgrade in the first stage is the old quantity and the old quality, the manifestations being mainly quantitative. What is on the upgrade is the new quantity and the new quality, the manifestations being mainly qualitative. It is the second kind of change that provides a basis for our ability to fight a protracted war and win final victory.

In the first stage, changes of two kinds are also occurring on the enemy's side. The first kind is a change for the worse and manifests itself in hundreds of thousands of casualties, the drain on arms and ammunition, deterioration of troop morale, popular discontent at home, shrinkage of trade, the expenditure of over ten thousand million yen, condemnation by world opinion, etc. This trend also provides a basis for our ability to fight a protracted war and win final victory. But we must likewise reckon with the second kind of change on the enemy's side, a change for the better, that is, his expansion in territory, population and resources. This too is a basis for the protracted nature of our War of Resistance and the impossibility of quick victory, but at the same time certain people will use it as a basis for their theories of national subjugation and of compromise. However, we must take into account the transitory and partial character of this change for the better on the enemy's side. Japan is an imperialist power heading for collapse, and her occupation of China's territory is temporary. The vigorous growth of guerrilla warfare in China will restrict her actual occupation to narrow zones. Moreover, her occupation of Chinese territory has created and intensified contradictions between Japan and other foreign countries. Besides, generally speaking, such occupation involves a considerable period in which Japan will make capital outlays without drawing any profits, as is shown by the experience in the three northeastern provinces. All of which again gives us a basis for demolishing the theories of national subjugation and of compromise and for establishing the theories of protracted war and of final victory.

In the second stage, the above changes on both sides will continue to develop. While the situation cannot be predicted in detail, on the whole Japan will continue on the downgrade and China on the upgrade. For example, Japan's military and financial resources will be seriously drained by China's guerrilla warfare, popular discontent will grow in Japan, the morale of her troops will deteriorate further, and she will become more isolated internationally. As for China, she will make further progress in the political, military and cultural spheres and in the mobilization of the people; guerrilla warfare will develop further; there will be some new economic growth on the basis of the small industries and the widespread agriculture in the interior; international support will gradually increase; and the whole picture will be quite different from what it is now. This second stage may last quite a long time, during which there will be a great reversal in the balance of forces, with China gradually rising and Japan gradually declining. China will emerge from her inferior position, and Japan will lose her superior position; first the two countries will become evenly matched, and then their relative positions will be reversed. Thereupon, China will in general have completed her preparations for the strategic counter-offensive and will enter the stage of the counter-offensive and the expulsion of the enemy. It should be reiterated that the change from inferiority to superiority and the completion of preparations for the counter-offensive will involve three things, namely, an increase in China's own strength, an increase in Japan's difficulties, and an increase in international support; it is the combination of all these forces that will bring about China's superiority and the completion of her preparations for the counter-offensive.

Because of the unevenness in China's political and economic development, the strategic counter-offensive of the third stage will not present a uniform and even picture throughout the country in its initial phase but will be regional in character, rising here and subsiding there. During this stage, the enemy will not relax his divisive tricks to break China's united front, hence the task of maintaining internal unity in China will become still more important, and we shall have to ensure that the strategic counter-offensive does not collapse halfway through internal dissension. In this period the international situation will become very favorable to China. China's task will be to take advantage of it in order to attain complete liberation and establish an independent democratic state, which at the same time will mean helping the world anti-fascist movement.

China moving from inferiority to parity and then to superiority, Japan moving from superiority to parity and then to inferiority; China moving from the defensive to stalemate and then to the counter-offensive, Japan moving from the offensive to the safeguarding of her gains and then to retreat—such will be the course of the Sino-Japanese war and its inevitable trend.

Hence the questions and the conclusions are as follows: Will China be subjugated? The answer is, No, she will not be subjugated, but will win final victory. Can China win quickly? The answer is, No, she cannot win quickly, and the war must be a protracted one. Are these conclusions correct? I think they are.

At this point, the exponents of national subjugation and of compromise will again rush in and say, "To move from inferiority to parity China needs a military and economic power equal to Japan's, and to move from parity to superiority she will need a military and economic power greater than Japan's. But this is impossible, hence the above conclusions are not correct."

This is the so-called theory that "weapons decide everything," which constitutes a mechanical approach to the question of war and a subjective and one-sided view. Our view is opposed to this; we see not only weapons but also people. Weapons are an important factor in war, but not the decisive factor; it is people, not things, that are decisive. The contest of strength is not only a contest of military and economic power, but also a contest of human power and morale. Military and economic power is necessarily wielded by people. If the great majority of the Chinese, of the Japanese and of the people of other countries are on the side of our War of Resistance Against Japan, how can Japan's military and economic power, wielded as it is by a small minority through coercion, count as superiority? And if not, then does not China, though wielding relatively inferior military and economic power, become the superior? There is no doubt that China will gradually grow in military and economic power, provided she perseveres in the War of Resistance and in the united front. As for our enemy, weakened as he will be by the long war and by internal and external contradictions, his military and economic power is bound to change in the reverse direction. In these circumstances, is there any reason why China cannot become the superior? And that is not all. Although we cannot as yet count the military and economic power of other countries as being openly and to any great extent on our side, is there any reason why we will not be able to do so in the future? If Japan's enemy is not just China, if in future one or more other countries make open use of their considerable military and economic power defensively or offensively against Japan and openly help us, then will not our superiority be still greater? Japan is a small country, her war is reactionary and barbarous, and she will become more and more isolated internationally; China is a large country, her war is progressive and just, and she will enjoy more and more support internationally. Is there any reason why the long-term development of these factors should not definitely change the relative position between the enemy and ourselves?

The exponents of quick victory, however, do not realize that war is a contest of strength, and that before a certain change has taken place in the relative strength of the belligerents, there is no basis for trying to fight strategically decisive battles and shorten the road to liberation. Were their ideas to be put into practice, we should inevitably run our heads into a brick wall. Or perhaps they are just talking for their own pleasure without really intending to put their ideas into practice. In the end Mr. Reality will come and pour a bucket of cold water over these chatterers, showing them up as mere windbags who want to get things on the cheap, to have gains without pains. We have had this kind of idle chatter before and we have it now, though not very much so far; but there may be more as the war develops into the stage of stalemate and then of counter-offensive. But in the meantime, if China's losses in the first stage are fairly heavy and the second stage drags on very long, the theories of national subjugation and of compromise will gain great currency. Therefore, our fire should be directed mainly against them and only secondarily against the idle chatter about quick victory.

That the war will be protracted is certain, but nobody can predict exactly how many months or years it will last, as this depends entirely upon the degree of the change in the balance of forces. All those who wish to shorten the war have no alternative but to work hard to increase our own strength and reduce that of the enemy. Specifically, the only way is to strive to win more battles and wear down the enemy's forces, develop guerrilla warfare to reduce enemy-occupied territory to a minimum, consolidate and expand the united front to rally the forces of the whole nation, build up new armies and develop new war industries, promote political, economic and cultural progress, mobilize the workers, peasants, businessmen, intellectuals and other sections of the people, disintegrate the enemy forces and win over their soldiers, carry on international propaganda to secure foreign support, and win the support of the Japanese people and other oppressed peoples. Only by doing all this can we reduce the duration of the war. There is no magic short-cut.

Mobile Warfare, Guerrilla Warfare and Positional Warfare

Excerpt from *On Protracted War* by Mao Tse-Tung

A war will take the form of mobile warfare when its content is quick-decision offensive warfare on exterior lines in campaigns and battles within the framework of the strategy of interior lines, protracted war and defence. Mobile warfare is the form in which regular armies wage quick-decision offensive campaigns and battles on exterior lines along extensive fronts and over big areas of operation. At the same time, it includes "mobile defence," which is conducted when necessary to facilitate such offensive battles; it also includes positional attack and positional defence in a supplementary role. Its characteristics are regular armies, superiority of forces in campaigns and battles, the offensive, and fluidity.

China has a vast territory and an immense number of soldiers, but her troops are inadequately equipped and trained; the enemy's forces, on the other hand, are inadequate in number, but better equipped and trained. In this situation, there is no doubt that we must adopt offensive mobile warfare as our primary form of warfare, supplementing it by others and integrating them all into mobile warfare. We must oppose "only retreat, never advance," which is flightism, and at the same time oppose "only advance, never retreat," which is desperate recklessness.

One of the characteristics of mobile warfare is fluidity, which not only permits but requires a field army to advance and to withdraw in great strides. However, it has nothing in common with flightism of the Han Fu-chu brand. The primary requirement of war is to destroy the enemy, and the other requirement is self-preservation. The object of self-preservation is to destroy the enemy, and to destroy the enemy is in turn the most effective means of self-preservation. Hence mobile warfare is in no way an excuse for people like Han Fu-chu and can never mean moving only backward, and never forward; that kind of "moving" which negates the basic offensive character of mobile warfare would, in practice, "move" China out of existence despite her vastness.

However, the other view, which we call the desperate reckless-ness of "only advance, never retreat," is also wrong. The mobile warfare we advocate, the content of which is quick-decision offen-sive warfare on exterior lines in campaigns and battles, includes positional warfare in a supplementary role, "mobile defence" and retreat, without all of which mobile warfare cannot be fully carried out. Desperate recklessness is military short-sightedness, originat-ing often from fear of losing territory. A man who acts with desperate recklessness does not know that one characteristic of mobile warfare is fluidity, which not only permits but requires a field army to advance and to withdraw in great strides. On the positive side, in order to draw the enemy into a fight unfavourable to him but favourable to us, it is usually necessary that he should be on the move and that we should have a number of advantages, such as favourable terrain, a vulnerable enemy, a local population that can prevent the leakage of information, and the enemy's fatigue and unpreparedness. This requires that the enemy should advance, and we should not grudge a temporary loss of part of our territory. For the temporary loss of part of our territory is the price we pay for the permanent preservation of all our territory, includ-ing the recovery of lost territory. On the negative side, whenever we are forced into a disadvantageous position which fundamen-tally endangers the preservation of our forces, we should have the courage to retreat, so as to preserve our forces and hit the enemy when new opportunities arise. In their ignorance of this principle, the advocates of desperate action will contest a city or a piece of ground even when the position is obviously and definitely unfa-vourable; as a result, they not only lose the city or ground but fail to preserve their forces. We have always advocated the policy of "luring the enemy in deep," precisely because it is the most effec-tive military policy for a weak army strategically on the defensive to employ against a strong army.

Among the forms of warfare in the anti-Japanese war mobile warfare comes first and guerrilla warfare second. When we say that in the entire war mobile warfare is primary and guerrilla warfare supplementary, we mean that the outcome of the war depends mainly on regular warfare, especially in its mobile form, and that guerrilla warfare cannot shoulder the main responsibility in deciding the outcome. It does not follow, however, that the role of guerrilla warfare is unimportant in the strategy of the war. Its role in the strategy of the war as a whole is second only to that of mobile warfare, for without its support we cannot defeat the enemy. In saying this we also have in mind the strategic task of developing guerrilla warfare into mobile warfare. Guerrilla warfare will not remain the same throughout this long and cruel war, but will rise to a higher level and develop into mobile warfare. Thus the strategic role of guerrilla warfare is twofold, to support regular warfare and to transform itself into regular warfare. Considering the unprecedented extent and duration of guerrilla warfare in China's War of Resistance, it is all the more important not to underestimate its strategic role. Guerrilla warfare in China, therefore, has not only its tactical but also its peculiar strategic problems. I have already discussed this in *Problems of Strategy in Guerrilla War Against Japan.* As indicated above, the forms of warfare in the three strategic stages of the War of Resistance are as follows. In the first stage mobile warfare is primary, while guerrilla and positional warfare are supplementary. In the second stage guerrilla warfare will advance to the first place and will be supplemented by mobile and positional warfare. In the third stage mobile warfare will again become the primary form and will be supplemented by positional and guerrilla warfare. But the mobile warfare of the third stage will no longer be undertaken solely by the original regular forces; part, possibly quite an important part, will be undertaken by forces which were originally guerrillas but which will have progressed from guerrilla to mobile warfare. From the viewpoint of all three stages in China's War of Resistance Against Japan, guerrilla warfare is definitely indispensable. Our guerilla war will present a great drama unparalleled in the annals of war. For this reason, out of the millions of China's regular troops, it is absolutely necessary to assign at least several hundred thousand to disperse through all enemy-occupied areas, arouse the masses to arm themselves, and wage guerrilla warfare in co-ordination with the masses. The regular forces so assigned should shoulder this sacred task conscientiously, and they should not think their status lowered because they fight fewer big battles and for the time being do not appear as national heroes. Any such thinking is wrong. Guerrilla warfare does not bring as quick results or as great renown as regular warfare, but "a long road tests a horse's strength and a long task proves a man's heart," and in the course of this long and cruel war guerrilla warfare will demonstrate its immense power; it is indeed no ordinary undertaking. Moreover, such regular forces can conduct guerrilla warfare when dispersed and mobile warfare when concentrated, as the Eighth Route Army has been doing. The principle of the Eighth Route Army is, "Guerrilla warfare is basic, but lose no chance for mobile warfare under favourable conditions." This principle is perfectly correct; the views of its opponents are wrong.

At China's present technical level, positional warfare, defensive or offensive, is generally impracticable, and this is where our weakness manifests itself. Moreover, the enemy is also exploiting the vastness of our territory to bypass our fortified positions. Hence positional warfare cannot be an important, still less the principal, means for us. But in the first and second stages of the war, it is possible and essential, within the scope of mobile warfare, to employ localized positional warfare in a supplementary role in campaigns. Semi-positional "mobile defence" is a still more essential part of mobile warfare undertaken for the purpose of resisting the enemy at every step, thereby depleting his forces and gaining extra time. China must strive to increase her supplies of modern weapons so that she can fully carry out the tasks of positional attack in the stage of the strategic counter-offensive. In this third stage positional warfare will undoubtedly play a greater role, for then the enemy will be holding fast to his positions, and we shall not be able to recover our lost territory unless we launch powerful positional attacks in support of mobile warfare. Nevertheless, in the third stage too, we must exert our every effort to make mobile warfare the primary form of warfare. For the art of directing war and the active role of man are largely nullified in positional warfare such as that fought in Western Europe in the second half of World War I. It is only natural that the war should be taken "out of the trenches," since the war is being fought in the vast expanses of China and since our side will remain poorly equipped technically for quite a long time. Even during the third stage, when China's technical position will be better, she will hardly surpass her enemy in that respect, and so will have to concentrate on highly mobile warfare, without which she cannot achieve final victory. Hence, throughout the War of Resistance China will not adopt positional warfare as primary; the primary or important forms are mobile warfare and guerrilla warfare. These two forms of warfare will afford full play to the art of directing war and to the active role of man—what a piece of good fortune out of our misfortune!

Reading 10

The Landing at Inch'on

by Roy E. Appleman

The history of war proves that nine out of ten times an army has been destroyed because its supply lines have been cut off. . . . We shall land at Inch'on, and I shall crush them [the North Koreans].

Douglas MacArthur

It was natural and predictable that General MacArthur should think in terms of an amphibious landing in the rear of the enemy to win the Korean War. His campaigns in the Southwest Pacific in World War II—after Bataan—all began as amphibious operations. From Australia to Luzon his forces often advanced around enemy-held islands, one after another. Control of the seas gives mobility to military power. Mobility and war of maneuver have always brought the greatest prizes and the quickest decisions to their practitioners. A waterborne sweep around the enemy's flank and an attack in his rear against lines of supply and communications appealed to MacArthur sense of grand tactics. He never wavered from this concept, although repeatedly the fortunes of war compelled him to postpone its execution.

MacArthur's Early Plans

During the first week of July, with the Korean War little more than a week old, General MacArthur told his chief of staff, General Almond, to begin considering plans for an amphibious operation

From *South to the Naktong, North to the Yalu* by Roy E. Appleman, Center for Military History, 1986.

designed to strike the enemy center of communications at Seoul, and to study the location for a landing to accomplish this. At a Far East Command headquarters meeting on 4 July, attended by Army, Navy, and Air Force representatives, Generals MacArthur and Almond discussed the idea of an amphibious landing in the enemy's rear and proposed that the 1st Cavalry Division be used for that purpose. Col. Edward H. Forney of the Marine Corps, an expert on amphibious operations, was selected to work with the 1st Cavalry Division on plans for the operation.[1] The early plan for the amphibious operation received the code name BLUEHEARTS and called for driving the North Koreans back across the 38th Parallel. The approximate date proposed for it was 22 July, but the operation was abandoned by 10 July because of the inability of the U.S. and ROK forces in Korea to halt the southward drive of the enemy.[2]

Meanwhile the planning for an amphibious operation went ahead in the Far East Command despite the cancellation of BLUE-HEARTS. These plans were undertaken by the joint Strategic Plans and Operations Group (JSPOG), Far East Command, which General Wright headed in addition to his duties as Assistant Chief of Staff, G-3. One of Wright's deputies, Col. Donald H. Galloway, was directly in charge of JSPOG. This unusually able group of planners developed various plans in considerable detail for amphibious operations in Korea.

On 23 July, General Wright upon MacArthur's instructions circulated to the GHQ staff sections the outline of Operation CHROMITE. CHROMITE called for an amphibious operation in September and postulated three plans: (1) Plan 100-B, landing at Inch'on on the west coast; (2) Plan 100-C, landing at Kunsan on the west coast; (3) Plan 100-D, landing near Chumunjin-up on the east coast. Plan 100-B, calling for a landing at Inch'on with a simultaneous attack by Eighth Army, was favored.[3]

This same day, 23 July, General MacArthur informed the Department of the Army that he had scheduled for mid-September an amphibious landing of the 5th Marines and the 2d Infantry Division behind the enemy's lines in co-ordination with an attack by Eighth Army.[4] The North Korean successes upset MacArthur's plans as fast as he made them. He admitted this to the Joint Chiefs in a message on 29 July, saying, "In Korea the hopes that I had entertained to hold out the 1st Marine Division [Brigade] and the 2d Infantry Division for the enveloping counter blow have not been fulfilled and it will be necessary to commit these units to Korea on the south line rather than . . . their subsequent commitment along a separate axis in mid-September. . . . I now plan to commit my sole reserve in Japan, the 7th Infantry Division, as soon as it can be brought to an approximate combat strength.[5]

X Corps Troops Assembled

By 20 July General MacArthur had settled rather definitely on the concept of the Inch'on operation and he spoke of the matter at some length with General Almond and with General Wright, his operations officer. On 12 August, MacArthur issued CINCFE Operation Plan 100-B and specifically named the Inch'on-Seoul area as the target that a special invasion force would seize by amphibious assault.[6]

On 15 August General MacArthur established the headquarters group of the Special Planning Staff to take charge of the projected amphibious operation. For purposes of secrecy the new group selected from the GHQ FEC staff, was designated, Special Planning Staff, GHQ, and the forces to be placed under its control, GHQ Reserve. On 21 August, MacArthur requested the Department of the Army by radio for authority to activate Headquarters, X Corps, and, upon receiving approval, he issued GHQ FEC. General Order 24 on 26 August activating the corps. All units in Japan or en route there that had been designated GHQ Reserve were assigned to it.[7]

It appears that General MacArthur about the middle of August had made up his mind on the person he would select to command the invasion force. One day as he was talking with General Almond about the forthcoming landing, the latter suggested that it was time to appoint a commander for it. MacArthur turned to him and replied, "It is you." MacArthur told Almond that he was also to retain his position as Chief of Staff, Far East Command. His view was that Almond would command X Corps for the Inch'on invasion and the capture of Seoul, that the war would end soon thereafter, and Almond would then return to his old position in Tokyo. In effect, the far East Command would lend Almond and most of the key staff members of the corps for the landing operation. General Almond has stated that MacArthur's decision to place him in command of X Corps surprised him, as he had expected to remain in Tokyo in his capacity as Chief of Staff, FEC. General MacArthur officially assigned General Almond to command X Corps on 26 August.[8]

General Almond, fifty-eight years old when he assumed command of X Corps, was a graduate of Virginia Military Institute. In

World War I he had commanded a machine gun battalion and had been wounded and decorated for bravery. In World War II he had commanded the 92d Infantry Division in Italy. Almond went to the Far East Command in June 1946, and served as deputy chief of staff to MacArthur from November 1946 to February 1949. On 18 February 1949 he became Chief of Staff, Far East Command, and, on 24 July 1950, Chief of Staff, United Nations Command, as well.

General Almond was a man both feared and obeyed throughout the Far East Command. Possessed of a driving energy and a consuming impatience with incompetence, he expected from others the same degree of devotion to duty and hard work that he exacted from himself. No one who ever saw him would be likely to forget the lightning that flashed from his blue eyes. To his commander, General MacArthur, he was wholly loyal. He never hesitated before difficulties. Topped by iron-gray hair, Almond's alert, mobile face with its ruddy complexion made him an arresting figure despite his medium stature and the slight stoop of his shoulders.

The corps' chief of staff was Maj. Gen. Clark L. Ruffner, who had arrived from the United States on 6 August and had started working with the planning group two days later. He was an energetic and diplomatic officer with long experience and a distinguished record in staff work. During World War II he had been Chief of Staff, U.S. Army Forces, Pacific Ocean Areas, in Hawaii. The X Corps staff was an able one, many of its members hand-picked from among the Far East Command staff.

The major ground units of X Corps were the 1st Marine Division and the 7th Infantry Division. In the summer of 1950 it was no easy matter for the United States to assemble in the Far East a Marine division at full strength. On 25 July, Maj. Gen. Oliver P. Smith assumed command and on that day the Commandant of the Marine Corps issued an order to him to bring the division to war strength, less one regiment, and to sail for the Far East between 10 and 15 August. This meant the activation of another regiment, the 1st Marines, and the assembly, organization, and equipment of approximately 15,000 officers and enlisted men within the next two weeks. On 10 August, the Joint Chiefs of Staff decided to add the third regiment to the division, and the 7th Marines was activated. It was scheduled to sail for the Far East by 1 September. The difficulty of obtaining troops to fill the division was so great that a battalion of marines on duty with the Sixth Fleet in the Mediterranean was ordered to join the division in the Far East.[9]

General Smith and most of the staff officers of the 1st Marine Division arrived in Japan from the United States on 22 August. The division troops, the 1st Marines, and the staff of the 7th Marines arrived in Japan between 28 August and 6 September. A battalion of marines in two vessels, the *Bexar* and the *Montague*, departed Suda Bay, Crete, in the Mediterranean on 16 August, and sailing by way of Suez arrived at Pusan on 9 September to join the 7th Marines as its 3d Battalion. The remainder of the 7th Marines arrived at Kobe on 17 September. The 5th Marines, in Korea, received a warning order on 30 August to prepare for movement to Pusan to join the division.[10]

Bringing the 7th Infantry Division up to war strength posed an even more difficult problem. During July, FEC had taken 140 officers and 1,500 noncommissioned officers and enlisted men from the division to augment the strength of the 24th and 25th Infantry and the 1st Cavalry Divisions as they in turn had mounted out for Korea. At the end of July the division was at less than half strength, but in noncommissioned officer weapons leaders and critical specialists the shortage was far greater than that proportion. On 27 July, the 7th Infantry Division was 9,117 men understrength—290 officers, 126 warrant officers, and 8,701 enlisted men. The day before, FEC had relieved it of all occupation duties and ordered it to prepare for movement to Korea.[11]

From 23 August to 3 September the Far East Command allotted to the 7th Division the entire infantry replacement stream reaching FEC, and from 23 August through 8 September the entire artillery replacement stream. By 4 September the division had received 390 officers and 5,400 enlisted replacements. General MacArthur obtained service units for the X Corps in the same way by diverting them from scheduled assignments for Eighth Army. The Far East Command justified this on the ground that, while Eighth Army needed them badly, X Corps' need was imperative.[12]

In response to General MacArthur's instructions to General Walker on 11 and 13 August to send South Koreans to augment the 7th Infantry Division, 8,637 of them arrived in Japan before the division embarked for Inch'on. Their clothing on arrival ranged from business suits to shirts and shorts, or shorts only. The majority wore sandals or cloth shoes. They were civilians—stunned, confused, and exhausted. Only a few could speak English. Approximately 100 of the South Korean recruits were assigned to each rifle company and artillery battery; the buddy system was used for training and control.[13]

The quality of the artillery and infantry crew-served weapons troops received from the United States and assigned to the 7th Division during August and early September was high. The superior training provided by the old infantry and artillery noncommissioned officers who arrived from the Fort Benning Infantry and the Fort Sill Artillery Schools brought the 7th Division to a better condition as the invasion date approached than could have been reasonably expected a month earlier. The 7th Division strength on embarkation, including the attached South Koreans, was 24,845.[14]

The Landing Controversy

All through July and August 1950 the Joint Chiefs of Staff gave implied or expressed approval of MacArthur's proposal for an amphibious landing behind the enemy's battle lines. But while it was known that MacArthur favored Inch'on as the landing site, the Joint Chiefs had never committed themselves to it. From the beginning, there had been some opposition to and many reservations about the Inch'on proposal on the part of General Collins, U.S. Army Chief of Staff; the Navy; and the Marine Corps. The FEC senior planning and staff officers—such as Generals Almond and Hickey, Chief of Staff and Deputy Chief of Staff; General Wright, the G-3 and head of JSPOG; and Brig. Gen. George L. Eberle, the G-4—supported the plan.[15]

The Navy's opposition to the Inch'on site centered largely on the difficult tidal conditions there, and since this opposition continued, the Joint Chiefs of Staff decided to send two of its members to Tokyo to discuss the matter with MacArthur and his staff. A decision had to be reached. On 20 July General Collins and Admiral Forrest P. Sherman, Chief of Naval Operations, left Washington for their conference with MacArthur. Upon arrival in Japan, Collins and Sherman engaged in private conversations with MacArthur and key members of his staff, including senior naval officers in the Far East. Then, on the afternoon of 23 July, a full briefing on the subject was scheduled in General MacArthur's conference room in the Dai Ichi Building.[16]

The conference began at 1730 in the afternoon. Among those present in addition to General MacArthur were General Collins, Admiral Sherman, Vice Admirals Joy and Struble, Generals Almond, Hickey, and Wright, some members of the latter's JSPOG group, and Rear Adm. James H. Doyle and some members of his staff who were to present the naval problems involved in a landing at Inch'on.

After a short introduction by General MacArthur, General Wright briefed the group on the basic plan. Admiral Doyle then presented the naval considerations. His general tone was pessimistic, and he concluded with the remark, "The operation is not impossible, but I do not recommend it." The naval part of the briefings lasted more than an hour.

During the naval presentation MacArthur, who had heard the main arguments many times before, sat quietly smoking his pipe, asking only an occasional question. When the presentation ended, MacArthur began to speak. He talked as though delivering a soliloquy for forty-five minutes, dwelling in a conversational tone on the reasons why the landing should be made at Inch'on. He said that the enemy had neglected his rear and was dangling on a thin logistical rope that could be quickly cut in the Seoul area, that the enemy had committed practically all his forces against Eighth Army in the south and had no trained reserves and little power of recuperation. MacArthur stressed the strategical, political, and psychological reasons for the landing at Inch'on and the quick capture of Seoul, the capital of South Korea. He said it would hold the imagination of Asia and win support for the United Nations. Inch'on, he said, pointing to the big map behind him, would be the anvil on which the hammer of Walker's Eighth Army from the south would crush the North Koreans.

General MacArthur then turned to a consideration of a landing at Kunsan, 100 air miles below Inch'on, which General Collins and Admiral Sherman had favored. MacArthur said the idea was good but the location wrong. He did not think a landing there would result in severing the North Korean supply lines and destroying the North Korean Army. He returned to his emphasis on Inch'on, saying that the amphibious landing was tactically the most powerful military device available to the United Nations Command and that to employ it properly meant to strike deep and hard into enemy-held territory. He dwelt on the bitter Korean winter campaign that would become necessary if Inch'on was not undertaken. He said the North Koreans considered a landing at Inch'on impossible because of the very great difficulties involved and, because of this, the landing force would achieve surprise. He touched on his operations in the Pacific in World War II and eulogized the Navy for its part in them. He concluded his long talk by declaring unequivocally for Inch'on and saying, "The Navy has never turned me down yet, and I know it will not now."

MacArthur seems to have convinced most of the doubters present. Admiral Sherman was won over to MacArthur's position. General Collins, however, seemed still to have reservations on Inch'on. He subsequently asked General Wright if the Far East Command had firm plans for a Kunsan landing which could be used as an alternate plan if the Inch'on operation either was not carried out or failed. Wright assured him that there were such plans and, moreover, that it was planned to stage a feint at Kunsan.[17]

Among the alternate proposals to Inch'on, in addition to the Kunsan plan favored by the Navy, was one for a landing in the Posung-myon area thirty miles south of Inch'on and opposite Osan. On the 23d, Admiral Doyle had proposed a landing there with the purpose of striking inland to Osan and there severing the communications south of Seoul. On the 24th, Lt Gen. Lemuel C. Shepherd, Jr. (USMC), called on General MacArthur and asked him to change the landing site to this area—all to no avail. MacArthur remained resolute on Inch'on.

Upon their return to Washington, Collins and Sherman went over the whole matter of the Inch'on landing with the other members of the Joint Chiefs of Staff. On 28 August the Joint Chiefs sent a message to MacArthur which seemingly concurred in the Inch'on plans yet attached conditions. Their message said in part: "We concur in making preparations for and executing a turning movement by amphibious forces on the west coast of Korea, either at Inch'on in the event the enemy defenses in the vicinity of Inch'on prove ineffective, or at a favorable beach south of Inch'on if one can be located. We further concur in preparations, if desired by CINCFE, for an envelopment by amphibious forces in the vicinity of Kunsan. We understand that alternative plans are being prepared in order to best exploit the situation as it develops."[18]

MacArthur pressed ahead unswervingly toward the Inch'on landing. On 30 August he issued his United Nations Command operation order for it. Meanwhile, the Joint Chiefs in Washington expected to receive from MacArthur further details of the pending operation and, failing to receive them, sent a message to him on 5 September requesting this information. MacArthur replied the next day that his plans remained unchanged. On 7 September, the Joint Chiefs sent another message to MacArthur requesting a reconsideration of the whole question and an estimate of the chances for favorable outcome. The energy and strength displayed by the North Koreans in their early September massive offensive had evidently raised doubts in the minds of the Joint Chiefs that

General Walker's Eighth Army could go over successfully to the attack or that X Corps could quickly overcome the Seoul defenses. In the meantime, General MacArthur on 6 September in a letter to all his major commanders confirmed previous verbal orders and announced 15 September as D-day for the Inch'on landing.[19]

In response to the Joint Chiefs' request for a reconsideration and an estimate of the chances for a favorable landing at Inch'on, General MacArthur on 8 September sent to Washington a final eloquent message on the subject. His message said in part:

> There is no question in my mind as to the feasibility of the operation and I regard its chance of success as excellent. I go further and believe that it represents the only hope of wresting the initiative from the enemy and thereby presenting an opportunity for a decisive blow. To do otherwise is to commit us to a war of indefinite duration, of gradual attrition, and of doubtful results. . . . There is no slightest possibility . . . of our force being ejected from the Pusan beachhead. The envelopment from the north will instantly relieve the pressure on the south perimeter and, indeed, is the only way that this can be accomplished. . . . The success of the enveloping movement from the north does not depend upon the rapid juncture of the X Corps and the Eighth-Army. The seizure of the heart of the enemy distributing system in the Seoul area will completely dislocate the logistical supply of his forces now operating in South Korea and therefore will ultimately result in their disintegration. This, indeed, is the primary purpose of the movement. Caught between our northern and southern forces, both of which are completely self-sustaining because of our absolute air and naval supremacy, the enemy cannot fail to be ultimately shattered through disruption of his logistical support and our combined combat activities. . . . For the reasons stated, there are no material changes under contemplation in the operation as planned and reported to you. The embarkation of the troops and the preliminary air and naval preparations are proceeding according to schedule.

The next day the Joint Chiefs, referring to this message, replied tersely to MacArthur, "We approve your plan and President has been so informed."[20] It appears that in Secretary of Defense Johnson, MacArthur had in Washington a powerful ally during the Inch'on landing controversy, for Johnson supported the Far East commander.[21] Thus on 8 September Washington time and 9 September Tokyo time the debate on the projected Inch'on landing ended.

A co-ordinate part of MacArthur's Inch'on plan was an attack by the Eighth Army north from its Pusan Perimeter beachhead simultaneously with the X Corps landing. This action was intended to tie down all enemy forces committed against Eighth Army and prevent withdrawal from the south of major reinforcements for the North Korean units opposing X Corps in its landing area. The plan called for the Eighth Army to break out of the Perimeter, drive northward, and join forces with X Corps.

On 30 August, General Smith had sent a dispatch to X Corps requesting that the 1st Provisional Marine Brigade in Korea be released from Eighth Army on 1 September to prepare for mounting out for Inch'on. MacArthur ordered that the Marine brigade be available on 4 September for that purpose. But no sooner was this order issued than it was rescinded on 1 September because of the crisis that faced Eighth Army after the great North Korean attack had rolled up the southern front during the night.[22]

Eighth Army's use of the 1st Provisional Marine Brigade in the battle near Yongsan threatened to disrupt the Inch'on landing according to Marine and Navy opinion. A tug of war now ensued between General Smith, supported by the U.S. Naval Forces, Far East, on the one hand and General Walker on the other for control of the 5th Marines. The Marine commander insisted he must have the 5th Marines if he were to make the Inch'on landing. General Walker in a telephone conversation with General Almond said in effect, "If I lose the 5th Marine Regiment I will not be responsible for the safety of the front." Almond sided with Walker despite the fact that he was to be commander of the Inch'on landing force, taking the view that the X Corps could succeed in its plan without the regiment. He suggested that the 32d Infantry Regiment of the 7th Division be attached to the 1st Marine Division as its second assault regiment. General Smith and NAVFE remained adamant. The issue came to a head on 3 September when Admirals Joy, Struble, and Doyle accompanied General Smith to the Dai Ichi Building for a showdown conference with Generals Almond, Ruffner, and Wright.

When it became clear that the group could not reach an agreement, General Almond went into General MacArthur's private office and told MacArthur that things had reached an impasse—that Smith and the Navy would not go in at Inch'on without the 5th Marines. Hearing this, MacArthur told Almond, "Tell Walker he will have to give up the 5th Marine Regiment." Almond returned to the waiting group and told them of MacArthur's decision.[23]

The next day, 4 September, General MacArthur sent General Wright to Taegu to tell General Walker that the 1st Provisional Marine Brigade would have to be released not later than the night of 5–6 September and moved at once to Pusan. At Taegu Wright informed Walker of MacArthur's instructions and told him that the Far East Command was loading the 17th Regiment of the 7th Infantry Division for movement to Pusan, where it would be held in floating reserve and be available for use by Eighth Army if necessary. (It sailed from Yokohama for Korea on 6 September.) He also said that MacArthur intended to divert to Pusan for assignment to Eighth Army the first regiment (65th Infantry) of the 3d Infantry Division arriving in the Far East, the expected date of arrival being 18–20 September. General Walker, in discussing his part in the projected combined operation set for 15 September, requested that the Eighth Army attack be deferred to D plus 1, 16 September. Wright agreed with this timing and said he would recommend it to MacArthur, who subsequently approved it.[24]

Naval Plans

In making ready its part of the operation, the Commander, NAVFE outlined the tasks the Navy would have to perform. These included the following: maintain a naval blockade of the west coast of Korea south of latitude 39° 35′ north; conduct pre-D-day naval operations as the situation might require; on D-day seize by amphibious assault, occupy, and defend a beachhead in the Inch'on area; transport, land, and support follow-up and strategic reserve troops, if directed, to the Inch'on area; and provide cover and support as required. Joint Task Force Seven was formed to accomplish these objectives with Admiral Struble, Commander, Seventh Fleet, as the task force commander. On 25 August, Admiral Struble left his flagship, USS *Rochester*, at Sasebo and proceeded by air to Tokyo to direct final planning.[25]

On 3 September, Admiral Struble issued JTF 7 Operational Plan 9-50. Marine aircraft from two escort carriers, naval aircraft from the U.S. carrier *Boxer*, and British aircraft from a light British carrier would provide as much support aircraft as could be concentrated in and over the landing area, and would be controlled from the amphibious force flagship (AGC) *Mt. McKinley*. An arc extending inland thirty miles from the landing site described the task force objective area.[26] In order to carry out its various missions, Joint Task Force Seven organized its subordinate parts as follows:

TF 90	Attack Force, Rear Adm. James H. Doyle, USN
TF 92	X Corps, Maj. Gen. Edward M. Almond, USA
TF 99	Patrol & Reconnaissance Force, Rear Adm. G. R. Henderson, USN
TF 91	Blockade & Covering Force, Rear Adm. W. G. Andrews, R.N.
TF 77	Fast Carrier Force, Rear Adm. E. C. Ewen, USN
TF 79	Logistic Support Force, Capt. B. L. Austin, USN
TF 70.1	Flagship Group, Capt. E. L. Woodyard, USN

For the naval phases, the command post of Admiral Struble was on the *Rochester;* that of Rear Admiral Doyle, second in command, was on the *Mt. McKinley.* More than 230 ships were assigned to the operation. Surface vessels of JTF 7 were not to operate within twelve miles of Soviet or Chinese territory nor aircraft within twenty miles of such territory.[27]

MacArthur had selected Inch'on as the landing site for one paramount reason: it was the port for the capital city of Seoul, eighteen miles inland, and was the closest possible landing area to that city and the hub of communications centering there.

Inch'on is situated on the estuary of the Yom-ha River and possesses a protected, ice-free port with a tidal basin. The shore line there is a low-lying, partially submerged coastal plain subject to very high tides. There are no beaches in the landing area—only wide mud flats at low tide and stone walls at high tide. Because of the mud flats, the landing force would have to use the harbor and wharfage facilities in the port area. The main approach by sea is from the south through two channels 50 miles long and only 6 to 10 fathoms deep (36–60 feet). Flying Fish Channel is the channel ordinarily used by large ships. It is narrow and twisting.

The Inch'on harbor divides into an outer and an inner one, the latter separated from the former by a long breakwater and the islands of Wolmi and Sowolmi which join by a causeway. The greater part of the inner harbor becomes a mud flat at low tide leaving only a narrow dredged channel of about 12–13 feet in depth. The only dock facilities for deep draft vessels were in the tidal basin, which was 1,700 feet long, 750 feet wide, and had an average depth of 40 feet, but at mean low tide held only 14 feet of water.[28]

Inch'on promised to be a unique amphibious operation—certainly one very difficult to conduct because of natural conditions. Tides in the restricted waters of the channel and the harbor have a maximum range of more than 31 feet. A few instances of an extreme 33-foot tide have been reported. Some of the World War II landing craft that were to be used in making the landing required 23 feet of tide to clear the mud flats, and the LSTs (Landing Ship, Tank) required 29 feet of tide—a favorable condition that prevailed only once a month over a period of three or four days. The narrow, shallow channel necessitated a daylight approach for the larger ships. Accordingly, it was necessary to schedule the main landings for the late afternoon high tide. A night approach, however, by a battalion-sized attack group was to be made for the purpose of seizing Wolmi-do during the early morning high tide, a necessary preliminary, the planners thought, to the main landing at Inch'on itself.[29]

Low seas at Inch'on are most frequent from May through August, high seas from October through March. Although September is a period of transition, it was considered suitable for landing operations. MacArthur and his planners had selected 15 September for D-day because there would then be a high tide giving maximum water depth over the Inch'on mud flats. Tidal range for 15 September reached 31.2 feet at low water. Only on this day did the tide reach this extreme range. No other date after this would permit landing until 27 September when a high tide would reach 27 feet. On 11–13 October there would be a tide of 30 feet. Morning high tide on 15 September came at 0659, forty-five minutes after sunrise; evening high tide came at 1919, twenty-seven minutes after sunset. The Navy set 23 feet of tide as the critical point needed for landing craft to clear the mud flat and reach the landing sites.[30]

Another consideration was the sea walls that fronted the Inch'on landing sites. Built to turn back unusually high tides, they were 16 feet in height above the mud flats. They presented a scaling problem except at extreme high tide. Since the landing would be made somewhat short of extreme high tide in order to use the last hour or two of daylight, ladders would be needed. Some aluminum scaling ladders were made in Kobe and there were others of wood. Grappling hooks, lines, and cargo nets were readied for use in holding the boats against the sea wall.

The initial objective of the landing Force was to gain a beachhead at Inch'on, a city of 250,000 population. The 3d Battalion, 5th Marines, was to land on Wolmi-do on the early morning high tide at 0630 15 September (D-day, L-hour). With Wolmi-do in friendly hands, the main landing would be made that afternoon at the next high tide, about 1730 (D-day, H-hour), by the 1st and 5th Marines.

Three landing beaches were selected—Green Beach on Wolmi-do for the preliminary early morning battalion landing, and Red Beach in the sea wall dock area of Inch'on and Blue Beach in the mud flat semi-open area at the south edge of the city for the two-regimental-size force that would make the main landing in the evening. Later, 7th Infantry Division troops would land at Inch'on over what was called Yellow Beach.

The 5th Marines, less the 3d Battalion, was to land over Red Beach in the heart of Inch'on, north of the causeway which joined Wolmi-do with Inch'on, and drive rapidly inland 1,000 yards to seize Observatory Hill. On the left of the landing area was Cemetery Hill, 130 feet high, on which three dual-purpose guns reportedly were located. On the right, a group of buildings dominated the landing area. The 5th Marines considered Cemetery and Observatory Hills as the important ground to be secured in its zone.

Simultaneously with the 5th Marines' landing, the 1st Marines was to land over Blue Beach at the base of the Inch'on Peninsula just south of the city. This landing area had such extensive mud flats that heavy equipment could not be brought ashore over it. It lay just below the tidal basin of the inner harbor and an adjacent wide expanse of salt evaporators. Its principal advantage derived from the fact that the railroad and main highway to Seoul from Inch'on lay only a little more than a mile inland from it. A successful landing there could quickly cut these avenues of escape or access at the rear of Inch'on.[31]

An early objective of the 1st Marine Division after securing the beachhead was Kimpo Airfield, sixteen road miles northeast of Inch'on. Then would follow the crossing of the Han River and the drive on Seoul.

As diversions, the battleship *Missouri* was to shell east coast areas on the opposite side of the Korean peninsula, including the rail center and port of Samch'ok, and a small force was to make a feint at Kunsan on the west coast, 100 air miles south of Inch'on.

Intelligence Estimate

General MacArthur's view at the end of August that the North Koreans had concentrated nearly all their combat resources against Eighth Army in the Pusan Perimeter coincided with the official G-2 estimate. On 28 August the X Corps G-2 Section estimated the enemy strength in Seoul as approximately 5,000 troops, in Inch'on as 1,000, and at Kimpo Airfield as 500, for a total of 6,500 soldiers in the Inch'on-Seoul area. On 4 September the estimate remained about the same except that the enemy force in the Inch'on landing area was placed at 1,800–2,500 troops because of an anticipated build-up there. This estimate remained relatively unchanged four days later, and thereafter held constant until the landing.[32]

American intelligence considered the enemy's ability to reinforce quickly the Inch'on-Seoul area as inconsequential. It held the view that only small rear area garrisons, line of communications units, and newly formed, poorly trained groups were scattered throughout Korea back of the combat zone around the Pusan Perimeter. Aerial reconnaissance reported heavy movement of enemy southbound traffic from the Manchurian border, but it was not clear whether this was of supplies or troops, or both. Although reports showed that the Chinese Communist Forces had increased in strength along the Manchurian border, there was no confirmation of rumors that some of them had moved into North Korea.[33]

The Far East Command considered the possibility that the enemy might reinforce the Inch'on-Seoul area from forces committed against Eighth Army in the south. If this were attempted, it appeared that the North Korean *3d, 13th,* and *10th Divisions,* deployed in either side of the main Seoul-Taejon-Taegu highway, could most rapidly reach the Inch'on area.

North Korean air and naval elements were considered incapable of interfering with the landing. On 28 August the Far East Command estimated there were only nineteen obsolescent Soviet-manufactured aircraft available to the North Korean Air Force. The U.N. air element, nevertheless, had orders to render unusable any known or suspected enemy air facilities, and particularly to give attention to new construction at Kimpo, Suwon, and Taejon. North Korean naval elements were almost nonexistent at this time. Five divisions of small patrol-type vessels comprised the North Korean Navy; one was on the west coast at Chinnamp'o, the others at Wonsan on the east coast. At both places they were bottled up and rendered impotent. On the morning of 7 September a ROK patrol vessel (PC boat) north of Inch'on discovered and sank a small craft engaged in mine laying; thus it appeared that some mines were to be expected.[34]

As a final means of checking on conditions in Inch'on harbor, the Navy on 31 August sent Lt. Eugene F. Clark to Yonghung-do, an island at the mouth of the ship channel ten sea miles from

Inch'on. There, Clark used friendly natives to gather the information needed. He sent them on several trips to Inch'on to measure water depths, check on the mud flats, and to observe enemy strength and fortifications. He transmitted their reports by radio to friendly vessels in Korean waters. Clark was still in the outer harbor when the invasion fleet entered it.[35]

The Ships Load Out

At the end of August the ports of Kobe, Sasebo, and Yokohama in Japan and Pusan in Korea had become centers of intense activity as preparations for mounting the invasion force entered the final stage. The 1st Marine Division, less the 5th Marines, was to outload at Kobe, the 5th Marines at Pusan, and the 7th Infantry Division at Yokohama. Most of the escorting vessels, the Gunfire Support Group, and the command ships assembled at Sasebo.

The ships to carry the troops, equipment, and supplies began arriving at the predesignated loading points during the last days of August. In order to reach Inch'on by morning of 15 September, the LSTs had to leave Kobe on 10 September and the transports (APs) and cargo ships (AKs) on 12 September. Only the assault elements were combat-loaded. Japanese crews manned thirty-seven of the forty-seven LSTs in the Marine convoy.[36]

The loading of the 1st Marine Division at Kobe was in full swing on 2 September when word came that the next morning a typhoon would strike the port, where more than fifty vessels were assembled. All unloading and loading stopped for thirty-six hours. At 0600 on 3 September, Typhoon *Jane* screeched in from the east. Wind velocity reached 110 miles an hour at noon. Waves forty feet high crashed against the waterfront and breakers rolled two feet high across the piers where loose cargo lay. Seven American ships broke their lines and one of the giant 200-ton cranes broke loose. Steel lines two and a half inches thick snapped. Only by exhausting and dangerous work did port troops and the marines fight off disaster. By 1530 in the afternoon the typhoon began to blow out to sea. An hour later relative calm descended on the port and the cleanup work began. A few vessels had to go into drydock for repairs, some vehicles were flooded out, and a large quantity of clothing had to be cleaned, dried, and repackaged.[37]

Despite the delay and damage caused by *Jane*, the port of Kobe and the 1st Marine Division met the deadline of outloading by 11 September. On the 10th and the 11th, sixty-six cargo vessels cleared Kobe for Inch'on. They sailed just ahead of another approaching typhoon. This second typhoon had been under observation by long-range reconnaissance planes since 7 September. Named *Kezia,* it was plotted moving from the southwest at a speed that would put it over the Korean Straits on 12–13 September.

On the 11th, the 1st Marine Division sailed from Kobe and the 7th Infantry Division from Yokohama. The next day the 5th Marines departed Pusan to rendezvous at sea. The flagship *Rochester* with Admiral Struble aboard got under way from Sasebo for Inch'on at 1530, 12 September. That afternoon a party of dignitaries, including Generals MacArthur, Almond, Wright, Maj. Gen. Alonzo P. Fox, Maj. Gen. Courtney Whitney, and General Shepherd of the Marine Corps, flew from Tokyo to Itazuke Air Base and proceeded from there by automobile to Sasebo, arriving at 2120. Originally, the MacArthur party had planned to fly from Tokyo on the 13th and embark on the *Mt. McKinley* at Kokura that evening. But Typhoon *Kezia's* sudden change of direction caused the revision of plans to assure that the party would be embarked in time. The *Mt. McKinley,* sailing from Kobe with Admiral Doyle and General Smith aboard, had not yet arrived at Sasebo when MacArthur's party drove up. It finally pulled in at midnight, and departed for the invasion area half an hour later after taking MacArthur's party aboard.[38]

Part of the invasion fleet encountered very rough seas off the southern tip of Kyushu early on 13 September. Winds reached sixty miles an hour and green water broke over ships' bows. In some cases, equipment shifted in the holds, and in other instances deck-loaded equipment was damaged. During the day the course of *Kezia* shifted to the northeast and by afternoon the seas traversed by the invasion fleet began to calm. The aircraft carrier *Boxer,* steaming at forced speed from the California coast with 110 planes aboard, fought the typhoon all night in approaching Japan. At dusk on the 14th, it quickly departed Sasebo and at full speed cut through the seas for Inch'on.[39]

Preliminary Bombardment

Air attacks intended to isolate the invasion area began on 4 September and continued until the landing. On the 10th, Marine air elements struck Wolmi-do in a series of napalm attacks. Altogether, sixty-five sorties hit Inch'on during the day.[40]

The main task of neutralizing enemy batteries on Wolmi-do guarding the Inch'on inner harbor was the mission of Rear Adm. J. M. Higgins' Gunfire Support Group. This group, composed of United States heavy cruisers, 2 British light cruisers, and 6 U.S. destroyers, entered the approaches to Inch'on harbor at 1010, 13 September. Just before noon the group in Flying Fish Channel sighted an enemy mine field, exposed at low water. It destroyed some of the mines with automatic fire. At 1220, the 4 cruisers anchored from seven to ten miles offshore, while 5 destroyers—the *Mansfield, DeHaven, Swenson, Collett,* and *Gurke*—proceeded on to anchorages close to Wolmi-do under cover of air strikes by planes from Fast Carrier Task Force 77. The destroyers began the bombardment of Wolmi-do at 1230.[41]

Five enemy heavily revetted 75-mm. guns returned the fire. In the intense ship-shore duel, the *Collett* received nine hits and sustained considerable damage. Enemy shells hit the *Gurke* three times, but caused no serious damage. The *Swenson* took a near miss which caused two casualties: one was Lt. (jg.) David H. Swenson, the only American killed during the bombardment. The destroyers withdrew at 1347.

At 1352 the cruisers, anchored out of range of the Wolmi-do batteries, began an hour and a half bombardment. Planes of Task Force 77 then came in for a heavy strike against the island. After the air strike terminated, the cruisers resumed their bombardment at 1610 for another half hour. Then at 1645 the Gunfire Support Group got under way and withdrew back down the channel.[42]

The next day, D minus 1, the Gunfire Support Group returned. Just before 1100, planes of Task Force 77 again delivered heavy strikes against the island. The heavy cruisers began their second bombardment at 1116, this time also taking under fire targets within Inch'on proper. The destroyers waited about an hour and then moved to their anchorages off Wolmi-do. The cruisers ceased firing while another air strike came in on the island. After it ended, the five destroyers began their bombardment at 1255 and in an hour and fifteen minutes fired 1,732 5-inch shells into Wolmi-do and Inch'on. When they left there was no return fire—the Wolmi-do batteries were silent.[43]

Securing the Inch'on Beachhead

The X Corps expeditionary troops arriving off Inch'on on 15 September numbered nearly 70,000 men.[44] At 0200 the Advance

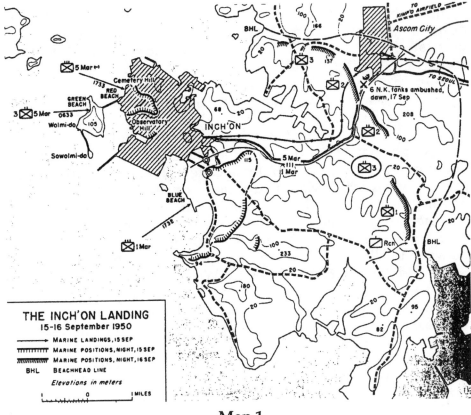

Map 1

Attack Group, including the Gunfire Support Group, the rocket ships (LSMRs) and the Battalion Landing Team, began the approach to Inch'on. A special radar-equipped task force, consisting of three high speed transports (APDs) and one Landing Ship Dock (LSD), carried the Battalion Landing Team—Lt. Col. Robert D. Taplett's 3d Battalion, 5th Marines, and a platoon of nine M26 Pershing tanks from A Company, 1st Tank Battalion—toward the transport area off Wolmi-do. Dawn of invasion day came with a high overcast sky and portent of rain.[45]

Wolmi-do, or Moon Tip Island, as it might be translated, is a circular hill—(Hill 105) about 1,000 yards across and rising 335 feet above the water. A rocky hill, it was known to be honeycombed with caves, trenches, gun positions, and dugouts. (*Map 1*)

The first action came at 0500. Eight Marine Corsairs left their escort carrier for a strike on Wolmi-do. The first two planes caught an armored car crossing the causeway from Inch'on and destroyed it. There was no other sign of life visible on the island as the flight bombed the ridge line. At 0530 the Special Task Force was in its designated position ready to land the assault troops. Twenty minutes later, Taplett's 3d Battalion began loading into 17 landing craft (LCVPs); the 9 tanks loaded into 3 landing ships (LSVs). L-hour was fifty minutes away.

Air strikes and naval gunfire raked Wolmi-do and, after this, three rocket ships moved in close and put down an intense rocket barrage. The landing craft straightened out into lines from their circles and moved toward the line of departure. Just as a voice announced over the ship's loud speaker, "Landing force crossing line of departure," MacArthur came on the bridge of the *Mt. McKinley*. It was 0625. The first major amphibious assault by American troops against an enemy since Easter Sunday, 1 April 1945, at Okinawa was under way. About one mile of water lay between the line of departure and the Wolmi-do beach.[46]

The 3d Battalion moved toward Wolmi-do with G and H Companies in assault and I Company in reserve. Even after the American rocket barrage lifted there was still no enemy fire. The first wave of troops reached the bathing beach on the northern arm of the island unopposed at 0633.

The first troops ashore moved rapidly inland against almost no resistance. Within a few minutes the second wave landed. Then came the LSVs carrying the tanks, three of which carried dozer blades for breaking up barbed wire, filling trenches, and sealing caves; three other tanks mounted flame throwers. One group of marines raised the American flag on the high ground of Wolmi-do half an hour after landing. Another force crossed the island and sealed off the causeway leading to Inch'on. The reduction of the island continued systematically and it was secured at 0750.[47]

A little later in the morning, Colonel Taplett sent a squad of marines and three tanks over the causeway to Sowolmi-do where they destroyed an estimated platoon of enemy troops; some surrendered, others swam into the sea, and still others were killed. Taplett's battalion assumed defensive positions and prepared to cover the main Inch'on landing later in the day.

In the capture of Wolmi-do and Sowolmi-do the Battalion Landing Team killed 108 enemy soldiers and captured 136. About 100 more in several caves refused to surrender and were sealed by tank dozers into their caves. Marine casualties were light—seventeen wounded.[48]

The preinvasion intelligence on Wolmi-do proved to be essentially correct. Prisoners indicated that about 400 North Korean soldiers, elements of the *3d Battalion, 226th Independent Marine*

Regiment, and some artillery troops of the *918th Artillery Regiment* had defended Wolmi-do.

After the easy capture of Wolmi-do came the anxious period when the tide began to fall, causing further activity to cease until late in the afternoon. The enemy by now was fully alerted. Marine and naval air ranged up and down the roads and over the countryside isolating the port to a depth of twenty-five miles, despite a rain which began to fall in the late afternoon. Naval gunfire covered the closer approaches to Inch'on.

Assault troops of the 5th and 1st Marines began going over the sides of their transports and into the landing craft at 1530. After a naval bombardment, rocket ships moved in close to Red and Blue Beaches and fired 2,000 rockets on the landing areas. Landing craft crossed lines of departure at 1645, and forty-five minutes later neared the beaches. The first wave of the 5th Marines breasted the sea wall on Red Beach at 1733. Most of the A Company men in the fourteen boats of the first three waves climbed over the sea wall with scaling ladders; a few boats put their troops ashore through holes in the wall made by the naval bombardment.[49]

On the left flank of the landing area, the 3d Platoon of A Company encountered enemy troops in trenches and a bunker just beyond the sea wall. There in an intense fight the marines lost eight men killed and twenty-eight wounded. Twenty-two minutes after landing, the company fired a flare signaling that it held Cemetery Hill. On top of Cemetery Hill, North Koreans threw down their arms and surrendered to the 2d Platoon. Other elements of the battalion by midnight had fought their way against sporadic resistance to the top of Observatory Hill.

The 2d Battalion, 5th Marines, landing on the right side of Red Beach, encountered only spotty resistance, and at a cost of only a few casualties gained its objective.

Assault elements of the 1st Marines began landing over Blue Beach at 1732, one minute ahead of the 5th Marines at Red Beach. Most of the men were forced to climb a high sea wall to gain exit from the landing area. One group went astray in the smoke and landed on the sea wall enclosing the salt flats on the left of the beach. The principal obstacle the 1st Marines encountered was the blackness of the night. Lt. Col. Alan Sutter's 2d Battalion lost one man killed and nineteen wounded in advancing to the Inch'on-Seoul highway one mile inland. The landing force had taken its final D-day objectives by 0130, 16 September.[50]

Following the assault troops, eight specially loaded LSTs landed at Red Beach just before high tide, and unloading of equip-

ment to support the forces ashore the next day continued throughout the night. Beaching of the LSTs brought tragedy. Just after
1830, after receiving some enemy mortar and machine gun fire,
gun crews on three of the LSTs began firing wildly with 20-mm.
and 40-mm. cannon, and, before they could be stopped, had killed
1 and wounded 23 men of the 2d Battalion, 5th Marines. The
Marine landing force casualties on D-day were 20 men killed, 1
missing in action, and 174 wounded.[51] The U.N. preinvasion estimate of enemy strength at Inch'on was accurate. Prisoners dis-
closed that about 2,000 men had comprised the Inch'on garrison.
Some units of the N.K. *22d Regiment* moved to Inch'on to reinforce
the garrison before dawn of the 15th, but they retreated to Seoul
after the main landing that evening. To the rank and file of the
North Korean soldiers in Seoul the landing came as a surprise.[52]

On the morning of 16 September the two regiments ashore
established contact with each other by 0730. Thereafter a solid line
existed around Inch'on and escape for any enemy still within the
city became unlikely. The ROK Marines now took over mop-up
work in Inch'on and went at it with such a will that hardly anyone
in the port city, friend or foe, was safe.[53]

Early in the morning of the 16th, Marine aircraft took off from
the carriers to aid the advance. One flight of eight Corsairs left the
Sicily at 0548. Soon it sighted six enemy T34 tanks on the Seoul
highway three miles east of Inch'on moving toward the latter
place. Ordered to strike at once, the Corsairs hit the tanks with
napalm and 500-pound bombs, damaging three of them and scat-
tering the accompanying infantry. The enemy returned the fire,
hitting one of the Corsairs. Capt. William F. Simpson's plane
crashed and exploded near the burning armor, killing him. A
second flight of eight Corsairs continued the attack on the tanks
with napalm and bombs and, reportedly, destroyed them all. Later
in the morning, however, when the advance platoon of the 1st
Marines and accompanying tanks approached the site, three of the
T34s began to move, whereupon the Pershings engaged and destroyed them.[54]

Both Marine regiments on the second day advanced rapidly
against light resistance and by evening had reached the Beachhead
Line, six miles from the landing area. Their casualties for the day
were four killed and twenty-one wounded.

Thus, within twenty-four hours of the main landing, the 1st
Marine Division had secured the high ground east of Inch'on,
occupied an area sufficient to prevent enemy artillery fire on the
landing and unloading area, and obtained a base from which to

mount the attack to seize Kimpo Airfield. In the evening of 16 September General Smith established his command post east of Inch'on and from there at 1800 notified Admiral Doyle that he was assuming responsibility for operations ashore.[55]

Capture of Kimpo Airfield and Advance to the Han River

During the advance thus far the boundary between the 5th and 1st Marines had followed generally the main Inch'on-Seoul highway, which ran east-west, with the 5th Marines on the north and the 1st Marines astride and on its south side. Just beyond the beachhead line the boundary left the highway and slanted northeast. This turned Colonel Murray's 5th Marines toward Kimpo Airfield, seven miles away, and the Han River just beyond it. Col. Lewis B. Puller's 1st Marines, astride the Inch'on-Seoul highway, headed toward Yongdungp'o, the large industrial suburb of Seoul on the south bank of the Han, ten air miles away.

During the night of 16–17 September, the 2d Battalion, 5th Marines, occupied a forward defensive position commanding the Seoul highway just west of Ascorn City. Behind it the 1st Battalion held a high hill. From a forward roadblock position, members of an advanced platoon of D Company, at 0545 on the 17th, saw the dim outlines of six tanks on the road eastward. Infantry accompanied the tanks, some riding on the armor.

The enemy armored force moved past the hidden outpost of D Company. At 0600, at a range of seventy-five yards, rockets fired from a bazooka set one of the tanks on fire. Pershing tanks now opened fire on the T34s. The recoilless rifles joined in. Within five minutes combined fire destroyed all six enemy tanks and killed 200 of an estimated 250 enemy infantry. Only one man in the 2d Battalion was wounded.[56]

Early that morning, General MacArthur, accompanied by Admiral Struble, and Generals Almond, Wright, Fox, Whitney, and others came ashore and proceeded to General Smith's command post, and from there went on to the position of the 2d Battalion, 5th Marines, where they saw the numerous enemy dead and the still-burning T34 tanks. On the way they had passed the six tanks destroyed the morning before. The sight of twelve destroyed enemy tanks seemed to them a good omen for the future.[57]

The 5th Marines advanced rapidly on the 17th and by 1800 its 2d Battalion was at the edge of Kimpo Airfield. In the next two hours the battalion seized the southern part of the airfield. The 400–500 enemy soldiers who ineffectively defended it appeared surprised and had not even mined the runway. During the night several small enemy counterattacks hit the perimeter positions at the airfield between 0200 and dawn, 18 September. The marines repulsed these company-sized counterattacks, inflicting heavy casualties on the enemy troops, who finally fled to the northwest E Company and supporting tanks played the leading role in these actions. Kimpo was secured during the morning of 18 September.[58]

The capture on the fourth day of the 6,000-foot-long, 150-foot-wide, hard surfaced Kimpo runway, with a weight capacity of 120,000 pounds, gave the U.N. Command one of its major objectives. It broadened greatly the capability of employing air power in the ensuing phases of the attack on Seoul; and, more important still, it provided the base for air operations seeking to disrupt supply of the North Korean Army.

On the 18th, the 2d Battalion, 5th Marines, sent units on to the Han River beyond the airfield, and the 1st Battalion captured Hill 99 northeast of it and then advanced to the river. At 1409 in the afternoon a Marine Corsair landed at Kimpo and, later in the day, advance elements of Marine Air Group 33 flew in from Japan. The next day more planes came in from Japan, including C-54 cargo planes, and on 20 September land-based Corsairs made the first strikes from Kimpo.[59]

Continuing its sweep along the river, the 1st Battalion, 5th Marines, on the 19th swung right and captured the last high ground (Hills 118, 80, and 85) a mile west of Yongdungp'o. At the same time, the 2d Battalion seized the high ground along the Han River in its sector. At nightfall, 19 September, the 5th Marines held the south bank of the Han River everywhere in its zone and was preparing for a crossing the next morning. (*Map VII*)

Meanwhile, the 2d Engineer Special Brigade relieved the ROK Marines of responsibility for the security of Inch'on, and the ROKs moved up on the 18th and 19th to the Han River near Kimpo. Part of the ROKs Marines extended the left flank of the 5th Marines, and its 2d Battalion joined them for the projected crossing of the Han River the next day.[60]

In this action, the 1st Marines had attacked east toward Yongdungp'o astride the Seoul highway. Its armored spearheads destroyed four enemy tanks early on the morning of the 17th. Then, from positions on high ground (Hills 208, 107, 178), three miles short of Sosa, a village halfway between Inch'on and Yong-dungp'o, a regiment of the N.K. *18th Division* checked the advance. At nightfall the Marine regiment dug in for the night a mile from Sosa. At Ascom City, just west of Sosa, American troops found 2,000 tons of ammunition for American artillery, mortars, and machine-guns, captured there by the North Koreans in June, all still in good condition.[61]

Not all the action that day was on and over land just after daylight, at 0550, two enemy YAK planes made bombing runs on the *Rochester* lying in Inch'on harbor. The first drop of four 100-pound bombs missed astern, except for one which ricocheted off the airplane crane without exploding. The second drop missed close to the port bow, causing minor damage to electrical equipment. One of the YAKs strafed H.M.S. *Jamaica*, which shot down the plane but suffered three casualties.[62]

Ashore, the 1st Marines resumed the attack on the morning of the 18th and passed through and around the burning town of Sosa at midmorning. By noon the 3d Battalion had seized Hill 123, a mile east of the town and north of the highway. Enemy artillery fire there caused many casualties in the afternoon but neither ground nor aerial observers could locate the enemy pieces firing from the southeast. Beyond Sosa the North Koreans had heavily mined the highway and on 19 September the tank spearheads stopped after mines damaged two tanks. Engineers began the slow job of removing the mines and, without tank support, the infantry advance slowed. But at nightfall advanced elements of the regiment had reached Kalch'on Creek just west of Yong-dungp'o.[63]

Other elements of the X Corps had by now arrived to join in the battle for Seoul. Vessels carrying the 7th Infantry Division arrived in Inch'on harbor on the 16th. General Almond was anxious to get the 7th Division into position to block a possible enemy movement from the south of Seoul, and he arranged with Admiral Doyle to hasten its unloading. The 2d Battalion of the 32d Regiment landed during the morning of the 18th; the rest of the regiment landed later in the day. On the morning of 19 September, the 2d Battalion, 32d Infantry, moved up to relieve the 2d Battalion, 1st Marines, in its position on the right flank south of the Seoul highway. It completed the relief without incident by noon. The total effective strength of the 32d Infantry when it went into the line was 5,114 men—3,241 Americans and 1,873 ROKs. Responsibility for the zone south of the highway passed to the 7th Division at 1800, 19 September. During the day, the 31st Regiment of the 7th Division came ashore at Inch'on.[64]

The Navy had supported the ground action thus far with effective naval gunfire. The *Rochester* and *Toledo* had been firing at ranges up to 30,000 yards in support of the marines and the ROKs on their left flank. Now, on the 19th, the *Missouri* arrived in Inch'on harbor from the east coast of Korea and began delivering naval gunfire support to the 7th Division on the right flank. Despite difficult tide conditions and other restrictive factors in Inch'on harbor, the Navy by the evening of 18 September had unloaded 25,606 persons, 4,547 vehicles, and 14,166 tons of cargo.[65]

The battle for Seoul lay ahead. Mounting indications were that it would be far more severe than had been the action at Inch'on and the advance to the Han. Every day enemy resistance had increased on the road to Yongdungp'o. Aerial observers and fighter pilots reported large bodies of troops moving toward Seoul from the north. The N.K. *18th Division,* on the point of moving from Seoul to the Naktong front when the landing came at Inch'on, was instead ordered to retake Inch'on, and its advanced elements had engaged the 1st Marines in the vicinity of Sosa. On the 17th, enemy engineer units began mining the approaches to the Han River near Seoul. About the same time, the N.K. *70th Regiment* moved from Suwon to join in the battle. As they prepared to cross the Han, the marines estimated that there might be as many as 20,000 enemy troops in Seoul to defend the city. The X Corps intelligence estimate on 19 September, however, undoubtedly expressed the opinion prevailing among American commanders—that the enemy was "capable of offering stubborn resistance in Seoul but unless substantially reinforced, he is not considered capable of making a successful defense."[66]

Not until their 18 September communiqué did the North Koreans mention publicly anything connected with the Inch'on landing and then merely stated that detachments of coastal defense had brought down American fighter planes.[67]

Notes

1. Interv, author with Almond, 13 Dec 51; MS review comments, Almond for author, 23 Oct 53; Hq X Corps, Opn CHROMITE, G-3 Sec, 15 Aug–30 Sep 50, p. 1; Lynn Montross and Capt. Nicholas A. Canzona, USMC, *U.S. Marine Operations in Korea, 1950–1953,* vol. II, *The Inchon-Seoul Operation* (Washington: Historical Branch, G-3, Headquarters, U.S. Marine Corps, 1954), pp. 4–7.

2. Schnabel, FEC, GHQ Support and Participation in the Korean War, ch. V, pp. 1–18.

3. *Ibid.*, ch. 5, pp. 12–13; Interv with Wright, 7 Jan 54. The landing at Kunsan called for a drive inland to Taejon; that at Chumunjin-up included a ROK division and called for an advance down the coastal road to Kangnung and then west to Wonju.

4. GHQ FEC, Ann Narr Hist Rpt, Jan–Oct 50, p. 11.

5. Schnabel, FEC, GHQ Support and Participation in the Korean War, ch. V, p. 25, quoting Rad C58993, CINCFE to JCS, 29 Jul 50.

6. Diary of CG X Corps, Opn CHROMITE; Interv, author with Wright, 7 Jan 54; interv, author with Maj Gen Clark L. Ruffner, 27 Aug 51.

7. Schnabel, Theater Command, ch. VIII. This volume will treat in detail the planning of the Inch'on landing and the policy debate on it. Hq X Corps, Opn CHROMITE.

8. Interv, author with Almond, 13 Dec 51; Hq X Corps, Opn CHROMITE; Almond biographical sketch.

9. 1st Mar Div SAR, Sep 50; Lt Gen Oliver P. Smith, MS review comments with ltr to Maj Gen Albert C. Smith, Chief Mil Hist, 25 Feb 54; Karig, *et al., Battle Report, The War in Korea*, pp. 123, 172.

10. 1st Mar Div SAR, vol. III, pp. 1–2; Smith, MS review comments.

11. EUSAK WD, 31 Jul 50, Memo for CofS, Strategic Status of 7th Inf Div; Schnabel, FEC, GHQ Support and Participation in the Korean War, ch. V, p. 5, citing Ltr, CINCFE to CG Eighth Army, 4 Aug 50; Maj Gen David G. Barr (CG 7th Inf Div), Notes, 1, 6, 31 Jul 50 (copies furnished author by Barr).

12. Schnabel, FEC, GHQ Support and Participation in the Korean War, ch. V, pp. 31–32; GHQ FEC, Ann Narr Hist Rpt, 1 Jan–31 Oct 50, p. 45; 7th Div WD, Aug–Sep 50; Barr, Notes, 4 Sep 50.

13. 7th Inf Div WD, 1 Sep 50; Diary of CG X Corps, Opn CHRONIITE, 1 Sep 50; Barr, MS review comments, 1957.

14. Interv, author with Barr, 1 Feb 54; Barr, Notes, 4 Sep 50.

15. Interv, author with Wright, 7 Jan 54; Interv, author with Eberle, 12 Jan 54; Ltr, Wright to author, 22 Mar 45; Almond, MS review comments for author, 23 Oct 53; Schabel, FEC, GHQ support and Participation in the Korean War, ch. V, p. 23; Interv, author with Lutes (FEC Planning Sec), 7 Oct 51.

16. Schnabel, Theater Command ch. VIII; *New York Times*, August 19, 1950.

17. The account of the 23 July conference is based on the following sources: Ltr, Wright to author, 22 Mar 54; Ltr, joy to author, 12 Dec 52; Ltr, Almond to author, 2 Dec 52; Smith, MS review comments; Montross and Canzona, *The Inch'on-Seoul Operation*, pp. 40–47; Karig, *et al., Battle Report, the War in Korea*, p. 169. General MacArthur's MS review comments show no comment on this section.

18. Schnabel, FEC, GHQ Support and Participation in the Korean War, ch. V, p. 6, citing Msg JCS 89960, JCS to CINCFE, 28 Aug 50.

19. Schnabel, FEC, GHQ Support and Participation in the Korean war, ch. VIII; Smith MS review comments 25 Feb 54.

20. Rad C62423, CINCFE to JCS, 8 Sep 50, and Rad 90958, JCS to CINCFE, 8 Sep 50.

21. In the course of the MacArthur hearings the next year, Secretary Johnson, in response to an inquiry from Senator Alexander Wiley, said, "I had been

carrying along with General MacArthur the responsibility for Inch'on. General Collins—maybe the censor will want to strike this out—did not favor Inch'on and went over to try to argue General MacArthur out of it.

"General MacArthur stood pat. I backed MacArthur, and the President has always, had before backed me on it." See Senate Committees on Armed Services and Foreign Relations, 82d Cong., 1st sess., June 1951, Hearings on *Military Situation in the Far East and the Relief of General MacArthur*, pt. 4, p. 2618.

22. Smith, MS review comments, 25 Feb 54.

23. Interv, author with Almond, 13 Dec 51; Smith, MS review comments, 25 Feb 54; Diary of CG X Corps, Opn CHROMITE, 2 Sep 50; Schnabel, FEC, GHQ Support and Participation in the Korean War, ch. V, pp. 26–27.

24. GHQ FEC, G-3 Sec, Wright, Memo for Record, 041930K Sep 50, reporting on his discussions with Walker and subsequent report to General Almond; Barr, Notes, 6 Sep 50.

25. Commander, Joint Task Force Seven and Seventh Fleet, Inch'on Report, September 1950, I-B-1 (hereafter cited as JTF 7, Inch'on Rpt).

26. JTF 7, Inch'on Rpt, p. 1; Ltr, Wright to author, 22 Mar 54.

27. JTF 7, Inch'on Rpt, p. 4, I-D-3, and ans. I and K.

28. JTF 7, Inch'on Rpt, an. E, p. 6; Mossman and Middleton, Logistical Problems and Their Solutions. The Navy's operation plan underestimated the size of the basin.

29. JTF 7, Inch'on Rpt. I-C-1 E-6.

30. 1st Mar Div SAR, Inch'on-Seoul, 18 Sep-7 Oct 50, p. 12, and G-3 Sec, an. C.

31. JTF 7, Inch'on Rpt, B-2 Opn Plan and an. B; 1st Mar Div SAR, vol. III, p. 4, and vol. I, p. 13.

32. Hq X Corps, Opn CHROMITE, p. 5; X Corps WD, G-2 Sec, Hist Rpt, 15 Aug–30 Sep 50, p. 1; 1st Mar Div SAR, vol. III, p. 5.

33. X Corps WD, G-2 Sec, Hist Rpt, 15 Aug–30 Sep 50; JTF 7, Inch'on Rpt, II, E-2.

34. JTF 7, Inch'on Rpt, an. E; Schnabel, FEC, GHQ Support and Participation in the Korean War, ch. V, pp. 36–37; Karig, *et. al., Battle Report, The War in Korea*, p. 195.

35. karig, *et. al., Battle Report, The War in Korea*, pp. 176–91, relates the Clark mission in detail.

36. 1st Mar Div SAR, 15 Sep–7 Oct 50, an. D, p. 4; 7th Inf Div WD, Sep 50.

37. JTF 7, Inch'on Rpt, I-D-3; 1st mar Div SAR, 15 Sep–7 Oct 50, an. D, p. 6; SFC William J. K. Griffen, "Typhoon at Kobe," *Marine Corps Gazette* (September 1951); "Operation Load-up," *The Quartermaster Review* (November–December, 1950), p. 40.

38. JTF 7, Inch'on Rpt, II 1; 1st Mar Div SAR, vol. I, pp. 15–18; Diary of CG X Corps, Opn CHROMITE, 12 Sep 50; Ltr, Wright to author, 22 Mar 54; Barr, Notes, 11 Sep 50.

39. Diary of CG X Corps, Opn CHROMITE, 13 Sep 50; Karig, *et al., Battle Report, The War in Korea*, p. 197.

40. GHQ FEC, G-3 Opn Rpt 79, 11 Sep 50; Ernest H. Giusti, "Marine Air Over Inchon-Seoul," *Marine Corps Gazette* (June 1952), p. 19.

41. JTF 7, Inch'on Rpt, I-E-1, Recon in Force; EUSAK WD, 24 Oct 50, G-2 Sec, ADVATIS 1225, Interrog of Sr Lt Cho Chun Hyon.

42. JTF 7, Inch'on Rpt, I-E-1, and II-1; GHQ FEC Sitrep, 14 Sep 50.

43. JTF 7, Inch'on Rpt, I-E-2; Karig, *et al.*, *Battle Report, The War in Korea*, p. 210.

44. Hq X Corps, Opn CHROMITE, G-3 Sec Hist Rpt, (gives strength of X Corps as 69,450); 1st Mar Div SAR, vol. 1, an. A, 5.

The major units were the 1st Marine Division, the 7th Infantry Division, the 92d and 96th Field Artillery Battalions (both 155-mm. howitzers), the 50th Antiaircraft Artillery (Automatic Weapons) Battalion (SP), the 56th Amphibious Tank and Tractor Battalion, the 19th Engineer Combat Group, and the 2d Engineer Special Brigade. The 1st Marine Division on invasion day had a strength of 25,040 men—19,494 organic to the Marine Corps and the Navy, 2,760 Army troops attached, and 2,786 Korean marines attached. Later, after the 7th Marines arrived, the organic Marine strength increased about 4,000 men. On invasion day the GHQ UNC reserve consisted of the 3d Infantry Division and the 187th Airborne Regimental Combat Team (composed of troops from the 11th Airborne Division). The ROK 17th Regiment was in the act of moving from Eighth Army to join X Corps.

45. JTF 7, Inchon Rpt, I-L-1 and I-F-1; 1st Mar Div SAR, vol. 1, p. 13.

46. X Corps WD, Opn CHROMITE, 15 Sep 50: 1st Mar Div SAR, vol. III, an. P, p. 4; Lynn Montross, "The Inchon Landing," *Marine Corps Gazette* (July 1951), pp. 26ff; Geer, *The New Breed*, pp. 213–25.

47. 3d Bn, 5th Mar, Special Act Rpt, an. P to 5th Mar Special Rpt, in 1st Mar Div SAR; JTF 7, Inch'on Rpt, I-F-1, 15 Sep 50.

48. 1st Mar Div SAR, vol. I, an. B, App. 1, 1; JTF 7, Inch'on Rpt, I-H-2; X Corps WD, G-2 Sec, Hist Rpt, Intel Estimate 8.

49. 1st Bn, 5th Mar SAR, p. 3; 1st Mar Div SAR, vol. III; Geer, *The New Breed*, pp. 24–25. Montross and Canzona, *The Inchon-Seoul Operation* covers the 1st Marine Division part of the Inch'on operation in detail. Much of this fine work is based on extensive interviews with participants.

50. 1st Mar Div SAR, Vol. I, an. P, p. 6, and an. C, p. 6; X Corps WD, Opn CHROMITE, 15 Sep 50; Diary of CG X Corps, 15 Sep 50.

51. Montross and Canzona, *The Inch'on-Seoul Operation*, pp. 110–11; Geer, *The New Breed*, p. 128.

52. ATIS Supp Enemy Documents, Issue 2, pp. 114–16, Opn Ord 8–10 Sep 50, CO *226th Unit*, captured 16 Sep 50; ATIS Interrog Rpt (N.K.) Issue 10, p. 7; *Ibid.*, Issue 8, Rpt 1345, Lt Il Chun Son, and Rpt 1346 Lt Lee San Kak; X Corps WD, Opn CHROMITE, p. 26, interrog of Capt Chan Chul, and p. 30), interrog of Lt Col Kim Yonh Mo.

53. Diary of CG X Corps, 16 Sep 50; Montross, "The Inchon Landing," *op. cit.*

54. X Corps WD, G-3 Sec, Msgs J-2, 4, 6, 7 from 160705 to 160825, Sep 50; 1st Mar Div SAR, vol. II, an. OO, p. 15; Geer, *The New Breed*, p. 128; ATIS Enemy Documents, issue 10, Rpt 1529, Hang Yong Sun, and Rpt 1534, Lt Lee Song Yol.

55. 1st Mar Div SAR, vol. I. p. 22, and an. C, p. 7; Smith, MS review comments, 25 Feb 54.

56. 5th Mar SAR, pp. 7–8, in 1st Mar Div SAR, vol. III; 1st Mar Div SAR, vol. II, an. OO, p. 16; Montross and Canzona, *The Inchon-Seoul Operation*, pp. 147–51.

57. Ltr, Wright to author, 22 Mar 54; Diary of CG X Corps, 17 Sep 50.

58. 5th Mar SAR, 17 Sep 50, pp. 7–8, in the 1st Mar Div SAR, vol. III; 1st Mar Div SAR, vol. I, p. 18; X Corps WD, G-3 Sec, 18 Sep 50; New York *Herald Tribune*, September 18, 1950, Bigart dispatch.

59. 1st Mar Div SAR, G-3 an. C, vol. 1, p. 10; JTF 7, Inch'on Rpt, 18 Sep 50; USAF Hist Study 71, p. 66; New York *Herald Tribune*, September 19, 1950, Bigart dispatch.

60. 1st Mar Div SAR, vol. I, G-3 Sec, an. C, pp. 10–13, 18–19 Sep 50; Geer, *The New Breed*, pp. 133–34.

61. 1st Mar Div SAR, vol. I, G-3 Sec, an. C, p. 8 and an. B, app. 2, p. 1; New York *Herald Tribune*, September 18, 1950, Bigart dispatch; CINCFE, Sitrep, 250600–260600 Sep 50.

62. JTF 7, Inchon Rpt, I-F-2 and IV-1.

63. 1st Mar Div SAR, vol. I, G-3 Sec, an. C, pp. 10–13, 18–19 Sep 50; Geer, *The New Breed*, p. 136; Montross and Canzona, *The Inchon-Seoul Operation*, p. 178.

64. 32d Inf WD, 16–19 Sep 50; Diary of CG X Corps, 18–19 Sep 50; JTF 7, Inchon Rpt, I-F-2; 1st Mar Div SAR, G-3 Sec, an. C, p. 13, 19 Sep 50; Almond, MS review comments for author, 23 Oct 53; 7th Inf Div WD, 16–19 Sep 50; 31st Inf WD, 19 Sep 50.

65. JTF 7, Incho'n Rpt, 18 Sep 50, and II-6.

66. JTF 7, Inch'on Rpt, I-F-2 and an. B, app. 2, p. 2, 18 Sep 50; ATIS Interrog Rpts (N.K.) Issue 8, Rpt 1300, p. 1, Hon Gun Mun, p. 40, Kim So Sung; Rpt 1336, p. 45, Kim Won Yong; Rpt 1365, p. 90, Kan Chun Kil; Rpt 1369, p. 96, Maj Chu Yong Bok: Ibid., Issue 9, p. 29, Kim Te Jon; X Corps PIR 1, 19 Sep 50; Giusti, "Marine Air Over Inch'on-Seoul," *op. cit.*, p. 19.

67. New York *Times*, September 19, 1950.

Reading 11

From Total War to Limited War

by D. Clayton James

Limits on the Ground War

The limitations imposed on both sides were of various types, consisting of both unilateral and bilateral restrictions and covering ground, sea, and air operations, as well as a host of nonoperational factors. Most were specifically designed to avert general war, but some were forced by enemy moves or by miscellaneous obstacles, such as logistical shortages, terrain or weather difficulties, and adverse public opinion.

One of the most persistent demands of MacArthur from the summer of 1950 until his removal the next spring was to take advantage of the offers of Chiang Kai-shek to use his troops in Korea or in operations against the Chinese mainland. The State Department, along with the British and other Allied governments, strongly believed that the introduction of Nationalist Chinese forces in Korea would help to bring the Communist Chinese into the fray, or if the CCF was already engaged, would cause Peking to commit even more of its estimated 4.5 million troops into the Korean conflict. During the Chinese civil war, moreover, the United States had gradually decreased its support of Chiang's regime from the peak assistance during World War II. Following the Nationalist move to Formosa, State officials had expected the island to be overrun shortly by Mao's forces, and the American relationship to Chiang had become even more tepid. Soon after the Korean hostilities began Truman had, in effect, set forth a policy of acknowledging two Chinas and of neutralizing Formosa by means of the Seventh Fleet patrol in the Formosa Strait. Among America's coalition members and, indeed, throughout the UN, the use of Nationalist troops in Korea would be viewed as a return by Washington to its close identification with Chiang during the war against Japan.

The JCS, in addition, did not need much persuasion to reject Chiang's offer because, as military chiefs, they were sharply critical of the low state of combat readiness of Chiang's soldiers. Collins testified at the Senate hearings in May 1951 that the Joint Chiefs "were highly skeptical that we would get anything more out of these [Nationalist] Chinese than we were getting out of the South Koreans, because these were the same people that were run off [mainland] China, in the first place." They also foresaw the Nationalist troops causing a heavy drain on American logistics in Korea, which were never adequate to satisfy altogether the supply needs of all the American units and the ROK and Allied forces that were also dependent upon those stores.

Chiang, in turn, clung to several small offshore islands, mainly Quemoy, Matsu, and the Tachens, in the vain hope during the Korean War as well as in the later 1950s, that communist shellings of the islands' garrisons might draw the Seventh Fleet and ultimately more American forces into entanglements with Communist China in those areas. Formosa's strategic location complicated the war's contingencies enough without the addition of Chiang's forces in action in Korea or on the Chinese mainland. Unlike Rhee, Chiang was sufficiently isolated on his island redoubt so that, whatever his discontent about American policy, he had little chance to disrupt the armistice negotiations or to intervene by force on his own.

At Panmunjom on November 27, 1951, the UN and communist truce delegations ratified an agreement that the military demarcation line was to be the line of contact, with a demilitarized zone formed by both armies pulling back two kilometers when the armistice was signed. Combat casualties on both sides had been heavy since July when the truce talks had begun, but now Ridgway, on orders from Washington, kept the UNC ground forces on a short leash, permitting Van Fleet to launch no major ground operations after the agreement on the demarcation line. The casualty rate would reach high levels again at times when one army or the other would try to improve its outpost lines or main defensive positions by seizing certain key points of high terrain, such as the ferocious battles over Pork Chop Hill. But by and large, combat operations were kept at small-unit levels after Panmunjom.

The demarcation issue had been settled principally on terms that the communist side had pushed, with Washington leaders hoping that the UN concession would lead to an armistice soon. This proved illusory, but the UN demarcation gesture and the abandonment of large-scale offensive operations by the UN forces were efforts at restricting the war and hastening a cease-fire that the civilian leaders in Washington appreciated far more than did Van Fleet and his commanders, who felt that their forces were unnecessarily restricted in their operations after November 1951.

While the UN side's refusal to employ Nationalist Chinese forces seems to have been an ameliorating influence on Red China's further escalation of the Korean combat, the deliberate limitation on UN major assaults after the settlement of the demarcation line was not followed by a corresponding willful restriction on the enemy side. Instead, the CCFs offensive possibilities were limited usually by the tremendous artillery and air firepower the UNC could focus upon large preassault assemblies of enemy troops. But willfully or not, the CCF and UNC remained in a stalemate. On only one occasion, the CCF offensive of June 10–July 20, 1953, did the enemy gain considerable ground, and that was achieved against relatively weak ROK forces.

The refusal of the Truman administration to condone any form of American ground operations outside Korea was significant because it apparently signaled Moscow and Peking that the United States was anxious to avoid an expansion that could trigger a global holocaust. On June 27, 1950, when Truman ordered the Seventh Fleet to the Formosa Strait, he ordered more military forces and matériel to the Philippines as well, together with greater military assistance to the French forces in the Indochina war and the dispatch of an American military mission there. Truman and his lieutenants might have decided to contribute more substantial military aid to the French in Indochina, which might have turned the advantage to the French and provoked Red China to divert more aid to the North Vietnamese. In fact, however, America had no viable option of sending considerable aid to the French at the time because logistically the U.S. military establishment was already seriously overextended in meeting its global commitments. Also, upon the strong urging of Britain and others of the UN coalition fighting in Korea, America remained adamant against any ground operations in the Far East outside Korea.

An important corollary to the refusal to send troops into combat beyond Korea's borders was the administration's decision to
demonstrate just how severely it was willing to keep the Korean
conflict a "police action" by its negligible reinforcements of the UN
Command after the first stages of the war. Washington's position
was made clearer when the four divisions for which MacArthur
had begged were assigned, instead, to Eisenhower's new NATO
command in 1951 and no new divisions were assigned to the
Korean fighting. (Two National Guard divisions were sent to
Korea in the winter of 1951–1952, but in fulfillment of a pledge
much earlier to MacArthur.)

Thus the United States sent an emphatic message to the communist powers that, regardless of the fighting under way in Korea,
it was not interested in escalating that conflict and that its top
global strategic priority remained the containment of Soviet advances in Europe. The limits on the ground war in Korea made it
possible for NATO to develop a reasonably strong deterrent to
Soviet expansion in West Europe. In essence, the limits on the
ground operations in Korea left the United States with more options in deploying its relatively meager forces globally, especially
in the security of its key European allies.

Limits on the Sea War

With its sizable Far East fleet stationed at Vladivostok, the
Soviet Union had the capability by loan, lease, or direct dispatch
of these vessels to Korean waters of turning the naval operations
into high-risk, costly ventures for the UNC. As it was, for reasons
of its own, the USSR refrained, and UNC naval functions were
important but not comparatively costly adjuncts of the ground
fighting. If MacArthur had gotten his wish, however, the naval
side of the war would have been greatly accelerated, so much so
that his superiors feared a third world war would result.

MacArthur had made two proposals involving naval surface
forces that he believed would be useful in pressuring Communist
China to remove its troops from the Korean peninsula: a naval
blockade of Communist China and the shelling of targets along the
Red Chinese coast. Neither of these was a viable alternative. The
blockade was too provocative and would not have been effective
without the cooperation of Britain and the USSR. America's allies
would not support it. The bombardment along the coast was also
deemed unfeasible because there were not enough available com-

bat ships to make an impact. In addition, there was the problem that, though much of Communist China's heavy industry was located in port cities within range of naval guns, it was sparse and most of her military hardware came from the USSR. Moreover, her mainland military and air bases were located largely beyond the reach of naval gunfire. Shelling of the heavily populated Chinese coastal cities would cause widespread civilian casualties, produce reactions of horror in world opinion, and might well anger the Soviet Union into providing more combat aircraft and a submarine fleet to Peking, if not actually entering the war. There was little question in Washington and other Western capitals that such naval action would be widely perceived as a deliberate American step to enlarge the war with Communist China.

The refusal to allow UNC naval operations beyond the Korean combat zone, except in the Formosa Strait, and the decision to reinforce NAVFE rather adequately in the long run but only for Korean and Formosa Strait missions were the main restrictions applied by the United States and its coalition in the naval realm. Beyond that, the Seventh Fleet and the Allied sea units supported ground and air forces in a myriad of ways, ranging from carrier-based air raids to transportation of troops and war matériel. Virtually all of the war's personnel and supplies arrived by sea.

Limits on the Air War

Air operations, of course, cannot be separated from the Navy's story in the war because much of the air action was undertaken by carrier aircraft. Much of the following, however, will concern issues of strategic bombing that were mainly in the realm of the ground-based Far East Air Forces. Even at the very beginning of the Korean War, American airmen were complaining about restrictions, a practice that was to become a habit for the remainder of the conflict, though the specific focus of the complaints changed. Throughout the war a variety of aerial limits were deliberately imposed by the American-led alliance. In his diary two days after the outbreak of hostilities, Lieutenant General Earle E. Partridge, head of the Fifth Air Force, was already discontented: "FEAF handicapped in this shooting war by not being permitted to cross the 38th parallel to destroy enemy at its source of staging." This restriction was lifted shortly, but as the hostilities evolved through various phases, numerous other handicaps were added while others were withdrawn. Although a number of important restrictions on UNC air operations had been removed by the end of the war, they were in effect during crucial periods when many airmen were convinced that their lifting could have been conclusive.

One of the most important restrictions which prevented a total refighting of World War II was the unwillingness to employ aerial delivery of nuclear, chemical, and biological weapons. The use of unconventional weapons was considered by the United States at various times during the Korean War, particularly during periods when the UNC forces were on the defensive. As the armistice talks dragged on, the Joint Chiefs studied the possibility of using nuclear, chemical, and biological weapons in the event that the negotiations broke down irrevocably. In December 1950, Prime Minister Attlee's hasty visit to confer with Truman after the latter's suggestion that he would not rule out consideration of any weapons in Korea, however, did not keep Pentagon planners from often mulling contingency situations where nuclear bombs might seem necessary. In the spring of 1953, President Eisenhower let it be known that he was considering the use of nuclear bombs if the communist negotiators at Panmunjom did not agree to an armistice soon, though such intimidation did not appear to figure significantly in the final outcome that summer.

The atomic bomb, or worse, the newly developed hydrogen bomb of late 1952, symbolized the total war that America had finally resorted to against Japan in the Second World War. A major reason it was not used in Korea undoubtedly was because it was such a powerful symbol of total war and thus entirely inappropriate for a limited conflict such as that in Korea. Nuclear warfare was a very sensitive issue with America's partners in the Korean struggle and with the United Nations in general, partly because of the threat of general war but also because of the symbolism and the prospect of using nuclear destruction again on Asian people. Washington decision-makers concluded that it was questionable whether such unconventional weapons would have been decisive if dropped on the rugged Korean battlegrounds or if used in bombing Red China. Lack of suitable targets, terrain problems, and powerful negative symbolism, as well as the impetus for a Soviet atomic counterstrike, made the "doomsday" bombs only a background emergency consideration in Washington.

According to Air Force General Jack J. Catton, "Available to General MacArthur and later General Ridgway, was the atomic capability of a unit of the 43d Wing, which we put on the island of Guam. . . . We could have had atomic weapons if the President decided to use them. We could have had atomic weapons very reliably and very accurately delivered within a period of about sixteen hours." Another source maintains that nonassembled nuclear weapons were placed aboard an American carrier off Korea in December 1950, and that simulated nuclear air raids were made over Pyongyang, the North Korean capital. On April 6, 1951, five days before MacArthur's dismissal, Truman authorized the Atomic Energy Commission to transfer nine nuclear bombs to the Air Force for possible use in Korea.

As late as May 1953, the Joint Chiefs recommended that if the truce talks were halted and the war expanded, all necessary courses of action against Communist China and North Korea should be pursued, including "extensive strategical and tactical use of atomic bombs." Surely the most important weapons limit by the UNC was its decision not to resort to nuclear warfare.

Charges of UNC aerial attacks using poison gas and germ warfare were hurled by communist negotiators at Panmunjom, as well as through propaganda leaflets and broadcasts from Peking and Pyongyang and speeches before the United Nations in 1952. No evidence of worth was ever forthcoming, however, and both the UNC and Washington vehemently denied the allegations, citing their strict orders against keeping deadly gases or germs in stock. According to the JCS official history, Ridgway, at the time, "suggested three possible motives for this unusually vitriolic propaganda program. The enemy might merely be manufacturing propaganda, either for home consumption . . . or to sway world opinion. He might be putting up a smoke screen to conceal his inability to control epidemics in his territories. . . . Most ominously of all, the enemy might be establishing justification for biological warfare when it appeared advantageous."

Nevertheless, when the JCS studied the possible options for action if the armistice negotiations broke down in the spring of 1953 and hostilities escalated, one of its assumptions was that chemical, biological, and radiological weapons would not be used except to retaliate." This suggests that by that time there may have been stores of all three of those weapons in the Far East Command. It does appear that if the communists had used any of these types of unconventional warfare, the UNC had the capacity by the spring of 1953 to retaliate in kind. But, afraid of the terrible consequences, they hoped not to resort to these weapons.

Another limitation on air power was the restriction against "hot pursuit," which was chasing enemy aircraft for two or three minutes' flight across the Yalu River over Manchuria. During the autumn of 1950 particularly, many heated messages passed back and forth between Tokyo and Washington regarding such transboundary pursuit. It was an important morale issue to UNC airmen, but it is questionable how militarily significant hot pursuit might have been if allowed. The Joint Chiefs, Truman, Marshall, and Acheson all appeared to agree with MacArthur that limited pursuit of enemy planes across the Manchurian border should be permitted, but America's coalition partners were strongly opposed to it.

Even before China came into the war, the borders of Communist China and the Soviet Union were considered very sensitive by the UNC. Once the Red Chinese entered the conflict, it was very clear to everyone that the bombing of mainland Chinese targets would be a drastic expansion of the hostilities. Communist China was placed off limits for UNC aerial attacks because of fear of Soviet entry into the war; enemy bombing of vulnerable strategic targets like the ports of South Korea or even targets in Japan or Okinawa; strong opposition from America's partners; and concern that American air strength was not adequate to do much serious damage or to absorb heavy losses in attacking Red China.

No aerial campaign against mainland China was undertaken, but in its final report on recommended courses of action if the truce talks collapsed and the war accelerated, the Joint Chiefs in May 1953 proposed to include air and naval operations directly against China and Manchuria. This idea, earlier advanced by MacArthur, was only seriously considered by the JCS after two frustrating years of truce talks and continued, indecisive fighting.

There were also UNC limits on bombing targets along the Yalu River that were felt to be especially sensitive to the Chinese and Soviets, such as urban centers, bridges, dams, and hydroelectric facilities. At first, certain cities near the Chinese or Soviet borders were forbidden to UNC bombers, notably Sinuiju, North Korea, which lay across the Yalu from Antung, Manchuria, where a complex of Chinese army and air installations was located; and Rashin, which was a port and road-rail hub in northeastern North Korea close to the Soviet border. Later restrictions on attacking both cities were removed.

One of the war's most controversial restrictions forbade UNC aircraft from attacking the north end of Yalu bridges. They had to follow set runs on their small targets without violating the border along the snaking Yalu while facing intense antiaircraft fire from gunners who could aim with confidence about their line of approach. The airmen's problems were compounded by the facts that MiG-15s often rose to intercept them from nearby Manchurian bases; many of the bridges had been sturdily built by the Japanese during their occupation; dropped spans were repaired quickly; pontoon bridges were added to assist in moving the large numbers of CCF units into North Korea; and once winter arrived, the Yalu froze over and the enemy troops could walk across the river during the night when UNC aircraft were usually absent.

Although the UNC strove to limit its aggression, there were times when all attempts at restraint broke down. After gaining the approval that Washington had denied earlier UNC commanders in chief, Clark approved Weyland's request to bomb a number of facilities in North Korea. Beginning in late June 1952, Weyland's FEAF bombers destroyed hydroelectric installations on the Yalu that supplied a considerable amount of the electrical power to North Korea and southern Manchuria. The FEAF bombers then launched a strategic bombing offensive against North Korea that summer which targeted virtually every possible industrial, transportation, or military facility of considerable size in the country, together with a number of irrigation dams that caused extensive flooding. The raids devastated countless nonmilitary structures and civilian dwellings. In the biggest bombing attack of the war, over 1,400 FEAF planes raided Pyongyang on August 29.

The heavy air assault continued on into the autumn of 1952 but without any noticeable effects on the Communist Chinese and North Korean determination to continue the war or their negotiators' wills to persist in obstructing the completion of an armistice agreement at Panmunjom. Except for not violating the Manchurian and Soviet borders and for not hurling even more aircraft into the strategic bombing campaign, the UNC land-based and carrier-based planes exercised no restraint in the summer and autumn of 1952. The massive air assault gradually wound down, largely for want of targets, leaving the North Korean cities and towns in ruins but the defensive entrenchments along the front line almost intact. Air Force leaders were dismayed and felt that further activity of this sort would weaken American air power potential in case of an emergency elsewhere. To conserve air resources, more restraints were imposed until suitable targets could be found.

The ability of the North Korean and Communist Chinese troops to operate with far fewer supplies and to move logistical matériel without great dependence on roads and rail lines was also a crucial factor in handicapping the UNC's air interdiction operations. Not only did the enemy's tactics of dispersing supplies hinder effectiveness, but his unconventional logistical techniques spelled trouble for the conventional war that the UNC ground, air, and sea forces, shaped by their World War II experiences, fought. For the UNC airman, foot soldier, and sailor, the Korean War was a very different war both in its limited and its unconventional nature.

Other Limits

Besides the limits on ground, sea, and air operations set forth by the UN side, other restrictions did not directly involve command decisions by the UNC. Some limitations on the UNCs combat activities were imposed primarily through the diplomatic dimension. Britain and the Allies exercised great influence on Washington policy-making. The Truman administration did pay careful heed to the views of its partners, especially the British. But there were many decisions by Washington on the direction of the war, both as to its acceleration and limitation, that were unilateral and left the Allies feeling far less than equal members of the coalition. Ultimately, America acted as it wished. Britain's post-World War II dependence on America precluded serious disagreement over Korea.

Meanwhile, in Washington, diplomatic as well as military policy was being decided by the State Department in a notable change from the practices in World War II. Then, the officials at Foggy Bottom, even Secretary of State Hull, were relegated largely to Western Hemispheric and United Nations matters. The era of the Korean conflict, however, was marked by extremely close ties between the President and his diplomatic advisers. Secretary Acheson, in particular, was given a powerful hand in the making of military strategy and the conduct of the war. There were no major military moves made without extensive consultation with and endorsement by Acheson and his lieutenants.

The enormous shift in influence of the State Department in military affairs had begun with the National Security Act of 1947 and had been strongly demonstrated in 1947–1949 in State's new impact on American programs in occupied Japan, Korea, and Germany. American command decisions in the Korean and Vietnam conflicts normally came down from policy decisions worked out jointly by the White House and the State and Defense departments. Civilian supremacy over the military took on new meaning with the State Department's key roles in the limitations enacted during both those wars. This enhanced position of the State Department in war-making should have meant more attention to political economic, social, and psychological restraints on the war that transcended the usual realm of command decisions. In the case of the Korean War, it did produce more attention to Allied interests and to postwar consequences, though not to the extent desired by other members of the UN coalition.

President Truman and Congress made conscientious efforts to convey to the enemy, as well as to the all-important "neutral" power, the USSR, that the U.S. government regarded the Korean hostilities as a "police action" in the sense of being a combat situation that did not require a declaration of war against either North Korea or Communist China, that was not seen as a war for survival by America, and that required only partial mobilization. By limiting the war and portraying it in propaganda as a localized conflict, however, the Truman administration sometimes became enmeshed in contradictory moves. The war was alternately portrayed as localized and as the key to the survival or downfall of the Communist Chinese regime itself.

Other restrictions were imposed by the enemy and were fully as significant in averting global war as those laid down by the American-led coalition. Communist China, North Korea, and their background co-belligerent, the Soviet Union, maintained a disciplined form of restrictions and did not wage all-out war any more than the UNC did. The United States and its coalition were fully aware that both sides were observing mutual restraints.

The Soviets did provide a considerable number of combat aircraft to the Chinese and North Koreans, most formidable of which was the MiG-15 fighter, but the enemy air forces were never large enough to wrest control of the skies over Korea from the FEAF and UNC carrier aircraft. The Soviets simply did not supply enough aircraft for that. Moreover, they never undertook strategic bombing campaigns against the highly vulnerable targets in South Korea, such as the ports of Pusan and Inchon. General Weyland commented, "The outcome of the conflict would have been vastly different had enemy domination of the air reversed the military positions of the Communists and the United Nations Command." In a sobering and lengthy diary entry in October 1950, Stratemeyer reflected on the UNCs benefits from the enemy's restrictions on air warfare:

> We must keep in mind that our home bases in Japan, and even in South Korea, have not been interfered with by enemy air.... If there had been an enemy air force [of comparable strength], it is questionable—to my way of thinking—that the ground

troops could have ever been supplied by long truck columns and trains as they were from Pusan [operating through the nights with lights on]. . . . All of us must be careful not to draw wrong conclusions from this small, "police action" war . . . We have had no communications' jamming. . . . We have not considered in all-out night operations the fact that the enemy could well employ night intruders against our light and medium bomber activities.

Besides aerial restraints, the communists did not utilize submarines or major combatant surface ships against the UNC. Such vessels, especially undersea craft, were a source of great anxiety to Joy, Struble, and other Seventh Fleet and Allied commanders—and for sound reasons: Not only was the Soviet submarine fleet large but also the antisubmarine warfare capabilities of NAVFE were unimpressive. Two of the turning points of the war were amphibious operations, Inchon and Hungnam, and both could have been greatly handicapped, if not defeated, by Soviet surface ships and submarines on loan to the North Koreans or Communist Chinese.

Like the United States and its coalition, the communist belligerents did not issue formal declarations of war, perhaps intending to signal that they, too, did not desire an expanded conflict. Indeed, Peking officially identified its troops in action in Korea as volunteers, claiming that its regular units had not been ordered into the combat.

Like the West, the communist powers made no attempt to initiate operations beyond the borders of Korea. When the Korean War began, the Red Chinese had been busily preparing for an invasion of Formosa, but that operation was suspended once it became apparent the North Korean offensive had failed and Red Chinese intervention would be required to save the Pyongyang regime. If Communist China, with its vast manpower reserves, had obtained Soviet vessels and had gone ahead with its amphibious assault on Formosa, the Seventh Fleet patrol would have become embroiled and other UNC forces from the Korean theater of operations might have been transferred to aid Chiang, creating an unbelievably complex international situation.

Few Chinese ground forces from South and Southwest China appear to have been transferred to Manchuria and North Korea, as were the crack Third and Fourth Field armies of North and East China. It is possible that Chinese troops and war matériel in the southern regions of China, as well as shipments of military equipment and supplies from the Soviet Union, could have been sent to

North Vietnam in sufficient strength to enable Ho Chi Minh's forces to turn the tide of battle against the French in 1950–1953 rather than after the Korean War.

If the West had been confronted by local wars in Korea, Formosa, and Indochina simultaneously, it is likely that even the vaunted American production capability would have been unable to maintain effective lines of resupply to all three theaters. Korea undoubtedly would have taken precedence because of the preponderance of strength already in action there, but it would have been a painful dilemma for Washington and Allied leaders to choose between Formosa and Indochina as the next-ranking priority of defense in the Far East. With additional Soviet assistance, the communists could have made the Asian situation much more complicated and menacing for the West.

After the hostilities ceased in Korea, the war gradually came to be accepted as a stalemate by all but the deeply committed on both sides. In the communist camp the faithful boasted that Communist China had emerged as one of the great powers, while in the western camp the true believers saw communist aggression contained and South Korea saved for democracy and capitalism. At a distance from the ideological and emotional aspects of the Korean conflict, the consequences were not so clear. Red China remained an isolated and backward giant but now alienated from the Soviet Union in many spheres of mutual interest; communism flooded into critical areas of Southeast Asia, especially Indochina and Indonesia; North Korea remained primitive and dictatorial, with growing ties to Peking rather than to Moscow; and South Korea learned more about making money than practicing freedom. Both Koreas underwent many years of slow recuperation from the devastation of the war, the ruination matching the worst suffered by any peoples in World War II.

While this strange and ugly limited war at times bore similarities to a microcosmic Second World War, the most remarkable phenomenon of the Korean conflict was the inexplicable communication, neither oral nor written, between implacably hostile camps who signaled restraint to each other. Without a single word of formal agreement they set up an intricate system of limitations amid the fighting of 1950–1953 that kept Korea from becoming the fiery fuse of Sarajevo in 1914 or Poland in 1939. The armed forces of the United States in Korea were supplied with commanders, troops, tactics, weapons, and equipment heavily drawn from World War II. If they had been able to conduct a war as their experience in 1941–1945 prompted them to, it would have been a war of overwhelming firepower and annihilation. Even though restricted to operations on the Korean peninsula, it is likely that in such a war the Communist Chinese and North Korean troops would have been mauled below the Yalu. But it is also probable that a decisive triumph of World War II proportions would have guaranteed the eruption of another and more terrible global war. As it was, the silent agreement on limitations worked, but it was a risk of perilous magnitude. It is astounding that only a decade later a gamble on unspoken limits would be tried again in another Asian war and that the world would be spared once more.

Reading 12

The Strategy of Revolutionary War

by Lt. Gen. Phillip B. Davidson, USA (Ret.)

Revolutionary war is a bold new form of aggression which could rank with the discovery of gunpowder.

Hubert Humphrey, 1965

In my first book, Vietnam at War, I attempted to show in both the first and last chapters the dominant role played in the Vietnam conflict by the enemy's Strategy of Revolutionary War. From a study of the reviews of the book and from the many informal questions and comments submitted by readers, I know now that I failed to establish the unique significance of this enemy strategy in the Vietnam War. I suppose that I should not be too harsh on myself; after all, the enemy's Strategy of Revolutionary War was the great "secret" of the Vietnam War. It was a "secret" then, and in most quarters is a "secret" now. Let me try once more, then, to reveal this "secret" and its monumental impact on the conflict.

The Vietnam War can be understood only, in terms of North Vietnam's Strategy of Revolutionary War. This book will not make many categorical statements, but that is one of them. The reason for the dominance of the enemy's Strategy of Revolutionary War lay in their possession of the strategic initiative. We danced to the North Vietnamese strategic tune, for it was the Communists who determined the style and scale of the war.

Reprinted with permission from *Secrets of the Vietnam War* by Lt. Gen. Phillip B. Davidson © 1990. Published by Presidio Press, 505-B San Marin Drive, Novato, CA 94945-1340.

The United States gave North Vietnam the strategic initiative, a prize of singular value, by the restraints the various American administrations placed on our forces in Vietnam. In the ground war, the United States Army and Marines were restricted to South Vietnam and could not attack enemy sanctuaries and bases in southern North Vietnam, Laos, or, until too late, in Cambodia. Nor could the ground forces sever the Ho Chi Minh Trail, the Communists' logistical lifeline from North Vietnam to its army in the South. Our air assault against North Vietnam was hampered throughout most of the war by target restrictions and bombing pauses which permitted the enemy to build effective defenses against our halfhearted attacks.

We conceded the strategic initiative to the enemy in other ways. Our political and diplomatic offenses were halting and ineffective. Our ambiguity as to our objectives and strategy in Vietnam contrasted with the enemy's singleness of purpose and the sure grasp of his own strategy, which allowed the Communists to gain and keep the initiative. Not until the so-called "Christmas bombings" of December 1972 did the United States fleetingly seize the strategic initiative from Hanoi.

Three North Vietnamese strategists formulated this dominant Strategy of Revolutionary War. They were: Senior General Vo Nguyen Giap, the North Vietnamese minister of Defense and commander in chief of all North Vietnamese forces; Truong Chinh, the North Vietnamese theoretician; and, of course, that wily old revolutionist, Ho Chi Minh. This trio derived their potent concepts from a mixture of the theories and actions of Mao Tse-tung, Lenin, Lawrence of Arabia, Napoleon, Clausewitz, and the Chinese military philosopher of antiquity, Sun Tzu. It is a powerful strategy, and one for which no successful countermeasures have yet appeared.

The Strategy of Revolutionary War has as its objective the seizure of political power in a nation-state. In operation, it totally integrates two principal forms of force, armed conflict and political conflict, which the North Vietnamese call military *dau tranh* (struggle) and political *dau tranh*. Their integration creates a kind of war heretofore unseen: a war waged on several fronts, not geographical fronts, but programmatic fronts, all conducted by one authority, all carefully meshed to serve one end—the seizure of national power.

Military *dau tranh* encompasses all types of conflict, from the assassination of a single government official, to a full scale conventional war of divisions, tanks, artillery, antiaircraft missiles, tactical air forces, and naval armadas. Due to its nature, the military aspects of revolutionary war progress (at least theoretically) through three distinct phases. In Phase I the state to be overthrown is militarily stronger than are the revolutionists, so the latter avoid combat, resorting to guerrilla warfare composed of small raids, ambushes, sabotage, and terrorism. As the revolutionists gain strength, they enter into Phase II of the Strategy of Revolutionary War, a stage of rough military parity with the state's forces. This phase is characterized by a combination of guerrilla actions and conventional war. Finally, in Phase III the military power of the revolution exceeds that of the state, and the revolutionary forces go over almost totally to conventional war. Military *dau tranh* culminates in the "General Counteroffensive" or "General Offensive," which aims at the total military defeat of the armed forces of the state.

Political *dau tranh* encompasses a much broader spectrum of nonmilitary power than the term implies to Westerners. It includes not only political and diplomatic elements, but psychological, ideological, sociological, and economic components as well. Political *dau tranh* consists of three separate programs: The first, *dan van*, is action to mobilize the people in Communist controlled areas and to use them as an instrument of war. Included in this program is an elaborate procedure to indoctrinate and motivate Communist troops. The second program, *dich van*, encompasses actions aimed at undermining the morale and loyalty of the enemy population. The third, *binh van*, are actions aimed at disaffecting the enemy soldiers. All of these programs utilize a mixture of terrorism, subversion, propaganda, disinformation, riots, and uprisings.

As military *dau tranh* moves through three overlapping stages, so too does political *dau tranh*. In the early stages of an insurrection, when the military power of the revolution is weak, political *dau tranh* predominates. The revolutionist agitates and mobilizes the people, and the political infrastructure is recruited and trained. As the military power of the revolution grows, armed force plays a more key role, but nevertheless, in Phase I, political *dau tranh* is predominant. In Phase II, a combination of guerrilla war and conventional war, there is a rough equivalence of effort between military *dau tranh* and its political mate. In the final Phase III stage, conventional war is emphasized and the political effort fades—never completely, for revolutionary war is always a political war. In fact, the North Vietnamese version of revolutionary war sees a great political climax, a final spontaneous uprising of the masses, the "Great Uprising." This "Great Uprising," linked with the

"Great Offensive," overthrows the state and brings the revolutionary group to power.

While in theory there is a steady progression through the three stages of revolutionary war, in practice this does not necessarily occur. Due to the actual situation, the revolutionists may find it desirable, or even necessary, to revert to an earlier phase—for example, from Phase II back to the emphasis on political *dau tranh* and guerrilla warfare of Phase I.

The Strategy of Revolutionary War (North Vietnamese style) has certain inevitable characteristics.

1. It is a *total war*. It mobilizes all the people whom the revolutionists control. It uses to the utmost every available facet of power.

2. It is waged with *total unity of effort*, every element of power coordinated with the others to gain the objective. Douglas Pike, the foremost expert on Vietnamese communism in the West, calls it "a seamless web." Truong Nhu Tang, one-time Viet Cong Minister of Justice, described this unified effort thusly, "Every military clash, every demonstration, every propaganda appeal was seen as part of a unified whole; each had consequences far beyond its immediately apparent results."[1]

3. It is by necessity and choice a *protracted war*. In the beginning, the revolution needs time to build a political base and to develop military power. In the later stages of revolutionary war, protracted war erodes an opponent's will to continue the conflict.

4. It stresses the gaining and keeping of *the initiative*. This pertains not only to the military initiative, but to the political and psychological initiatives as well. For example, after the Tet offensive, the North Vietnamese abandoned the *tactical* military initiative in South Vietnam and launched a psychological offensive aimed at the destruction of the will of the American people to continue the war. Revolutionary war teaches that only by holding the initiative and utilizing the offensive can the revolutionists take advantage of an opponent's weaknesses.

5. It is a *changing war*, featuring a constant shift between Phases with consequent changes in the mix and importance of military and political *dau tranh*. During the Vietnam War, the most critical problem faced by the North Vietnamese was to determine what phase of revolutionary war they were in at any given

time and toward what phase they were moving. As will be seen, these questions dominated the debates within the North Vietnamese Politburo and led to the most bitter disputes within that body.

6. Revolutionary war is a *"mosaic"* war. In one area it may be in Phase III, conventional war, while nearby it may be in Phase II, and somewhere else it may be a Phase I insurgency. For example, in late 1967 a large-scale conventional war (Phase III) raged along the Laotian border of northern South Vietnam and around the DMZ. At the same time, a Phase II situation (conventional war/insurgency) prevailed in mid-South Vietnam, while a pure Phase I insurgency existed in the Mekong Delta of southern South Vietnam. Under the North Vietnamese Strategy of Revolutionary War, each situation required different military tactics and a different mixture of military and political *dau tranh*.

The three different phases of revolutionary war could exist in even closer proximity to each other. In 1967-1968, the South Vietnamese I Corps area, also known as Military Region I (MR I), the northern five provinces of South Vietnam, had a Phase I insurgency in its southern coastal province of Quang Ngai, a Phase II (combination) in the two adjoining provinces to the north, and a good size conventional war (Phase III) in the two northern provinces of Quang Tri and Thua Thien. Truong Chinh in his seminal work, *Primer for Revolt*, described revolutionary war as "disordered and muddled," and he was right.

This understanding of the Strategy Revolutionary War will place most of the disputes about strategic concepts (both North Vietnamese and American) in a comprehensible perspective. From the earliest days of their war against the French, the Vietnamese Communists (then known as the Viet Minh) debated about what phase of revolutionary war they were in at the moment of argument and to which phase they were then moving. As far back as 1944, Giap, then in command of a small poorly armed rabble, in Ho's absence planned to launch a "military offensive" in the remote mountainous area of northern North Vietnam. Ho Chi Minh resumed and promptly canceled the offensive because he deemed it premature. To Ho, the Viet Minh were in early Phase I, the political building phase, not in Phase II, as Giap believed. In 1951, with Ho's approval, Giap launched a "General Counteroffensive," a Phase III attack, to drive the French from the Tonkin

Delta, and if successful, from North Vietnam. The Viet Minh offensive, misconceived and mismanaged, collapsed with heavy Communist casualties. Again, Giap was premature. In 1951 the Viet Minh were in Phase II, and Giap's attempt to move them into the final stages of Phase III, for which the prerequisites did not exist, proved disastrous. The necessary prerequisites for a Phase III offensive did exist in 1953-1954, and at Dien Bien Phu the Communists won Indochina War I.

In Indochina War II (against the South Vietnamese and the Americans), the Communist debate about the phases of revolutionary war centered on the war in South Vietnam. From 1954 (the end of Indochina War I) until 1961, there was agreement throughout the Communist leadership in Vietnam that the Communist revolution in South Vietnam was a Phase I insurgency. From 1961 until mid-1965, the members of the North Vietnamese Politburo argued bitterly as to whether the insurgency in the South was in Phase I or Phase II. Strangely enough, the arguments were publicized in the Hanoi press and over Radio Hanoi. Giap and Truong Chinh, the theoreticians of revolutionary war, held that the war in South Vietnam during the early Sixties was a Phase I insurgency. Conversely, Nguyen Chi Thanh, the Communist commander in South Vietnam, plus Le Duan and Le Duc Tho (the so-called "southern clique") contended that the southern war had entered Phase II.

The "southern clique" triumphed in these debates of 1961-1965, and their victory moved the war into Phase II in 1965, as both United States and North Vietnamese ground units joined the conflict. In early 1968, with the Tet offensive and the siege of Khe Sanh, the North Vietnamese moved into Phase III, conventional war. Giap and Truong Chinh opposed this escalation of the war, maintaining that the Communists in South Vietnam had not progressed far enough militarily or politically to support this final phase of the General Offensive—General Uprising. Giap and Truong were right. The General Offensive collapsed with ghastly casualties, and the General Uprising never arose.

Faced with the military debacle of the Tet offensive in mid-1968, Giap and Truong argued for a retrogression into Phase II of revolutionary war, a combination of insurgency and small unit conventional war. Again, the southern clique adamantly disputed them, insisting on a continuation of the large scale conventional operations of Phase III. This time Giap and Truong won. In mid-1968 the Communists moved backward into Phase II and in early 1969, further retrogressed into Phase I. This Phase I insurgency, however, differed from the previous Phase I insurgency in two ways. First, the small, insurgency-type operations were carried out, not by the Viet Cong guerrillas, but by North Vietnamese sappers, who were elite commandos. Second, waiting in the sanctuaries of Laos, Cambodia, and the DMZ, were the divisions and corps of the VC and NVA Main Forces, ready to move the war back into Phase III instantly.

By 1972 the Communists had rebuilt their forces in the South and, following the withdrawal of United States ground forces, moved into Phase III with their so-called Easter offensive. Giap and Truong Chinh again opposed this escalation, arguing, for a delay of another year. They lost the argument—the offensive took place. But Giap and Truong won the consolation prize of having been right—the offensive failed with bloody casualties.

Following the Easter offensive, the North Vietnamese reverted again to Phase II operations against the South Vietnamese. By early 1975 they had regained their offensive strength and launched the final campaign, a Phase III all-out conventional war with over twenty divisions, hundreds of tanks, and even a small tactical air force. This array won the war.

American leaders disputed about the proper strategy as vigorously and as acrimoniously as did the North Vietnamese Politburo. Between the Americans and the North Vietnamese, however, there was one tremendous difference—disputes within the Politburo concentrated, properly, on which phase of revolutionary war existed at any given time. The arguments among the Americans, on the other hand, dwelt on the viability and desirability of various strategic options open to the United States, without reference to, or knowledge of, the governing factor of the conflict—the Strategy of Revolutionary War. United States strategy should have been based solidly on the fact that the enemy had the strategic initiative, which left the United States with two options—first, take the strategic initiative away from the Communists, or second, counter whatever phase of revolutionary war the enemy was carrying out. Since the American leaders elected not to seize the strategic initiative until Christmas 1972, they selected by the same token the second alternative. But they failed here too. Not understanding revolutionary war, they were unable to determine the current phase of the enemy's strategy, and from this base, to fashion the proper American countermeasures.

To this day, debates rage as to what should have been the correct American ground strategy in Vietnam. Should we have elected as the predominant concept clear and hold strategy, the enclave strategy, the strategy of attrition, the strategy of limited war, or even a modified version of the strategy of annihilation? The disputes were, and are, muddled by two aspects of revolutionary war—its changing nature, and its "mosaic" character. Thus, each of the American disputants is able to cite a situation in a given time frame or in a particular area showing that the war was really an insurgency, or a Phase II combination, or a Phase III conventional war. Then, armed with *his* special situation, the disputant argues for the general application of this particular American counterstrategy to the ground war as a whole.

A comprehension of the Strategy of Revolutionary War with its changing and mosaic nature would have indicated that the proper United States counterstrategy, like the strategy with which it contended, had to be changing and mosaic in character itself. For example, from 1954 to 1961, the United States, then advising the South Vietnamese government, should have based its concepts on countering a Phase I Communist insurgency. In this phase, the strategy of clear and hold and the enclave strategy were both valid. From 1961 until 1965, as the war moved from Phase I to Phase II (a combination of insurgency and conventional war), a different American/South Vietnamese counterstrategy was appropriate. The correct strategy during this period was a combination of clear and hold and attrition, with the weight of the effort given to clear and hold.

From 1965 to 1968, as the war shifted from Phase II toward Phase III (conventional war), the same strategy was appropriate, although now concentrating more on attrition. In 1968 the American counterstrategy should have shifted again towards all-out conventional war. In late 1968 and 1969-1972, as the enemy retrogressed into Phase II and then into Phase I (sapper version), American strategy should have shifted to meet the new situation. In 1972 with the enemy's Easter offensive, American strategy, correctly, shifted to conventional war (Phase III).

There is another aspect of this complicated business of countering the changing nature of revolutionary war. The authors of the American counterstrategy must know not only what phase of revolutionary war the conflict is in, but toward what phase it is moving. The counterstrategy to a given phase of revolutionary war determines such by-products as tactics, organization, training, intelligence operations, equipment, logistics, and base construction, to name only a few activities dependent on the adopted strategy. To counter a Phase I insurgency, for example, requires different tactics, organization, equipment, etc., than does the opposition to a Phase III conventional war. Now, it takes time to make the necessary adjustments of organization, equipment, and training, etc., to meet each new enemy phase. So, just as the strategist of revolutionary war must anticipate the next phase of revolutionary war, so too must the counterstrategist.

These shifts of American counterstrategy just discussed deal only with one facet of revolutionary war—its *changing* nature. United States concepts had also to deal with the *mosaic* character of revolutionary war. While the overall United States counterstrategy should have been based on the progressions and retrogressions of the North Vietnamese Strategy of Revolutionary War, there would have had to be a variation of strategies to counter the problems arising from differing situations in various areas. For example, in 1967-1968, one American counterstategy was appropriate to meet the Phase III conventional war along the DMZ, but this concept would be totally inappropriate to contend with the Phase I insurgency deep in the Mekong Delta.

An example of the controversy which the mosaic nature of revolutionary war can cause was, and still is, the acrimonious dispute between the United States Marine Corps and General Westmoreland as to the proper ground strategy for 1967. The marines maintain that the war was essentially an insurgency, and that some form of a clear and hold or enclave strategy was appropriate. To this end they formed the Combined Action Platoons (CAPs), composed of fifteen marines and thirty-four local South Vietnamese militia. This platoon permanently occupied a village or hamlet, giving protection to the inhabitants. By the end of 1967, the marines had sixty-seven such teams in the villages of their area of tactical responsibility.

General Westmoreland and the other army leaders decried the CAP concept as a form of defensive strategy. As they saw things, it surrendered the tactical initiative to the Communists. Beyond that it allowed the enemy's large regular units, concentrated largely in the two northern provinces of the marine's area, to move about at will, while the marines hunkered down in their enclaves around Chu Lai and Da Nang. Westmoreland urged the marines to take the offensive and seek out the large enemy units and destroy them.

In actuality, both the marines and Westmoreland were right—they were just looking at different pieces of the mosaic. Westmoreland, from his overall view as the senior commander in South Vietnam in 1967, sensed that countrywide the enemy was in Phase II, moving rapidly to Phase III. This was particularly true in the two *northern* provinces of the marines' area of responsibility. On the other hand, the marines were concentrating on their *three southern* provinces, where a particularly virulent and longstanding brand of insurgency flourished. Westmoreland's emphasis on large unit search and destroy operations didn't make much sense in the guerrilla infested southern part of the marines' area. Conversely, the CAPs were inappropriate to the Phase II/Phase III situation around the DMZ. But neither in 1967—nor now—did any of the disputants recognize that they were looking at different parts of the mosaic of revolutionary war.

Thus, the great "secret" of the Vietnam conflict was the enemy's Strategy of Revolutionary War. Most people knew, or sensed, parts of it, but only a handful saw this "secret" clearly and wholly, and then, generally well after the end of the war. Most critics of the war have not seen it even yet. And so, some two decades later, the bootless arguments and controversies continue.

One of the controversies developed around another "secret" of the Vietnam War—with the word, "secret," being used again to mean something which has been made confused or obscure to the general public. And this is strange, for this controversy developed into one of the most memorable trials in American history—*Westmoreland v. CBS. Welcome, therefore, to the "numbers game."*

Reading 13

Fight at Ia Drang

by John A. Cash

Up to the fall of 1965 the fighting by U.S. troops in Vietnam had been characterized, for the most part, by hit-and-run counterinsurgency operations against Viet Cong irregulars. It was during the week before Thanksgiving, amidst the scrub and stunted trees of the Ia Drang River valley in the western sector of Pleiku Province along the Cambodian border, that the war changed drastically. For the first time regular North Vietnamese regiments, controlled by a division-size headquarters, engaged in a conventional contest with U.S. forces. The 1st Battalion, 7th Cavalry, 1st Cavalry Division (Airmobile), took the lead in this battle. (*Map 1*)

North Vietnamese General Chu Huy Man's Western Highlands Field Front headquarters had conceived a bold plan for operations in the Central Highlands of the Republic of Vietnam. To be carried out in the fall of 1965 and designated the Tay Nguyen Campaign, the enemy plan called for an offensive against the western plateau encompassing Kontum, Pleiku, Binh Dinh, and Phu Bon Provinces. It specified the destruction of Special Forces camps at Plei Me, Dak Sut, and Duc Co, the annihilation of the Le Thanh District headquarters, and the seizure of the city of Pleiku. Assault forces included the 32d and 66th North Vietnamese Army Regiments.

By the end of October, following an unsuccessful attempt to capture the Plei Me Special Forces Camp, the 32d and 33d Regiments were being pursued by units of the 1st Cavalry Division's 1st Brigade in the Pleiku area. The American forces had deployed westward from the division base camp at An Khe when the Plei Me Camp was threatened and for twelve days had engaged in

From *Seven Firefights in Vietnam* by John A. Cash, Center for Military History, 1970.

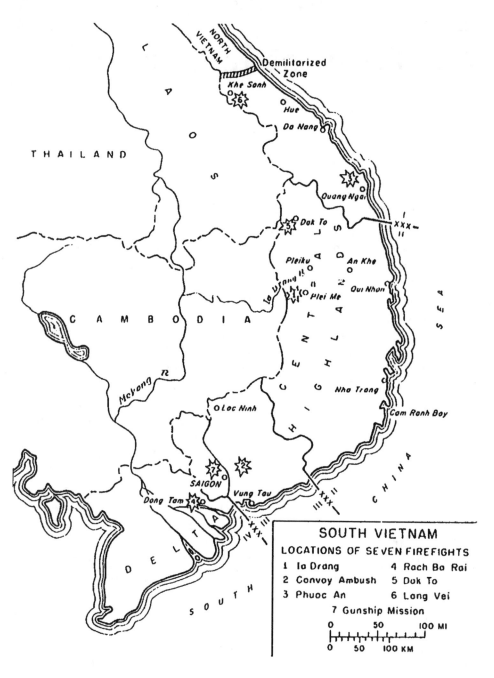

Map 1

intensive search and destroy as well as reconnaissance in force operations, most of them involving fierce fighting and most of them successful.

On 9 November the 1st Brigade was relieved by the 3d, known as the Garry Owen Brigade. This name was a matter of no small pride to the troopers of the 3d Brigade. Originally a Gaelic song once sung by the Irish Lancers, Garry Owen was adopted by the 7th Cavalry Regiment of Lt. Col. George A. Custer during the American Indian wars in the nineteenth century. A mark of the *esprit* of the 7th Cavalry, the name and new words to the song came to Vietnam with the brigade. The 3d's forces consisted of the 1st and 2d Battalions, 7th Cavalry, joined for this operation by the 2d Battalion, 5th Cavalry.

Concerned that the North Vietnamese might slip away entirely, Maj. Gen. Harry W. O. Kinnard, the 1st Cavalry Division commander, directed Col. Thomas W. Brown, the 3d Brigade commander, to employ his units south and southeast of Plei Me. Colonel Brown, a tall, lean officer, well schooled in airmobile techniques and with plenty of experience in infantry tactics, began on 10 November to press the search vigorously with squad and platoon saturation patrolling.

When three days of patrolling turned up few North Vietnamese, General Kinnard ordered Colonel Brown to search westward toward the Cambodian border. Anxious to engage an enemy that was proving to be more and more elusive, Brown focused his attention on the densely wooded area south of the Ia Drang River at the base of the Chu Pong massif, a rugged mountain mass straddling the South Vietnamese-Cambodian border.

To Brown the prospect of finding the enemy near the banks of the slowly meandering Ia Drang River seemed good. This sector had been a bastion of the Viet Minh who earlier had fought the French in Indochina. And during a recent intelligence briefing Brown had seen on the G-2 situation map a big red star indicating a probable major base for at least one North Vietnamese regiment, which could be using it as a way station for soldiers infiltrating South Vietnam. Friendly troops, furthermore, had not been in this area for some time. If his efforts failed, Colonel Brown planned to search farther south even closer to the Cambodian border.

On 10 November General Chu Huy Man, undismayed by his heavy loses in the failure at Plei Me, decided to try again on 16 November. The staging area his headquarters selected in preparation for the new attack included the very terrain Colonel Brown had chosen to search.

The 33d North Vietnamese Army Regiment, originally a 2,200-man fighting force, had lost 890 killed, 100 missing, and 500 wounded during the Plei Me debacle. It now began reorganizing its meager ranks into a single composite battalion in the valley between the Ia Drang River and Hill 542, the most prominent peak of Chu Pong in this area. Thirteen kilometers westward on the northern bank of the Ia Drang was the 32d North Vietnamese Army Regiment, still a formidable fighting force despite some losses during the recent battle. The *force majeure* for the second enemy attempt on Plei Me Special Forces Camp was the newly arrived 66th North Vietnamese Army Regiment. By 11 November its three battalions were positioned along both banks of the Ia Drang, a few kilometers west of the 33d Regiment. Although General Chu Huy Man intended to reinforce the three regiments with a battalion each of 120-mm. mortars and 14.5-mm. twin-barrel antiaircraft guns, both units were still on the Ho Chi Minh Trail in Cambodia, en route to the staging area.

Colonel Brown's plan, meanwhile, was developing. On 13 November he directed his operations officer, Maj. Henri-Gerard ("Pete") Mallet, who until a few weeks before had been the 2d Battalion, 7th Cavalry, executive officer, to move the 1st Battalion, 7th Cavalry, to a new area of operations southwest of Plei Me and to prepare a fragmentary order that would put the battalion at the base of the Chu Pong peak (Hill 542) as a jump-off point for search and destroy operations in the vicinity.

On the same day Major Mallet, grease pencil in hand, outlined an area comprising roughly fifteen square kilometers on the situation map. Heretofore the search areas assigned to the infantry battalions had been color-designated. Having run out of primary colors at this point, he designated the sector, which was shaped like an artist's pallet, Area LIME.

At 1700 on the 13th Colonel Brown was with Lt. Col. Harold G. Moore, Jr., the 1st Battalion, 7th Cavalry, commander, at his Company A command post south of Plei Me. He told Moore to execute an airmobile assault into the Ia Drang valley north of the Chu Pong peak early the next morning and to conduct search and destroy operations through 15 November. Although the brigade had been allocated 24 helicopters a day, Colonel Brown could provide the 1st Battalion, 7th Cavalry, with only 16 for the move because his other two battalions needed 4 each for resupply purposes and some local movement of elements of squad and platoon size. Fire support, so important to an air assault, was to be provided by two 105-mm. howitzer batteries of the 1st Battalion, 21st Artillery. They would be firing from Landing Zone FALCON, nine kilometers east of the search area. One battery was to be airlifted from Plei Me to FALCON early on the 14th before the assault; the other was already in position. A note of concern in his voice, Colonel Brown reminded Moore to keep his rifle companies within supporting range of each other. Both men were sharply conscious that the battalion had yet to be tested in battle against a large enemy force.

Colonel Moore returned to his command post at Plei Me, where his headquarters soon buzzed with activity. Radioing his Company A and Company C commanders, whose troops were engaged in saturation patrolling throughout their sectors, the tall Kentuckian told them to concentrate their men at first light on 14 November at the largest pickup zones in each sector and to be ready themselves to take a look at the target area. He arranged for the helicopters to lift Company B back to Plei Me early on the morning of the 14th from brigade headquarters, twenty minutes away to the southwest. The unit had just been placed there on the evening of the 13th to secure Colonel Brown's command post and other administrative and logistical facilities. Setting 0830 the following morning as the time for issuing the order, which would be preceded by a reconnaissance flight, Moore continued supervising preparations until by 2200 everything had been accomplished that could be done before the actual reconnaissance.

That night before going to bed Colonel Moore reviewed his plan and decided on a fresh approach for this operation. Instead of setting down each company on a separate landing zone as he had been doing for the past few days, he would use one landing zone for the entire battalion. His whole force would then be available if he encountered the enemy on landing. Although American units had not engaged a sizable enemy force for some time, the big red star designating a possible enemy base that both he and Colonel Brown had seen on the map loomed large in his mind.

Colonel Moore considered his assets. Firepower would be no problem. The 21st Artillery, tactical air, and gunships had given him excellent support in previous operations, and he knew that Colonel Brown would provide additional fire support if he needed it.

The manpower situation was somewhat different. Of the twenty-three officers authorized for his three rifle companies and one combat support company, twenty were available and practically all had been with the battalion since air assault testing days at Fort Benning, Georgia. In the enlisted ranks the scene was less encouraging, for the 1st Battalion, 7th Cavalry, would be at only two-thirds strength. During the unit's first two months in Vietnam, malaria and individual service terminations had taken their toll. At the moment, 8 to 10 men from the battalion were in transit for rest and recuperation, and each company had kept 3 to 5 men each back at Camp Radcliff, the An Khe permanent base camp, for various reasons—minor illness, guard duty, administrative retention, base camp development. Colonel Moore was not unduly concerned, however, for he had accomplished previous search and destroy missions with approximately the same numbers. Besides, rarely did any commander field a unit at 100 percent strength.

The 14th dawned bright and clear and by 0630 Company B had been lifted to Plei Me from brigade headquarters by CH-47 Chinook helicopters. Since it had already been assembled in one location, Colonel Moore had selected Company B to land first.

While he supervised preparations, Capt. John D. Herren, Company B commander, chewed on his pipe and thought of the impending operation. He and his men had gone without sleep the night before, having had to cope with an understandably jittery brigade command post. A few minutes before midnight on the 12th the post had been attacked by a local Viet Cong force that killed seven men and wounded twenty-three. Herren could only trust that the lack of rest would have little effect on the fighting ability of his men.

Amid a deafening roar of helicopters, the reconnaissance party assembled. The ships, finished with Herren's company, had begun to move Battery A, 1st Battalion, 21st Artillery, to FALCON, where it would join Battery C as planned. Standing there to hear Colonel Moore were the Company B, Company D, and headquarters company commanders; a scout section leader from Troop C, 1st Squadron, 9th Cavalry; the commander of Company A, 229th Aviation Battalion (Airmobile), Maj. Bruce P. Crandall; and the battalion S-3, Capt. Gregory P. Dillon. Moore briefed the group on the battalion's mission, the flight route, and what to look for. Then, using two UH-1D Huey helicopters and escorted by two UH-1B gunships, the reconnaissance party departed.

Flying at 2,500 feet and following a pattern that would both provide some deception and allow for maximum viewing of the target area, the four helicopters headed southwest to a point about eight kilometers southeast of the Ia Drang River. Then they turned and flew due north to Duc Co where they circled for five minutes, reversed course, and by 0815 returned to Plei Me. (*Map 2*)

Once on the ground, the members of the party discussed possible landing zones to be chosen from open areas observed during

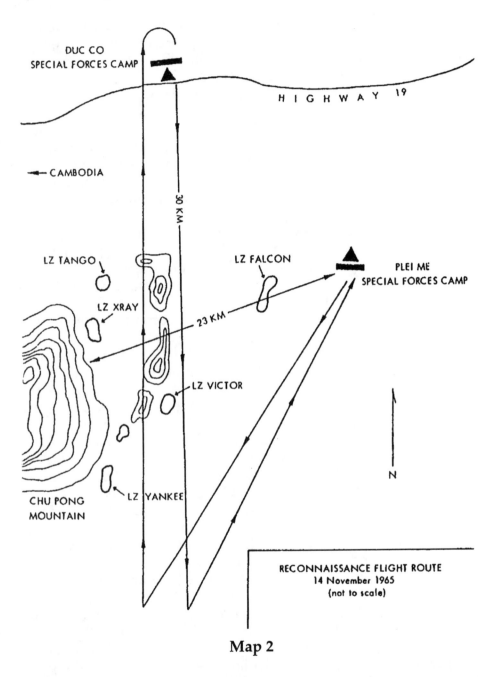

DUC CO
SPECIAL FORCES CAMP

H I G H W A Y   19

◂— CAMBODIA

30 KM

LZ TANGO

LZ FALCON

PLEI ME
SPECIAL FORCES CAMP

LZ XRAY

23 KM

LZ VICTOR

N

CHU PONG
MOUNTAIN

LZ YANKEE

RECONNAISSANCE FLIGHT ROUTE
14 November 1965
(not to scale)

Map 2

the flight. While they were debating, the brigade fragmentary order, which specified Area LIME as the primary zone of interest, arrived. Within a few minutes the choice narrowed to three landing zones: TANGO, X-RAY, and YANKEE. Colonel Moore wanted the largest site available, one that would not unduly restrict the helicopters. This ruled out TANGO as inadequate. Surrounded by tall trees, it could accommodate three, perhaps four, Hueys at most, or half a rifle platoon. Both YANKEE and X-RAY seemed likely choices, for either could take eight to ten ships at a time; at least a platoon and a half could be put on the ground at the start, that most crucial of all moments during an airmobile assault. Announcing X-RAY as his tentative choice, Colonel Moore turned to the scout section leader from the 9th Cavalry and instructed him to fly another reconnaissance mission at "nap-of-the-earth" level along the Ia Drang valley. He was to obtain more details about X-RAY, YANKEE, and the surrounding terrain and to look for any signs of enemy activity.

The scout section was back in forty minutes. Although the pilots had seen several trails during their low-level flight, they had drawn no enemy fire. YANKEE, they reported, was usable but risky because it had too many high tree stumps. X-RAY, they confirmed, could easily take eight to ten ships, and just a few hundred meters north of it they had seen communications wire stretched along an east-west trail. This last bit of intelligence was all Colonel Moore needed. X-RAY was to be the primary site, with YANKEE and TANGO as alternates to be used only on his order.

By this time it was 0855 and with the planning completed Colonel Moore reassembled the company commanders, his staff, and representatives of supporting forces to hear his order.

According to the latest available intelligence, an enemy battalion was located five kilometers northwest of X-RAY. Another hostile force of undetermined size was probably just southwest of the landing zone itself, and a secret base was believed to be three kilometers to the northwest. To develop these targets, Moore explained, the 1st Battalion was going to make an air assault into X-RAY, then search for and destroy enemy forces, concentrating on stream beds and wooded high ground. The low-level reconnaissance had no doubt alerted any enemy in the area. To keep the enemy guessing up to the last as to where an actual landing would occur, the 21st Artillery was to fire an 8-minute diversionary preparation on YANKEE and TANGO. This was to be followed by a 20-minute rain of fire on X-RAY, with emphasis on the slopes of a finger with a contiguous draw that jutted out from Chu Pong just northwest of X-RAY. Gunships of the 2d Battalion, 20th Artillery (Aerial Rocket) (Airmobile), were to follow the tube artillery barrage for thirty seconds with rocket and machine gun fire, after which the escort gunships of Company A, 229th Aviation Battalion, were to sweep the area.

Using sixteen Hueys, Herren's Company B was to follow close on the heels of the fire preparation, land, and secure X-RAY, followed in turn and on order by Companies A, C, and D. Once on the ground Companies A and B were to assemble in attack formation just off the north and northeastern sectors of X-RAY, prepared to search east or northeast on order, with Company A on the right. Designated at first as the reserve force, Company C was upon landing to assume the security mission from Company B on order with a "be prepared" task to move west and northwest, searching the lower portion of Chu Pong. If Company C did hit anything, Moore reasoned, at least he would have his entire force readily available as a backup. Company B had priority of fire at the start, but once the westward Push from X-RAY began the priority was shifted to Company A.

Colonel Moore directed each rifle company to bring one 81-mm. mortar tube and a maximum ammunition load and Company D to bring its three tubes. When all companies had closed at X-RAY, their mortars were to revert to control of the Company D mortar platoon.

Just as he completed his briefing, Colonel Moore learned that the artillery was in position. Setting 1030 as touchdown time at X-RAY for the air assault, with the 20-minute artillery preparatory fires to be completed by H minus 1 minute, Moore knew that it would be a split-second affair.

For this mission the troops of the 1st Battalion, 7th Cavalry, would be well prepared. Standing operating procedure dictated that each rifleman carry at least 300 rounds of M16 ammunition, and each grenadier was ordered to bring between two and three dozen high-explosive shells for his 40-mm. grenade launcher. Machine gun crews were to transport at least 800 rounds of linked 7.62-mm. ammunition, and every man was to have no less than two M26 fragmentation grenades. There were to be at least two 66-mm. M72 light assault weapons per squad and five to six smoke grenades in each platoon. Every soldier was to carry one C ration meal and two canteens of water, as well as an ample supply of intrenching tools and machetes.

Colonel Brown arrived as Moore finished giving the order and Moore briefed him separately. The brigade commander liked the tactical plan, agreed with the selection of X-RAY as the primary landing zone, and was satisfied that Moore's concept of the operation followed the guidance he had given him the previous afternoon.

At 1017, after a brief delay resulting from the too hasty positioning of the artillery pieces at FALCON, the preparatory fires began. Thirteen minutes later the leading elements of Company B lifted off the Plei Me airstrip with a thunderous roar in a storm of red dust. With volleys of artillery fire slamming into the objective area, the sixteen Hueys, four platoons of four each, filed southwestward across the midmorning sky at two thousand feet. Two kilometers out, they dropped to treetop level. The aerial rocket artillery gunships meanwhile worked X-RAY over for thirty seconds, expending half of their loads, then circled nearby, available on call. The 229th's escort gunships came next, rockets and machine guns blazing, immediately ahead of the lift ships. As the lead helicopters braked for the assault landing, their door gunners and some of the infantrymen fired into the trees and tall grass.

Lunging from the ships, the men of Company B, Colonel Moore among them, charged into the trees, snap-firing at likely enemy positions. By 1048 the helicopters were already returning to Plei Me for the rest of Company B and advance contingents of Company A.

Relatively flat and open as seen from above, X-RAY took on a different appearance when viewed by the infantryman on the ground. Ringed by sparse scrub brush with occasional trees ranging upward to a hundred feet, the landing zone was covered with hazel-colored, willowy elephant grass as high as five feet, ideal for the concealment of crawling soldiers. Interspersed throughout were anthills, some considerably taller than a standing man, all excellent as crew-served weapons positions. Along the western and northeastern edges of the landing zone the trees were especially thick and extended up the slopes of Chu Pong peak, which was 542 meters high and whose thick vegetation offered good concealment for enemy troops. A dry creek bed with waist-high banks ran along the western edge of the landing zone.

Captain Herren watched with satisfaction as his 1st Platoon leader, 2d Lt. Alan E. Deveny, went about the business of securing the landing zone. In line with orders from Colonel Moore, Herren was using a new technique. Rather than attempt a 360-degree perimeter coverage of the entire area as in previous operations, Herren concealed most of his force in a clump of trees and tall grass near the center of the landing zone as a reaction striking force, while Deveny's squads struck out in different directions, reconnoitering the terrain fifty to a hundred meters from the western side of X-RAY. A sound technique, it allowed Captain Herren to conserve his forces while he retained a flexible option, which, in view of the 30-minute turnaround flight time for the rest of the battalion, appeared prudent.

As Lieutenant Deveny's soldiers pressed the search, Herren became fully convinced that if there was to be a fight the proximity of X-RAY to the enemy haven across the Cambodian border made X-RAY the likely site. Yet the leading elements of the 1st Battalion, 7th Cavalry, had landed successfully and were thus far unopposed.

Where was the enemy?

The helicopter landing had been spotted. Although elements of the North Vietnamese units that had been scheduled to participate in the 16 November Plei Me attack had left their Ia Drang valley staging areas at dawn the morning of 14 November, the landing of Captain Herren's infantrymen in X-RAY a few hours later had prompted General Chu Huy Man to change course swiftly. Plei Me would have to wait. The 66th and 33d Regiments would attack the landing zone and destroy the Americans. By noon two battalions of the 66th and the newly formed composite battalion of the 33d were preparing for the assault from positions at the base of Chu Pong and the low ground immediately to the west.

At X-RAY the 1st Platoon, Company B, continued to probe. At 1120 Lieutenant Deveny's troops made a discovery: searching the brush, a rifleman surprised an enemy soldier only fifty meters from the landing zone. The North Vietnamese tried to lose himself in the thicket, but the Americans soon captured him. He was unarmed, dressed in trousers and a dirty khaki shirt with a serial number on one of the epaulets, and carried only an empty canteen.

Notified of the catch, Colonel Moore rushed to the spot with his intelligence officer, Capt Thomas C. Metsker, and his Montagnard interpreter, a Mr. Nik. Questioning the prisoner, they learned that he was a deserter from the North Vietnamese Army and had been subsisting on bananas for five days. He declared that three North Vietnamese battalions were on Chu Pong mountain, anxious to kill Americans but as yet unable to find them.

Elated but cautious, for getting the rest of the battalion in quickly and safely was now doubly important, Colonel Moore told Captain Herren to intensify his search and prepare to assume Company C's mission of exploring the terrain at the foot of Chu Pong, giving special attention to the finger and draw to the northwest. Moore radioed his S-3, Captain Dillon, who was circling the landing zone in the command helicopter, to land and pick up the prisoner and fly him back to 3d Brigade headquarters for additional interrogation.

Hardly had Moore given Herren his mission when the commander of Company A, Capt. Ramon A. Nadal II, reported. A former Special Forces officer on a second Vietnam tour, Nadal begged permission for his company to follow the lead opened up by Company B's find. Moore had already given the job to Herren, whose men now knew the terrain and were tensed for an approaching fight; he told Nadal to assume the mission of providing security for the landing zone.

For the move northwest Captain Herren directed Lieutenant Deveny's 1st Platoon toward the finger, with 2d Lt. Henry T. Herrick's 2d Platoon on the right. He told both officers to advance abreast. Positioning 2d Lt. Dennis J. Deal's 3d Platoon behind the 1st as a reserve, captain Herren and his company moved out.

Deveny got ahead of Herrick's platoon after crossing the dry creek bed which ran along the eastern flank of the finger. At 1245 his platoon encountered an enemy force of about platoon size which attacked both his flanks with small arms fire. Pinned down and suffering casualties, he asked for help. Captain Herren, in an attempt to relieve the pressure, radioed Lieutenant Herrick to establish contact with the 1st Platoon's right flank.

Anxious to develop the situation, Herrick maneuvered his 27-man force in that direction. A few minutes after Herren issued the order, the point of Herrick's 2d Platoon bumped into a squad of North Vietnamese soldiers moving toward X-RAY along a well-used trail, parallel to the platoon's direction of advance. The startled enemy turned and scurried back along the trail; firing, the 2d Platoon followed in close pursuit with two squads forward. The platoon soon began to receive sporadic but ineffective enfilade fire from the right. The lead squads were now at the crest of the finger, about a hundred meters from the dry creek bed. To the right and farther downhill was the 3d Squad.

Lieutenant Herrick intended to continue his sweep, with all three squads on the line and machine guns on the flanks. Although he could no longer see the enemy soldiers, he knew that they were somewhere in front of him. He was about to give the signal to continue when men in his 3d Squad spotted about twenty North Vietnamese scrambling toward two large anthills off the platoon's left flank. As the last of the enemy disappeared behind the anthills, the 3d Squad opened fire. The North Vietnamese returned it, but a 3d Squad grenadier found the range and in less than a minute was pumping round after round into their ranks. Screams mingled with the sound of the explosions.

Without warning, a blistering volley of enemy fire suddenly erupted from the right flank. The opening fusillade killed the grenadier and pinned down the rest of the squad.

Deploying his two M60 machine guns toward the harassed force, Herrick yelled to the 3d Squad leader, S. Sgt. Clyde E. Savage, to pull back under covering fire of the machine guns. Yet even as the gunners moved into firing position and Herrick radioed word of his predicament to his company commander, the situation grew worse. Within a few minutes fire was lashing the entire 3d Platoon from all sides. Covered by the blazing M60's, Sergeant Savage managed to withdraw his squad toward the platoon, carrying the M79 of the dead grenadier, who lay sprawled where he had fallen, a .45-caliber pistol clutched in his right hand. Amid increasingly heavy fire of all calibers, including mortars and rockets, the squad reached the main body of the platoon and joined the other men in hastily forming a 25-meter perimeter.

The machine gunners were less fortunate in making their way into the perimeter. Although the closer team managed to disengage and crawl into the small circle of prone infantrymen, enemy fire cut down all four in the other team. Seizing the fallen team's M60, the North Vietnamese turned it against Herrick's positions.

Except for the artillery forward observer, 1st Lt. William O. Riddle, who soon caught up with Lieutenant Deal, Captain Herren and his command group had dropped behind the leading platoons while Herren radioed a situation report to Colonel Moore. To the Company B commander, who could hear the firefight going on in the jungle ahead, the enemy appeared to be in two-company strength and fully capable of cutting off Lieutenant Herrick's 2d Platoon. Yet Captain Herren had few resources to turn to Herrick's assistance. Already he had committed his 3d Platoon to go to the aid of Lieutenant Deveny, and the company's lone 81-mm. mortar was in action, making quick work of the meager forty rounds of high-explosive ammunition the crew had brought to the landing zone.

Since Deveny appeared to be less closely engaged than Herrick, Captain Herren ordered him to try to reach Herrick. If Deal's force could reach Deveny soon enough, together they stood a good chance of reaching Herrick.

Having reported the action to Colonel Moore, Captain Herren turned from his radio just in time to see a North Vietnamese soldier not more than fifteen meters away with a weapon trained on him. Rapidly, Herren fired a burst from his M16, ducked for cover, and tossed a grenade.

Off to his left, Herren could just make out men crouched in the dry stream bed, firing toward the finger. Believing them to be members of the 3d Platoon and anxious to get them linked up with his 1st Platoon, he headed toward them.

At the landing zone Colonel Moore had meanwhile alerted Captain Nadal to be prepared to assist Herren as soon as Company C was on the ground. The heavy firefight had barely commenced when Company A's last platoon and the lead forces of Company C landed. It was 1330. A few rounds of enemy 60-mm. and 81-mm. mortar fire slammed into the tall elephant grass in the center of the landing zone as Colonel Moore turned to Nadal and ordered him to rush a platoon to Herren to be used in getting through to Herrick. Captain Nadal was to follow with his remaining two platoons and link up with Company B's left flank. Colonel Moore then turned to Capt. Robert H. Edwards, who had just landed with some of his troops, and directed him to set up a blocking position to the south and southwest of X-RAY, just inside the tree line, where he could cover Company A's exposed left flank. Moore knew that this was a risky move because he had only Company D left as a reaction force and still had to defend an entire landing zone in all directions. By this positioning of Edwards' company he would be exposing his rear, but in the light of the rapidly developing situation, which bore out what the prisoner had told him, it seemed the only sensible thing to do.

The S-3, Captain Dillon, had by now returned from brigade headquarters and was hovering above X-RAY, relaying the course of the battle to Colonel Brown's headquarters.

Colonel Moore had established his command post near a prominent anthill in the center of the landing zone. He radioed Dillon to request air strikes, artillery, and aerial rocket fire, starting on the lower fringes of the Chu Pong slopes and then working first over the western and then over the southern enemy approaches to X-RAY. Secondary targets would be the draws leading down from the mountain and any suspected or sighted enemy mortar positions. Priority was to be given to requests for fire from the fighting companies.

Dillon passed the fire requests to Capt. Jerry Whiteside, the 21st Artillery liaison officer, and Lt. Charles Hastings, the Air Force forward air controller, who were seated beside him. A few minutes later, Pleiku-based aircraft were blasting the target area, and two strikes were made on the valley floor to the northwest, near the suspected location of the enemy battalion.

Although the artillery also responded quickly, the fire was at first ineffective. Since there were no well-defined terrain features that could be used as reference points to the fighting troops, now hidden by a heavy pall of dust and smoke that hung in the air, it was hard to pinpoint locations for close-in support. Aware of the difficulty, Colonel Moore radioed Whiteside to use the technique of "walking" the fires down the mountain toward the landing zone from the south and the west, and fires were soon close enough to aid some of the embattled infantrymen.

Anxious to assist Company B, Captain Nadal radioed his 2d Platoon leader, 2d Lt. Walter J. Marm, to move foreward. Marm formed his platoon into a skirmish line and started out immediately from the landing zone toward the sound of the firing. Since there was no time to consult with Captain Herren, Lieutenant Marm planned to join the Company B left flank and push through to Lieutenant Herrick's perimeter. No sooner had he crossed the dry creek bed when two North Vietnamese appeared before his platoon and surrendered. A few moments later, just as he reached Deal's 3d Platoon, troops of both units spotted a force of khaki-clad enemy soldiers moving across their front, left to right. Both Deal and Marm had apparently met the left enveloping pincer which had initially flanked Herrick and which was now attempting, it seemed, to surround all of Company B. A fierce firefight ensued, both sides taking casualties. The enemy soldiers then peeled off to the left, breaking contact momentarily and, unknown to Marm, trying to maneuver behind Marm via the dry creek bed.

Taking advantage of the lull, Marm collected all of his and Deal's wounded and ordered one of his squad leaders, S. Sgt. Lonnie L. Parker, to take them back to the landing zone. Parker tried but returned in twenty minutes to report that the platoon was surrounded. Marm doubted that the enemy could have moved that fast but he could not be sure, since enemy troops were now maneuvering to his flank also.

When the North Vietnamese of the flanking force, estimated as company size, entered the dry creek bed they ran headlong into the rest of Company A; Nadal, eager to join the fray, had moved his remaining two platoons forward. First to meet the enemy in the creek bed was the 3d Platoon. The firing was at very close range, the fighting savage. The platoon leader, 2d Lt. Robert E. Taft, going to the aid of one of his squad leaders who, unknown to Taft, was already dead, was himself hit in the throat and died instantly. Recoiling from the first shock, the men of the left half of the 3d Platoon climbed onto the creek bank where, along with the men of the 1st Platoon, they poured a murderous fire into the enemy. A seriously wounded rifleman lay near the body of Lieutenant Taft beneath the deadly cross fire.

As the firefight erupted in the dry creek bed, additional elements of Company C and the lead troopers of Company D landed at X-RAY in the first eight Hueys of the fifth airlift. They touched down in a heavy hail of enemy small arms fire that wounded a pilot and a door gunner.

Capt. Louis R. LeFebvre, the Company D commander, in the lead helicopter, could see the air strikes and artillery fire slamming into the ground around X-RAY. Leaning forward to unhook his seat belt as the aircraft touched down, he felt a bullet crease the back of his neck. Instinctively, he turned to the right just in time to see his radio operator slump forward, still buckled in his seat, a bullet hole in the left side of his head. Grabbing the dead man's radio, LeFebvre jumped from the helicopter, told those assembled who had landed in other ships to follow, and raced for the tree line to the west, seventy-five meters away. Only four men followed him. Under fire all the way, they reached the relative safety of the dry creek bed, thirty-five meters short of the tree line.

So heavy was the fire, particularly in the northwestern area, that Colonel Moore radioed the remaining eight helicopters not to land. Sporadic rocket and mortar fire, the crash of artillery volleys, and the thunderclap of air strikes that were now ringing the small clearing blended in one continuous roar.

Captain LeFebvre heard firing in front of him and on both sides. His small group had moved into position just to the right of Company A's two platoons, which were still battling the force that had attempted to flank Marm's platoon. LeFebvre and his men joined the firing from their positions in the creek bed, their immediate targets twenty-five to thirty North Vietnamese moving to the left across their front. Soon realizing the need for more firepower, LeFebvre called for his antitank platoon (which had been reorganized into a rifle platoon) to join him. It had come in with him on the last flight and was 150 meters to his rear, assembled on the landing zone, awaiting instructions. The acting platoon leader, S. Sgt. George Gonzales, answered that he was on the way. LeFebvre then yelled to his mortar platoon leader, 1st Lt. Raul E. Requera-Taboada, who had accompanied him in the lead ship and lay a few feet away from him, to send his radio operator forward to replace the man who had been killed in the helicopter.

Just as the radio operator joined him, Captain LeFebvre looked up to see Captain Herren. The Company B commander told him that there were enemy soldiers south in the direction from which he had come. He and his radio operator took positions beside LeFebvre and began firing along with the others. In rapid succession, Herren's radio operator was killed, LeFebvre's right arm shattered by a fusillade of enemy small arms fire, and Taboada received a bad leg wound. Herren applied a tourniquet to LeFebvre's arm and then resumed firing.

With half of the fifth lift landed, Company C had all of its troops except three Huey loads. While the Company A firefight raged, Captain Edwards, in accordance with Colonel Moore's guidance, quickly moved his platoons into a blocking position occupying 120 meters of ground immediately adjacent to Nadal's right flank. Edwards was none too soon. A few minutes later a strong enemy force struck Company C from the southwest and west. Lying prone, the Americans put out a withering volley of fire. The North Vietnamese soldiers, estimated at a reinforced company, wore helmets and web equipment and, like those who had hit Companies A and B, were well camouflaged. With the help of well-placed air strikes and artillery fire, however, Company C held them off, killing many. The 1st Platoon managed to capture a prisoner, who was quickly evacuated.

Colonel Moore's gamble in positioning Edwards' forces south of Nadal's rather than to the north proved sound, for by the timely commitment of Companies A and C he had so far succeeded in frustrating enemy attempts to overrun the landing zone. But with his rear still exposed, he directed Edwards to tie in and co-ordinate with Company D to his left extending the perimeter south and southeast into the brush.

Edwards found Sergeant Gonzales, who had assumed command of Company D after Captain LeFebvre had been evacuated. Leaving skeleton crews to man the mortars, together they quickly moved the antitank platoon and some of the mortar platoon alongside Company C. The reconnaissance platoon had not yet arrived.

While coordinating with Gonzales, Captain Edwards learned that the mortars had not been centrally organized. With Colonel Moore's approval, Edwards placed them under his own section leader's control until the battalion mortars platoon leader should arrive with his fire direction centers. But the mortars were unable to provide effective fire support because smoke, noise, and confusion made it difficult for the forward observers to adjust. The intensity of the fighting increased as did the noise. Hit by heavy enemy ground fire while making a low-level firing pass over X-RAY, an A-1E Skyraider, trailing smoke and flames, crashed two kilometers northeast of the landing zone, killing the pilot. When enemy soldiers tried to reach the wreckage, helicopter gunships destroyed it with rocket fire.

By this time it was a few minutes before 1500 and, judging by reports from his companies, Colonel Moore estimated that a North Vietnamese force numbering at least 500 to 600 opposed his battalion, with more on the way. Calling Colonel Brown, he asked for another rifle company.

At brigade headquarters, Colonel Brown was following developments closely. Monitoring the 1st Battalion, 7th Cavalry, tactical situation by radio, he had realized from the report of Company B's contact and what followed that the battalion was going to have its hands full. By 1430 he was in the air above X-RAY to see the situation for himself. Below him as the battle raged, he noticed that the artillery was firing halfway up Chu Pong. He radioed Colonel Moore to bring it in closer where it could be more effective. He did not know that Colonel Moore had arranged for the artillery to fire farther out at secondary target areas when not shooting specific close-in missions.

Convinced of the seriousness of the situation Colonel Brown had given careful consideration to what action to take if Colonel Moore asked for help. Of his two other battalions only one company was assembled at one place—Company B, 2d Battalion, 7th Cavalry, whose troops had just begun to arrive at brigade headquarters for perimeter security duty. These troops were, therefore, the logical choice, and when Moore called for assistance Colonel Brown in midafternoon attached Company B to the 1st Battalion, 7th Cavalry. Another company replaced the troops as perimeter guard at brigade headquarters.

It seemed obvious to Colonel Brown as the afternoon wore on that the enemy was trying to annihilate the 1st Battalion, 7th Cavalry. Looking to the future, he prepared for further reinforcements. Shortly after approving the use of Company B, 2d Battalion, 7th Cavalry, Colonel Brown called Lt. Col. Robert B. Tully, who commanded the 2d Battalion, 5th Cavalry, and directed him to assemble his unit as quickly as possible at Landing Zone VICTOR, which lay three kilometers to the southeast. Since he did not relish the idea of moving a steady stream of helicopters into what might still be a hot landing zone, and since he felt certain that the enemy would expect such a maneuver and would probably be prepared to deal with it, Brown told Tully that he would move by foot to reinforce Moore's battalion at X-RAY the next morning. He then directed the remainder of the 2d Battalion, 7th Cavalry, to move to Landing Zone MACON, a few kilometers north of X-RAY, where it would be close to the fight and available if needed.

By 1500 Colonel Moore had decided that it was absolutely essential, and safe enough, for the remaining tactical elements of the 2d Battalion to land. Although the eastern sector of the perimeter was still under enemy fire, the fire had slackened considerable because of the action of Company C and Company D. In minutes after receiving the landing order, the battalion reconnaissance platoon, Company C's three loads of troops, and the executive officer and the first sergeant of Company D were on the ground. Colonel Moore directed 2d Lt. James L. Litton, the executive officer, to take over from Sergeant Gonzales, who had been wounded, co-ordinate all mortars in the battalion under one central fire direction center, and deploy the reconnaissance platoon around the northeastern fringe of the landing zone as a battalion reserve and to provide security in the area.

Although by this time Colonel Moore, in an attempt to minimize the ships' exposure to enemy fire, was personally directing the helicopter traffic into X-RAY, two helicopters were disabled during the landing. One received enemy fire in the engine compartment while lifting off and had to make a forced landing in an open area just off the northern edge of X-RAY. Another clipped the treetops with the main rotor blade when landing and could not be flown out. Both crews, who were uninjured, were evacuated almost immediately while the helicopters, secured by Company D troopers, awaited lift-out later. Other helicopter crews nevertheless continued to fly missions into X-RAY, exhibiting great courage and audacity under fire.

On the ground the welfare of men who were wounded was considerably improved by the fact that four airmen and the battalion surgeon had landed with medical supplies early in the afternoon. They had set up an emergency aid station near Moore's command post. Rather than expose medical evacuation helicopters to enemy fire, Colonel Moore arranged with the helicopter lift company commander, Major Crandall, to evacuate casualties to FALCON by loading them on departing lift ships. With the help of a pathfinder team which arrived by 1600, the system worked well.

Within a half hour after the rest of the battalion had closed into X-RAY, the forces of Company A and Company B that had been attempting to reach Lieutenant Herrick's platoon pulled back to the dry creek bed under covering artillery and mortar fire at Colonel Moore's direction, bringing their dead and wounded along. Although Company B's 1st Platoon (with 2d Lt. Kenneth E. Duncan, the company executive officer, overseeing the operation) had advanced to a point within seventy-five meters of the isolated force and had eventually linked up with the 3d Platoon, all attempts to reach Herrick had been unsuccessful. The 1st Battalion, 7th Cavalry, clearly was facing an aggressive, expertly camouflaged, and well-armed enemy force that could shoot well and was not afraid to die. Nevertheless, Colonel Moore decided to give it another try. He ordered Companies A and B to prepare for a coordinated attack, supported by heavy preparatory fires, to reach the beleaguered platoon, while Companies C and D, the former still engaged in a violent fight, continued to hold the line on the perimeter.

The predicament of the isolated force meanwhile grew progressively worse. Lieutenant Herrick and his men sorely needed the reinforcements that Colonel Moore was attempting to send. The North Vietnamese laced the small perimeter with fire so low to the ground that few of Herrick's men were able to employ their intrenching tools to provide themselves cover. Through it all the men returned the fire, taking a heavy toll of the enemy. Sergeant Savage, firing his M16, hit twelve of the enemy himself during the course of the afternoon. In midafternoon Lieutenant Herrick was hit by a bullet which entered his hip, coursed through his body, and went out through his right shoulder. As he lay dying, the lieutenant continued to direct his perimeter defense, and in his last few moments he gave his signal operation instructions book to S. Sgt. Carl L. Palmer, his platoon sergeant, with orders to burn it if capture seemed imminent. He told Palmer to redistribute the ammunition, call in artillery fire, and at the first opportunity try to make a break for it. Sergeant Palmer, himself already slightly wounded, had no sooner taken command than he too was killed.

The 2d Squad leader took charge. He rose on his hands and knees and mumbled to no one in particular that he was going to get the platoon out of danger. He had just finished the sentence when a bullet smashed into his head. Killed in the same hail of bullets was the forward observer for the 81-mm. mortar. The artillery reconnaissance sergeant, who had been traveling with the platoon, was shot in the neck. Seriously wounded, he became delirious and the men had difficulty keeping him quiet.

Sergeant Savage, the 3d Squad leader, now took command. Snatching the artilleryman's radio, he began calling in and adjusting artillery fire. Within minutes he had ringed the perimeter with well-placed concentrations, some as close to the position as twenty meters. The fire did much to discourage attempts to overrun the perimeter, but the platoon's position still was precarious. Of the 27 men in the platoon, 8 had been killed and 12 wounded, leaving less than a squad of effectives.

After the first unsuccessful attempt to rescue the isolated force, Company B's two remaining platoons had returned to the creek bed where they met Captain Herren. Lieutenants Deveny and Deal listened intently as their company commander explained that an artillery preparation would precede the two-company assault that Colonel Moore planned. Lieutenant Riddle, the company's artillery forward observer, would direct the fire. The platoons would then advance abreast from the dry creek bed.

The creek bed was also to serve as a line of departure for Captain Nadal's company. The Company A soldiers removed their packs and received an ammunition resupply in preparation for the move. Aside from the danger directly in front of him, Nadal believed the greatest threat would come from the left, toward Chu Pong, and accordingly he planned to advance with his company echeloned in that direction, the 2d Platoon leading, followed by the 1st and 3d in that order. Since he was unsure of the trapped platoon's location, Captain Nadal decided to guide on Company B. If he met no significant resistance after traveling a short distance, he would shift to a company wedge formation. Before embarking on his formidable task, Nadal assembled as many of his men as possible in the creek bed and told them that an American platoon was cut off, in trouble, and that they were going after it. The men responded enthusiastically.

Preceded by heavy artillery and aerial rocket fire, most of which fell as close as 250 meters in front of Company B, which had fire priority, the attack to reach the cutoff platoon struck out at 1620, Companies A and B abreast. Almost from the start it was rough going. So close to the creek bed had the enemy infiltrated that heavy fighting broke out almost as soon as the men left it. Well camouflaged, their khaki uniforms blending in with the brownish-yellow elephant grass, the North Vietnamese soldiers had also concealed themselves in trees, burrowed into the ground to make "spider" holes, and dug into the tops and sides of anthills.

The first man in his company out of the creek bed, Captain Nadal had led his 1st and 2d Platoons only a short distance before they encountered the enemy. The 3d Platoon had not yet left the creek bed. 2d Lt. Wayne O. Johnson fell, seriously wounded, and a few moments later a squad leader yelled that one of his team leaders had been killed.

Lieutenant Marm's men forged ahead until enemy machine gun fire, which seemed to come from an anthill thirty meters to their front, stopped them. Deliberately exposing himself in order to pinpoint the exact enemy location, Marm fired an M72 antitank round at the earth mound. He inflicted some casualties, but the enemy fire continued. Figuring that it would be a simple matter to dash up to the position and toss a grenade behind it, he motioned to one of his men to do so. At this point the noise and confusion was such that a sergeant near him interpreted the gesture as a command to throw one from his position. He tossed and the grenade fell short. Disregarding his own safety, Marm dashed quickly across the open stretch of ground and hurled the grenade into the position, killing some of the enemy soldiers behind it and finishing off the dazed survivors with his M16. Soon afterward he took a bullet in the face and had to be evacuated. (For this action he received the Medal of Honor.)

Captain Nadal watched the casualties mount as his men attempted to inch forward. All of his platoon leaders were dead or wounded and his artillery forward observer had been killed. Four of his men were killed within six feet of him, including Sfc. Jacke Gell, his communications sergeant, who had been filling in as a radio operator. It was a little past 1700 and soon it would be dark. Nadal's platoons had moved only 150 meters and the going was tougher all the time. Convinced that he could not break through, he called Colonel Moore and asked permission to pull back. The colonel gave it.

Captain Herren's situation was little better than Captain Nadal's. Having tried to advance from the creek bed by fire and maneuver, Herren too found his men engaged almost immediately and as a result had gained even less ground than Company A. Understrength at the outset of the operation, Herren had incurred thirty casualties by 1700. Although he was anxious to reach his cutoff platoon, he too held up his troops when he monitored Captain Nadal's message.

Colonel Moore had little choice as to Captain Nadal's request. The battalion was fighting in three separate actions—one force was defending X-RAY, two companies were attacking, and one platoon was isolated. To continue under these circumstances would be to risk the battalion's defeat in detail if the enemy discovered and capitalized on Moore's predicament. The forces at X-RAY were liable to heavy attack from others directions, and to continue to push Companies A and B against so tenacious an enemy was to risk continuing heavy casualties. The key to the battalion's survival as Moore saw it was the physical security of X-RAY itself, especially in the light of what the first prisoner had told him about the presence of three enemy battalions. Moore decided to pull his forces back, intending to attack again later that night or early in the morning or to order the platoon to attempt to infiltrate back to friendly lines.

But the move was not easy to make. Because of the heavy fighting, Company A's 1st Platoon had trouble pulling back with its dead and wounded. Captain Nadal committed the 3d Platoon to help relieve the pressure and assist with the casualties. Since he had lost his artillery forward observer, he requested through Colonel Moore artillery smoke on the company to screen its withdrawal. When Moore relayed the request, the fire direction center replied that smoke rounds were not available. Recalling his Korean War experience, Moore approved the use of white phosphorus instead. It seemed to dissuade the enemy; fire diminished immediately thereafter. The success of the volley encouraged Nadal to call for another, which had a similar effect. Miraculously, in both instances, no friendly troops were injured, and both companies were able to break away.

By 1705 the 2d Platoon and command group of Company B, 2d Battalion, 7th Cavalry, were landing in X-RAY. Amidst cheers from the men on the ground, Capt. Myron Diduryk climbed out of the lead helicopter, ran up to Colonel Moore, and saluted with a "Garry Owen, sir!" Colonel Moore briefed Diduryk on the tactical situation and then assigned him the role of battalion reserve and instructed him to be prepared to counterattack in either Company A, B, or C sector, with emphasis on the last one. An hour or so later, concerned about Company C's having the lion's share of the perimeter, Colonel Moore attached Diduryk's 2d Platoon to it.

Captain Diduryk's 120-man force was coming to the battle as well prepared as the 1st Battalion, 7th Cavalry, troops already there. Each rifleman had 15 to 20 magazines, and every M60 machine gun crew carried at least 4 boxes of ball ammunition. The 40-mm. grenadiers had 30 to 40 rounds each, and every man in the company carried at least 1 fragmentation grenade. In addition to a platoon-size basic load ammunition supply, Diduryk had two 81-mm. mortars and forty-eight high-explosive rounds.

When 2d Lt. James L. Lane, leader of the 2d Platoon, Company B, reported to Company C with his platoon for instructions, Captain Edwards placed him on the right flank of his perimeter where he could link up with Company A. Edwards directed all the men to dig prone shelters. Other than for close-in local security, Edwards established no listening posts. The thick elephant grass would cut down on their usefulness, and the protective artillery concentrations that he planned within a hundred meters of his line would endanger them.

Rather than dig in, Company A took advantage of the cover of the dry creek bed. Captain Nadal placed all his platoons in it, except for the four left flank positions of his 3d Platoon, which he arranged up on the bank where they could tie in with Company C.

Company B elected not to use the creek bed. Instead, Captain Herren placed his two depleted platoons just forward of it, along 150 meters of good defensive terrain, an average of five meters between positions, with his command post behind them in the creek bed. He began immediately to register his artillery concentrations as close as possible to his defensive line and ordered his men to dig in.

Company D continued to occupy its section of the perimeter without change.

By 1800 all of Company B, 2d Battalion, 7th Cavalry, had landed. A half hour later Colonel Moore, figuring that the reconnaissance platoon was a large enough reserve force, readily available and positioned near the anthill, changed Captain Diduryk's mission, directing him to man the perimeter between Companies B and D with his remaining two platoons. 2d Lt. Cyril R. Rescorla linked his 1st Platoon with Company B, while 2d Lt. Albert E. Vernon joined his flank with Company D on his left. Diduryk placed his two 81-mm mortars with the 1st Battalion, 7th Cavalry, and allowed some of the crew to man the perimeter. Soon his men were digging in, clearing fields of fire, and adjusting close-in concentrations.

Except for completing registration of artillery and mortar fire, Colonel Moore had organized his battalion perimeter by 1900. Fighting had long since died down to the tolerable level of sporadic sniper fire, and as night came on the last of the dead and wounded were being airlifted to FALCON from the collecting point in the vicinity of the battalion command post, near the anthill. Just before dark a resupply of much needed ammunition, water, medical supplies, and rations was flown in. The aid station had been dangerously low on dexadrine, morphine, and bandages, and the water supply had reached such a critical stage at one point that a few soldier had eaten C ration jam for its moisture content to gain relief from the heat. A two-ship zone for night landing was established in the northern portion of X-RAY. Although under enemy observation and fire, it was much less vulnerable than other sectors of X-RAY where most of the fighting had occurred.

At 1850 Colonel Moore radioed his S-3, Captain Dillon, to land as soon as possible with two more radio operators, the artillery liaison officer, the forward air controller, more small arms ammunition, and water. Except for refueling stops Dillon had been in the command helicopter above X-RAY continuously, monitoring the tactical situation by radio, relaying information to brigade headquarters, and passing on instructions to the rifle companies; the helicopter itself served as an aerial platform from which Captain Whiteside and Lieutenant Hastings directed the artillery fire and air strikes. In order to carry out Colonel Moore's instructions, Dillon requested two helicopters from FALCON. By 2125 Dillon was nearing X-RAY from the south through a haze of dust and smoke. Just as his helicopter approached for touchdown, he glanced to the left and saw what appeared to be four or five blinking lights on the forward slopes of Chu Pong. The lights hovered and wavered in the darkness. He surmised that they were North Vietnamese troops using flashlights to signal each other while they moved, for he recalled how an officer from another American division had reported a similar incident two months earlier during an operation in Binh Dinh Province. Upon landing, Dillon passed this information on to Whiteside and Hastings as target data.

During the early hours of darkness, Colonel Moore, accompanied by his sergeant major, made spot visits around the battalion perimeter, talking to the men. Although his troops were facing a formidable enemy force and had suffered quite a few casualties, their morale was clearly high. Moore satisfied himself that his companies were tied in, mortars were all registered, an ammunition resupply system had been established, and in general his troops were prepared for the night. (*Map 3*)

During the evening the 66th North Vietnamese Regiment moved its 8th Battalion southward from a position north of the Ia Drang and charged it with the mission of applying pressure against the eastern sector of X-RAY. Field Front headquarters meanwhile arranged for movement of the H-15 Main Force Viet Cong Battalion from an assembly area well south of the scene of the fighting. The 32d Regiment had not yet left its assembly area, some twelve kilometers away, and the heavy mortar and antiaircraft units were still en route to X-RAY.

At intervals during the night, enemy forces harassed and probed the battalion perimeter in all but the Company D sector,

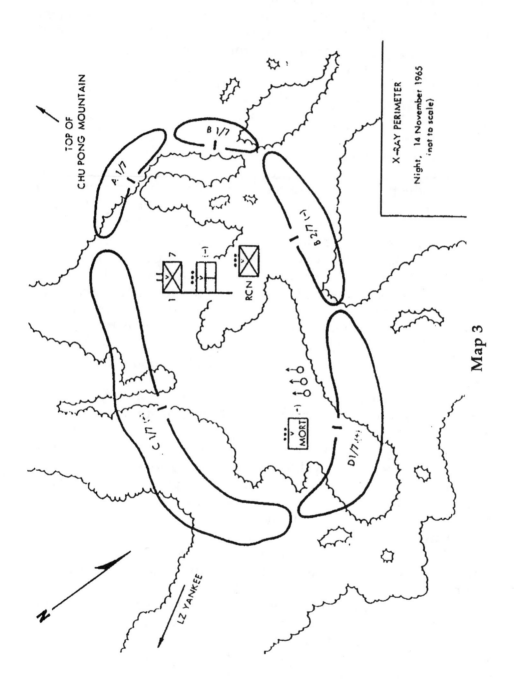

TOP OF
CHU PONG MOUNTAIN

B 1/7

A 1/7

B 2/7 (-)

RCN

C 1/7 (-)

MORT (-)

D1/7 (-)

N

LZ YANKEE

X-RAY PERIMETER

Night, 14 November 1965
(not to scale)

Map 3

and in each instance well-placed American artillery from FAL-CON blunted the enemy's aggressiveness. Firing some 4,000 rounds, the two howitzer batteries in that landing zone also laced the fingers and draws of Chu Pong where the lights had been seen. Tactical air missions were flown throughout the night.

The remnants of Sergeant Savage's isolated little band meanwhile continued to be hard pressed. Three times the enemy attacked with at least a reinforced platoon but were turned back by the artillery and the small arms fire of the men in the perimeter, including some of the wounded. Spec. 5 Charles H. Lose, the company senior medical aidman (whom Captain Herren had placed with the platoon because of a shortage of medics), moved about the perimeter, exposed to fire while he administered to the wounded. His diligence and ingenuity throughout the day and during the night saved at least a half-dozen lives; having run out of first-aid packets as well as bandages from his own bag, he used the C ration toilet tissue packets most of the men had with them to help stop bleeding. Calm, sure, and thoroughly professional, he brought reassurance to the men.

Before the second attack, which came at 0345, bugle calls were heard around the entire perimeter. Some sounds seemed to come from Chu Pong itself, 200 to 400 meters distant. Sergeant Savage could even hear enemy soldiers muttering softly to each other in the sing-song cadence of their language. He called down a 15-minute artillery barrage to saturate the area and followed it with a tactical air strike on the ground just above the positions. Executed under flareship illumination, the two strikes in combination broke up the attack. The sergeant noted that the illumination exposed his position and it was therefore not used again that night.

A third and final attack came over an hour later and was as unsuccessful as the previous two. Sergeant Savage and his men, isolated but still holding throughout the night, could hear and sometimes see the enemy dragging off his dead and wounded.

At brigade headquarters, Colonel Brown continued to assess the significance of the day's activities. Pleased that the 1st Battalion, 7th Cavalry, had been able to hold its own against heavy odds, and with moderate casualties, he was convinced that the fight was not yet over. He radioed General Kinnard for another battalion, and Kinnard informed him that the 1st Battalion, 5th Cavalry, would begin arriving at brigade headquarters the following morning.

Having decided much earlier to try again for the third time to reach the isolated platoon and at the same time to secure the perimeter, Colonel Moore was ready by the next morning. Both he and his S-3 felt that the main enemy effort would be against the platoon. This time he intended to use three rifle companies instead of two. Since Captain Herren's men were most familiar with the ground, he planned to reinforce Company B with a platoon from Company A and to use Company B as the lead force again. Colonel Moore and his command group were to follow Herren's force. Companies A and C were to follow behind on the right and left, respectively, protecting the flanks and prepared to assist the main effort on order. The S-3, Captain Dillon, was to stay behind with the remainder of the battalion at the perimeter, ready to command it as a reserve force if necessary.

Ten minutes after first light, Colonel Moore directed all company commanders to meet him at the Company C command post where he would discuss final plans and view the attack route with them. He also told them to patrol forward and to the rear of their perimeter positions, looking for possible snipers or infiltrators that might have closed in during the night.

Upon receiving these instructions, Captain Edwards of Company C radioed his platoon leaders and told them to send at least squad-size forces from each platoon out to a distance of 200 meters. No sooner had they moved out when heavy enemy fire erupted, shattering the morning stillness. The two leftmost reconnaissance elements, those of the 1st and 2d Platoons, took the brunt of the fire, which came mainly from their front and left front. They returned it and began pulling back to their defensive positions. Well camouflaged, and in some cases crawling on hands and knees, the North Vietnamese pressed forward. In short order the two reconnaissance parties began to suffer casualties, some of them fatal, while men in each of the other platoons were hit as they attempted to move forward to assist.

When he heard the firing, Captain Edwards immediately attempted to raise both the 1st and 2d Platoons on the radio for a situation report, but there was no answer; each platoon leader had accompanied the reconnaissance force forward. He called Lieutenant Lane, the attached platoon leader from Company B, 2d Battalion, and his 3d Platoon leader, 2d Lt. William W. Franklin, and was relieved to discover that most of their forces had made it back to the perimeter unscathed; a few were still attempting to help the men engaged with the enemy.

From his command post, Edwards himself could see fifteen to twenty enemy soldiers 200 meters to his front, moving toward him. He called Colonel Moore, briefed him on the situation, and requested artillery fire. Then he and the four others in his command group began firing their M16's at the advancing enemy. Edward called battalion again and requested that the battalion reserve be committed in support.

Colonel Moore refused, for both he and Captain Dillon were still unconvinced that this was the enemy's main effort. They expected a strong attack against the isolated platoon and wanted to be prepared for it. Also, from what they could hear and see, Edwards' company appeared to be holding on, and they had given him priority of fires.

The situation of Company C grew worse, however, for despite a heavy pounding by artillery and tactical air and despite heavy losses the enemy managed to reach the foxhole line. Captain Edwards attempted to push Franklin's 3d Platoon to the left to relieve some of the pressure, but the firing was too heavy. Suddenly two North Vietnamese soldiers appeared forty meters to the front of the command post. Captain Edwards stood up and tossed a fragmentation grenade at them, then fell with a bullet in his back.

At 0715, seriously wounded but sill conscious, Edwards asked again for reinforcements. This time Moore assented; he directed company A to send a platoon. Company C's command group was now pinned down by an enemy automatic weapon that was operating behind an anthill just forward of the foxhole line. 2d Lt. John W. Arrington, Edwards' executive officer, had rushed forward from the battalion command post at Colonel Moore's order when Edwards was wounded. As Arrington lay prone, receiving instructions from Captain Edwards, he was shot in the chest. Lieutenant Franklin, realizing that both his commanding officer and the executive officer had been hit, left his 3d Platoon position and began to crawl toward the command group. He was hit and wounded seriously.

Almost at the same time that the message from Edwards asking for assistance reached the battalion command post, the enemy also attacked the Company D sector in force near the mortar emplacements. The battalion was now being attacked from two different directions.

As soon as Captain Nadal had received the word to commit a platoon, he had pulled his right flank platoon, the 2d, for the mission since he did not want to weaken that portion of the perimeter nearest Company C. He ordered his remaining platoon to extend to the right and cover the gap. The 2d Platoon started across the landing zone toward the Company C sector. As it neared the battalion command post, moving across open ground, it came under heavy fire that wounded two men and killed two. The platoon deployed on line, everyone prone, in a position just a few meters behind and to the left of the 3d Platoon of Company A's left flank and directly behind Company C's right flank. The force remained where it had been stopped. It was just as well, for in this position it served adequately as a backup reserve, a defense in depth against any enemy attempt to reach the battalion command post.

The heavy fighting continued. At 0745 enemy grazing fire was crisscrossing X-RAY, and at least twelve rounds of rocket or mortar fire exploded in the landing zone. One soldier was killed near the anthill, others were wounded. Anyone who moved toward the Company C sector drew fire immediately. Still the men fought on ferociously. One rifleman from Company D, who during the fighting had wound up somehow in the Company C sector, covered fifty meters of ground and from a kneeling position shot ten to fifteen North Vietnamese with his M16.

Colonel Moore alerted the reconnaissance platoon to be prepared for possible commitment in the Company D or Company C sector. Next, he radioed Colonel Brown at brigade headquarters, informed him of the situation, and requested another reinforcing company. Colonel Brown approved the request and prepared to send Company A, 2d Battalion, 7th Cavalry, into the landing zone as soon as the intensity of the firing diminished.

At 0755 Moore directed all units to throw colored smoke grenades so that ground artillery, aerial rocket artillery, and tactical air observers could more readily see the perimeter periphery, for he wanted to get his fire support in as close as possible. As soon as the smoke was thrown, supporting fires were brought in extremely close. Several artillery rounds landed within the perimeter, and one F-105 jet, flying a northwest-southeast pass, splashed two tanks of napalm into the anthill area, burning some of the men, exploding M16 ammunition stacked in the area, and threatening to detonate a pile of hand grenades. While troops worked to put out the fire, Captain Dillon rushed to the middle of the landing zone under fire and laid out a cerise panel so that strike aircraft could better identify the command post.

Despite the close fire support, heavy enemy fire continued to lash the landing zone without letup as the North Vietnamese troops followed their standard tactic of attempting to mingle with the American defenders in order to neutralize American fire support. A medic was killed at the battalion command post as he worked on one of the men wounded during the napalm strike. One of Colonel Moore's radio operators was struck in the head by a bullet; he was unconscious for a half hour, but his helmet had saved his life.

By 0800 a small enemy force had jabbed at Company A's left flank and been repulsed, but Company D's sector was seriously threatened. Mortar crewmen were firing rifles as well as feeding rounds into their tubes when a sudden fusillade destroyed one of the mortars. The antitank platoon was heavily engaged at the edge of the perimeter. With the battalion under attack from three sides now, Colonel Moore shifted the reconnaissance platoon toward Company D to relieve some of the pressure there. He radioed Colonel Brown for the additional company and alerted Company B, 2d Battalion, 7th Calvary, for action. He would have Company B on call until the battalion's Company A could put down in the landing zone.

Moore ordered Captain Diduryk to assemble his command group and his 1st Platoon at the anthill. Since he had already committed his 2d Platoon to Company C the previous night, Diduryk had left only the 3d Platoon to occupy his entire sector of the perimeter. He told the platoon leader, Lieutenant Vernon, to remain in position until relieved. Diduryk's 1st Platoon had lost one man wounded and one killed from the extremely heavy grazing fire and had not yet even been committed.

By 0900 the volume of combined American fires began to take its toll; enemy fire slacked. Ten minutes later, elements of Company A, 2d Battalion, 7th Cavalry, landed. Colonel Moore directed the company commander, Capt. Joel E. Sugdinis, to occupy Diduryk's original sector, which he did after coordinating with Diduryk.

By 1000 the enemy's desperate attempts to overwhelm the perimeter had failed and attacks ceased. Only light sniper fire continued. A half hour later Diduryk's company joined Lieutenant Lane's platoon in the Company C sector, Diduryk's force was augmented by the 3d Platoon of Company A, 2d Battalion, 7th Cavalry, which had rushed there immediately upon landing. Colonel Moore elected to allow it to remain.

Meanwhile, less than three kilometers southeast of the fighting, additional reinforcements were en route to X-RAY. Having departed Landing Zone VICTOR earlier that morning, Colonel Tully's 2d Battalion, 5th Cavalry, was moving on foot toward the sound of the firing.Because of the scarcity of aircraft on 13 November as well as the dispersion of his companies over a relatively large area, Colonel Tully had been able to send only two of his companies into VICTOR before dark on the 14th. At that, it had been a major effort to get one of them, Company C, picked up and flown to VICTOR, so dense was the jungle cover. In clearing a two-helicopter landing zone, the soldiers of Company C had used over thirty pounds of plastic explosives and had broken seventeen intrenching tools.

By the early morning hours of the 15th, Colonel Tully nevertheless had managed to assemble his three rifle companies in accordance with Colonel Brown's instructions. The task force moved out at 0800, Companies A and B abreast, left and right, respectively, with Company C trailing Company A. Colonel Tully used this formation, heavy on the left, because of the Chu Pong threat. He felt that if the enemy struck again it would be from that direction. He had no definite plan as to what he would do when he arrived at X-RAY other than reinforce. Details would come later. (*Map 4*)

Shortly after the fighting died down at X-RAY, enemy automatic weapons fire pinned down the two lead platoons of Company A, 2d Battalion, 5th Cavalry, as they approached from the east, 800 meters from the landing zone. The North Vietnamese were in trees and behind anthills. The company commander, Capt. Larry T. Bennett, promptly maneuvered the two lead platoons, which were in a line formation, forward. Then he swung his 3d Platoon to the right flank and pushed ahead; his weapons platoon, which had been reorganized into a provisional rifle platoon, followed behind as reserve. The men broke through the resistance rapidly, capturing two young and scared North Vietnamese armed with AK47 assault rifles.

Soon after midday lead elements reached X-RAY. Colonel Moore and Colonel Tully coordinated the next move, agreeing that because they were in the best position for attack and were relatively fresh and strong upon arriving at the landing zone, Companies A and C, 2d Battalion, 5th Cavalry, would participate in the effort to reach the cutoff platoon. Company B, 1st Battalion, 7th Cavalry, would take the lead since Herren knew the terrain between X-RAY and the isolated platoon. Moore would receive Company B, 2d Battalion, 5th Cavalry, into the perimeter and would remain behind, still in command, while Colonel Tully accompanied the attack force. The incoming battalion's mortar sections were to remain at X-RAY and support the attack.

Colonel Tully's co-ordination with Captain Herren was simple enough. Tully gave Herren the appropriate radio frequencies and call signs, told him where to tie in with his Company A, and

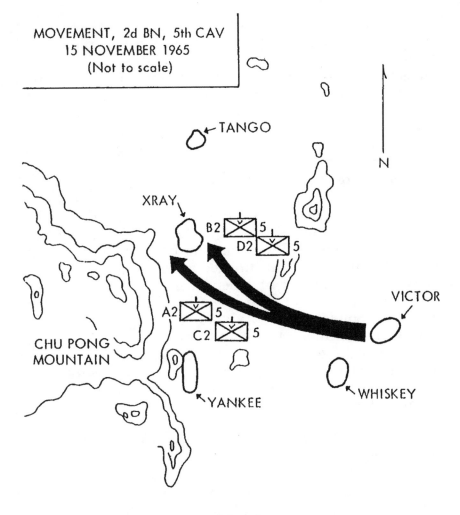

Map 4

instructed him to move out when ready. At 1315, preceded by artillery and aerial rocket strikes, the rescue force started out, Herren's company on the right, Company A, 2d Battalion, 5th Cavalry, on the left.

Fifteen minutes after the relief force had left the perimeter, Colonel Moore directed all units to police the battlefield to a depth of 300 meters. They soon discovered the heavy price the enemy had paid for his efforts: enemy bodies littered the area, some stacked behind anthills; body fragments, weapons, and equipment were scattered about the edge of the perimeter; trails littered with bandages told of many bodies dragged away.

The cost had also been heavy for the 1st Battalion, 7th Cavalry, which had lost the equivalent of an American rifle platoon. The bodies of these men lay amongst the enemy dead and attested to the intensity of the fight. One rifleman of Company C lay with his hands clutched around the throat of a dead North Vietnamese soldier. Company C's 1st Platoon leader died in a foxhole surrounded by five enemy dead.

The relief party, meanwhile, advanced cautiously, harasses by sporadic sniper fire to which the infantrymen replied by judiciously calling down artillery fire. As they neared Savage's platoon, lead troops of Captain Herren's company found the captured M60 machine gun, smashed by artillery fire. Around it lay the mutilated bodies of the crew, along with the bodies of successive North Vietnamese crews. They found the body of the M79 gunner, his .45-caliber automatic still clutched in his hand.

A few minutes later, the first men reached the isolated platoon; Captain Herren stared at the scene before him with fatigue-rimmed eyes. Some of the survivors broke into tears of relief. Through good fortune, the enemy's ignorance of their predicament, Specialist Lose's first-aid knowledge, individual bravery, and, most important of all, Sergeant Savage's expert use of artillery fire, the platoon had incurred not a single additional casualty after Savage had taken command the previous afternoon. Each man still had adequate ammunition.

Colonel Tully did not make a thorough search of the area, for now that he had reached the platoon his concern was to evacuate the survivors and casualties to X-RAY in good order. Accordingly, he surrounded the position with all three companies while Captain Herren provided details of men to assist with the casualties. The task was arduous, for each dead body and many of the wounded required at least a four-man carrying party using a makeshift poncho litter.

As he walked the newly established outer perimeter edge to check on the disposition of one of his platoons, Captain Bennett, the commander of Company A, 2d Battalion, 5th Cavalry, fell, severely wounded by a bullet in his chest fired at close range by a hidden North Vietnamese sniper. A thorough search for the enemy rifleman proved fruitless, and Colonel Tully directed his force to return to X-RAY. With Herren's company in single file and the casualties and Tully's units on either flank, the rescue force arrived at the landing zone without further incident.

Colonel Moore now redisposed his troops. Since he had two battalions to employ, he worked out an arrangement with Colonel

Tully that allowed him to control all troops in the perimeter. He took Company D, minus the mortar platoon, off of the line and replaced it with Colonel Tully's entire battalion. Tully's force also occupied portions of the flanking unit sectors. The wounded and dead were evacuated and everyone dug in for the night.

That evening at Brigade headquarters Colonel Brown again conferred with General Kinnard, who told Brown that the 1st Battalion, 7th Cavalry, would be pulled out on the 16th and sent to Camp Holloway just outside Pleiku for two days of rest and reorganization.

Although the North Vietnamese had suffered heavy casualties, not only from their encounter with the 1st Battalion, 7th Cavalry, but also as a result of a B-52 strike on Chu Pong itself that afternoon, they had not abandoned the field entirely. Sporadic sniper fire continued at various points along the perimeter during the earlier part of the night. The moon was out by 2320 in a cloudless sky. American artillery fired continuously into areas around the entire perimeter and on Chu Pong where secondary explosions occurred during the early evening. At 0100 five North Vietnamese soldiers probed the Company B, 1st Battalion, 7th Cavalry, sector; two were killed and the others escaped. Three hours later, a series of long and short whistle signals were heard from the enemy, and a flurry of activity occurred in front of Company B, 2d Battalion, 7th Cavalry. Trip flares were ignited and anti-intrusion alarms sprung, some as far out as 300 meters. At 0422 Diduryk's attached Company A leader, 2d Lt. William H. Sisson, radioed that he could see a group of soldiers advancing toward his positions. He was granted permission to fire and at the same time his platoon was fired on by the enemy. In less than ten minutes Diduryk was under attack along his entire sector by at least a company-size force. His company met the attack with a fusillade of fire from individual weapons, coupled with the firepower of four artillery batteries and all available mortars. Calling for point-detonating and variable time fuzes, white phosphorus, and high-explosive shells, Diduryk's forward observer, 1st Lt. William L. Lund, directed each battery to fire laterally and in depth in 100-meter adjustments. This imaginative effort, along with illumination provided by Air Force flareships, proved highly effective. Enemy soldiers nevertheless attempted to advance during the brief periods of darkness between flares and in some cases managed to get within five to ten meters of the foxhole line, where they were halted by well-aimed hand grenades and selective firing.

At 0530 the enemy tried again, this time shifting to the southwest, attacking the 3d Platoon and some left flank positions of the 2d Platoon. This effort, as well as another launched an hour later against the 1st Platoon's right flank, was also repulsed.

During the firefight, the Company B executive officer, radio operators, and troops from the reconnaissance platoon of the 1st Battalion, 7th Cavalry, made three separate ammunition resupply runs under fire to the anthill. At one point the supply of M79 ammunition dropped to such a dangerously low level that Diduryk restricted its use to visible targets, especially enemy crew-served weapons and troop concentrations. By dawn of the 16th the enemy attack had run its course. Diduryk's company had only six men slightly wounded, while piles of enemy dead in front of the positions testified to the enemy's tactical failure.

Still concerned with possible enemy intentions and capabilities and no doubt wary because of what had happened to Company C on the previous morning's sweep, Colonel Moore directed all companies to spray the trees, anthills, and bushes in front of their positions to kill any snipers or other infiltrators—a practice that the men called a "mad minute." Seconds after the firing began, an enemy platoon-size force came into view 150 meters in front of Company A, 2d Battalion, 7th Cavalry, and opened fire at the perimeter. An ideal artillery target, the attacking force was beaten off in twenty minutes by a heavy dose of high-explosive variable time fire. The "mad minute" effort proved fruitful in other respects. During the firing one North Vietnamese soldier dropped from a tree, dead, immediately in front of Captain Herren's command post. The riddled body of another fell and hung upside down, swinging from the branch to which the man had tied himself in front of Diduryk's leftmost platoon. An hour later somebody picked off an enemy soldier as he attempted to climb down a tree and escape.

Company C, 1st Battalion, 7th Cavalry, and the reconnaissance platoon meanwhile made a detailed search of the interior of X-RAY itself. There were three American casualties unaccounted for, and Colonel Moore was still concerned about infiltrators. The search turned up nothing.

An hour later Moore considered it opportune to push out from the perimeter on a co-ordinated search and to sweep out to 500 meters. The move commenced at 0955. After covering fifty to seventy-five meters, Company B, 2d Battalion, 7th Cavalry, platoons met a large volume of fire, including hand grenades thrown by enemy wounded still lying in the area. Diduryk quickly lost a weapons squad leader killed and nine other men wounded, including the 2d Platoon leader and platoon sergeant. Under artillery cover, he withdrew his force to the perimeter. Colonel Moore and Lieutenant Hastings, the forward air controller, joined him. A few minutes later tactical air, using a variety of ordnance that included rockets, cannon, napalm, cluster bomb units, white phosphorus, and high explosive, blasted the target area. The strike ended with the dropping of a 500-pound bomb that landed only twenty-five meters from the 1st Platoon's positions.

The sweep by Company B, 2d Battalion, 7th Cavalry, began again, this time using fire and maneuver behind a wall of covering artillery fire and meeting scattered resistance which was readily eliminated. Twenty-seven North Vietnamese were killed. The sweep uncovered the three missing Americans, all dead. The area was littered with enemy dead, and many enemy weapons were collected.

By 0930 the lead forces of the remainder of the 2d Battalion, 7th Cavalry, reached X-RAY, and an hour later Colonel Moore received instructions to prepare his battalion, along with Company B, 2d Battalion, 7th Cavalry, and the 3d Platoon, Company A, 2d Battalion, 7th Cavalry, for the move to Camp Holloway. The remainder of the 2d Battalion, 7th Cavalry, and 2d Battalion, 5th Cavalry, were to be left behind to secure the perimeter. Moore did not want to leave, however, without another thorough policing of the battle area, particularly where Company C had been attacked on the morning of the 15th. Captain Diduryk therefore conducted a lateral sweep without incident to a distance of 150 meters.

As the 1st Battalion, 7th Cavalry, began its move to Camp Holloway, the casualties with their equipment, as well as the surplus supplies, were also evacuated. Captured enemy equipment taken out included 57 Kalashnikov AK47 assault rifles, 54 Siminov SKS semi-automatic carbines with bayonets, 17 Degtyarev automatic rifles, 4 Maxim heavy machine guns, 5 model RPG2 antitank rocket launchers, 2 81-mm. mortar tubes, 2 pistols, and 6 medic's kits.

Great amounts of enemy weapons and equipment had been previously destroyed elsewhere in the battle area, and Moore arranged with the commanding officer of the 2d Battalion, 7th Cavalry, to destroy any enemy matériel left behind at X-RAY. Included were 75 to 100 crew-served and individual weapons, 12 antitank rounds, 300 to 400 hand grenades, an estimated 5,000 to 7,000 small arms rounds, and 100 to 150 intrenching tools.

American casualties, attached units included, were 79 killed, 121 wounded, and none missing. Enemy losses were much higher and included 634 known dead, 581 estimated dead, and 6 prisoners.

Reading 14

A Strategy of Tactics

by Andrew F. Krepinevich, Jr.

The Strategy of Attrition

With the deployment of American combat troops to South
Vietnam in large numbers, the Army applied the doctrine and
force structure it had developed for conventional contingencies in
Europe and Korea against insurgent forces practicing a form of
revolutionary warfare. The lack of progress in defeating the insurgents during the period 1965–68 can be attributed, in part, to an
Army strategy reflecting traditional methods of operation in a
conflict that was dramatically different from its wars over the
previous half-century. Deeply embedded in the service's psyche,
conventional operations held sway over the Army even as its
civilian superiors lost faith in their effectiveness for counterinsurgency operations.

In a sense, simple attrition of insurgent forces and support
systems was a natural strategy for MACV to pursue. It emphasized
the Army's strong suits in firepower and strategic mobility and
offered the prospect of minimizing U.S. casualties. The Army,
being denied the opportunity to win a decisive battle of annihilation by invading North Vietnam, found the attrition strategy best
fit the kind of war it had prepared to fight.

Basically, a strategy of attrition offered the Army the prospect
of winning the war quickly, or at least more quickly than with
traditional counterinsurgency operations, which promised to be
long and drawn out. Attrition is a product of the American way of
war: spend lavishly on munitions, materiel, and technology to save
lives. How many citizens or governmental and military leaders

Krepinevich. *The Army and Vietnam*, pp. 164-193. © 1986 by Johns Hopkins University
Press. Reprinted by permission.

would (or could) choose the other side of the coin? U.S. military leaders believed in the morale-raising and life-saving value of massive firepower whose success they had witnessed in World War II and Korea.

An attrition strategy was a natural outgrowth of the force structure and doctrine developed by the Army. Units deployed to Vietnam in the summer of 1965 were not the Special Warfare task forces that the Army purportedly had formed for counterinsurgency contingencies but heavy units trained and equipped for mid-intensity warfare. As one general put it, "The infantry divisions of the Army were very, very heavy and difficult to deploy and . . . had limited mobility if they weren't in an area where there were roads." The Army, said General Taylor, felt compelled to adopt a strategy of attrition because of the political ground rules that confined the Army's operations within the RVN. If the Army was denied a battle of annihilation through an invasion of North Vietnam, then attrition was the closest approximation available.

Some have stated that the strategy of attrition was not a strategy at all but actually reflected the absence of one. The sheer weight of American materiel and resources seemed sufficient to the military leadership to wear down the North Vietnamese and their VC allies; thus, strategy was not necessary. All that was needed was efficient application of firepower. It had worked against the Japanese and the Germans in World War II and against the Chinese in Korea. It would be tried again in Vietnam.

Attrition as Strategy

Initially, the Army had an open field in deciding how the war in South Vietnam would be fought. The president, concerned primarily with keeping the war contained, focused his attention on the bombing campaign against the North. So long as MACV restricted its operations to South Vietnam proper, interference would be minimal. McNamara, feeling that his expertise did not measure up to that of the Joint Chiefs, was similarly reluctant to get involved.

Westmoreland's proposed strategy envisioned a three-phase process culminating in the destruction of all insurgent forces and base areas by the end of 1967. Phase I would see the stabilization of the situation by the end of 1965 using the 44-battalion commitment; phase 2 involved the 24-battalion add-on projected for 1966 and called for "the resumption of the offensive"; phase 3 was viewed as a mop-up period in which remaining insurgent forces would be eliminated. Westmoreland recalled that he "came up with the concept of leveling off our buildup to achieve a well-balanced, hard-hitting force designed to fight in sustained combat and just grind away against the enemy on a sustained basis—something [the enemy] was not capable of doing, since he didn't have the logistics."

Westmoreland explicitly rejected the alternative of paying less attention to the enemy's big units and breaking down U.S. units into smaller groups to concentrate on pacification. His position was rooted in the military operations conducted by the VC in November 1964, when they mounted a limited offensive in Binh Dinh Province. In their attacks, two VC regiments defeated a number of smaller ARVN units engaged in pacification operations. Speaking of this defeat in detail, Westmoreland maintained that "it was a lesson long to be remembered." He cited it as an example, saying that if he broke any U.S. forces down to engage in pacification, they would suffer the same fate. Yet the incident was more a rationalization for the big-unit operations favored by MACV than an objective lesson against the perils of maintaining insufficient quick-reaction reserves, the real cause of the ARVN's November debacle. That MACV possessed these quick-reaction units in the form of its airmobile forces and thus could afford to concentrate heavily on pacification was a point that was lost on the MACV Staff and their superiors.

Westmoreland's approach was seconded by the chairman of the Joint Chiefs, Gen. Earle Wheeler. As Wheeler saw it, "the ground operations in the South would increase the communists' consumption and the bombing would reduce [their] supply." MACV simply developed a strategy to suit the Army's preferred *modus operandi*, force structure, and doctrine. According to Westmoreland, "Superior American firepower would be most advantageously employed against the big units, and using it in remote regions would mean fewer civilian casualties and less damage to built-up areas." Again General Wheeler agreed, contending that U.S. combat power and mobility "will enable us to find the enemy more often, fix him more firmly when we find him, and defeat him when we fight him . . . our objective will be to keep the combat tempo at such a rate that the Viet Cong will be unable to take the time to recuperate or regain their balance." It was Harkins's old Plan Explosion all over again. This approach, Wheeler concluded, "provides a strategy which, in my opinion, gives the best assurance of military victory in South Vietnam."

Westmoreland, like Taylor, argued that given the geographical limitations involved, there was no alternative to attrition. He claimed that population security could not be provided if the enemy's big units were at large. When it was pointed out that 90 percent of the country's population lived along the narrow coastal plain and in the Delta and that VC battalions in the remote, sparsely populated Highlands would be isolated from the people, Westmoreland demurred, contending that "it was not enough merely to contain the big units. They had to be pounded with artillery and bombs and eventually brought to battle on the ground if they were not forever to remain a threat."

This was essential if the Army's strategy of attrition was to succeed. Yet Westmoreland himself revealed the fatal flaw in this strategy. What if the enemy's big units refused to fight? What if they continued to wage an insurgency in the traditional sense, with the people, instead of the opponent's military forces being the objective? The general conceded that "unlike the guerrillas, if we avoided battle, we could never succeed. We could never destroy the big units by leaving them alone." Yet *the guerrillas avoided battle* and drew the Americans away from the population. As Westmoreland later admitted, "From the first the primary emphasis of the North Vietnamese focused on the Central Highlands and the central coastal provinces, with the basic end of drawing American units into remote areas and thereby facilitating control of the population in the lowlands." By focusing on population control, Westmoreland might have forced the guerrillas to come to him. As things turned out, the Army would neither secure the population nor get its decisive battles with the insurgents.

Furthermore, either out of organizational hubris or slavishness to the Concept (or both), COMUSMACV ignored the lack of success of previous search-and-destroy operations. Even in the recent quasi-phase 3 period of the insurgency they had proved largely ineffective, as found in a MACV staff report submitted in March 1965 which found that ARVN search-and-destroy operations frequently "failed to establish any contact with major VC units." Despite the ARVN's shortcomings, the report concluded, "the ability of the VC to break contact and 'disappear' from view does not depend upon luck or some special technique" but on the inherent advantages that accrued to skilled insurgent forces.

For Westmoreland, this process of fitting the war to the Concept led to his perception of the insurgency as somewhat akin to a previous war in which standard Army operations had prevailed. As he saw it: "Vietnam was a war of movement, an area war. It was somewhat analogous to the [American] Civil War. There were certain troops in static positions, around base areas and airfields, but other than that it was a war of movement. Instead of having a horse, as was the case in the Civil War, we had the helicopter. It was a war of fluid situations. It was impossible for us to seize and hold terrain after seizing it because we didn't have the troops. . . . You 'homed' on the enemy as in the Civil War and tried to bring the enemy to combat. Once you've done that, then you regroup, move, and continue to try and find the enemy and force him to combat."

The result of viewing the war through the perceptual lens of the Concept was the perpetuation of search-and-destroy operations from the advisory era into the period of intervention. While men like Sir Robert Thompson argued for concentrating on the local guerrilla forces, which provided sustenance to the VC's main-force units, MACV claimed that it was the other way around—the big units were supporting the local guerrillas. Not only did the Army's assertion turn insurgency doctrine on its head but it was untrue. A Pentagon study conducted in 1966, when VC forces were even larger than in the previous year, estimated that VC support requirements from outside South Vietnam totaled *only twelve tons per day!* Obviously, the bulk of insurgent support was provided from *within* the RVN. The Army leadership, however, refused to acknowledge this. There was no questioning of Westmoreland's approach by the Army brass back in Washington; both Wheeler and Harold Johnson were in agreement with the commander in the field. The JCS also supported the Army's approach. In JCS Memorandum 652-65, dated 27 August, the Chiefs called for increased pressure on the North and seizing the initiative as posited by COMUSMACV in the South. This was followed by JCS Memorandum 811-65, dated 10 November, in which the Chiefs visualized the use of U.S. ground forces as providing "heavy assault strength against VC forces and bases" in search-and-destroy operations. The ARVN was to be consigned to the unglamorous duty of population security, a role in which they had demonstrated considerable ineptitude in the past. Thus the Army left counterinsurgency to the RVNAF, while U.S. commanders went out in search of the big battles.

The Chiefs appeared to have cause for satisfaction over their endorsement of MACV's strategy when, shortly after the forwarding of their memo, Army forces defeated the Communists in a major battle in the Ia Drang Valley.

The Ia Drang Valley and Validation of the Concept

While the attrition strategy was formulated in the summer of 1965, U.S. ground forces continued arriving in South Vietnam: two Army brigades in July, followed by a corps headquarters. A Marine regiment landed in August, and by the end of September the entire 1st Air Cavalry Division had been deployed to the Central Highlands. The remainder of the 1st Infantry Division was deployed by 7 October, and, finally, an entire ROK division was in-country on 8 November. U.S. strength at that time stood at 184,314 men. The pride of the U.S. forces, however, was the Army's 1st Cavalry Division. It was deployed as the Army had wanted, to the Central Highlands, where insurgent strength was most formidable.

On 14 November elements of the 1st Cavalry encountered regimental-size formations of North Vietnamese in the Ia Drang Valley. The ensuing battle was both bloody and savage, with the Communists suffering over 1,200 killed, while U.S. losses exceeded 200. To General Westmoreland and the MACV Staff (particularly his G-3, Gen. William Depuy) the Ia Drang Valley campaign represented the successful application of the attrition strategy. Here were large enemy formations willing to go toe to toe with the Americans, and their big units were being smashed by the Army's firepower and high-tech mobility. Standard operations were working; therefore, no alternative strategies need be explored. No more feedback was required for MACV save the body counts that measured the attrition strategy's progress. For Westmoreland, "the ability of the Americans to meet and defeat the best troops the enemy could put on the field of battle was once more demonstrated beyond any possible doubt, as was the validity of the Army's airmobile concept." General Johnson felt that "the worst was behind us."

Indeed, from this point on, the Army began to discard any reluctance that it had concerning the deployment of heavy forces, such as armor. Whereas Westmoreland had originally questioned the utility of deploying armored formations in a low-intensity conflict environment, this soon gave way to a feeling of enthusiasm toward the use of tanks against insurgents. As early as the beginning of 1966 the Army Staff in Washington was pressing MACV to accept the new Sheridan tank for use in the RVN. By then the M48 Patton tank had already been deployed with the 1st Infantry Division to test the effectiveness of armor against insurgents. Westmoreland's initial resistance to armor was overcome primarily by its ability to provide the firepower that he felt was needed for his strategy of attrition. Armor had the additional advantage, from the Army's point of view, of allowing mechanized infantry to fight mounted, employing their armored personnel carriers (APCs) or tanks as assault vehicles in closing with and destroying the enemy. Of course, it was not very difficult for the VC to determine when an armored unit was trying to close with them; thus, the American tanks were easily avoided. Often, APCs and tanks were employed in "jungle busting," plodding noisily ahead of the infantry, clearing a path through the jungle and setting off mines and booby traps. One disillusioned colonel remarked, "I saw personally only one example of jungle-busting: four kilometers progress in 16 hours by a troop and attached rifle company. The costs in maintenance (then and later) certainly outweighed the knowledge that a serpentine jungle path a few feet wide might have been temporarily freed of VC."

The use of armored formations went against many principles of classical counterinsurgency doctrine. Armored units rarely operated at night, when the guerrillas were most active; they allowed for easy evasion of U.S. forces by the guerrillas; they encouraged the infantry to operate "buttoned up" inside their vehicles instead of out on patrol; they were "maintenance-intensive" pieces of equipment, requiring large numbers of support troops, who did not actively participate in operations; and finally, compared with the infantry, they were grossly indiscriminate in the application of firepower. In short, they were a blunt instrument for combating insurgency—save in its most advanced stages—but quite appropriate to the Army's notion of how wars should be fought.

A further addition to the Army's arsenal of firepower was the air support provided by tactical fighters and helicopters. The rationale for the lavish application of such firepower (and, in the case of the helicopter, additional mobility) was not for counterinsurgency operations but to support the Army's strategy of attrition. All this firepower and mobility, claimed General Wheeler, made traditional concerns relating to counterinsurgency inoperative: "These two air weapons—helicopters and fighter bombers—provide to South Vietnamese and to US forces an advantage in mobility and firepower—the fundamentals of combat—greatly exceeding that available to counterinsurgency forces in any other guerrilla war. Frankly, I do not know what is the required ratio of government to guerrilla forces in order for the government to prevail. I do know that it is not eight or ten-to-one in South

Vietnam because we can achieve the preponderance of force required with less than that ratio."

Despite the general's confidence in the Army's attrition strategy, students of insurgency warfare were uneasy over this radical departure from classical counterinsurgency strategy. Sir Robert Thompson, in evaluating the Army's approach to the insurgency, stated, "The major criticism I had tactically in Vietnam was that the one element in which you [the Army] were never mobile was on your feet. You got landed from helicopters and the battle took place, but when the battle was over and you had won the battle, you even went out by helicopter. No one ever walked out. Now the enemy, who was mobile on his feet, could actually decide whether he was going to have a battle with you in the first place, and he could break it off whenever he wanted to." Thompson felt that victory could be achieved only through a long process involving the denial of enemy access to the people through intensive ambushing and patrolling in and around the populated areas and by the use of long-range patrols to harass the guerrillas in more remote areas. Sooner or later the VC, denied access to their primary source of supply, the population, would have to come out in the open and contest the government's control of the people. At that point the insurgent main forces could be defeated. Barring a gross error in judgment on the part of the insurgents, however, annihilation of the VC's main units would not happen before these conditions occurred. By adopting a strategy of attrition, the Army placed the VC in the position of merely having to survive in order to prevail.

Strategic approaches such as Thompson's did not gain a receptive ear within the Army, even as it became apparent to many civilian observers that the Army Concept was inappropriate for insurgency conflict. General Williams, author of the McNamara directive that gave birth to Army airmobility, recalled a discussion with an American correspondent while in Vietnam:

> Sitting and talking to him, he made the charge. He said, "You are doing more in your helicopters to prevent our side from winning this war than anyone else." I said, "How's that?" He said, "Well, let me illustrate it this way. Everybody agrees that this is a war for the hearts and minds of the people. How do you expect our forces to win the hearts and minds of the people when all they do is take off from one Army base and fly overhead at 1500 feet while Charlie is sitting down there and he's got 'em by the testicles jerking, and every time he jerks their hearts and minds follow. Now, until the Americans are

willing to get down there with Charlie, he's got their hearts and minds."

Reflecting upon this, General Williams agreed that "if you really want to be cost-effective, you have to fight the war the way the VC fought it. You have to fight it down in the muck and in the mud and at night, and on a day-to-day basis." Yet, the general told the correspondent, "that's not the American way, and you are not going to get the American soldier to fight that way."

Although Williams felt that a true counterinsurgency strategy was not possible, junior officers in Vietnam, less indoctrinated in the ways of the Concept, were more inclined to support it. On a trip to Vietnam in December 1965, after supper one night General Johnson engaged in a gab session with lieutenants and captains of the 1st Infantry Division. The discussion quickly turned to strategy and tactics. The young platoon leaders and company commanders told the Chief of Staff that they could not engage the enemy if they were moving around in big outfits. What was needed, they said, was to operate in many small units, constantly moving and patrolling. Although Johnson "agreed with their philosophy," he rejected their ideas, since "we [the Army] were not going to be able to respond to the public outcry in the United States about [the] casualties" that might result.

There was, however, one segment of the American ground forces in South Vietnam that opted for a close approximation of traditional counterinsurgency strategy. These combat units did not belong to the Army but were U.S. Marine units deployed in I Corps. As Sir Robert Thompson pointed out, "Of all the United States forces the Marine Corps alone made a serious attempt to achieve permanent and lasting results in their tactical area of responsibility by seeking to protect the rural population."

Combined Action Platoons (CAPs): A Marine Challenge to the Concept

The Marine approach to counterinsurgency in Vietnam had its roots in the heritage of the service. A history of Marine participation in small wars had given them a background in the type of conflict environment they faced in South Vietnam. As early as 1940 the Marines had put out a manual on small wars which stated:

In regular warfare, the responsible officers simply strive to attain a method of producing the maximum physical effect with the force at their disposal. In small wars, the goal is to gain decisive results with the least application of force and the consequent minimum loss of life. The end aim is the social, economic, and political development of the people subsequent to the military defeat of the enemy insurgent. In small wars, tolerance, sympathy, and kindness should be the keynote of our relationship with the mass of the population.

Once the Marines arrived in South Vietnam, they put their doctrine into practice. Gen. Lewis Walt, commander of the Marine forces under COMUSMACV, issued orders for all Marine combat units to conduct vigorous patrols and ambushes from sundown to sunup, when insurgent activity was greatest. Walt issued stringent orders regarding the application of firepower, keeping it to an absolute minimum. Reflective of the manner in which the Marines viewed the conflict was a story told by General Walt of some Marines who came upon an old woman mining a road used by U.S. forces. They discovered that the woman harbored no particular hatred toward Americans. She planted the mines because the VC threatened to kill her granddaughter, the only surviving member of her family, if she refused. Since neither the Marines nor the Saigon regime protected her from this form of revolutionary "justice," observed Walt, he could hardly condemn her actions.

Although it would have been easy for the Marines to vent their frustration against the victims of insurgent coercion, Walt realized that that would only be playing into the enemy's hands. If the Marines were going to succeed, they would have to get close to the people and provide them with security from communist intimidation. Therefore, rather than hopping around in airmobile search-and-destroy operations or use helicopters for movement and logistical support, the Marines relied on the same roads used by the population. Walt observed that the Marines "could have depended almost entirely on sealift and airlift between major points on the north-south road through our area, but like many other things in Vietnam, the purely military consideration was never fully adequate. It was important that the roads be kept open for the people as well as for ourselves."

The Marine approach to counterinsurgency was further refined through the efforts of Capt. Jim Cooper, commander of a Marine company operating near the Vietnamese town of Chulai. After a period in which his unit conducted repeated sweeps, patrols, and attempted ambushes, Cooper became frustrated at his inability to separate the guerrillas from the population in the hamlet of Thanh My Trung. He decided to deploy his Marines inside the hamlet and announced that henceforth the people would be protected from the VC, for he had come to stay. Cooper increased the number of night patrols and ambushes and brought the villages' paramilitary Popular Forces (PF) unit under his wing, gradually making the local force assume a greater share of responsibility for village security. Before long the PFs, along with the Marines, were engaged in continuous night patrols in the area immediately surrounding the village, stalking the VC, setting ambushes, disrupting the insurgents' plans and activities. The result was the VC's abandonment of the village.

It did not take long for CAPs to catch on with the Marines. By 1966 there were fifty-seven such units in I Corps, and the number expanded to seventy-nine in 1967. As it worked out, each CAP consisted of fifteen marines and 34 PFs living in one particular village or hamlet. Their mission called for giving high priority to the traditional elements of counterinsurgency strategy: destruction of the insurgent infrastructure, protection of the people and the government infrastructure, organization of local intelligence nets, and training of the PFs. If CAPs suffered from problems, they centered on the language barrier between the Americans and their Vietnamese counterparts and the failure of the Marine Corps leadership to arrange the CAPs to provide for an interlocking network of units that would conform to the "oil spot" principle.

The CAPs produced results, but like all successful counterinsurgency programs, it took time. By the summer of 1967 a DOD report noted that the Hamlet Evaluation System (HES) security score gave CAP-protected villages a score of 2.95 out of a possible 5.0 maximum, as compared with an average of 1.6 for all I Corps villages. Furthermore, there was a direct correlation between the time a CAP stayed in a village and the degree of security achieved, with CAP-protected villages progressing twice as fast as those occupied by the PFs alone.

All this was achieved at a casualty rate *lower* than that found in units operating in search-and-destroy missions. Gen. Richard Clutterbuck, a British counterinsurgency expert, noted that "although [Marine] casualties are high, they are only 50% of the casualties of the normal infantry or marine battalions being flown around by helicopters on large scale operations." Thus, the actual data on casualties belied Army concerns that such operations produced intolerably high American losses.

The Marines also initiated a program called GOLDEN FLEECE, which was rooted in traditional counterinsurgency doctrine. It invoked saturating coastal farming areas with Marine guards and

patrols during the harvest season so that the farmers could harvest, store, and eventually sell their crop free from VC taxation.
Although the VC fought the system, they were no longer the fish
swimming in a sea of cooperative people. They instructed the
farmers to let the food rot in the fields or risk reprisals. When the
farmers, emboldened by the long-term presence of the Marines
and their assurance that they had come to stay, went ahead with
the harvest, the VC tried to make good their threat, first attacking
in small patrols but eventually moving up to battalion-size assaults. Each time, the Marines, assisted by local paramilitary units,
beat them back. "Each catty of rice," wrote General Walt, "not
going into Viet Cong bins meant that another catty had to be grown
in North Vietnam and brought over the hundreds of miles of
mountain trail by human bearers."

Even though only a small percentage of the total Marine force
in South Vietnam was utilized in these operations (a mere ten
companies were involved in the CAP program during 1967), the
results were impressive. Sir Robert Thompson noted that "the use
of CAPs is quite the best idea I have seen in Vietnam, and it worked
superbly." At the same time, DOD survey teams observing the
operations of CAPs went away concluding that then current Army
training simulations (the "Vietnam villages") were "not by any
means representative of real situations."

The Army's reaction to the CAP program was ill-disguised
disappointment, if not outright disapproval, from the top down.
Gen. Harry Kinnard was "absolutely disgusted" with the Marines.
"I did everything I could to drag them out," he said, "and get them
to fight. . . . They just wouldn't play. They just *would not play*. They
don't know how to fight on land, particularly against guerrillas."
Major General Depuy observed sarcastically that "the Marines
came in and just sat down and didn't do anything. They were
involved in counterinsurgency of the deliberate, mild sort."

Brigadier General Hunt of Great Britain, an expert on insurgency warfare, recounted his experience with the Army on one of
his trips to I Corps: "The Marines had never been able to sell the
idea of CAPs to the rest of the Americans [i.e., the Army]. It was
only in the north where the CAPs were operating, and when I went
down to MACV and referred to this [limitation of the program],
they said that I had been fixed by the Marines—brainwashed! They
did not agree and in any case said it would be too expensive. [They
did not realize that] when you get an RF or PF man out in the
village he is like the chicken's neck; he is in an extremely danger-

ous position. You have to make it clear to him that he is going to be supported if there is need."

General Westmoreland was particularly upset over the Marines' use of CAPs, challenging as they did the concept of operations that he had drawn up. He stated in his memoirs that "they were assiduously [sic] combing the countryside within the beachheads, trying to establish firm control in hamlets and villages, and planning to expand the beachhead gradually up and down the coast. . . . Yet the practice left the enemy free to come and go as he pleased throughout the bulk of the region and, when and where he chose, to attack the periphery of the beachheads." Westmoreland did not realize that the Marines were operating in the densely populated areas, leaving the VC little to recruit or exploit in the remote, largely uninhabited region they controlled. Furthermore, through long-range STINGRAY patrols, the Marines gained intelligence on the movements of large insurgent forces close to the populated areas. The efficacy of the Marine approach is borne out by the results: throughout the history of the program only *one* CAP was ever overrun.

Westmoreland later conceded that the Marines achieved some "noteworthy results," but he continued to defend the Army approach, claiming that he "simply had not enough numbers to put a squad of Americans in every village and hamlet." This was not supported by the facts. First, it was not necessary to place army squads in *every* village simultaneously; indeed, the "oil spot" principle called for gradual expansion outward from selected areas. Westmoreland's argument is more reflective of the Army's impatience for quick results in a conflict environment that would not produce them.

Second, even if encadrement of every village and hamlet had been the requirement, a 1967 DOD report found that it could be met by utilizing 167,000 U.S. troops, far fewer than the 550,000 eventually assigned to South Vietnam. Some argue that of the 550,000 only about 80,000 represented the "foxhole strength" of American forces, that is, those men actually involved in the fighting. The counterargument, of course, is that the force mix was grossly overweighted in favor of support personnel necessary to maintain the firepower-intensive U.S. forces deployed in South Vietnam. Tanks, APCs and helicopters require considerable numbers of maintenance support personnel, along with a large logistical tail of soldiers to keep the flow of spare parts and munitions moving. Light infantry units, on the other hand, require far fewer support troops, enabling a greater percentage of soldiers to participate in the actual fighting. Such light infantry units, however, were few and far between in the heavy, firepower-oriented force structure of the Army. To strip down the ROAD divisions to fight a light infantry war would have required the Army to go against everything it had worked for during the lean years of the Eisenhower administration.

Given a 550,000-man ceiling, a force mix providing for CAP operations could have been effected, with several airmobile or ROAD divisions held in reserve to counter any large-scale VC/NVA incursions into areas undergoing pacification. Casualties would have been minimized, and population security enhanced.

While Westmoreland was just as disgusted as Depuy with the Marines' approach to the war, he realized that the carrot would work better than the stick in moving them toward MACV's strategic approach to the conflict. The marines, after all, were not a part of the Army; furthermore, if they wanted, they could drag their feet in complying with MACV directives or seek support from the Navy in resisting the Army's intrusion into their operations. Therefore, Westmoreland, with Depuy's help, wrote General Walt a note in an effort to persuade the Marines to conform to the Army strategy. In it, Westmoreland told Walt that he was "impressed with the professional competence of all echelons and with the grasp which your officers and men display regarding the problems of long term security and pacification." He was concerned, however, "about the situation throughout the part of I Corps which lies beyond the three Marine enclaves. Outside your enclaves the VC are largely able to move at will and they are rapidly consolidating very large areas. . . . The longer the VC have a free hand in the rest of the Corps, the more area they will consolidate, and the more difficult it will be for us in the long run. . . . Therefore, I believe very strongly that we must . . . seek out and destroy large VC forces." The discussion focused on consolidation of terrain, not the population. In any event, the purpose of search-and-destroy operations was not to occupy territory but to engage in battle.

MACV did initiate an Army version of CAP involving mobile training teams (MTTs). This approach involved four-man Army teams and an ARVN officer working with village paramilitary forces for about a month and then moving on. The program reflected the Army's quick-fix approach to counterinsurgency and its desire for quick results. Four men providing hamlet security for one month was hardly the same as thirteen men involved over a prolonged period of time. The Army would not accept the fact that getting people to believe you were going to protect them required an effective government security force that was always going to be there, as well as a lot of time and resources. Counterinsurgency on the cheap would not work.

It must be said, however, that the Army succeeded in meeting the challenge to its preferred strategy that CAPs represented. In the end, the Marine CAP program remained limited, despite its demonstrated effectiveness. The bulk of Marine forces in I Corps remained involved in border surveillance and interdiction operations, one example being the Marine base at Khe Sanh.

How Much Is Enough? (Revisited)

For its chosen strategy to work, the Army gambled that it could attrite insurgent forces faster than the enemy could replace them, either by infiltration from the North or by recruitment within the South. In opting for this approach, the Army wagered that a strategy playing to its strong suits instead of the insurgents' weak points would be enough to provide victory.

The key to success in this strategic approach was forcing the VC and the NVA to fight. Having eschewed the traditional approach of having the insurgents fight to maintain access to the population, the Army relied on its technological and logistical strong suits—it would use sensors, infrared photography, helicopters, and a host of technological wonders to find the enemy, and firepower and mobility to destroy him. The Communists, however, had been and would continue to be successful in dictating the tempo of operations and, therefore, their level of casualties as well. The Army, faced with the potential bankruptcy of its strategy, responded, not by abandoning it, but by insisting, as it had during the advisory years, that the only necessary change was an increase in the scope and intensity of operations.

It became evident quite early on that the insurgents would stick to their strategy of protracted conflict: drawing U.S. units away from the populated areas to allow continued access to their logistical base (the population); generating U.S. casualties to attrite the will of the United States to continue the war; keeping U.S. forces in remote, static positions when possible (Khe Sanh, for example) to inhibit their operational effectiveness; and deploying sufficient NVA forces to entice the Army away from populated areas.

Evidence of the insurgents' strategic continuity was present early in the Army's intervention phase in Vietnam. It will be recalled that COMUSMACV authorized the 173d Airborne Brigade to participate in search-and-destroy operations in the Iron Triangle, a Communist redoubt northwest of Saigon, in late June, before the final decision was made on the 44-battalion request. During the three-day operation the brigade failed to make any significant contact with the enemy, although the unit was sweeping through an area long recognized as a VC stronghold.

A little over three months later the 173d was again involved in search-and-destroy operations in the Iron Triangle, this time from 8 to 14 October. The after-action report submitted by the brigade indicated that the VC were avoiding U.S. forces and were retreating into phase 2 guerrilla warfare rather than slugging it out with the Americans in Phase 3-type operations. Nevertheless, Brigadier General Williamson, the 173d's commander, wrote that his unit had "torn apart" the Iron Triangle and destroyed "all enemy troops." The unit claimed forty-four enemy killed. Yet within a year the Army was again trying to clear the area of VC. Ignoring the implications of operations such as these, MACV chose to rest its estimate of enemy intentions on the victory of the 1st Cavalry in the Ia Drang Valley.

By late November MACV realized that the force ratios that the Army had creatively arrived at earlier did not reflect the true situation. On 23 November, Westmoreland notified the JCS that "the VC/PAVN buildup rate is predicted to be double that of US Phase II forces [now the 28-battalion add-on]." The increase in enemy forces would leave the allied forces with a ratio of only 2.1:1 in "battalion equivalents" by the end of 1966. Rather than reevaluate the strategy of attrition, MACV forwarded a request for an additional 41,500 troops, raising Army phase 2 deployments to 154,000 men, for a total of nearly 375,000 by mid-1967. Meanwhile, the myth that the insurgents' main-force units were the principal source of support for local guerrilla forces persisted.

Despite the victory in the battle of the Ia Drang Valley, Westmoreland quickly realized that his attrition strategy would take time and the infusion of large numbers of U.S. troops to reach the *crossover point*, the point where the enemy's losses in battle would exceed his capability to replace them. At a high-level conference in Honolulu from 7 to 9 February, William Bundy and John McNaughton drafted a program for increased U.S. forces for South Vietnam. While President Johnson and Prime Minister Ky were involved in their meetings the program was ironed out at Camp Smith by Westmoreland, Wheeler, Admiral Sharp, the CINCPAC, Bundy, and McNaughton.

Reacting to the president's exhortation to "nail the coonskin to the wall" in South Vietnam, the plan called for U.S. troop levels to be increased from 184,300 at the close of 1965 to some 429,000 by the end of 1966. The number of U.S. maneuver battalions would jump from 35 to 79. The intent was to more than double the rate of U.S. offensive operations, and primary emphasis was placed on achieving that objective, as opposed to pacification. The goal was to reach the crossover point by year's end.

In March McNamara authorized JCS planning for deployment of the additional forces, with their deployment stretched out through mid-1967 to avoid a callup of the reserves. On 11 April McNamara approved, with minor exceptions, the deployment plan proposed; there would be seventy U.S. maneuver battalions in the RVN by year's end, and the remaining nine would be deployed by June 1967. Thus, between July 1965 and the Honolulu Conference, Westmoreland upped the number of maneuver battalions required to do this job from fifty-eight (the number called for in the 24-battalion add-on) to seventy-nine.

In fact, the Army was pushing for an increase not only in the intensity of the war but in its scope as well. The JCS felt that the president "was not doing enough" and advocated carrying the war into the insurgent sanctuaries in Laos and Cambodia, if not North Vietnam itself. General Johnson supported an operation into Laos to cut the Ho Chi Minh Trail, as did General Westmoreland, and in early 1966 MACV developed plans for such a maneuver. The desire to expand the war was largely the result of impatience and frustration on the part of many senior officers at their inability to force the enemy to stand and fight. Lieutenant General Kinnard, commander of the 1st Cavalry Division, expressed the views of most of his contemporaries when he said, "We were fighting their kind of war, and I wanted to make them fight our kind of war. I wanted to turn it into a conventional war—boundaries—and here we go, and what are you going to do to stop us?"

The initial plan, EL PASO 1, saw the 1st Cavalry Division establishing an airhead on the Bolovens Plateau in the Laotian panhandle, supported by one incursion by the 3d Marine Division pushing west from Quang Tri Province and another by the 4th Infantry Division driving up from the Central Highlands. Here again the Army was falling back on old, familiar plans and ideas. General Johnson had commissioned a study in March 1965 to determine the feasibility of such an operation. As it turned out, it was not feasible. Westmoreland's airhead was basically something that had been advanced during the Laotian crisis in 1961–62.

MACV, however, was continually frustrated in its efforts to win presidential approval for the operation.

Rejection of the plan notwithstanding, the attrition strategy persisted; during the last five months of 1966, MACV invested 95 percent of its combat battalion resources in search-and-destroy operations. Westmoreland recalled one typical operation: "I called on the 1st Brigade, 101st Airborne Division, under Brigadier General Willard Pearson to join the search and later the entire 1st Cavalry Division, commanded by Major General Jack Norton. Patrolling relentlessly through the trackless jungle, catapulting from one hastily built hilltop firepower support base to another, those units through the summer killed close to 2,000 of the enemy; when the cavalry division returned for another sweep in October, a thousand more of the enemy would never make it into the populated region." Unfortunately, the enemy *already was* in the populated regions. While the Army chased its elusive quarry through the country's interior the insurgents continued operating along the densely populated Coastal Plains. Over half of all significant contact with Communist forces in the first half of 1966 took place, not in the interior regions, but along the Coastal Plains. The inference was clear: the insurgents would fight to maintain access to the population while leading the Army on a wild-goose chase inland, drawing MACV's maneuver battalions away from the people they were purportedly protecting.

One year after the commitment of U.S. ground forces the Army had made little headway against the enemy. VC forces, numbering 160,000 the year before, now stood at some 220,000, not including some 38,000 NVA troops. It was estimated that the enemy could recruit internally or infiltrate into the RVN the equivalent of fifteen battalions a month. During this period, in March 1966, a study commissioned by General Johnson in July 1965 was completed by the Army Staff. Entitled "Program for the Pacification and Long-Term Development of South Vietnam" (PROVN), it was the product of an eight-month effort of some of the brightest minds on the Army Staff, charged by the Chief of Staff with "developing new sources of action to be taken in South Vietnam by the United States and its allies which will lead in due time to successful accomplishment of US aims and objectives."

The study was not received favorably by the Army leadership, and its conclusions and recommendations make the reasons clear. The authors of the report contended that there was "no unified effective pattern" to the Army's war effort, that the situation in Vietnam had "seriously deteriorated," and that 1966 might be the final opportunity to modify MACV's strategy before victory became impossible. The PROVN group recommended that pacification be given top priority in the war effort. Nevertheless, it stated that "the bulk of US and FWMA [Free World Military Assistance] Forces and designated RVNAF units should be directed against enemy base areas and against their lines of communication in SVN, Laos and Cambodia, as required; the remainder of Allied force assets must assure adequate momentum to activity in priority Rural Construction areas." While PROVN was less than a ringing endorsement for a traditional counterinsurgency strategy, it at least acknowledged the need for direct Army participation in population security programs. PROVN also called for greater efforts to achieve some sort of unity of command and for development of a single, integrated plan for the counterinsurgency forces.

The study was briefed to COMUSMACV on 17 May in Honolulu. Westmoreland contended that most of PROVN's recommendations had been acted on and that the United States could not foist unity of command on the Vietnamese or force adherence to U.S. plan without risking the Saigon regime's being tagged as U.S. puppets. Thus, even though the study allowed for the continuance of current Army operations while the ARVN bore the brunt of pacification, the very notion that the Army had a major obligation to Revolutionary Development, as it was called, made the Army leadership uneasy. Nor was the Army brass thrilled with the idea that the U.S. ambassador (particularly one such as Lodge, with his apparent preference for traditional counterinsurgency doctrine) would set priorities and objectives for the Army.

The upshot of all this furor over PROVN and its recommendations was its suppression by the Army. The document was downgraded from a study to a "conceptual document," in no way binding on MACV or the Army; furthermore, for a period after its completion Army officers were forbidden to discuss the study, or even acknowledge its existence, outside DOD. Despite Westmoreland's claims that MACV had responded to the PROVN study, the second half of 1966 saw MACV utilize its maneuver battalions almost exclusively in search-and-destroy operations.

Evidence of PROVN's negligible impact is found in another Army study completed in May 1967, entitled "Review and Analysis of the Evaluation of the US Army Mechanized and Armor Combat Operations in Vietnam" (MACOV). Prepared by CDC, the evaluation found that "approximately 25% of all operations are security or minor pacification missions, and approximately 75% are search and destroy." Furthermore, "of 170 battalion task force size US initiated offensive operations by armor-mech units examined in the study, only one (0.59%) took place at night. . . . Of 509 company team size similar operations, fourteen took place at night (2.75%)."

While the Army might have been successful in side-stepping the implications of the PROVN study, it had less luck with the civilians at OSD, where doubt and concern over the Army strategy for winning the war began manifesting themselves. On 18 June CINCPAC forwarded MACV's force request for calendar year 1967. Citing the proposed increases as "rounding out forces," the request called for U.S. strength in the RVN to increase to 90 maneuver battalions and 542,588 personnel. It was received by McNamara on 5 August with the Chiefs' stamp of approval. The secretary of defense balked at approving yet another increase, requesting "a detailed line by line analysis for these requirements to determine that each is truly essential to the carrying out of our war plan." McNamara included in his memo to the JCS issue papers prepared by the Whiz Kids at Systems Analysis (OSA) questioning the need for additional troops.

On 10 August Westmoreland bluntly notified his superiors, "I cannot justify a reduction in requirements submitted." Given the strategy he had adopted, COMUSMACV was correct. The JCS labored over the objections presented by Alain Enthoven and the people at Systems Analysis and forwarded their defense on 24 September. Enthoven remained unpersuaded. The JCS had cut over half of the 70,000 slots to which OSA had objected, but this still left projected U.S. force levels at some 20,000 over the limits in OSA's Program 4. Before presenting this contentious issue to the president for a decision, McNamara decided on a trip to South Vietnam for a first hand evaluation of the situation, in the hope of avoiding an open clash between the generals and OSD's civilian brain trust.

McNamara was accompanied on his trip by General Wheeler, Robert Komer (the president's special assistant for pacification), and Assistant Secretary of Defense John McNaughton, among others. The mission arrived in Saigon on 10 October and departed on the 13th. The visit had a sobering effect on McNamara, confirming many of his doubts about the progress of the war. In a pessimistic memorandum to the president the day after his return, McNamara surveyed the situation in South Vietnam. He saw "no reasonable way to bring the war to an end soon [as the enemy] has adopted a strategy of keeping us busy and waiting us out (a strategy of attriting our national will)." Pacification was "a bad disappointment" that had, "if anything, gone backward"; the ROLLING THUNDER bombing campaign had produced insignificant benefits, if any. As for the strategy of attrition, McNamara stated that

> *the one thing demonstrably going for us in Vietnam over the past year has been the large number of enemy killed-in-action resulting from the big military operations.* Allowing for possible exaggeration in reports, the enemy must be taking losses—death in and after battle—at the rate of more than 60,000 a year. The infiltration routes would seem to be one-way trails to death for the North Vietnamese. *Yet there is no sign of an impending break in enemy morale and it appears that he can more than replace his losses by infiltration from North Vietnam and recruitment in South Vietnam.*

Since the war effort appeared to be going nowhere, McNamara offered some recommendations for improvement. He suggested leveling off U.S. forces at 470,000 and a vigorous pacification effort. McNamara strongly challenged Westmoreland's rationale for search-and-destroy operations in lieu of an emphasis on pacification, contending that "the large-unit operations war, which we know best how to fight and where we have had our successes, is largely irrelevant to pacification as long as we do not lose it."

Finally, McNamara proposed constructing a barrier across the 17th-parallel DMZ dividing the two Vietnams. Some scientists, along with Harvard Law School professor Roger Fisher and John McNaughton, had sold McNamara on the idea of an electronic barrier that could be manned by some 10,000–15,000 troops. The barrier proposal was in some respect a scaled-down version of the Army proposal for eliminating infiltration by moving a four-division blocking force into northern South Vietnam and Laos. The military's reaction to McNamara's idea can best be summed up by the words of former marine officer William Carson, who wrote that "the only way to describe the barrier is to recognize it as just one more 'happening' in the Defense Department's Alice in Wonderland approach to insurgency."

The barrier proved an expensive error in terms of both money and manpower expended. It tied down U.S. troops along the DMZ, subjecting them to harassing fire from VC and NVA forces. The Marines estimated that eighteen engineer battalions would be required on a sustained basis just to build and maintain the necessary access roads if the barrier were to run the entire length of the DMZ. The most interesting aspect about the McNamara Line, however, was that while the military dismissed it as an idiotic civilian fantasy, MACV could still seriously plan for the establishment of an anti-infiltration barrier across the 17th parallel and the Laotian panhandle!

While McNamara staked out his position for stabilized force levels, a strong commitment to pacification, and a barrier across the DMZ, the Joint Chiefs responded rapidly and angrily to his proposals. In a JCS memorandum sent to the president on the same day as McNamara's report, the Chiefs objected to the 470,000-man force level advanced by McNamara, as well as the planned diversion of ARVN forces away from offensive operations into pacification activities, citing the increased burden on U.S. forces that would result.

Despite their disagreement with the McNamara proposals, the Chiefs were prepared to yield to pressure from above—but only a little. They maintained that the military situation had "improved substantially over the past year." Thus, they would agree to the use of a "substantial fraction" of the ARVN for pacification purposes, and they recommended that COMUSMACV be placed at the head of the pacification program "to achieve early optimum effectiveness." Several weeks later, after the Manila Conference, the Chiefs recommended that they be allowed to begin "mining ports, [a] naval quarantine, spoiling attacks and raids against the enemy in Cambodia and Laos, and certain special operations [to] support intensified and accelerated revolutionary development and nation building programs." The Chiefs, it seems, just could not get the hang of counterinsurgency warfare.

By early November the military's willingness to accommodate McNamara had filtered down to COMUSMACV's Combined Campaign Plan (CCP) for 1967, issued on 7 November. The plan called for the RVNAF to support pacification with the majority of its forces; however, the ARVN formed only one component of the RVNAF, with the PFs and RFs making up the remainder. The primary mission of the U.S. and FWMA force contingencies would remain the destruction of VC/NVA main forces and base areas through a series of offensives. The emphasis on attrition continued. As General Taylor explained, the CCP "had language in it that seemed to indicate Westy's responsibility for clearing the enemy out of every square foot of soil in all [of] South Vietnam and probably accounted for his willingness to engage the enemy in places where terrain and distance to base areas was very favorable to him [the VC]; that is, they were right up against the border. The defense of Khe Sanh seemed to confirm the impression that he felt he had to control those worthless valleys way over there toward Laos."

On 11 November, Program 4, as it was called, was published by OSD. The program provided the military with authorization to increase U.S. force levels in Vietnam to the 470,000 troops Enthoven had recommended to McNamara the previous month. This represented a shortfall of 7 Army maneuver battalions and roughly 53,000 troops requested in the JCS package. Six days later McNamara laid out the reasons for his decision in a Draft Presidential Memorandum (DPM). The significance of the memorandum lies in the concerns voiced by McNamara over the strategy the military was pursuing in Southeast Asia. McNamara felt that the United States had two choices: (1) to continue pouring combat forces into South Vietnam in an effort to reach the elusive crossover point through search-and-destroy operations; or (2) to level off U.S. forces at a point where they could keep the enemy's big units "neutralized," that is, away from the populated regions. McNamara advocated the latter course, arguing that "if MACV estimates of enemy strength are correct, we have not been able to attrite the enemy forces fast enough to break their morale and more US forces are unlikely to do so in the foreseeable future." The secretary of defense supported his decision by citing the inability Of MACV to reach the crossover point. The Army, McNamara said, had reached the point of diminishing marginal returns, where the commitment of additional troops had only a negligible impact on the enemy casualty rate.

Thus did the civilians in OSD conclude that the Army's attrition strategy was not working and that its prospects for producing an eventual victory were exceedingly dim. The nonprofessionals, the Whiz Kid analysts whom the Army brass detested so much, were actually out in front on the "learning curve" of what was really transpiring in Vietnam. The Army leadership, burdened by its rigid conceptual approach to the conflict, echoed the familiar refrain: "more of the same." The Chiefs filed a JCS memorandum disputing the force levels set and the secretary of defense's priorities the day following his DPM, but to no avail. In the coming months the Army Concept would come under increasing criticism from civilians in the Defense community, with the Army, as always, promising results if given more resources to grind the enemy down.

As the war moved into 1967, Westmoreland's need for additional forces remained acute. The general believed more than ever that with enemy strength continually on the increase, U.S. forces had to fight in the remote border regions to prevent the Communists from interfering with the pacification program. On 18 March, Westmoreland forwarded a request to the JCS for an increase in U.S. forces of at least 2 1/3 divisions, with 4 2/3 divisions considered an optimal addition to MACV's order of battle. The request saw U.S. troop strength in South Vietnam reaching at least 559,000 (108 maneuver battalions) by mid-1968, with 676,000 men (130 maneuver battalions) included in the "optimum" package. Westmoreland stated that unless the 2 1/3 divisions were forthcoming, he would have to divert ARVN forces engaged in pacification operations to help take up the shortfall in offensive operations.

MACV's list of troop requirements was formally reported to McNamara on 20 April. Five days later Westmoreland arrived in Washington to discuss the situation in Vietnam with President Johnson. In their meeting the general pressed for the introduction Of ARVN forces into the Laotian panhandle and the eventual development of southern Laos into a major battlefield to take pressure off the South. When Westmoreland brought up the 2 1/3-division request, Johnson replied, "When we add divisions can't the enemy add divisions?" Westmoreland contended that the attrition strategy was working and observed, "It appears last month we reached the crossover point in areas excluding the two northern provinces." Westmoreland maintained that MACV had forced that enemy's main-force units into remote areas just as planned; however, extra forces were needed to protect the northern provinces against a possible incursion by North Vietnamese units.

President Johnson, as evidenced by his discussion with Westmoreland, doubted that the Army could reach the crossover point. These doubts were fed by a number of key civilians and civilian organizations—OSD, the CIA, and Robert Komer (the designated head of Civil Operations and Revolutionary Development Support [CORDS]) among them—who were increasingly skeptical of MACV's ability to achieve victory using the current strategy.

Komer had penned a memo to the president prior to departing for South Vietnam on 24 April. Never known to mince words (a characteristic that earned him the sobriquet "Blowtorch"), Komer called for a redirection of U.S. strategic emphasis toward pacification, upgrading the paramilitary forces, jacking up the ARVN and letting them take on the bulk of the fighting, and placing all forces in a unified command under the Americans. Thus Komer, who had been the president's special assistant for pacification since March

1966, implicitly rejected the call for more U.S. forces and the strategy that mandated their request.

Meanwhile, the CIA had published a study that concluded that no decisive advantage could be gained from U.S. incursions of the sort Westmoreland was advocating. The CIA maintained that the vast majority Of VC/NVA supplies continued to be generated from *within* South Vietnam. MACV was incensed over the CIA's contention, particularly with respect to Cambodia, where, the Army claimed, over a thousand metric tons of military supplies from the PRC had arrived in the port of Sihanoukville in 1966. Yet, even if *all* the supplies had been destined for South Vietnam, it would have amounted to *less than three tons per day* for a force of over 285,000 guerrillas, hardly a make-or-break operation.

Perhaps the most damning evidence against the Army Concept came from the Systems Analysis people at OSD. In their efforts to measure progress in a war with no fronts, Alain Enthoven and his Whiz Kids applied their form of analysis to the struggle in Southeast Asia. Having no independent means of acquiring information on the war, they based their studies on data supplied by MACV itself. Using that statistical base, in January 1967 OSA began issuing a series of monthly Southeast Asia Analysis Reports that, to the annoyance of the Army, elaborated on the failure of the attrition strategy. In two memos to the secretary of defense on 1 and 4 May, OSA challenged MACV's force request and Westmoreland's contention that progress was being made in South Vietnam. Using the Army's Armored Combat Operations in Vietnam (ARCOV) study and MACV after-action reports, OSA showed that if the Army's strategy remained the same, force increases would have very little impact on the war.

The ARCOV report showed that 88 percent of all engagements were initiated by the enemy. Thus the VC had the initiative. They could either refuse or accept battle on their terms and, in doing so, could control their casualty level. Hence, the attrition strategy was unfeasible, since MACV could not force the enemy to do battle. The OSA report went on to say that while MACV was still prosecuting the war as though phase 3 insurgency operations were being conducted, the numbers of VC/NVA attacks of battalion size had been decreasing since the arrival of U.S. ground forces in the latter part of 1965. Indeed, the monthly average of such attacks had decreased from 9.7 per month in the final quarter of 1965 to 1.3 per month in the final quarter of 1966. Meanwhile, the number of small-scale enemy attacks had increased by 150 percent over the same period. The implication was obvious to OSA: the Communists had reverted to phase 2 operations.

While MACV had been out in the border regions chasing the enemy in fruitless attempts to drive up insurgent casualties, it had not provided a shield for pacification, as Westmoreland contended, but had actually left the population exposed to the guerrillas. Indeed, OSA noted that *fully 90 percent of all incidents in any given quarter were occurring in the 10 percent of the country that held over 80 percent of the population.* What was even more distressing, the 1967 incident rate was roughly the same as in 1966 and 1965. Search-and-destroy operations had not succeeded in assisting the government to effect better control of the people. As one OSA report noted, the big-unit war was irrelevant to the pacification effort as long as the enemy could not initiate big battles and win them. As for the Army's contention that if units were broken down to assist in pacification, they risked being defeated in detail, OSA observed that "our forces routinely defeat enemy forces outnumbering them two or three to one. In no instance has a dug-in US company been overrun, regardless of the size of the attacking force, and nothing larger than a company has come close to annihilation when caught moving." Thus, shifting the bulk of U.S. and ARVN forces into pacification efforts hardly constituted the threat that the Army claimed it did. Beginning in November 1966, OSA maintained that a change in tactics was needed if the attrition strategy was to succeed. MACV needed to focus on an effective population security program to deny the VC their sources of recruitment rather than attempt to obliterate enemy forces on the battlefield.

Turning to the MACV request, Enthoven expressed amazement at the absence of any coherent rationale to support the additional deployments, observing that the MACV requirement was based on "unselective and unquantified goals. . . . What is surprising to me is that MACV has ignored this . . . information in discussing force levels." The OSA report concluded by recommending rejection of Westmoreland's request and calling for the Army to commence serious efforts to upgrade the RVNAF before they assumed a greater role of the defense burden.

Enthoven's analysis carried the day with McNamara. On 19 May a DPM was drawn up recommending that no additional forces be dispatched to South Vietnam other than those already called for in Program 4. The Chiefs, however, persisted. The Army rejected the OSA evaluation out of hand. Furthermore, it sought to exclude other individuals and organizations from having access to the SEA Reports. On at least two occasions General Wheeler strongly recommended to McNamara that the reports "be limited for internal OSD use only" in order to "reduce the dissemination of incorrect and/or misleading information to senior officials of other government agencies, as well as commanders in the field." The day after the DPM was drafted, the Chiefs, in their "Worldwide Posture Paper," reaffirmed their support of Westmoreland's request, claiming that such forces would help "regain the Southeast Asia initiative and exploit our military advantage."

The wrangling over what additional forces should be sent to MACV continued over the next two months. During this period the State Department also became involved in the debate, in the form of a series of options presented by Under Secretary of State Nicholas Katzenbach. Katzenbach initially offered two alternatives, one supporting the JCS position, the other the stand taken by OSA. Predictably, a stalemate quickly ensued. Additional alternatives followed, representing the all-too-familiar practice of finding the middle ground acceptable to all. On 12 June, McNaughton sent a DPM to the president outlining three courses of action. Before a decision was made, however, McNamara visited Saigon on 7 July armed with data from Enthoven showing that 3-2/3-division equivalents could be provided Westmoreland by 31 December 1968 without calling up the reserves.

McNamara arrived in a war zone that had experienced the attrition strategy for nearly two years without any appreciable results. The prototypical military operation since the 173d Airborne Brigade had conducted its first assault on the Iron Triangle back in June of 1965 remained search and destroy. In June 1967, fully 86 percent of MACV's battalion operations time was dedicated to such operations.

Large search-and-destroy operations such as ATTLEBORO (September–November 1966), CEDAR FALLS (January 1967) and JUNCTION CITY (February–May 1967) attempted to bring the enemy to battle so that his forces could be attrited by U.S. firepower. To MACV, attacking enemy strongpoints or base areas was the best way to bring the elusive guerrillas out into the open. For example, ATTLEBORO saw 22,000 U.S. and ARVN troops, complete with B-52 bomber air support and massive artillery fire, conduct a drive into War Zone C, the VC stronghold northwest of Saigon. The seventy-two-day operation was declared a success, since the enemy suffered an estimated 1,100 dead and lost a considerable amount of supplies. Yet, before long the VC reoccupied the area and were operating as before. Major General Depuy, then commander of the 1st Infantry Division, a participant in the operation, recalled the difficulties involved in locating the enemy: "They metered out their casualties, and when the casualties were getting too high . . . they just backed off and waited. I really thought that the kind of pressure they were under would have caused them to perhaps knock off the war for awhile, as a minimum, or even give up and go back north. But I was completely wrong on that. I was surprised a little bit, too, after I took over the division [at] the difficulty we had in trying to find the VC. We hit more dry holes than I thought we were going to hit. They were more elusive. They controlled the battle better. They were the ones who decided whether there would be a fight."

ATTLEBORO was followed by CEDAR FALLS, an incursion into the Iron Triangle. Two infantry divisions participated in the nineteen-day operation that saw U.S. forces kill over 700 VC and capture 613 weapons. The Army's "success" in generating enemy casualties and capturing enemy supplies in these operations led to another large-scale assault into War Zone C, JUNCTION CITY. The operation utilized the Army's 1st Infantry Division, the 173d Airborne Brigade, the 11th Armored Cavalry Regiment (ACR), and a brigade of the 9th Infantry Division. Their mission was to destroy VC/NVA forces and installations in the northern and eastern portions of the War Zone. As General Westmoreland noted, JUNCTION CITY completed the Army's transition of the insurgency into a mid-intensity conflict: "The operation employed for the first time all our different types of combat forces, including paratroopers and large armored and mechanized units."

JUNCTION CITY lasted for nearly two months, from 22 February to 15 April. U.S. forces killed 1,776 VC while capturing vast amounts of ammunition, medical supplies, and more than 800 tons of rice. The Army claimed that CEDAR FALLS and JUNCTION CITY "confirmed the ATTLEBORO experience that such multi-division operations have a place in modern counterinsurgency warfare." Yet the operation was anything but a success. The target, the 9th VC Division, was not rendered ineffective, and with one exception, the only significant engagements were those initiated by the VC. One general stated that "it was a sheer physical impossibility to keep the enemy from slipping away whenever he wished if he were in terrain with which he was familiar—generally the case." The Army utilized massive amounts of firepower: 3,235 tons of bombs and over 366,000 rounds of artillery. Thus, several tons of ordnance were required to kill one VC.

Although Westmoreland claimed that operations like JUNC-TION CITY convinced the enemy that basing units near populated areas was "foolhardy," such was not the case. As one Army general conceded, "In neither instance were we able to stay around, and it was not long before there was evidence of the enemy's return." Captured enemy documents and statements issued by the North Vietnamese leadership indicated that not only had the Army failed to seize the initiative but there was every indication that MACV was playing into the hands of the Communist strategy of pro-tracted warfare. For example, VC documents captured during CEDAR FALLS revealed that the enemy strategy was based on concentrating North Vietnamese Army and VC main forces in numerous remote areas to prevent concentration of American forces in the populated Coastal Plain. The objective, as Giap stated at the time, was to draw American forces away from pacification and engage them in inconclusive battles along the frontiers, inflict-ing U.S. casualties in the process and sapping U.S. will to continue the war. Yet MACV continued to claim that search-and-destroy operations were a success, that they forced the enemy away from the populated areas so that the pacification program could be carried out.

Again, the information available did not bear this out. An analysis of enemy activity in III Corps Tactical Zone (CTZ) during the period 1965–67 showed a dramatic increase in engagements in the four border provinces, from 38 in 1966 to 273 in 1967. While MACV claimed that this proved the validity of search-and-destroy operations, OSA concluded otherwise, noting that "if allied forces had pushed the enemy to the border provinces, we would expect the attack rates elsewhere in III CTZ to have diminished. They doubled." Even worse, the big battles the Army was seeking were not occurring, despite the purported success of operations such as JUNCTION CITY. The enemy was moving away from direct as-saults on U.S. positions in favor of hit-and-run mortar attacks which were more effective in inflicting U.S. casualties. Although MACV refused to admit it, the Army was in a small-unit war: by 1967 over 96 percent of all engagements with enemy forces oc-curred at company strength or less.

Although this information was available to MACV and the Army Staff, it was never systematically evaluated. The only infor-mation or feedback that the Army required concerned how well the service was implementing its strategy of attrition, that is, factors such as the body count, weapons captured, enemy supplies destroyed, and so on. The Army, having convinced itself of the validity of its Concept for insurgency warfare in the battle of the Ia Drang Valley, was concerned only with the need to apply it with greater intensity.

This, then, was the operational environment and the organizational attitude McNamara found upon his arrival in Saigon. During his visit Westmoreland reluctantly agreed to a force level of 525,000 troops, an increase that would provide MACV with an additional 19 maneuver battalion equivalents. In the end, the 3-2/3 division equivalents outlined by Enthoven as the maximum available were whittled down by only some 14,400 spaces. On 14 August a memo from OSD initiated Program 5, directing the chiefs to bring U.S. troop strength in South Vietnam to 525,000 as expeditiously as possible.

As the conflict moved into 1968, Westmoreland forwarded MACV'S year-end assessment of the situation in Vietnam. The tone of the report was optimistic. The general held that the arrival of the Program 5 forces would allow for increased offensive operations The VC, said Westmoreland, had lost control "over large areas and population" in 1967. So confident was Westmoreland that in January he dispatched two brigades belonging to the 1st Cavalry Division to the I CTZ border region around Khe Sanh, drawing them away from the populated region only days before the enemy's biggest offensive to date, the nationwide assault on the populated areas during Tet, the Vietnamese New Year's celebration. The stage was now set for the enemy to deliver a shock that would see the civilian leadership openly challenge the Army's strategy for the war.

Reading 15

Giap's Dream, Westmoreland's Nightmare

by Timothy J. Lomperis

Dienbienphu, madame . . . Dienbienphu . . . history doesn't always repeat itself. But this time it will. We won a military victory over the French, and we'll win it over the Americans, too. Yes, madame, their Dienbienphu is still to come. And it will come. The Americans will lose the war on the day when their military might is at its maximum . . . we'll beat them at the moment when they have the most men, the most arms and the greatest hope of winning.

General Vo Nguyen Giap[1]

The eventual goal throughout was Saigon, but from the first the primary emphasis of the North Vietnamese focused on the Central Highlands and the central coastal provinces . . . [Also, the] most logical course for the enemy, it seemed to me, was to make another and stronger effort to overrun the two northern provinces . . . the most vulnerable part of the country.

General Wm. C. Westmoreland[2]

Lewis Carroll had his character Alice awaken from her bizarre and somewhat frightening Wonderland with the reassuring exclamation, "Things are not as they seem in dreams." So too, it appears,

From *Parameters*, June 1988, pp. 19-32. Copyright © 1988. Reprinted by permission.

with the Vietnam War: things were not as they seemed. This article probes the ironic twists of fate dealt to Giap's dream of another triumphant Dienbienphu against the Americans, and Westmoreland's nightmare of ignominious defeat before two simultaneous conventional thrusts by the North Vietnamese across the Demilitarized Zone in the north and through the Central Highlands.[3] In the world of events, Giap's dream of a Dienbienphu against the Americans, even in the triumph of his forces in 1975, was dashed, but Westmoreland's nightmare, after the departure of the last American GIs from Vietnam in 1973, was fully visited on the hapless remaining South Vietnamese defenders two years later.

Put simply, then, as a demonstration of a successful people's war strategy (of which a Dienbienphu was to be the culmination), the triumphant Ho Chi Minh Campaign of the North Vietnamese in 1975 was a fraud, whereas, ironically enough, the fears of the American command of a South Vietnam succumbing to a conventional invasion proved, prophetically, to be well-founded.

To make such claims obviously risks confusing the already difficult task of drawing lessons from Vietnam because such claims run counter to received truth. The first of these "truths" is that the North Vietnamese victory was a virtuoso exhibition of people's war. The lesson is that such a strategy can serve as a model for profitable emulation by beleaguered insurgents in El Salvador, the Philippines, Peru, and elsewhere. The second "truth" is that the United States was so blinded to the guerilla nature and underlying political issues of the conflict that it erringly chose to focus on the conventional threat of the North Vietnamese army. The lesson emerging therefrom is that the United States cannot be counted on ever to develop a foreign policy capable of dealing with insurgencies and the grievances that undergird them. Whether these emergent lessons prove right or wrong, the point of this article is that in order to establish themselves, they will have to look elsewhere for their fundamental truths. There is no simple Munich in the Vietnam War.

Few wars can compare with Vietnam as an example of a Clausewitzian fog that has become even soupier after the war's conclusion than when it was actually being fought. The North Vietnamese claim they won by a strategy they actually abandoned after the 1968 Tet Offensive. Most Americans have come to believe they lost a guerrilla war though they in fact crushed it. Ironically, the winning strategy was an American one used by the North Vietnamese in the name of Marxist people's war. It is not a story from which lessons readily emerge.

Tet 1968: The End of a Dream and the Beginning of a Nightmare

We have passed the 20th anniversary of the 1968 Tet Offensive. Few students of the Vietnam War quarrel with the notion that the offensive was a major—if not the central—turning point of the war, but many still debate its significance, the intentions behind it, and its outcome. Militarily, it was a series of coordinated shock assaults on a national scale.[4] Starting with their preliminary siege of the Khe Sanh Combat Base (near the DMZ) on 21 January, the communists launched their country-wide attacks on the nights of 30 and 31 January, which, in the first week, enveloped 34 province capitals, all seven autonomous cities, and 64 district towns. For this first wave the communists had amassed a force of some 84,000 men.[5] Though by 31 March the offensive had been beaten back, the defenses of many of these towns and cities had been breached. Parts of Saigon were held by Viet Cong shock units for two weeks, and the entire city of Hue was occupied for three weeks. Even the grounds of the U.S. Embassy in Saigon had been briefly penetrated. The physical destruction was enormous; the fighting was fierce; and the casualties were heavy. The communists lost nearly 60,000 in killed and wounded, the Americans and South Vietnamese about 10,000.[6] Fifteen Americans won the Medal of Honor.[7] A second wave called "Mini-Tet" was launched in May, but despite another break into Saigon it quickly fizzled. A final wave in August hardly attracted attention, and the communists themselves have readily acknowledged that this last round was a failure. When it was all over, official American figures showed that the communists had suffered 92,000 deaths.[8]

Despite these heavy communist losses, the most obvious effect of the Tet Offensive was that it marked the end of the escalation ladder for the Americans. In brief, a war effort designed to induce Hanoi to come to the conference table and desist from further attempts at forcible takeover of the south was instead blown apart by these shocking attacks ordered by Hanoi. The Pentagon, to say nothing of the American public, was obviously shaken by the offensive. An after-action assessment by General Earle G. Wheeler, Chairman of the Joint Chiefs of Staff, concluded that "it was a very near thing."[9]

In the same report, Wheeler endorsed what he said was an add-on request by the U.S. military command in Saigon (MACV) for 206,756 men to turn the war around and exploit the military advantages the defeat of the offensive afforded.[10] Such a request clearly amounted to a proposal for a significant change in strategy as well. An analysis of this request in the *Pentagon Papers* reveals a full understanding of the strategic Rubicon that would be crossed in responding to it favorably:

> The alternatives stood out in stark reality. To accept General Wheeler's request for troops would mean a total U.S. military commitment to SVN (South Vietnam)—an Americanization of the war, a callup of reserve forces, vastly increased expenditures. To deny the request for troops, or to attempt to again cut it to a size which could be sustained by the thinly stretched active forces, would just as surely signify that an upper limit to the U.S. military commitment in SVN had been reached.[11]

To help him think through his response, President Lyndon Johnson called together a group of his most trusted advisers, inside and outside the government—dubbed the Wise Men—who agonized over the request in February and March. In the meantime, the domestic American reaction to the offensive was not promising for any contemplated expansion of the war. On 12 March Senator Eugene McCarthy, one of the most vocal critics of the war, garnered 42 percent of the vote in the New Hampshire presidential primary. Just four days later, a dithering Senator Robert Kennedy announced his candidacy for the presidency on an antiwar platform, giving the antiwar movement a luster it had previously lacked. The polls also began to show signs of a demonstrable shift away from support for the war. While 40 percent of the respondents of a 1967 Harris poll had supported Johnson's conduct of the war, that support had plummeted to 26 percent in March 1968.[12] Surveying the military options and the domestic political carnage, the Wise Men advised Johnson to deescalate and seek a negotiated settlement. Reluctantly concurring, Johnson, in a televised address on 31 March, explained to the American public his decisions to freeze the war by keeping the American troop commitment at existing levels and to order a partial bombing halt of North Vietnam as a step toward negotiation. Further, he dramatically announced that he was dropping out of the presidential campaign. Militarily, America had won the battle of Tet, but politically it was a defeat for Lyndon Johnson.

Had Johnson and his Wise Men's survey encompassed the perspective of the communists, their assessments might not have been so gloomy. Whatever the intentions of the communist leaders (which will be discussed shortly), the Tet Offensive certainly did not go according to the plans they had given to their cadres and military commanders. Directives went out to all commands to instill in their troops a sense of ultimate sacrifice for this "decisive hour." All the long years of revolutionary activity had led up to this moment: "We only need to make a swift assault to secure the target and gain total victory."[13] Victory was to be achieved in three stages: first, a shock assault would be carried into the cities by largely local (i.e., southern) forces; second, a tide of both popular uprisings by the people and massive defections by ARVN units triggered by those assaults would bring about the collapse of the South Vietnamese government;[14] and finally, regular units of the North Vietnamese army would enter the cities as a triumphant mopping-up force, obliging the outflanked and thoroughly disoriented Americans to negotiate their own withdrawal.[15]

In the event, of course, the offensive never got beyond stage one. The responsibility for this stage, one recalls, fell heavily on locally recruited southerners. Pentagon sources estimated that in the first wave of Tet (January to March) only 20 to 25 percent of the North Vietnamese forces in the south were committed, whereas virtually all Viet Cong combatants were engaged.[16] With the failure of any popular uprisings and mass ARVN defections to develop in accordance with stage two plans, Hanoi decided to husband its own resources. Though it used many of its own troops in the Mini-Tet launched in May, this second wave was much smaller than the first. The third wave in August reverted back to entire reliance on local forces. As a standard of comparison, there were 29 battalion-sized attacks in the first wave, six in the second, and only two in the third.[17] This is not to say that northerners went completely unscathed—they bore the brunt of the fighting at Khe Sanh and in Hue, for example—but it was the southern insurgent ranks that were decimated. The ultimate military result of Tet, therefore, was that if the war was to continue, the responsibility for its prosecution shifted to the northerners.[18] Before the offensive, 55 percent of the main force communist ranks were filled by northern regulars, but in April 1968 over 70 percent of these positions had to be provided by northerners. Even such a fervent believer in the revolutionary unity of the communist side as Frances FitzGerald admitted that after Tet the "southern movement was driven to become almost totally dependent on the North."[19]

If southern communists might be forgiven for wondering aloud about the asymmetry of regional sacrifice during Tet, northerners felt they had reason to fear for the fatherland itself and were therefore justified in conserving their troops for this challenge.[20]

Indeed, after the siege of Khe Sanh was lifted by American troops in Operation Pegasus in April, two North Vietnamese divisions withdrew from the south altogether.[21] What they feared was a repeat of the Inchon landings.[22] Despite aspersions from southerners about the northern preoccupation with safeguarding "the great socialist rear," Hanoi's fears were not unfounded. American military planning (and desires) for cross-border operations into Laos and Cambodia to cut the Ho Chi Minh Trail and even to disrupt the north by amphibious landings that would slice across North Vietnam's slender southern panhandle was of long standing. In his memoir Westmoreland relates that he first proposed such cross-border operations in 1964. His staffers continued to draw up contingency plans for these operations in 1966 and 1967. Throughout his account he expresses frustration over his failure to get clearance for these attacks, which he saw as a natural extension of his strategy.[23] It is clear from the *Pentagon Papers* (as well as from the memoirs both of Westmoreland and of Admiral Ulysses. S. Grant Sharp) that a petition for moves into Laos, Cambodia, and North Vietnam was imbedded in the 206,000-troop request.[24]

That an expanded war strategy was behind the troop request was no mystery to Vietnamese communists. Indeed a lead article in the 10 March 1968 issue of *The New York Times* outlined the essential features of the debate over the request. Though the tenor of the article was that the request was unrealistic, the article admitted that if it were granted Vietnam could "no longer be called 'a limited war.'"[25] The communists, in fact, had been worried about such an expansion for at least as long as Westmoreland had been planning it. The key December 1963 resolution of the Lao Dong party to intervene directly in the war in the south contained the warning: "At the same time, we should be prepared to cope with the eventuality of the expansion of the war into North Vietnam."[26] An intriguing 1984 interview conducted by William Turley with the deputy editor of the North Vietnamese journal *People's Army* corroborates this preoccupation. The editor said that the siege of Khe Sanh was actually intended as a probe to see if the Americans would send troops north in response to attacks across the DMZ. When no such attacks came, Hanoi went ahead with Tet.[27] It can also be inferred that with the huge losses, the failure to incite any response from the South Vietnamese populace, and the rumblings of a 206,000-troop request (even when it was turned down), Hanoi got nervous and decided not to send "good money after bad"—even if it meant splitting the revolution and abandoning a strategy.

The meaning of Tet 1968 turns, then, essentially on the intentions of the communists. If their intentions were not to win on the battlefield but rather to launch a dramatic and devastating assault (sacrificing, incidentally, a fair proportion of their southern comrades) that would rekindle the antiwar movement to the point where the American will could no longer be mobilized for a response—and thereby inducing American policymakers to deescalate the war—then the communists clearly could have called Tet a victory, and even hailed it as another Dienbienphu. Indeed, it is in precisely these terms that an official account of the war portrays the offensive as a victory: Tet "bankrupted the aggressive will of the U.S. imperialists, and forced them to deescalate the war and negotiate with us at the Paris Conference."[28]

Though such intentions square well with subsequent events, it can be readily inferred from other communist writings and statements that, with such enormous sacrifices, they intended to achieve much more than a gradual American deescalation. If Tet was considered to have been such a victory, it is strange that as early as 1969 and 1970 there were thinly disguised public recriminations over the offensive at even the politburo level among such venerables as Truong Chinh, Le Duan, and Vo Nguyen Giap. In the middle of a eulogy on Karl Marx, for example, Truong Chinh pointedly reminded his colleagues that "our strategy is to protract the war; therefore, in tactics we should avoid unfavorable fights to the death."[29]

Since the war, some leading communist figures have become even more candid about Tet. That the war could have been won by pulling on the fickle heartstrings of American domestic moral sentiment and opinion is not something too many communists are eager to claim. Such a claim would almost vitiate all the sacrifices made on the battlefield, where, according to the strategy of people's war, the final test must come. Despite his praise for the U.S. antiwar movement, General Giap emphasized to Stanley Karnow "that the 'decisive' arena was Vietnam itself, where communist success hinged on 'changing the balance of power in our favor.'" Indeed, communist General Tran Do told Karnow, "In all honesty, we didn't achieve our main objective, which was to spur uprisings throughout the south . . . As for making an impact in the U.S., it had not been our intention—but it turned out to be a fortunate result."[30] Truong Nhu Tang, a southerner who was a founding member of the National Liberation Front and the Justice Minister of the NLF's Provisional Revolutionary Government, doesn't even concede the "fortunate result." What Tet succeeded in doing, he points out, was to bring Richard Nixon, a far more formidable adversary than Lyndon Johnson, into the White House.[31]

For purposes of settling the question of intentions, the postmortem of Tet by Tran Van Tra, the leading southern general among the communist forces, is poignantly revealing:

> However, during Tet of 1968 we did not correctly evaluate the specific balance of forces between ourselves and the enemy . . . In other words, we did not base ourselves on scientific calculation or a careful weighing of all factors, but in part on an illusion based on our subjective desires. For that reason, although that decision was wise, ingenious, and timely . . . we suffered large sacrifices and losses . . . which clearly weakened us. Afterwards, we were not only unable to retain the gains we had made, but had to overcome a myriad of difficulties in 1969 and 1970 so that the resolution could stand firm in the storm . . . If we had weighed and considered things meticulously, taken into consideration the balance of forces of the two sides . . . less blood would have been spilled . . . and the future development of the revolution would certainly have been far different.[32]

More than a battlefield loss, then, the Tet Offensive was a failure of strategy and politics as well. Even the official account of the war drops its overweening tone of euphoria in its narration of Tet and does not resume its pro forma optimism until the Easter invasion of 1972.[33] Truong Nhu Tang, more forthrightly, describes the period from the Tet Offensive to the Laotian cross-border operation of 1971 as one of hardship and of serious tensions between southern and northern communists. These tensions, he insists, could have been profitably exploited by Henry Kissinger had he the political perspicacity to see them.[34]

Thus, there was no Dienbienphu in the Tet Offensive. Even such an admirer of the communist cause as Gabriel Kolko concedes, "Never again was the Tet 1968 strategy repeated."[35] People's war, as a banner that had led the party through a generation of trials, was finished. Without it, the communists thrashed about in their jungles for two years without a strategy to guide them. Then hope trickled back as the glimmerings of another strategy began to emerge, an American one.

Success in Failure: Hanoi's American Strategy

Though it may have been *terra incognita* to the American public in the post-World War II years, Vietnam was no stranger to contingency planners in the Pentagon. As early as 1952 the Joint Chiefs of Staff mulled over the possibility of sending eight American combat divisions to Indochina's Red River delta to free French forces for offensive actions against the Viet Minh. With the withdrawal of the French and the partitioning of Vietnam at the 17th parallel as a result of the Geneva Accords of 1954, a Korean War mindset settled in on the military planners of the 1950s. Assuming the North Vietnamese were bent on reunifying the country, they identified three invasion routes which could link up for a culminating assault on the capital city of Saigon: the first, and most direct, was a drive across the DMZ and down Highway One along the coast; the second passed through the Laotian panhandle and cut across the Central Highlands; and the third was a grand flanking movement originating in the northern Laotian mountains that would sweep down to the Mekong River and follow it to Saigon. To counter such a presumed strategy, American planners envisioned a three-staged operation of their own. The first involved securing coastal and inland bases to establish an infrastructure of logistical support. The second called for U.S. forces to push inland and set up blocking positions astride these three invasion routes: the DMZ, the Central Highlands, and an arc around Saigon's northern and western approaches. The final stage was a counteroffensive of combined airborne, amphibious, and ground attacks into North Vietnam.[36]

With the coming of the Kennedy Administration in 1961, a concern for counterinsurgency began to play a role in military planning. Indeed, the JCS had recognized the need to incorporate counterinsurgency capabilities into the South Vietnamese armed forces as early as March 1960.[37] The Kennedy era, however, ushered in a crew of enthusiasts for counterinsurgency strategy. Men like General Maxwell Taylor, Walt Rostow, and Roger Hilsman guaranteed that there would indeed be a debate with the more conventional planning of the military establishment. Michael Brown categorizes the debate as being between two schools who viewed the nature of the war according to diametrically opposite concepts: the war school and the insurgency school.[38]

It was this tug-of-war that caused such initial indecision in 1965 over how to deploy forces in the impending troop buildup. Nominally, the debate was between advocates of a cautious pacification/enclave strategy and those of a big-unit/aggressive strategy.[39] In fact, however, the military debate was overlaid by a welter of political concerns that were argued out in this period.[40] What emerged by July 1965 was a compromising strategy, here described by Westmoreland in his memoir:

> *Phase One:* Commit those American and Allied forces necessary "to halt the losing trend" by the end of 1965.
>
> *Phase Two:* "During the first half of 1966," take the offensive with American and Allied forces in "high priority areas" to destroy enemy forces and reinstitute pacification programs.
>
> *Phase Three:* If the enemy persisted, he might be defeated and his forces and base areas destroyed during a period of a year to a year and a half following Phase II.[41]

This seemingly innocuous strategy contained important ramifications. In the strategy of attrition, provision was made for the incorporation of "pacification programs." Indeed the PROVN study of the Army Staff, completed in March 1966, insisted that pacification be given top priority in the war. Although there was a variety of programs and missions undertaken under the rubric of pacification, when all was said and done Westmoreland's strategy reflected the conventional-war emphasis that Andrew Krepinevich convincingly argues is at the core of the U.S. Army's ethos.[42] His strategy, furthermore, was little more than a reiteration of the first two stages of the three-staged operation envisioned by JCS planners in the 1950s to throw back a North Vietnamese invasion. It is obvious, at least from a military point of view, that the success of Westmoreland's strategy ultimately depended on the implementation of an unstated fourth phase, the third stage of the JCS contingency plan calling for airborne, amphibious, and ground attacks into North Vietnam.

Putting the story of the two strategies together (Washington's and Hanoi's), the Tet Offensive meant two things. For the communists it was the end of people's war and, essentially, of any strategy built on guerrilla warfare. For the American command, with the refusal of the 206,000-troop request, it was the end of any possibility of a conventional military victory. Both sides, then, saw their strategies turn to ashes. For the Americans there was little else to do but to deescalate the war, turn it over to the Vietnamese, and find some palliative way to negotiate themselves home. For the communists, however, there remained, lying around still unused as a strategy, an acting out of the very conventional invasion that had animated the fears of the JCS planners of the 1950s.

Interestingly, Truong Nhu Tang cites the "incursion" into Cambodia by American forces in 1970 as the turning point of the war, rather than Tet. Although he concedes that the operation nearly succeeded in capturing COSVN headquarters intact and seriously disrupted operations in the south, it was "an enduring gift" because it decisively separated the American leadership from its domestic support.[43] The political uproar over Cambodia also ensured that there would be no unstated phase four to worry about from MACV. With a conventional victory for the Americans impossible, ARVN's debacle in its cross-border operation into Laos in February 1971 (Lam Son 710) proved to the communists that a conventional-war strategy was possible. Two of AVRN's best divisions, the 1st Division and the Airborne Division, were routed in their assault across the Ho Chi Minh Trail on Tehepone, Laos. Though there were no American ground troops involved, there was generous American air support for the ARVN forces, but the communists were successful despite it.

In the Easter invasion launched on 30 March 1972, the communists tried out their new strategy. They dubbed it the Nguyen Hue campaign, not even bothering to call it a popular uprising. This time the North Vietnamese unleashed practically everything they had: 14 divisions and 26 independent regiments (only a training division in Hanoi and two in Laos were held back.) They also concentrated their forces for four major attacks: one across the DMZ, one on Hue, another across the Central Highlands, and a final one on Saigon. An attempt to bring the invasion to the Mekong Delta ended in failure.[44] After seizing all of Quang Tri Province just south of the DMZ and overrunning Loc Ninh north of Saigon, the invasion stalled. The communists' bid for Hue was turned back. ARVN successfully defended the Central Highland towns of Kontum and Pleiku. And the drive on Saigon was stopped at An Loc. Though U.S. ground troops played little role in the Easter invasion, American air support was massive—and often decisive. On 15 September, South Vietnamese marines recaptured Quang Tri. With this the invasion was over, at a reported loss of 100,000 North Vietnamese killed.[45]

Plainly, the communists had not got their new strategy down right. General Giap and his staff made two strategic mistakes that were magnified by the tactical errors of their field commanders. Although this time Giap did nothing like Tet and scattered his forces to the four winds, he nevertheless failed to concentrate them into a single blow. Instead, he attacked on four fronts at staggered time intervals. Further, after overrunning Quang Tri he ordered a three-week pause. The effect of both these mistakes was to allow ARVN to regroup and consolidate its positions. Tactically, the North Vietnamese committed a variety of conventional blunders showing an inability to conduct combined-arms warfare, that is, they were unable to get armored, artillery, and infantry units to work together. On the ground, particularly in the Central Highlands, they often threw away an initial superiority by mounting desperate human-wave assaults that left their ranks depleted and forced them to retire from the field.[46]

In 1975, in their lightning 55-day Ho Chi Minh campaign, they got their strategy right. Though the communists were aided by disastrous mistakes of both strategy and tactics by the South Vietnamese and by the complete lack of U.S. air support that had always provided hefty margins for error in the past for both Americans and South Vietnamese, it was an epic military campaign culminating in the triumphant seizure of Saigon on 30 April 1975.[47] This time the communists concentrated their forces for one overwhelming thrust across the Central Highlands, choosing, shrewdly, to aim at the lightly defended provincial capital Ban Me Thuot. The town fell on 11 March, the day after it was attacked. On 13 March, South Vietnamese President Nguyen Van Thieu convened a fateful meeting in which he contradictorily ordered the simultaneous withdrawal from Pleiku and Kontum and the recapture of Ban Me Thuot. Ban Me Thuot was not recaptured and the withdrawal turned into a rout. Determined not to give ARVN forces any chances to recover and regroup, North Vietnamese forces now struck across the DMZ to link up with their comrades cutting across the Central Highlands. In a panic, Thieu ordered the Airborne Division south to Saigon just as the 1 Corps Commander was setting it up to anchor his defense of Hue. Shorn of this division and with the commander further confused by Thieu on whether to try to hold Hue and Danang, the north collapsed in chaos and panic. Hue fell on 28 March and Danang two days later. The link-up was now complete and the North Vietnamese steamroller inexorably advanced on Saigon, its tanks smashing through the gates of the Presidential Palace in Saigon on 30 April.[48]

Thus, in losing a people's war, the communists went on to win the war itself. But in adopting a conventional war strategy, they won by a means that should have brought defeat. The United States, on the other hand, won a war it thought it lost, and lost by default what it could have prevented.

Conclusion: The Stolen Strategy

The Vietnam War has been over now for 13 years. But whatever else Americans have done with Vietnam, they have certainly not put it behind them. Everywhere in the Third World where the remotest prospect for American intervention in some local squabble looms, the ghost of Vietnam casts its shadow. "Lessons" of Vietnam are invoked to justify virtually any policy. With respect to the question in the Middle East over whether to permit the continued presence of U.S. Marines in Lebanon, for example, Senator Charles Percy and Joseph Biden cited the "lessons" of Vietnam to justify opposite votes. People draw lessons from their memories, from a set of images that, in time, become highly selective. Some, with Ronald Reagan, remember Vietnam as a "noble crusade," while others in the antiwar community relive with Daniel Ellsburg his nightmare of the war as a heinous "crime."

The historian Ernest May, however, offers the reminder that historical lessons are properly drawn only from comparing one component of an event to a similar component in another event, not from application of an entire event wholesale.[49] Even in victory there are things done wrong and stupidly, and in defeat there are yet deeds of intelligence and glowing success. Hence, the lessons from any conflict do not derive from the general outcome of success or failure, but from the constituent components of the victory or defeat. The German blitzkrieg was not the origin of the German defeat in World War II, nor was the people's war the strategy by which the Vietnamese communists came to power in 1975. These facts may make no difference to the Vietnamese and Germans of today, but they do to the Salvadoran guerrilla *comman-dante*, for example, who may think that history is on his side because he is following a people's war strategy which had "soundly defeated" the Americans in Vietnam a decade earlier.

For the sake of lessons, two points from this tale of two strategies emerge. First, it was not at the hands of a guerrilla strategy or people's war by which the United States and South Vietnam were beaten. This is not to say the Americans are to be commended, therefore, for being intelligent and wise. Despite their abandonment of people's war in the Tet Offensive, the communists did enjoy for the duration of the war one of the key benefits of this strategy, an intelligence superiority in the field. Truong Nhu Tang insisted in an interview with Al Santoli that communist units always had advance warning of major allied operations.[50] Consequently, U.S. forces in the field were unable, most of the time, to fulfill the basic mission of the infantry, "to close with and destroy the enemy." Also, even had the United States intervened success-fully in 1975, there is no assurance Hanoi would not have kept trying. Indeed, Hanoi's ability to fight the Cambodians in 1977 and 1978, take on the Chinese in sharp border battles in 1979, and continue to occupy Cambodia in the 1980s should refute any latent hopes that Hanoi would have fallen immediately to a "phase four" attack. What this does say, however, is that by switching to a conventional war strategy, the internal political issues that fueled the defeated people's war were left unresolved by both sides, not just by the American and South Vietnamese.

Second, the Vietnam War was a frustrating contradiction in that it was simultaneously a conventional war and a guerrilla insurgency. Compared to other insurgencies of the postwar era, then, it is more unique than it is general in its applications.[51] As such, it was not wrong for American military planners or for General Westmoreland to concentrate on the conventional chal-lenge first. Larry Cable has pointed out that in Korea the United States faced both a conventional war and a guerrilla war but concentrated on the conventional war; the guerrilla war evapo-rated with the expulsion of the conventional North Korean army.[52] In Vietnam, the guerrillas largely disappeared after they rose to mount a conventional attack, and the war then had to be won by the communists in conventional, almost American, terms.

In concluding this discussion of strategy in Vietnam, we can agree with the venerable Chinese strategist Sun Tzu's dictum that "what is of supreme importance in war is to attack the enemy's strategy."[53] To this eternal verity General Giap can legitimately add the postscript that it is doubly clever to steal it.

Notes

1. Interview of North Vietnamese General Vo Nguyen Giap by Italian journal-ist Oriana Fallaci. Cited in Russell Stetler, ed., *The Military Art of People's War: Selected Writings of General Vo Nguyen Giap* (New York: Monthly Review Press, 1970), p. 3M.

2. William C. Westmoreland, *A Soldier Reports* (New York: Doubleday, 1976), pp. 194, 213.

3. Though Giap's dream of a Dienbienphu is clear enough, Westmoreland never fleshed out what I have chosen to call his nightmare. Nevertheless, his preoccupation with a threat to Saigon emanating from a conventional overrunning of the north of Sourth Vietnam is rife throughout his memoir, *A Soldier Reports*. His worries about the Central Highlands come out on pp. 144, 150, 156–58, 171, 178–79, 218–19 and 406. On p. 163 he forthrightly

acknowledges his fear of the country being cut in two, and on p. 406 he notes that Giap in his writings had viewed the Central Highlands as the key to solving "the problem of South Vietnam." His concerns for the DMZ emerge on pp. 150, 164, 168, 196–201, and 350–51. His fears of a link-up are most clearly expressed when he talks of the coastal cities of Hue, Danang, and Qui Nhon, as on p. 167.

4. By far the most comprehensive and balanced account of the Tet Offensive is in Don Oberdorfer, *Tet!* (New York: Doubleday, 1971).

5. Neil Sheehan, et al., *The Pentagon Papers as Published by the New York Times* (New York: Bantam, 1971), p. 617. See also Oberdorfer, p. 262; and William S. Turley, *The Second Indochina War. A Short Political and Military History, 1954–1975,* (Boulder, Colo.: Westview, 1986), p. 106.

6. Oberdorfer, dedication page; see also Turley, p. 108.

7. Oberdorfer, p. 332.

8. Robert S. Shaplen, *The Road from War: Vietnam 1965–1971*, rev. ed. (New York: Harper and Row, 1971), p. 219.

9. Sheehan, et al., p. 616.

10. Ibid, p. 620. Westmoreland writes that this request was not his idea, but Wheeler's. See Westmoreland, pp. 352–58.

11. *The Pentagon Papers*, the Senator Gravel edition (Boston: Beacon, 1975), IV, 549.

12. George C. Herring, *American's Longest War: The United States and Vietnam, 1950–1975*, 2nd ed. (New York: Alfred A. Knopf, 1986), pp. 201–02.

13. "'The Decisive Hour': Two Directives for Tet," Joint United States Public Affairs Office, (hereinafter JASPAO), *Viet-Nam Documents and Research Notes* (hereinafter VNDRN) Nos. 28–29 (April 1968), p. 4.

14. Turely, p. 99. Turley reports that the Lao Dong party had been led to believe that it had a popular support base of four million people in the south that would respond to its calls if only the communist troops could get around American forces.

15. Gabriel Kolko, *Anatomy of a War: Vietnam, the United States, and the Modern Historical Experience* (New York: Pantheon, 1985), p. 308.

16. *The Pentagon Papers*, Gravel edition, IV, 539.

17. Kolko, p. 328; and Hoang Ngoc Lung, *The General Offensives of 1968–69* (Washington: USACMH, 1981), pp. 103–04, 110.

18. "North Vietnam's Role in the South," JUSPAO, *VNDRN Nos. 36–37* (June 1968), pp. 1, 13. As the war progressed to its conclusion, these proportions became even more weighted with northerners.

19. Frances FitzGerald, *Fire in the Lake: The Vietnamese and the Americans in Vietnam* (New York: Random House, 1972), p. 527.

20. This "wondering" is noted by Turley, p. 113. In 1981 Stanley Karnow found persistent bitterness against northerners by southern communists over Tet. In an interview with Karnow in Saigon, one female commando in the offensive denounced it as a "grievous miscalculation" by Hanoi that "wantonly squandered the southern insurgent movement." See Karnow, *Vietnam: A History* (New York: Viking, 1983), p. 545.

21. Obendorfer, p. 304.

22. The Inchon landings would seem to offer a perfect example of Van Tien Dung's "blossoming lotus" tactics of "attacking on the rear to collapse the front," a supposed innovation that the communist general introduced in the 1975 campaign. See Hung P. Nguyen, "Communist Offensive Strategy and the Defense of South Vietnam," *Parameters*, 14 (Winter 1984), 11.

23. Westmoreland, pp. 148, 153.

24. *The Pentagon Papers*, Gravel edition, IV, 550–55; and Andrew Krepinevich, Jr., *The Army and Vietnam* (Baltimore: Johns Hopkins Univ. Press, 1986), pp. 242, 244.

25. The article was reprinted in the *Pentagon Papers*. See *The Pentagon Papers*, Gravel edition, IV, 586.

26. "The Viet-Nam Workers' Party's 1963 Decision to Escalate the War in the South," JUSPAO, *VNDRN No. 96* (July 1971), p. 40.

27. Turley, p. 105.

28. *The Anti-U.S. Resistance War for National Salvation 1954–1975: Military Events* (Hanoi: People's Army Publishing House, 1980 [Joint Publication Research Service Reel No. 80968, 3 June 1982]), pp. 104–05.

29. "Let Us Be Grateful to Karl Marx and Follow the Path Traced by Him," JUSPAO, *VNDRN No. 52* (February 1969), p. 1. For a brief account of these recriminations, see Timothy J. Lompert's, *The War Everyone Lost—And Won: America's Interventions in Vietnam's Twin Struggles* (Baton Rouge, La.: Louisiana State Univ. Press, 1984) pp. 152–54.

30. Karnow, pp. 523, 527.

31. Truong Nhu Iang, *A Vietcong Memoir* (San Diego, Calif.: Harcourt Brace Jovanovich, 1985), pp. 141–44.

32. Tran Van Tra, *Vietnam: History of the Bulwark B2 Theatre*, Vol. 5: *Concluding the 30-Years War* (Ho Chi Minh City: Van Nghe Publishing House, 1982 [JPRS Reel No. 82783, 2 February 1983]), pp. 35–36.

33. *Anti-U.S. Resistance War*, pp. 105–38.

34. Truong Nhu Tang, pp. 186–200, 213.

35. Kolko, p. 334.

36. Alexander S. Cochran, Jr., "American Planning for Ground Combat in Vietnam, 1952–1965," *Parameters*, 14 (Summer 1984), 63–65. It is nothing more than this plan that Harry Summers contends would have turned the war around. See Harry G. Summers, Jr., *On Strategy: A Critical Analysis of the Vietnam War* (New York: Dell, 1984), esp. pp. 126–32.

37. George M. Kahin, *Intervention: How America Became Involved in Vietnam* (New York: Alfred A. Knopf, 1986), p. 473.

38. Michael L. Brown, "Vietnam: Learning from the Debate," *Military Review*, 67 (February 1987), 49.

39. Cochran raises some legitimate questions as to whether there was such a dichotomous debate. Rather, he argues, the so-called debate over an enclave versus a big-unit war strategy was actually a discussion over retiming pre-existing plans (p. 67).

40. On the military side alone, Jeffrey Clarke catalogs a debate among conventional war advocates, enclave defenders, Vietnamization and guerilla war enthusiasts, and proponents of a beefed-up advisory and training effort.

See his "On Strategy and the Vietnam War," *Parameters*, 16 (Winter 1986), 39–46.

41. Westmoreland, p. 142.

42. Krepinevich, pp. 180–82, 232–33.

43. Truong Nhu Tang, pp. 212–13.

44. For an account of the failed offensive in the Mekong delta, see Ngo Quang Truong, *The Easter Offensive of 1972* (Washington: USACMH, 1980), pp. 137–56.

45. Guenter Lewy, *America in Vietnam* (New York: Oxford Univ. Press, 1978), p. 198.

46. For a litany of these mistakes, see ibid., p. 199; and Ngo Quang Truong, pp. 158–60.

47. The official communist account of the campaign is by General Van Tien Dung in his *Our Great Spring Victory*, trans. John Spragens, Jr. (New York: Monthly Review Press, 1977). An American acount that closely tracks Dung's narrative, and adds the political and diplomatic maneuvering to the military drama, is Frank Snepp's *Decent Interval: An Insider's Account of Saigon's Indecent End* (New York: Random House, 1977). William E. Le Gro provides a terse blow-by-blow account of the military action in his *Vietnam from Cease-Fire to Capitulation* (Washington: USACMH, 1981).

48. An insightful analysis of communist strategy and tactics in their victorious campaign can be found in Hung P. Nguyen, "Communist Offensive Strategy and the Defense of South Vietnam," *Parameters*, 14 (Winter 1984), 3–19. The present writer, however, remains to be convinced that the communist campaign exemplified Tran Van Tra's "war of sysntheses."

49. Ernest R. May, *"Lessons" of the Past: The Use and Misuse of History in American Foreign Policy* (New York: Oxford Univ. Press, 1973), pp. 127–41.

50. Al Santoli, "Why Viet Cong Flee," *Parade*, 11 July 1982, p. 5.

51. This point has been made by Samuel P. Huntington, among others, in Stanley Hoffman, Samuel P. Huntington, Richard N. Neustadt, and Thomas C. Schelling, "Vietnam Reappraised," *International Security*, 6 (Summer 1983), 6–7.

52. Barry E. Cable, *Conflict of Myths: The Development of American Counterinsurgency Doctrine and the Vietnam War* (New York: New York Univ. Press, 1986), pp. 177–78. The basic point of Cable's book, however—and it is a prescient one—is that the U.S. Army has failed to distinguish between *partisan* guerrillas (which are adjucts to conventional forces) and *insurgetn* guerillas (which are internally supported forces in their own right). See esp. pp. 5–7.

53. Sun Tzu, *The Art of War*, trans. Samuel B. Griffith (London: Oxford Univ. Press, 1963), p. 77.